# Business Enterprise
in Japan

# Business Enterprise in Japan: Views of Leading Japanese Economists

*edited by*
Kenichi Imai and
Ryutaro Komiya

*translation edited and*
*introduced by*
Ronald Dore and
Hugh Whittaker

The MIT Press
Cambridge, Massachusetts
London, England

This book was set in Palatino by Asco Trade Typesetting Ltd., Hong Kong, and was printed and bound in the United States of America.

Library of Congress Cataloging-in-Publication Data

Nihon no kigyō. English.
  Business enterprise in Japan: views of leading Japanese
  economists / edited by Kenichi Imai and Ryutaro Komiya; translation
  edited and introduced by Ronald Dore and Hugh Whittaker.
     p.    cm.
  Includes bibliographical references and index.
  ISBN 0-262-09032-5
  ████████████agement—Japan.  2. Business enterprises—Japan.
  ██████████. Komiya, Ryūtarō, 1928–    . III. Dore, Ronald Philip.  IV. Whittaker,

███████████ 1994

                                                                    94-11954
                                                                        CIP

# Contents

# Contributors

Masahiko Aoki (chapter 2)
Stanford University

Kenichi Imai (chapters 1 and 6)
Stanford University

Motoshige Ito (chapter 5)
University of Tokyo

Hiroyuki Itami (chapter 3)
Hitotsubashi University

Tadao Kagono (chapter 4)
Kobe University

Kazuo Kioke (chapter 13)
Hosei University

Tetsuya Kishimoto (chapter 16)
Kobe University

Takao Kobayashi (chapter 4)
University of Tokyo

Ryutaro Komiya (chapters 1 and 18)
Aoyama Gakuin University

Kazutoshi Koshiro (chapter 12)
Yokohama National University

Yoshiro Miwa (chapter 7)
University of Tokyo

Ikujiro Nonaka (chapter 11)
Hitotsubashi University

Isao Ohashi (chapter 14)
Nagoya University

Yoshiyasu Ono (chapter 10)
Osaka University

Hiroyuki Odagiri (chapter 9)
Tsukuba University

Naomi Saeki (chapter 17)
Niigata University

Masu Uekusa (chapter 15)
University of Tokyo

Ryuhei Wakasugi (chapter 8)
Yokohama National University

Hiroshi Yoshikawa (chapter 10)
University of Tokyo

# Acknowledgments

*Nihon no kigyo*, the original Japanese book, derives from a project by leading Japanese economists launched in 1986, culminating in conferences in Gotemba and Oiso in 1988 and 1989, and published by the Tokyo University Press in 1989. Two of the papers were subsequently published in English; Masahiko Aoki's "Toward an Economic Model of the Japanese Firm" in the *Journal of Economic Literature*, March 1990, and Isao Ohashi's "On the Determinants of Bonuses and Basic Wages in Large Japanese Firms" in the *Journal of the Japanese and International Economies*, December, 1989. We are grateful to the editors of these journals for permission to reprint the articles here.

The initial work of translation was a cooperative effort. The editors would like to thank all those who took part: Douglas Anthony (chapters 1 and 4), Martin Bronfenbrenner (chapter 13), Giorgio Brunello and Manuela Berlanda (chapter 12), Alice Lam (chapter 11), Brian MacLean (chapter 15), Colin McKenzie (chapters 16 and 18), Marcus Rebick (chapter 10), Mari Sako (chapter 5), Norihiko Shirouzu (chapter 6), Christoph Sieglen and Martha Lane (chapter 7), Susan Weiner (chapter 9), and Eleanor Westney (chapter 8), The remaining two (chapter 3—Dore; chapter 17—Whittaker) were our responsibility.

We would also like to extend our thanks to the Japan Industrial Policy Research Institute for a grant facilitating the translation, and to those who helped with the editing—Alison Chapman, Elizabeth Draper, and Steven Wilkinson. The only contribution to the original work not reproduced here is a theoretical note on the theory of the firm by Yosuke Okada, but many of the other papers have been substantially abbreviated. We believe that nothing of importance has been lost, but we crave the indulgence of authors who might feel otherwise and thank the original editors for their tolerance in permitting us to substantially reedit.

Ronald Dore
Hugh Whittaker

**Business Enterprise
in Japan**

# Introduction

Ronald Dore and
Hugh Whittaker

The importance of this book is twofold. First, it goes beyond the common emphasis in writings about "the Japanese firm" on the large industrial corporation; it includes papers, for instance, on cooperatives, on public enterprises, and on the (mostly mutual) life insurance companies. Second, because of the range of topics tackled and the variety of perspectives held by its contributors, the book offers a good overview of the wide spectrum of interpretative viewpoints among Japanese economists—the more useful in that the authors represented are generally regarded as the leading authorities in the field.

## Capitalism, Not Capitalism, or a Different Form of Capitalism?

Japanese firms may be renowned as models of consensus, but those who write about them are not. Perhaps the most fundamental line of contention divides those who say that the Japanese system is radically different from the familiar "Western" or "neoclassical" models, and those who would argue that given a few major differences in institutional arrangements, the Japanese system is in all essentials driven by the same market forces and competitive individualistic motivational drives as are assumed by neoclassical economists.

By and large—though the correlation of views is not perfect—the former attribute the high level of performance of Japanese firms to precisely those features that differentiate them from their foreign competitors, the latter to the ability to beat Westerners on their own ground.

The conferences at which these papers were first presented occurred too early for our authors to be able to comment on a new and related point of debate—between those who see the bursting of the recent speculative bubble at a time of more general recession as being merely a temporary trial that will be countered by the characteristic strengths of the Japanese firm and those who view it as a turning point in accelerating the inevitable process through which Japanese firms are increasingly forced (e.g., by the internationalization of financial markets) to become more and more like those of Western countries. But anyone who wants to make up his mind on that "change or no change" question will gain a lot from the analyses offered here, written, as they were, at a time when the economy was romping away.

Are Japanese firms governed by the same economic principles as they are understood in the West and the same capitalist assumptions about property rights? On the one hand is the view best epitomized in Komiya's remarks in the last chapter about the inapplicability of the word "capitalism" to the system that prevails in Japan. First, he says, there are not many capitalists in charge of business enterprises, and second, the maximization of the returns to capital plays a very small part in determining the motives of major decision makers. Japan is very different, in quite fundamental ways, from the United States.

Komiya is perhaps not the best representative of this school; he has too long a history as a leader in the diffusion of neoclassical economics in Japan. (A now eminent pupil recalls with delight the days when students who used the phrase "excessive competition"—then a favorite analytical tool of MITI—could be sure of getting a D, since rigorous economics allowed for no such concept.) A more overt champion is Itami whose paper in this volume neatly summarizes his view of the Japanese business firm as exemplary of "human-capital-ism"—an organization that gives pride of place to the owners of human capital rather than to the owners of physical capital. In fact Itami's paper is not just about the business firm but about the whole economic structure. His contribution is to show how certain consistent principles—the diffused sharing of information and the evocation of trust and cooperation—are characteristic both of the internal structure of firms and of the trading relations between them. These lead to a distinctive set of behavioral characteristics not explained by neoclassical theory.

In the opposing view the term capitalism is hardly ever used, but the assumption that managers are there to maximize the returns to shareholders and hire the necessary labor with that end in view—as company law *says* is the case as much in Japan as in Britain—is basic to the analysis. So also are the assumptions of the homogeneity, rationality, and the predominantly self-interested concerns of Man. The generalizations, the regularities of behavior, the laws built into economists' equations, follow inevitably from these assumptions and are therefore universal. Much of the English-language work by this school is designed to demonstrate that universality. The typical paper says: All right; to be sure, at first sight it looks as if the Japanese behave differently. But in fact they are just as self-interestedly rational as Americans. They just happen to have got a different set of institutions that change, slightly, the constraints on their behavior. But if you take, say, the lifetime employment convention, or, the seniority-constrained promotion system, or the investor's expectation of dividend levels, as the initial starting point, then you can see that our models of rational behavior apply *within those constraints* just as much as within the different constraints of, say, the American economy. In Japan, as elsewhere, it is *competition*—interpersonal as well as interorganizational—that is the engine of efficiency. One of our authors has subsequently written a book (Odagiri 1992) of which this is the very explicit theme.

In this volume Koike's paper about intellectual skills and the organization of shopfloor work is a good example. He argues that the motivation for acquiring skills can be ascribed to individualistic self-interest. Notions of Japanese "groupism" are redundant. They may be developed more cleverly, but individualistic competitive instincts are every bit as strong as in the West, perhaps stronger.

Much of the discussion, however, accepts that there are distinctively Japanese characteristics and centers on how summarily to characterize them. Most of the authors would agree that if you want to understand what goes on in Japanese boardrooms, you can throw most of the writings that go under the rubric "agency theory" out of the window. (One could probably say much the same about RJR Nabisco.) But should one lump managers with other employees and talk about "employee power," "employee sovereignty," a "labor-managed firm," or are managers the arbiters in a "dual sovereignty system"? Where does the *overall* balance of power between employees, managers, and shareholders lie?

This is not *just* a glass half full/half empty question, since, as Aoki suggests in his chapter, each label suggests a different maximand for the firm (on the assumption of self-interest), and econometric studies ought to confirm or refute hypotheses about maximands. His essay is the most systematic and comprehensive exploration of these issues, a synthesis of ideas he has been developing in two books already familiar to Western readers (1984a, 1988). He is quite clear about the differences between what he calls the J-mode firm and its American counterpart, the H-mode firm. He also clearly characterizes the standard "theory of the firm" (and the burgeoning literature applying game theory to principal-agency relations) as describing the H-mode firm but not the J-firm. But his three "duality principles" suggest that the difference might be seen as a difference in the choice among a range of "functional alternatives," with the range itself being defined by some overarching economic logic. He looks forward to the day when there might be an overarching "theory of the firm" that might embrace both J-firms and H-firms.

What would the overarching, culture-free (or rather all-cultures-embracing) theory of the firm be like? Vacuous, probably. As long as "utility" is an empty suitcase into which we each can pack our own fancy clothes, absolutely anything can be subject to economic analysis. The question is, whether we learn anything by rising to such stratospheric levels of generality. One may question whether Gary Becker on the economics of love and marriage enables us to understand better the relations between men and women either in the United States or in India, let alone the differences between them (Becker 1981). The same might be said of the theory of the firm.

### Culture, Altruism, and Cooperation

It is clear from his concluding remarks that for Aoki, the potential joker in the pack, the potential obstacle to a complete theory of the firm, is "culture." By culture he seems to mean behavior that is driven by the inertia of convention or by some absolute value preference, rather than by the deliberate choice of means to one of the utility-maximizing ends typically recognized in the (Western) economic literature. While the "collective memory of traditional agrarian customs and values" have played a part, it is historically clear that many of the features of modern Japanese firms are the product of managerial design, deliberate means of eliciting cooperation and diligence. "Many of the elements of the J-model should *now* be regarded as serious objects of economic analysis." (Our emphasis. But one question in passing, Didn't militant unions in the immediate postwar period play an important part in the inventions too?)

Actually the real joker in the pack, the real threat to rigorous neoclassical economics, is not "culture" as such but (to be sure, "culturally determined") altruism. Can we not detect this in Itami's "diffuse sharing"? Is there not just *a bit* of it—as well as all the self-interested calculations of long-run material profit—in the way Japanese workers accept subordination in hierarchies, give up their weekends so that the firm can get a new product out two days ahead of its rivals, take salary cuts when the firm is in difficulties? Game theory of course might find a way of explaining how the life-risking behavior of a tightly integrated, high-morale platoon in battle boils down to self-interest. Certainly it has been employed to show, in relation to employee and firm behavior, that rational calculation of self-interest under the expectation of repeated games is all that is required to explain *coopera-tion*. But can that really be all there is to it?

There are shadows here of the great political divide of the twentieth century—the division between the liberal vision of the invisible hand economy driven by *competition* and the socialist vision of a collective or a mixed economy rooted in *cooperation*. Now that the only economies that explicitly claimed to represent the latter ideal have been strangulated by their productive inefficiency, perhaps, in what Michel Albert calls the confrontation of capitalisms (1991), it is Japan that will take over the banner of cooperation. That does not necessarily mean that the Japanese have to acknowledge an affinity between their form of capitalism and the structure of Russian values—that affinity which Alan Blinder discerns when he recommends to the Russians that they take the shorter leap to a Japanese form of capitalism rather than the longer leap to the American one (1992). They would no doubt be loathe to do so. So would all those writers of the left who think that "Toyotism" is somehow even more morally objectionable than "Fordism" but are not quite sure why. Once one gets away from simple game theorist notions that cooperation arises only from self-interest/ repetition, one begins to make important distinctions: between egalitarian cooperation and hierarchical cooperation, between aloof authoritarian hierarchies and friendly all-dressed-in-the-same-uniform hierarchies, between cooperation for individual ends (which Anglo-Saxons generally approve of) and cooperation in the interests of some transcendental entity—"our company" or *"der Vaterland"* (Anglo-Saxons of left-wing persuasion always have had trouble coming to terms with the fact that Hitler's "national socialism" was not inaccurately described as a form of socialism).

## Capitalists and Workers: Risk and Control

That said, there is another sense in which Japan might be considered to represent a "left-wing" solution to the problems of running an industrial economy—the greater relative power of employees vis-à-vis the owners of capital, described in several of the contributions. In the labor-controlled firm, as Imai and Komiya spell it out in their opening paper, inputs and outputs are determined so as to maximize income per employee after paying a fixed share of profits to shareholders. This leads to growth orientation rather than short-term profit maximization, as well as limits on recruitment.

As Imai and Komiya, as well as Itami, and Kagano and Kobayashi point out, this is also a just recognition of the distribution of risk. Shareholders are necessary to provide capital, but given modern stockmarkets they can easily sell their holdings (if they are clever with only limited loss) and so face only limited risk. Employees, on the other hand, especially in the Japanese employment system, cannot easily transfer their skill resources without loss. It is also a recognition of the fact that in an age of high technology, human capital, built up through long years of experience and job rotation within the firm, is now *the* key resource.

Hence it is now right and rational that employees—or *their* representatives, the directors—make the key decisions and that they partake of the fruits of their endeavours. What is right and rational, however, does not always happen. The reason why it does happen in Japan, these authors suggest, is because of the pattern of shareholding (which so upset T. Boone Pickens as rampant *in*justice when he tried to get directors on the board of Koito) and because of the career tracks internal to firms that ensure a basic harmony between director policies and worker interests.

Capitalists, in this conception, do not control the firm, either directly or indirectly. Aoki disagrees, insisting on a duality of control between providers of finance—particularly banks which are both major shareholders and loan providers—and employees. Control by the former manifests itself when things go wrong; declining profit rates can invite bank intervention, including the removal of senior management. But, to evoke worker cooperation, managers do not have to be single-minded representatives of the employees. It is enough if they are seen to strike a fair balance between the interests of employees and the owners of capital. If they do, they can expect employees to contribute greater effort than they would under a competitive wage system, and to invest in their own training, with the result that a Pareto-superior outcome is achieved. This does not come about automatically, however, but rather through a nonhierarchical style of operations coordination, balanced by a hierarchical incentive system, contrasting with the representative Western firm which combines the hierarchical coordination of operations with a more nonhierarchical incentive system.

### Bonuses and Flexibility

For readers for whom this is all a bit metaphysical and who just want to know what gives with Japanese firms and how they work, there is plenty of meat, though the nature of this meat is still open to debate.

Several of the contributions offer evidence or interpretations of the bonuses paid by Japanese firms (twice yearly, amounting in the average large firm to the equivalent of four or five months' wages)—a question that attracted a great deal of attention when "stagflation" and "Eurosclerosis" were dominant topics of concern and the OECD was mobilizing economists for studies of the sources of rigidity and flexibility. Freeman and Weitzman (1987), for instance, are inclined to see the Japanese bonus system as an approximation to Weitzman's model of the "share economy" (1984), responsible for helping to weather shocks and hold down unemployment. Some of our authors—Komiya, Imai, and Itami, for instance—in line with their characterization of the Japanese firm as controlled by workers, or under "employee sovereignty"—also treat the bonus as a form of profit distribution, pointing out that bonuses actually vary with company performance more than do shareholder dividends.

Ohashi challenges the profit-distribution model as neglecting general labor market conditions in the determination of wage and bonus levels, a deficiency that he seeks to correct by using an efficiency wage model. He argues, using micro-level firm data as well as two-digit industry classifications, that bonuses reward intensity of work (as measured partly by sales and partly by overtime), and he assumes (though it is in the nature of regression analysis that he cannot prove it) that the prospect of increased bonuses motivates the extra intensity of work. (That is presumed to be managers' intention, rather than a mere ex post sharing out of the cake because bonuses correlate better with sales than with profits, which include nonoperating income.) Intensity of work is rewarded in the form of bonus because this saves on transaction costs required for measurement and negotiation.

Koshiro also emphasises labor market conditions but argues that the strong downward rigidity of bonuses compromises both the profit sharing and the flexibility effects. Bonus levels are, to be sure, related to profits, (more closely, he finds, as does Ohashi, than are wage increases), but bonuses and wages respond more strongly to labor market conditions and price movements than conventional wage theories would predict. However, bonuses should also be seen in their historical context as protecting workers' living conditions. His overall conclusion, which so neatly encapsulates the debates we have outlined, is that "the Japanese employment system can basically be explained by the neoclassical theory of human capital and the theory of internal labor markets, with the important qualification that this system is close to that of the labor-managed firm."

## Nonhierarchical Coordination

Hierarchy is slippery word. Consider the Aoki distinction quoted earlier: The J-firm is hierarchical in the sense that the incentive system depends on a hierarchy of status and pay which individuals seek to climb, but the coordination of decisions is nonhierarchical. The typical H-firm organization, by contrast, works by hierarchical coordination; orders go from upper to lower levels. The same term "hierarchy" is used, on the one hand, to describe a ranking in terms of status and material rewards and, on the other, a ranking in terms of differential power. Perhaps a better way of making the distinction that avoids the ambiguities of the word "hierarchy" would be "imperative coordination" (the H-firm) versus "collegial coordination" (the J-firm).

The two contributions on corporate R&D by Wakasugi and Nonaka are striking illustrations of this nonhierarchical, or nonimperative, collegial, coordination. Cooperation across job boundaries and departments is seen to foster rapid product development from conception through to marketing (but not basic research), encouraged by interdepartmental career development paths, and institutional factors such as flexible, market-oriented R&D budgeting. "Learning by intrusion," through a shared division of labor is an important feature of Nonaka's particular Japan versus West dichotomy—information/problem creation versus information processing/ problem solving.

Koike, who is well-known as one of the few economists to have undertaken detailed factory fieldwork and who has generated much of the discussion of job rotation and career development, has a rather different emphasis. He maintains that job assignments and responsibilities *are* clearly set, both for routine and nonroutine work. Whatever "teamwork" means, in Japanese factories it does not imply any vagueness about who does what. The crucial element of superiority in the Japanese firm, what gives it competitive strength, is the high level of firm-specific intellectual skills that individuals possess.

**Long-termism**

As noted earlier, Koike stresses that the incentives to acquire those firm-specific intellectual skills take the shape of prospects of preferential career advancement over the long term. The advancement for which employees compete takes place not in big decisive jumps but in small steps over a long period. Losers do not lose definitively; they still have opportunities that are worth competing for. As in Axelrod's model of repeated games, it is the long-term orientation of employees engaged in these rank-order contests (blue-collar workers in their career tracks as well as graduates competing to end their careers with the top salaries in top management) that induces cooperation through mere self-interest. Parsimony can rule out resort to any other (dangerously cultural) explanatory variables like a friendly desire to help out a colleague, or a sense of duty, or an interest in skill acquirement as a form of self-realization, or some kind of indentification with the firm and its goals.

The long-term orientation of individuals is also the central theme of Kagono and Kobayashi who very specifically take up the notion of "identification with the firm." They don't quite do the same sanitizing job on motivations as Koike; they take seriously both the expressions of worker loyalty and also, in apparent paradox, the expressions of dissatisfaction that are regularly turned up in attitude surveys of employees. But they do persuasively argue that identification with the firm has a self-interested logic. Their central concept is "logic of commitment" as opposed to a (U.S.) "logic of exit." Many of the investments made by employees and the assets they have developed over the long term are realizable only within the firm, and these assets would not be fully appreciated in the market place. Hence there is greater commitment, though not necessarily happy, satisfied commitment. Where the "logic of exit" prevails, however, the freedom of exit of uncommitted shareholders, and the insecurity thereby induced in managers by frequent takeovers, has a knock-on effect to reduce commitment, as much on the part of senior managers as on rank and file employees. Needless to say, the former is seen as more conducive to incremental innovation.

The long-term perspective is also, not surprisingly, a central concept of Ono and Yoshikawa's study of plant and equipment investment in the postwar period—the fluctuations in its volume, yields (distinctly lower in the 1970s than in other industrial countries), year-to-year stability, and relative cost. Why should Japan have had investment rates consistently four or five percentage points of GDP higher than that of the United States? Again, the answer is the long-term orientation of the decision-making managers and the attitudes toward technology and skill acquisition (holding out prospects that investments will be efficient) that long-term employment induces in the work force.

### Keiretsu

There are strong parallels between discussions of long-termism and *intra-firm* cooperation/competition, on the one hand, and the discussion of long-termism and *interfirm* relations in Ito's paper, one of the three on trading structures which illuminate one of the hotter themes in the perennially acrimonious U.S.–Japan negotiations about the closed nature of the Japanese economy.

Ten years ago *keiretsu* had the rather precise and limited meaning of a pyramidical structure of subsidiaries and highly dependent suppliers and subcontractors grouped around a large manufacturing firm. It was not used to describe the rather different groupings—neither similarly hierarchical nor imperatively coordinated—of firms derived from the old *zaibatsu* conglomerates, or of firms that share a connection with the same main bank. Foreigners tended to conflate the two in their attempt to put some name to that secret impenetrable conspiracy which denied them access to Japanese markets. *Keiretsu* became a word to conjure with, like freemasonry in some other societies. Gradually, tired of trying to make clear distinctions, the Japanese have accepted the conflation and now use *keiretsu* in the wider sense. But the distinction remains important, and Imai's paper clarifies it.

In fact he separates four phenomena: There is the pyramid or "solar system" type of real, hierarchical *keiretsu* built around a single dominant firm. In the second category are the three ex-*zaibatsu* enterprise groups (Mitsui, Mitsubishi, Sumitomo) whose firms often retain the old *zaibatsu* name, have fairly substantial cross-holdings of shares, occasionally exchange directors, usually contain only one major firm in any industry, and are in fact a cluster of independent firms that maintain (limited) preferential trading relations and technical cooperation relations with each other. The third category, the groups that share a main bank, have similar characteristics—and similarly define their boundaries in terms of membership in their presidents' lunch club, but they have a lesser density of cross-shareholdings, recognize less strong ties of obligation to trade preferentially with each other, and, indeed, may sometimes include competitors in the same industry. Unlike the old *zaibatsu* groups, moreover, membership is not exclusive. Hitachi belongs to two of the bank groups.

The fourth phenomenon Imai calls not an enterprise group but an enterprise network. Like the others it is a set of firms that has well-established trading relations which are expected to last over time. This group differs from the ex-*zaibatsu* groups in that there is none of the paraphernalia of presidents' lunches or cross-holdings of shares, and it differs from the *keiretsu* proper in not being dominated by a single firm and not being hierarchical. Dependence is mutual, rather than one-sided. The firms are usually organized round the production and distribution of particular products or services and are stable as long as, but only as long as, the market for those products or services is stable.

What all these *keiretsu* have in common is a pattern of trading relations. Much has been written about these trading arrangements in recent years, particularly about subcontracting in manufacturing. They are market relations to be sure, but customer markets not auction markets, relational contracting rather than spot contracting, relations based on an appreciation of the investment made in the relation itself, on a sense of obligation to take the rough with the smooth to continue it, and a trust in the trading partner's acceptance of the same obligation.

Ito's paper explores the way in which such relationships not only promote cooperation but also risk sharing and the joint creation and ownership of information. But at the same time there are safeguards against the abuse of trust (what economists often call "moral hazard" even when it is not clear whether it is A who is in danger of falling into sin, or B who is in danger from A's immorality). In the long run, getting benefit out of the relationship depends on performance. In the case of the hierarchical *keiretsu*, dependent subcontractors compete for preferential "ranking" in the system, just as employees compete for promotion within the firm.

All this is illustrated in detail in Miwa's study of subcontracting in the automobile industry. These trading relationships involve the development of relation-specific rather than general competences. The investments made, and the rents generated, cannot be realized in full if taken to the open marketplace. One again, voice is preferred to exit, and Miwa suggests greater efficiency results.

This gray zone between market and hierarchy has become a commonplace of transaction cost economics in recent years, but Imai's analysis sets these structures not only in the Williamsonian tradition but also in that of the much older literature on monopoly and vertical integration. Nowadays, with modern complications of the technical process of production and modern communications, to operate in that gray zone between market and hierarchy, he claims, gives a firm a competitive edge over the vertically integrated firm traditionally favored in the United States—superior information flows, better interaction with the market. Lack of the powers of ownership control that characterize the vertically integrated firm proves not to be essential. It may be historical accident that Japan has come one way, while the United States went the other. But Japan has been lucky; the system she has got stuck with is the more efficient one.

## Control and Accountability in the Absence of Shareholders

The papers of the last section of the book raise the issue of what shareholders do and corporate control in another form—by looking at three forms of business organization operating in, at least somewhat competitive, markets, that are not privately owned or joint stock companies—government and public enterprises (Uekusa), members of cooperatives (Saeki), and policyholders of mutual life insurance companies (Komiya). There is also a paper by Kishimoto on the big utility companies that *are* joint stock companies—regulated private monopolies—which gives a foretaste of what will result from some of the privatizations discussed by Uekusa.

The latter's paper, as well as giving an overview of the structure of public enterprise in Japan, concentrates on the three main post-1985 privatizations of former wholly public enterprises—telecommunications, the railways, and tobacco manufacture and distribution—and of the complete privatization of the former public-private, joint-stock-with-government-control company, Japan Air Lines. His analysis of the sources of inefficiency is particularly clear; Diet control over budgeting and accounts settlement was subject to pork-barreling influence and a source of inefficiency through the carry-over of rules such as purchase at list price and the need to exhaust budgets within the year. Growth and profit/cost reduction came to be overshadowed as managerial objectives, by the need to avoid conflict, controversy, or accidents that would evoke political interference. "Managerial slack" was induced partly by this lack of independence, partly by political control over appointments, and partly by political constraints on the handling of unions. "Slack" as compared to what, though? It may be an indication of the national X-efficiency norm—the standard by which managerial "slackness" or "tightness" is judged—that the national railway, held up to scorn in mid-1980s for its huge level of accumulated debts, in fact had a gap between earned revenue and outgoings far smaller than any of the subsidized railways of Europe—not to mention a better record for running trains on time. (In the case of some European railways, one needs to add, as the small print on the timetables does, "or at all.")

"Selling off the family silver to pay the butcher," as Harold Macmillan, the former prime minister, called Mrs. Thatcher's privatizations, takes on a rather different color when you can sell off a little over a third of the equity in your telecommunications company for ninety billion dollars, as the Japanese government managed to do with measurable impact on the public debt. Uekusa considers the privatizations a success, however, on more counts than that. Managerial independence, fewer restrictions on entrepreneurial initiatives, a bit of competition at the margins (he doesn't mention pressure from shareholders to make profits and pay dividends) have improved performance in all kinds of ways which he describes in concrete terms.

Anyone who has wondered how it is that the president of the Tokyo Electric Power Company gets to chair the main employers' confederation, and how it is that his company, which exports little more than a few packages of technology, can give such lavish parties in the world's capitals in the midst of a recession, will have had cause to reflect that the problems of control over natural monopoly are not easy problems. Obviously a case for eternal vigilance. It is not clear from Kishimoto's paper on the gas and power generation industry that vigilance is what they get. He assures us that, although, as "income-per-worker-maximizing" employee-controlled firms, as in the Imai/Komiya characterization of Japanese enterprises generally, the public regulation of tariffs (to give a "reasonable"—7 to 8 percent—return on "reasonable" costs) may induce less than a socially optimum supply, competition from other power sources and from self-generation by big volume users saves the day. One would like to see the econometric work that would fortify this reassurance.

There is no ambiguity, by contrast, over whom the mutual life insurance companies are formally responsible to—their policyholders. Nevertheless, that is hardly the way they behave, as Komiya's paper shows. As in other countries, they are major holders of equity, but they seem not to be concerned—as institutional investors are in the United States or in Britain and as, in theory, it is their fiduciary duty toward policyholders to be—primarily with maximizing the returns on their equity investments. There are regulatory constraints, but life insurance companies, just like the banks, have other ties with the companies whose shares they own, notably providing policies for their employees. It is through exploiting these ties that they get the growth in market share which is their more dominant objective. The mutual companies seem in fact to behave no differently from the minority of life insurance companies that take a joint-stock form. Both, Komiya claims, fit his characterization of the typical Japanese corporation as firms that behave as if they are controlled by their workers. Which is far from saying that they are not subject to efficiency-inducing market discipline. There *is* a competitive market for insurance services (though muted by state regulation of premiums). Komiya also points out another neglected but very important market—that for university graduates. Nothing worries the responsible elders of an enterprise community more than the prospect of a decline in the quality of new generations of recruits. Life insurance companies have usually figured strongly in the annually published league tables that show the employment preferences of graduates from the elite universities. A firm that has dropped from third place to thirteenth would have a very worried board of directors. The way to prevent that is not just better PR and recruitment drives but better published performance figures.

Paradoxically the enterprises that behave least like worker-controlled firms are the cooperatives discussed by Saeki. Not really a paradox, of course, since neither of the two very different kinds of organizations Saeki discusses are production organizations owned by their employees. First are consumer cooperatives owned by the users of their services. The much more important comprehensive agricultural cooperatives (a third of the members but many times the turnover) are cooperatives of agricultural producers who combine for the scale economies of cooperative marketing, credit, and input purchasing services—with agricultural credit expanding into all kinds of financial services, and input purchasing into general consumer cooperation. The former spring from the grass roots and have an anti-establishment flavor. The latter are buttressed by half a century's accretion of state subsidies and regulations that are very largely administered through, and provide a substantial part of the revenue for, the cooperatives.

Village cooperatives combine in a pyramidal structure of prefectural federations and the prefectural confederations in national-level organizations. The last can be very large and powerful; in the 1950s the Central Agricultural Credit Bank was so flush with funds that it could dominate the overnight money market. No shareholders, it would seem, could be more remote and more "captive" than the ultimate family-farmer owners of these cooperative organizations. Hence one would expect control to pass easily into the hands of an increasingly professionalized management and staff. But not entirely. In a Uruguay Round world where agricultural subsidies are under attack, these cooperatives are also lobbies. The ultimate owners are very interested indeed in those lobbying efforts and can read about them daily in their newspapers. Hence there is tension between the elected representatives' emphasis on the lobbying function and the professionals' on the specialist function—and a greater potential for conflict than in the typical joint-stock company.

Deregulation and trade liberalization will have no effect on the consumer cooperatives. It will hit the agricultural coop system hard.

**About the Future?**

It all reads like a picture of a very stable system. But is it? Once upon a time it was standard for works on Japanese enterprises to finish with the prediction that the whole system was about to change. We could be reassured that any peculiarities were transitory, that Japanese companies would become more Western—more normal. Some of our authors are more ambivalent here. Deregulation, internationalization, the aging of the work force, trade liberalization—or growing trade management—will produce a very different world, say some, though perhaps there will be mutual convergence. Others imply that Japanese enterprises will continue to respond to these pressures in their own characteristic way, which will maintain their competitiveness. They are a bit short, however, on precise predictions. They leave them to the reader's imagination. So do we.

# I     The Firm

# 1 Characteristics of Japanese Firms

Kenichi Imai and
Ryutaro Komiya

In this chapter we outline our overall approach, within the framework of economic analysis, to the elucidation of the basic characteristics of the structure and behavior of Japanese firms—especially large firms. This background should help with the understanding of the separate arguments that are developed in the chapters that follow.[1]

In what follows, we deal first with the significance of the "lifetime employment" and "seniority payment" systems in Japanese firms, the way in which they are economically rational, given their socioeconomic environment, and how they relate to the Japanese firm's concern with growth. Then, we explain how large firms in Japan have characteristics that resemble those of so-called worker-controlled firms in that, in a broad sense, profits are distributed to employees. In that discussion we consider the relationship between this characteristic and the tendency to create networks of subcontractors, subsidiaries, affiliates, and so on. Next we turn to the distribution of profits and the role of the shareholder as we spell out our basic approach to modern Japanese firms. Last, we touch upon a few problematical points and some prospects for the future.

## 1.1 Japanese Firms and Their Concern with Growth

Large Japanese firms are generally known to have certain employment practices—namely lifetime employment and the *nenko* (seniority and merit) principle of promotion by seniority—that differ from those of Western firms. These practices are thought to be connected with the strong growth orientation of Japanese firms. Where lifetime employment and *nenko* promotion prevail, the rapid growth of the firm benefits those who work for it.

---

1. Not all the authors in this book share the opinion as to what characteristics constitute the Japanese firm. The views in this chapter are strictly our own, but we believe they represent the "highest common denominator" of the views of the various authors.

It gives them opportunities for promotion, high salaries, and reemployment after retirement. As a consequence there is strong pressure from within the firm for growth. At the same time the means of growth—continual technological innovation—requires the buildup of human resources within the firm, the accumulation of the ability to learn and to solve problems, which the lifetime employment and *nenko* systems facilitate. There is mutual reinforcement.

The large firm in present-day Japan differs somewhat from the classical image of the firm, where capitalists—the suppliers of capital—employ labor and seek to maximize the returns on their capital. It is better defined as an organizational entity consisting of aggregations of managers, technologists, skilled workers, sales and clerical personnel who have accumulated the capacity to operate in some specific area of business activity. They are not simply aggregations of labor inputs employed by capital. They are integrated bodies of "human capital." The separation of ownership and control has probably gone further in the large firm sector (big business) in Japan than in any of the other advanced countries. The shareholders' say in the affairs of a firm and their power to influence its operations are weak. There is good ground for describing Japanese managers as representatives of the people who constitute the firm.

How did Japanese firms get to be like this? Our explanation is as follows. We use technical jargon only when it is inescapable.

## 1.2   The Lifetime Employment System and the *Nenko* Principle

By the lifetime employment system, we mean the custom whereby the "regular" employees of a firm do not have their employment terminated when the firm has no further use for them, nor are they laid off, temporarily or otherwise, except where the firm encounters serious operating difficulties. By "regular" employees, we mean those who are employed on a permanent basis, having been recruited from among new graduates of high schools and universities over a wide geographical area. We do not include irregular workers such as temporary and part-time employees, and "outsiders" such as those employed on despatch or secondment from other firms. However, if temporary workers satisfy certain conditions, they can become "fully" or "properly" employed and become "regular" workers.

Although we use the term *lifetime employment*, we do not mean literally that workers stay with one firm until they die. Most firms have a retirement age of between 55 and 66, and a fair number of younger workers, especially those in their twenties, voluntarily move from one firm to another.

It is difficult to provide a simple explanation of the legal basis for lifetime employment. There is, for example, no unambiguous contract that guarantees employment until retirement. However, in some instances a regional labor relations committee or a court may decide that a "regular" employee of a firm was dismissed without "reasonable" cause and order the firm to reemploy the worker.

The lifetime employment system is not necessarily peculiar to Japan. The leading firms in the United States and Europe operate on a similar system. There is also some debate as to whether the system in Japan is in the process of breaking down. At present, however, the traditional lifetime employment system is found in most large firms in Japan. Its existence is commonly accepted among those seeking employment with firms, those currently in employment, and among employers.

Unless something untoward happens, most firms try to avoid dismissing regular employees. Even when technical innovation or restructuring makes a cutback in personnel unavoidable, the normal pattern is first to transfer staff to subsidiary and associated firms, and then to seek voluntary redundancies by topping up retirement benefits. Only then, if the number of workers is still too great, will the firm resort to designated dismissals.

Most employees want to guarantee their livelihood and status by working as long as possible with one firm. In most Japanese universities a budding scholar assumes that he will pass through the positions of assistant and lecturer before becoming an assistant professor and then professor. In contrast to the United States, if an offer of tenure is not quickly forthcoming, he will not consider it necessary to seek a position elsewhere.

In most areas the lifetime employment system is likely to experience some change in the future. But, as long as socioeconomic rationality pertains (in the sense that we will explain it), it is likely to persist among Japanese firms as one of their distinctive features.

The *nenko* (seniority payment and advancement) system is the practice by which wages and salaries of regular employees increase in each specified interval of time. From the point of view of function and status, promotion is granted at fixed intervals of time. It would be a mistake, however, to interpret this term literally as meaning that positions within the firm, and wages or salaries, are determined merely according to length of service.

In terms of bonuses and company position, employees with similar academic records and length of service get increases in remuneration and are promoted at rates that are essentially the same for some time after being engaged by the firm. Thereafter, merit-related differences begin to appear in their pay increases, bonuses, and speed of promotions. In general, white-collar workers who have passed the age of forty are subject to a strict selection process if they wish to become managers (*bucho*) or section chiefs (*kacho*). Furthermore, not all *bucho* or *kacho* jobs are equally desirable. Some are good posts, some not so good, and some mere sinecures. From the time of employment onward, stiff competition takes place among those recruited in the same year with regard to future promotion. Nevertheless, the firm tries hard to give equal attention to raising the abilities and competence level of each employee and to keeping the evaluation process as fair as possible. A fairly large number of people take part in the lengthy evaluation process, and normally the firm takes a good deal of trouble to obtain the agreement of those parties interested in the evaluation. As a result promotions and pay increases take place in accordance with an evaluation with which most parties concur.

The *nenko* system in Japan is closely bound up with the in-firm policy for fostering talent and developing the capacities of the work force. In Europe and America employers typically take on workers from the external labor market, rather than engaging in periodic wage and salary increases, promotions, and job transfer. Or else they may seek out and promote a suitable person from within the organization irrespective of his place in the seniority ranking. This is fundamentally different from the personnel policy of Japanese firms.

The method of selecting top managers (*keieisha*) in Japanese firms is an extension of the *nenko* system for employees. Most top managers in large Japanese firms—directors (*torishimariyaku*), executive directors (*jomu*), managing directors (*senmu*), vice presidents (*fukushacho*), presidents (*shacho*), and chairmen of boards of directors (*kaicho*)—entered their company upon leaving school or university and were selected from among those who had been promoted through the seniority payment and advancement system. In most large firms the custom is that the man at the top of the management structure—the company president—decides who is to be the next president. It is true that in some American firms (GE, Exxon, IBM, and TI) the company president is chosen from among the long-serving members of the work force. However, the system as described —where nearly all the top managers, including the company president, are promoted from among the work force, and the company president chooses the next president—seems to be peculiar to Japan. It is because of these selection and promotion practices that managers in large Japanese firms come so strongly to take on the appearance of representatives of their employees.

## 1.3 Economic Rationality

It is clear that traditional Japanese principles for the formation of organizations and the Confucian concept of *seniores priores*—precedence to the old over the young—have been influential in producing those features of Japanese firms that we have referred to above as the lifetime employment system and the *nenko* system.[2] However, it is important from the economist's point of view to explain how it was that, against this historical and cultural background, Japanese firms formed their organizations, developed them, and adapted them to changes in the environment and, in dynamic terms, made them into efficient organizations. The fundamental reason for the organizational success of Japanese firms may be considered to be that, at least in the postwar economic and social environment, the systems of lifetime employment and seniority payment and advancement have a greater economic rationality than alternative organizational and employment mechanisms.

Had the lifetime employment system and the *nenko* system been formed only as the result of historical and cultural factors, then we would expect these practices always to have been present in large Japanese firms. But they only took root in Japanese industrial society—for the blue-collar workers—from the mid-1950s. Once large Japanese firms had improved their economic efficiency by adopting this formula, it spread to firms of middle-standing as an organizational form in the 1960s and was then adopted by many small- and medium-sized firms in the latter half of the 1970s.

What enabled the extension of these systems among large Japanese firms from the mid-1950s was the widespread support for the idea that if a firm's employees could come to look at the firm as a community, they would be better able to revive firms that had been weakened by the war. These attempts to create such communities (*kyodotai*), including the entire work force of a firm, had originally been made in the prewar period with the goal of developing the company in a way that would overcome the labor union movement. That union movement had gained power in 1945 and remained strong until the mid-1950s largely due to the influence of the Japanese Communist Party. In addition, however, the absorption of new technologies from Europe and America in this period necessitated greater

2. The president of a large Japanese company, as well as being a highly capable member of the organization, must be a model leader for the people of the organization. A president with these attributes is able to exercise powerful leadership.

labor and management cooperation. To make up for the postwar deficit in Japanese technological innovation, and to compete with European and American firms, companies imported new technologies and tailored them to the Japanese industrial system. Even if firms had attempted to resort to the external labor market for the technical and skilled workers they needed to use these new technologies, such workers were in scarce supply. So for large Japanese firms the most effective means of meeting the labor demands of the new technologies was to develop the skills of their own workers through so-called on-the-job training.

On-the-job training is not solely concerned with developing specialist skills within the firm related to a particular task, nor with training people externally at specialist schools and colleges. If it were, it is possible that specialists trained within the firm might eventually go independent on the basis of their skills or transfer to another firm. Instead, large firms in post-war Japan had their workers experience various kinds of work within the same workplace. This "all-rounder" formula was also extended to white-collar workers, who were attached to a succession of different sections and departments within the company as part of a promotion process, which resembled more a "spiral staircase" than a "ladder." This method of forming a wide range of skills useful to the firm's activities is not possible except when premised on a long-term and stable employment relationship. Work-ers trained in this fashion acquire skills that are more or less specific to the firm, so transfer to another firm would put them at a disadvantage.

It is not certain what prompted this work-rotation formula which accom-panied spiral promotion under the *nenko* system. However, it does seem to fit very well with the operational activities of contemporary large firms and the character of the technological innovation that takes place in them. Technological innovation takes a long time. Even after new core and re-lated technologies have been introduced, they must be continually im-proved. In the process the interconnections between various tasks must be harmonized in order to increase the efficiency of the whole system. For this to happen, there must be good communication and close understanding between different levels and positions within the organization. The fact that the people in charge transfer between positions and experience differ-ent kinds of work contributes greatly to process and raises the efficiency of the system overall. The present era is one in which technological innova-tion is rapid, and the danger is that if any person acquires only very limited skills within a single technological system, those techniques and that knowledge will become outdated. It is clearly to the advantage of the individual worker to acquire a wide variety of skills and knowledge by means of job rotation.

The fact that the information exchanged has a strong empirical character and can be passed on only in a single workplace has had a lot to do with the on-the-job-learning formula described above. Empirical, on-the-job learning has been a critical factor in Japan's evident success in adapting technologies produced in other advanced countries and in the Japanese firms' independent improvements to these technologies. The job rotation formula is practically indispensable in the exchange of this sort of knowledge and information and in its common ownership among workers. The *nenko* system may have ancient origins, but it was very appropriate as a method for developing the capacities of workers in the economic environment of postwar Japan, and it is clear that it was economically rational. While some workers might want to specialize in a particular skill or to be able to continue working as a specialist in any available company responsible only for the work that requires their skill, most workers prefer to be one of a group, able to bring to the firm a wide range of useful skills and knowledge. Of course they can hope to contribute to the development of their firm by applying themselves to these skills.

## 1.4 Human Capital and Managerial Resources

On the basis of the *nenko* system Japanese firms have developed a pool of "managerial resources" consisting of the engineering technology, production management, marketing, and research and development techniques needed in their operations. The pool also contains the skills needed to collect and analyze information relating to these techniques. To put it another way, Japanese firms are a repository of the "human capital" which possesses these kinds of skills. First-rate foreign firms share this attribute. But Japanese firms are not the simple sum of the individual units of human capital. In essence, they are organizational entities where, from top to bottom, groups of employees are elaborately linked together, and they wield coherent collective skills in the form of managerial resources. To build up these resources and thereby develop the firm, it is necessary that the employees individually and jointly possess relevant information, as well as develop the skills related to their respective tasks through continual training. From many standpoints, but especially from those of the firm and its employees, the *nenko* system and the system of lifetime employment represent favorable conditions for achieving this objective.

When it became evident in the postwar economy that this sort of enterprise management strengthened the firm for international interfirm competition, a virtuous circle was born where expectations of the future growth of firms further increased the efficiency of the long-term employment and the rotation formula. This occurred not only in large firms but also in second-rank and small- and medium-sized firms.

A major characteristic of managerial resources of this kind, originally created, as we have seen, in the actual work process amid postwar technological change, is their flexibility and ability to adapt to new waves of technological innovation and changes in the market. This is especially true of the last ten years; the microelectronic revolution especially depends on learning by doing, learning by using, and learning by diffusing.

As we have described them, large Japanese firms are agglomerations of managerial resources consisting of human capital. When we compare the number of employees that make up this human capital with those in foreign firms, we find that the number is remarkably low when measured against the volume of sales. Keeping the firm proper "lean" is another feature particular to Japanese firms, and it is connected with the Japanese form of industrial organization. Table 1.1 gives examples of this for some representative Japanese and U.S. firms. We see that while Toyota's level of sales is a little more than 42 percent that of GM's, it has less than 8 percent of GM's work force.

This difference is entirely attributable to the fact that Japanese firms try to keep the number of workers employed in the firm proper small and to make use of subsidiary firms, affiliated firms, subcontracting firms, and temporary and part-time workers in their operations. At Toyota, for example, we find that the firm proper has made itself leaner by lowering the ratio

**Table 1.1**
A comparison of the scale of Hitachi, Toyota, GE, and GM

|  | Value of sales (in ¥ trillions) | Number of employees (in 1,000s) | Number of shareholders (in 1,000s) |
|---|---|---|---|
| Hitachi | 2.9 | 78 | 210 |
| GE | 5.7 | 302 | 506 |
| Toyota | 6.0 | 64 | 63 |
| GM | 14.2 | 813 | 830 |

Source: 1987 data for each company. The value of scales for GE and GM are calculated at the rate of $1 : ¥140.

of the parts it produces itself to only 25 percent (the ratio for GM is about 70 percent).

## 1.5 A Simple Theoretical Model

Before we discuss the industrial organization of Japanese firms, we will look at a very simple model that should aid us in understanding the behavior of Japanese firms. Large Japanese firms distribute to their shareholders a fixed proportion of their profits (total profits multiplied by a fixed rate). They distribute the remainder, plus what is paid out as wages, to their staff (*shain*) (consisting of regular employees). We assume that on the basis of this formula they determine the volume of output and the volume of capital and labor inputs *so as to maximize the per-capita incomes of their staff*. This simple hypothesis is based on the assumption that employees of large Japanese firms may be considered to be receiving—in the form of better (or worse) pay than other firms, profit-linked bonuses, retirement allowances, fringe benefits (e.g., company housing and health), welfare facilities, expense allowances, and so on—a share in the firm's profits.

If a proportion of the firm's profits is distributed to employees (staff) in this fashion, then the optimum number of employees is smaller than it would be if the firm were to act so as to maximize profits. Restricting the confines within which profits are distributed as narrowly as possible would raises the incentive for employees to increase their efficiency. It may be considered that the fundamental reason why Japanese firms attempt to keep the firm proper small ("lean") stems from this fact.

Let us now show the output of commodities as $X$, price as $p$, the volume of labor (employees) as $L$, wages as $w$, the quantity of capital used as $K$, and the return on capital as $r$. If we assume that the proportion of profits distributed to employees is $\beta$ and therefore that the proportion distributed to shareholders who are the suppliers of capital is $(1 - \beta)$, then we can write the total income $W$ received by employees as

$$W = \beta(pX - wL - rK) + wL$$

and the total income $R$ accruing to shareholders as

$$R = (1 - \beta)(pX - wL - rK) + rK,$$

where $w$ and $r$ are the wage and the return-on-capital rates established in the external market, it being assumed that $W$ and $R$ are greater than $wL$ and $rK$. If we assume on the basis of this premise that the firm will conduct itself so as to maximize the per-capita income of its employees ($W/L$ in our notation), then the scale of employment will be determined, as it is in the so-called worker-controlled firm, by the point where marginal productivity of labor is equal to the average productivity of labor.[3] Then, if the average productivity of labor were to rise, the wages paid to labor would also rise. In the case of the firm that merely aims to maximize profits, the volume of employment is determined by the point where the marginal product of labor equals a wage that is determined in the external labor market. But in the simplified model of the Japanese firm that we have just outlined, the volume of labor employed is less than this, as it is also in the worker-controlled firm. This is advantageous in as much as it maximizes the per-capita income of employees. The volume of capital used under the assumptions of this simplified model will be determined at the point where the marginal productivity of capital (marginal efficiency) is equal to the rate of return on capital (capital cost or rate of interest) fixed in the capital market.

The firm trains human capital over a long period in order to enable its labor force to carry out complex, interrelated tasks. More simple tasks are performed by temporary and part-time workers whose wages are determined in "external" labor markets rather than being linked to profits. This division of labor is economically rational for the firm. Although an objection may be raised that it is discriminatory toward the temporary and part-time workers who are unable to share in the firm's profits, this arrangement is not necessarily disadvantageous for workers who are seeking short-term or part-time work. Temporary and part-time workers are usually housewives, people without the long periods of education and training undergone by regular employees, or people who have left other firms. The fact that firms have a mechanism for employing these people reduces the unemployment rate.

## 1.6   The Connection with the Organization of Industry

Japanese industrial organization extends this division of labor to relations between large firms and subsidiary and subcontracting firms. The firm proper, with its high-cost human capital, restricts itself to tasks of high marginal productivity and entrusts other tasks either to less qualified workers or to workers in "outside" firms.

These other tasks may be very important. The subcontractors in the automobile industry produce parts that are vital to maintaining the quality of the main product. Moreover these subsidiary tasks require the accumulation of specialized managerial resources. Such a relationship—in which

---

3. On this point, see Komiya (1988).

the outside firms work in accordance with standards set in the parent company—is only possible when there is an elaborate exchange of information. Most large Japanese firms work as one with their long-term subsidiary, subcontracting, and affiliated firms. Subsidiaries, subcontractors, and affiliates carry on their own education and training, and their staffs make up the "extended family" of the managerial resources of the large firms. (See Chapter 6 on enterprise groups.)

The same sort of relationship exists with respect to capital equipment. Just as human capital is accumulated through long-term education and training, so the efficiency of capital equipment is gradually raised through the exchange of information between the users and the manufacturers of machines, equipment, and plant. In most cases these suppliers are outside firms, but in many cases the firm proper and its suppliers jointly own the necessary information about the capital equipment, and employees of the supplier improve, repair, and maintain the machinery and equipment of the main firm with the same attitude as if they were its employees. In this way large Japanese firms endeavor to keep the firm proper "lean," while dealing with external organizations as if they were "internal."

## 1.7   Wage Differentials between Firms

In Japan "interscale wage differentials" between large firms, small- and medium-sized firms, and very small businesses are quite marked. In defining these differentials, we calculate not just the total of wages, allowances, and bonuses but also the various fringe benefits to arrive at the total remuneration paid to workers of the same capacities.[4] There are significant differences in such levels of remuneration even among the large firms quoted in the first section of the stock exchange. That these differences are larger than those in other advanced industrial countries can be explained by the fact that each firm accumulates a different quantity of "managerial resources," and not merely through its total quantities of labor and capital, and that consequently production functions differ from firm to firm. Each firm then determines its volume of employment at the point where it maximizes the per capita incomes of its "staff" (at the point where the

---

4. When he compared interfirm wage differentials for Japan and for various EC countries using a 1972 EC Survey, Koike (1984, 72–73) found that Japanese wage differentials were approximately the same as those in France (i.e., roughly the EC average). He took this to mean that Japanese interfirm wage differentials could not be said to be all that great. However, when all the fringe benefits described in this chapter are considered, we believe that there are fairly substantial interfirm wage differentials. Unfortunately, comprehensive data on this subject are scarce.

marginal and average productivity of labor are equal). Even with the same number of workers $L$ and the same value of capital $K$, fairly large differences can arise between firms in their accumulated "managerial resources" as $L$ and $K$ interact over a long period of time. Significant differences in wage levels between firms will arise over time corresponding to the marginal productivity (equal to average productivity) of labor of regular employees under different levels of "managerial resources."

The fact that wages may differ from large firm to large firm, and that some smaller firms pay wages higher than those of the large firms, implies that the commonly accepted "dual-structure" theory—for explaining marked variation of wage levels between large firms and medium and small firms—is inadequate. In a system where there are diverse needs for managerial resources from firm to firm, there will naturally be diverse wage levels. This is why, when we examine the "model wage patterns" of firms—the career wage progression for standard workers—we can detect marked differences in wage levels between firms that appear to be engaged in similar areas of industry.

## 1.8   Relationships with the Capital Market

Similarities with the Labor-Managed Firm

As we have stated above, large firms in Japan can be assumed to maximize the per-capita incomes of their regular employees. Regular employees receive a share of the firm's profits in the form of wages and salaries, bonuses and fringe benefits, and to that extent the firm possesses the characteristics of what we refer to as the "labor-managed firm." Originally this term referred to a firm whose core was composed of a group of workers who set the firm up, obtained the capital and employed managers, and so forth, when the need arose. The democracy inherent in this kind of firm might seem very different from the typical large firm in Japan, where decision making is carried out through a structured organization with the president (or the chairman of the board of directors) at its apex. They are similar, however, in that both have managers who are regarded as representatives of their employees, and who take the fundamental decisions, as well as regular employees who receive a fixed share of the profits of the firm.

However, we still have to explain how and why typical large Japanese firms can behave so as to maximize the per-capita incomes of their employees despite the existence of shareholders who originally supplied the equity capital and who have complete and ultimate right of claim on the profits of the firm. Why do the shareholders tacitly approve of the distribution to employees and officers of a sizable portion of the profits that ought really to revert to them?[5]

There are several factors. The Americans after the war tried to democratize the Japanese economy by weakening the power of the *zaibatsu*, who had hitherto been the largest shareholders in Japan's major joint-stock companies. This redistribution of shares led to a decline in shareholder influence over managers, whose position was strengthened. The postwar growth in Japanese capital accumulation, particularly in the household sector, created a plentiful supply of funds on which business could draw, either through the issuance of equity capital (shares) or debt, using the newly modernized money markets and capital markets. Firms with first-class managerial resources at their command, which were thus regarded as having strong prospects, were able to obtain funds without much difficulty, either through the capital market or from financial institutions.

The fact that investors could regard the distribution of profits to the work force as beneficial to their interests is also significant. This distribution raised the capabilities of workers and the accumulation of managerial resources, and thereby improved the prospects for the firm. Because share prices rose based on investors' calculations of these prospects, shareholders felt no need to interfere with the distribution of profits to employees. In fact Japanese shareholders were amply rewarded for this forbearance, and they received on average a rate of return substantially higher than the rate of interest.[6] To examine this question further, we need to consider more closely the role of the shareholder in the contemporary Japanese capital market and the factors that determine this influence.

Shareholders' Influence (To Whom Do Firms Belong?)

While it is true that the tendency among large firms in Japan is toward a marked separation of ownership and control, we should not draw the

---

5. The distribution of profits to employees is not a peculiarly Japanese phenomenon. There are also profit-sharing firms in other countries. However, we can in most cases regard the profits distributed in such firms essentially as bonuses paid out in proportion to profits, often in smaller U.S. firms essentially as a substitute for pensions. There appear to be no examples of the situation that pertains to large firms in Japan where profits are distributed routinely to the "staff." See D. W. Bell and C. Hansen (1987).

6. According to estimates made by Aoki, in the eleven-year period between 1966 and 1977, the rate of interest on the banks' one-year deferred (time) deposits was 5.95 percent. In contrast, the average after-tax rate of return on share investment was 17.0 percent. In the research conducted outside Japan mentioned in note 5, share prices of profit-sharing firms were found on average to be higher than those of non-profit-sharing firms.

conclusion that shareholders have absolutely no influence over the running of the firm. A share (stock) is primarily an instrument indicating a residual claim on the profits of a firm after all costs have been defrayed from its revenues. Shares are negotiable on the stock market. When shareholders conclude that a firm is run badly and offers little prospect of profits, they will sell their shares and buy those of a different firm. With large firms in Japan, the majority of their shareholders are so-called stable shareholders (*antei kabunushi*) who continue to hold the firm's shares over long periods irrespective of its short-term performance. Although this acts to set a floor for share prices, the prices can respond quite sensitively merely to dealings in the marginal amounts that shareholders put on the market as they perceive how one firm is performing relative to another.

In this sense share prices constantly "evaluate" the way in which a firm is being run. But how does such an evaluation actually influence the firm's decision making? It is just as wrong, on the one hand, to say that the shareholders own the firm and therefore are the ultimate dominant influence as it is, on the other, to say that because of the separation of ownership and control they have no influence.

As for how *much* influence they have, we need to look at actual processes and not just formalities. Large firms are complex mechanisms. Whatever may be the formal legal situation, from an economics viewpoint there can be no black-and-white assignment of ownership. One needs to look at who takes what share in the surplus (or loss) the firm generates and who takes what decisions. Formally, in a joint-stock company the shareholders who provide the equity capital are the people who have an overriding claim to its surplus and have the final say in the running of the firm through the medium of the shareholders' meeting. Employees are the owners of labor power taken on by the firm on long- or short-term contracts (or on tacit contracts) in accordance with the firm's needs. A section of these employees also have some say in the managerial decisions. Other firms, which supply it with technology, raw materials, physical capital, and so on, stand in a contractual relationship with the firm, where they sell to it on specified conditions the various inputs that they own. The organizational complex created by this accumulation of contracts is what we mean by a firm; an organization in which the varied participants—employees, shareholders, and associated companies—come together in pursuit of their own interests.

For judgments made in the stock market by shareholders to have a marked effect on managerial decision making in firms, there has to be a supplementary mechanism. In the United States it is normal for most large firms to select capable managers not from their own employees but from the managerial "labor" market. Managers' reputation in this labor market is strongly influenced by the performance of the share price of their companies. Where share prices fall, the market rating of the managers of the firm also declines. Likewise it is not unusual for the remuneration of managers to be determined by the profits of the firm and the price of its shares. There is obviously a strong incentive for managers to try and raise the price of their firm's shares. If they have not made sufficient profits, or if they have arrogated to themselves (or to their employees) a part of the profits that ought to have gone to the shareholders, then the firm's share prices will fall and the chances of a takeover will increase. The potential threat of a takeover becomes a "final deterrent" impelling managers toward maximizing share prices. American economists, especially those who see the relationship between shareholders and managers as a relationship between a principal and his agent, insist that in an efficient capital market, managers act, and indeed must act, so as to maximize share prices.

By contrast, in large firms in Japan, this supplementary pressure from the market either barely functions or does not exist. Japanese managers are chosen from the firm's employees through a competitive and lengthy process that has virtually no connection with the price of the firm's shares. Large firms in Japan prevent takeovers by means of "stable shareholder maneuvres" (kabunushi antei kosaku) in which they hold a proportion of each other's shares, and a further proportion is held by a firm's banker and (where applicable) by its trading company. The primary reason for doing this is to protect the firm's managers, but it is also intended to prevent takeover threats designed solely to blackmail the firm's managers into buying back their own firm's shares at inflated prices. When someone starts buying up the shares of a Japanese company, it is usually this which lies behind it, not an attempt to replace the weak management of an ailing company with a better one. But whatever the motives, stable shareholding blunts the direct influence of the stock market on the management of firms. This has given managers the autonomy to be able to distribute a proportion of the profits to the workers whom they represent and on whose support they depend.

This autonomy is not without its limits. Joint stock companies need additional share capital in order to grow, and this must come from a periodic increase in shares (or by the issue of convertible debentures). The rest has to come from undistributed reserves. Even if no new shares are issued, and funds are instead borrowed from financial institutions or through bond issues, the necessary condition is that management must ensure that profits rise sufficiently to pay interest and redeem the principal. The firm must also compare its operating performance, market share, and rate of growth with that of its competitors so that it can continue to attract first-class staff to build up its managerial resources. There is no simple formula for assessing which of these factors is the most important in the running of the Japanese firm, but it is clear that if the firm is not able at least to make sufficient profits, increase its share capital, and continue to grow and develop satisfactorily, then it will soon be unable to distribute profits to its work force.

We can assume that shareholders active in the stockmarket arrive at a valuation of a firm's share prices by asking whether the firm has a satisfactory level of investment, training, and research and development, and of course inquiring as to how its profits are distributed. Both individual investors and institutional investors (banks, trust companies, life insurance companies, etc.) are continually examining this sort of information and asking how these factors contribute to the long-term performance of the firm. (Bell and Hansen 1987 found that profit-sharing firms in fact enjoyed higher than average share prices.) Shares in a firm whose long-term performance is unsatisfactory and whose returns to its shareholders are poor will be sold, and its share prices will be depressed. Even though such a fall may not immediately prove an obstacle to the running of the firm or make a change in its management unavoidable, it will eventually place limitations on the firm's growth. It seems likely therefore that a firm's top managers, and those who aspire to top management, will aim to secure satisfactory profits and, if possible, maintain the firm's share price at a higher level than that of comparable firms. This leads us to the conclusion that while large firms in Japan may be characterized as managed by labor, this is not incompatible with the operation of the stockmarket.[7] Even though the Japanese system

---

7. We have taken the relationship between large firms in Japan, where ownership is separated from control, and their shareholders to be fundamentally a relationship between the firm and the market. We have therefore taken it that just as a firm sells its products in the product market to consumers and to other firms, it obtains the supply of equity or share capital it needs for growth in the capital market (or the market for share capital). We assumed previously that large firms in Japan distribute their profits in a given ratio between employees and shareholders, and that they maximize the per-capita income of their employees. In such a case firms will determine the amount of capital (share capital) that they will use so as to equate the marginal efficiency of that capital with its rate of return, which is determined in the capital market (see note 4). That is to say, we believe that the managers of a firm run it with the ex ante aim of keeping the rate of return (dividends and capital gains) to its shareholders at the same level, or slightly higher, than other firms in the same industry with a similar standing and business profile, and that the level of investment, the rate of increase in capital, and the level of retained reserves is determined on this basis.

differs greatly from that of the United States (especially in the frequency of takeovers) the modern joint-stock company system and a competitive capital market do perform a significant economic function in allocating resources.

## 1.9  Conclusion

In this chapter we have surveyed the distinctive characteristics of the Japanese firm, particularly the typical large firm. We have described how in postwar Japan, along with the increasing separation of ownership and control, the spread of the lifetime employment and the seniority payment and promotion systems and the development of the economy as a result of technological innovation, firms that have performed excellently have developed as elaborate human organizations with specialized abilities to operate in their individual fields.

Since in the Japanese firm the fruits of the firm's operations are distributed among its employees, they are positive in their approach to working diligently, vying with each other in terms of ingenuity and in producing fresh opportunities for profit. Because their employment is guaranteed, they have a positive attitude toward the introduction of new methods and constant technological innovation, and are enthusiastic about creating new markets so that the firm can continue to develop. Schumpeterian creative destruction and innovation is the goal, rather than static efficiency in the distribution of resources at a given point in time.

Technological and organizational innovation has been the goal during the violent changes in the economic environment marked by the recovery from postwar desolation, the rapid economic growth that followed, two oil crises, and recently the rapid rise in the price of the yen. What sustained this innovation was the power of firms as human organizational entities and an entrepreneurial spirit that pursued economic development by seeking opportunities in the market without being unduly constrained either by the "control of capital" or by political power. As economic growth and development proceeded, the scope for economic activity widened not only

---

However, although we stress that this relationship between the firm and its shareholders is fundamentally a market relationship, we do not deny that large shareholders perform an important function as the key players, both at the founding of the firm and when it runs into operating difficulties. Consequently they are always in the position of being potential holders of power. Nevertheless, as long as a firm is performing above a given level, it is rare even for large shareholders (other than those who founded the company or owner-managers in a family company) to exercise their power other than by buying and selling their shares in the market.

for large firms but also for small- and medium-sized firms. Companies emerged from the ranks of small- and medium-sized firms, some with good technological capabilities and managerial skills who had thrown off their former subordinate status. Among them there were quite a few that were able to develop into fully fledged "Japanese-type" large firms. From the point of view of individual firms in this category, the process was certainly not a smooth one. However, Japan's small- and medium-sized firms as a whole made great progress during the course of economic development. As a result of this large firms and small- and medium-sized firms now have a relationship of mutual complementarity.

Although we were not able to analyze it in depth in this chapter, it is important to pay attention to the fact that the close information transfer we observed between the large firms and the small- to medium-sized firms is replicated in Japanese firms as a whole. Technology and managerial know-how are also transferred between firms. The joint operations undertaken between firms accelerate this process. The exchange of information between firms can easily become a breeding ground for cartel-like behavior. But, when changes in technology and in the market are rapid and the boundaries delineating industries are blurred, technology transfer and technological cooperation is common and performs an ex ante coordinating function with respect to mutually undertaken, complementary undertakings. In addition this is something that can also be said of the situation between firms and financial organizations and firms and government. As well as lending large sums of money to firms, Japanese banks are providers of business information. The government has also tried to encourage the flow of information and thereby increase entrepreneurship and industrial efficiency.

However, for this very reason Japanese firms tend to move uniformly in a similar direction, respond sensitively to the smallest difference, and compete fiercely among themselves; they can thus be regarded internationally as exceptional entities. In addition, as a result of their pursuit of efficiency as human organizational entities, what they have sought from their individual employees is cooperativeness rather than strong individuality. They have therefore tended to place ability to contribute to the organization as a whole ahead of the exhibiting of individual capabilities. From now on individual skill will be much sought after in research and development, in design, and in the development of software, and these activities will come to have increasingly more important strategic status in firms' activities. It remains to be seen how the *nenko* system and the lifetime employment system will change and which diverse patterns of organization will emerge among Japanese firms.

The results of Japanese firms have been a good deal better than those of foreign firms, but to foreign eyes the expectations that Japanese firms have of their employees may appear unreasonable. Ronald Dore puts it as follows: "Economic efficiency is of course important. I am all in favour of increasing productivity. However, I myself would not want to be an employee of a Japanese firm. If I were expected to put my work before my personal and family life and my leisure to the same extent as Japanese workers, I would say "no thank you" (Dore 1973, Preface to Japanese translation). Perhaps Japanese workers would not like to work in a British factory either, but it may be that the seeds of social problems have been concealed by the results achieved by Japanese firms. Behind the long-term competition and the accumulation of managerial resources, there are the people who have sacrificed their family life to work. Whether the positive or negative aspects of the Japanese system will win out will be determined, in many instances, by minute differences in the composition of a firm's labor force and the way it is run. The future economic environment is likely to require of Japanese firms deep thought concerning these fine differences. As we have explained, the *nenko* and lifetime employment systems contain many things that are of positive worth from the point of view of both the operation of the firm and its economic activities. Nevertheless, there are things that can be seen as drawbacks from the point of view of the allocation of resources and the distribution of income. The fact that the interfirm mobility of personnel is low implies that large differences in the marginal productivities of various kinds of workers will persist over the long term. There is therefore a barrier to the efficient allocation of resources.

Furthermore the company in which a person was employed right after high school or university governs that person's entire career path and level of income. It would be an exaggeration to liken it is to the feudal period, when a man's entire destiny was determined by the status he was born into—samurai, peasant, artisan, merchant—or, if peasant, by the fief he was born into. Still, compared with other industrial societies which have high mobility (Europe and North America), Japan has probably had a lower level of equality of opportunity with respect to the distribution of income. This should serve as a caveat to the success story outlined above.

We have tried to show the way in which the firm is a social entity that develops within the historical and cultural context of a particular society. Because of this, rapid fundamental change is not possible. But we can be sure that in the future, Japanese firms will continue to transform themselves in response to changes in their economic and social environment.

# 2    Toward an Economic Model of the Japanese Firm

Masahiko Aoki

Over the last decade a considerable economic and management literature has been produced in English dealing with various aspects of Japanese firms compared with their Western counterparts. The literature is rich and wide-ranging.[1]

The list of representative papers is incomplete and possibly biased, but it is certainly sufficient to indicate the rich variety of subject matter studied in the growing literature on Japanese firms. My aim here is not to present an exhaustive survey of either that or of the comparable Japanese literature but rather to provide a "unified" treatment of various Japanese practices and to suggest a consistent economic model that explains how Japanese firms operate and what they achieve. I leave the more detailed assessment of their comparative efficiency to future studies, but the underlying assumption is that one of the important sources of the industrial strength

I am indebted to Professor Moses Abramovitz who suggested that I write this paper and provided constant encouragement and guidance throughout its preparation. I am also indebted to three anonymous referees of the *Journal of Economic Literature*, in which this paper first appeared (vol. 28, no 1, March 1990) and to Professors Komiya and Riordan for their critical comments and helpful suggestions.

1. Some of the most important contributions are the following: Abegglen and Stalk (1985, ch. 5) and Monden (1983) on the *kanban* system (just-in-time method) and other practices of manufacturing operations; Aoki (1986, 1989) and Itoh (1987) on the nonhierarchical mechanism of operational coordination; Leibenstein (1987), Lincoln, Hanada, and McBird (1987) and Tachibanaki (1987) on the nature of internal hierarchies; Koike (1984, 1988, 1989) and Shimada and Macduffie (1986) on skill formation systems on the job and on shop-floor industrial relations; Shirai (1984) on enterprise unionism; Hashimoto and Raisian (1985) and Mincer and Higuchi (1988) on employment duration and tenure-wage profile; Freeman and Weitzman (1987) and Taylor (1989) on the bonus system; Horiuchi, Packer, and Fukuda (1988), Sheard (1989), and Berglof (1989) on bank-oriented financing and the main bank system; Ando and Auerbach (1988) and Bernheim and Shoven (1989) on the cost of capital; Aoki and Rosenberg (1989), Imai, Nonaka, and Takeuchi (1985), and Westney and Sakakibara (1985) on R&D organization and rapid product development; Asanuma (1985, 1989) and Kawasaki and McMillan (1987) on subcontracting; Abegglen and Stalk (1985, ch. 8), Aoki (1984a, 1988a), and Komiya (1987) on the nature of Japanese management.

(and weakness in certain respects) of the Japanese economy can be found in the micro-micro (internal) structure of firms. Thus the theme of this essay is parallel to that of the MIT Commission on Industrial Productivity (Dertouzos, Lester, and Solow 1989) which in its comparative assessment of the American productive performance placed strong emphasis on the impact of organizational factors.

The questions I ask are: Is there any logical connection between the "Japanese" mode of internal operation and coordination, on the one hand, and the so-called Japanese employment system on the other? Is the bank-oriented business financing related to the internal structure of Japanese firms in any essential manner? If so, how, and what are its implications for the nature of management and behavior of firms? The model that emerges to answer these questions turns out to be somewhat at odds with the standard contractual model of the firm that prevails in the Anglo-American theoretical literature. Is this because the Japanese model is culturally unique? Or, given the competitive challenge posed by Japanese firms in global markets, does the difference suggest a need to broaden the scope and reorder the focus of the theory of the firm? Toward the end of this essay, I will touch briefly on these issues as well.

The organization of this chapter is as follows: Sections 2.1 and 2.2 describe a few important examples of operational practices in Japanese firms and suggest that horizontal coordination among operating units based on knowledge sharing, rather than skill specialization, is an important internal characteristic of Japanese firms. They also make an elementary inquiry into the efficiency implications of horizontal coordination. The employees of Japanese firms are nonetheless arranged in a hierarchy of rank, and section 2.3 argues that Japanese firms depend on employee competition to achieve higher status within their hierarchies of rank as a primary incentive device. The hierarchical nature of the incentive scheme therefore complements the nonhierarchical tendency of operational coordination and so helps maintain organizational effectiveness and integrity. Section 2.4 deals with the nature of financial control over Japanese firms in a bank-oriented financial system. It contends that the financial and internal characteristics of Japanese firms are closely related to, and complement, each other. Section 2.5 proposes that as a result of this complementarity, the managerial decisions of Japanese firms are subject to the dual influence of financial and employee interests. It discusses the nature and behavioral consequences of mutual commitments between management, on the one hand, and employees and banks, on the other. Fundamental theoretical propositions developed in Section 2.1 through 2.5 are summarized in the form of three duality principles. Section 2.6 contains concluding remarks. Because of space limitations, detailed data supporting stated stylized facts are not presented in this chapter. They appear in the works cited in note 1 and in my recent book.[2] Moreover I limit references to works available in English.

A key to an understanding of Japan's industrial performance can be found in the ability of firms in certain industries to coordinate their operating activities flexibly and quickly in response to changing market conditions and to changes in other factors in the industrial environment, as well as to emergent technical and technological exigencies. Representative Japanese firms have cultivated an ability for rapid response by developing an internal scheme in which emergent information is utilized effectively on site, and in which operating activities are coordinated among related operating units on the basis of information sharing. In the next section I first illustrate this claim with three examples drawn from operating practices in the automobile and steel industries and from R&D activities in manufacturing industry generally. I then characterize generic aspects of these and other examples as a mechanism of hierarchical coordination. I summarize some results of a comparative analysis of the relative information efficiency of the two coordination mechanisms, and finally I discuss their implications for understanding and interpreting Japanese industrial performance. I am aware that any attempt to draw general propositions from specific examples runs the risk of small sample bias. But the following examples are drawn from many observations made recently in the course of plant visits and interviews with engineers and managers, and I am reasonably confident that they represent widespread and generic elements of Japanese practice.[3] Also I believe that the significance of the comparative analysis to follow is very hard to grasp without breaking open the economists' black box of the production function and gaining a concrete image of how firms operate without a rigid hierarchical order.

---

2. Aoki (1988a).

3. Between September 1987 and August 1989, I interviewed managers and engineers of about 50 Japanese manufacturing firms and banks. My intensive studies included plant visits to the following firms: Nippon Steel Corporation, Matsushita Electric Industrial Col., Ltd., Sony Corporation, Honda Motor Co., Ltd., Toyota Motor Corporation, Omron Tateisi Electronics Co., Kyowa Hakko Kogyo Co., Ltd., Tonen Corporation, IBM Japan, Ltd., Kajima Corporation, Ohbayashi Corporation, Toray Corporation, the Sumitomo Bank, Ltd., and the Sanwa Bank, Ltd. A few of the interview records were published in Aoki, Koike, and Nakatani (1989).

## 2.1 Examples of Practices in Japanese Firms

Production Scheduling—An Automobile Industry Case

A number of studies based on rather crude accounting methods claim that the automobile industry represents a case in which Japan has caught up with the forerunners in production cost efficiency and is now itself running ahead very fast.[4] Fuss and Waverman (1985) have recently cast doubt on such assertions and have claimed, on the basis of elaborate econometric analysis, that even in 1980 Japanese industry was only slightly more productive "at normal capacity utilization rates" despite the apparent cost efficiency of Japanese producers. Because the automobile industry is characterized by significant quasi-fixed factors, such as capital plant, administrative and designing jobs, and product-specific manufacturing facilities, shifts in consumers' tastes or an economic downturn can have severe effects on cost efficiency. Fuss and Waverman maintain that long-run total factor productivity growth during the 1970s has been underestimated by an order of 30 to 40 percent for North American producers in accounts that neglect the effects of undercapacity utilization.

It may be questioned, however, whether it is appropriate to dismiss inadequate capacity utilization among North American producers at that time simply as "short-run disequilibrium" that had no bearing on understanding the nature of comparative cost efficiency. I rather maintain that the organizational ability of firms to generate a product mix attuned to unpredictable market demands and emerging technology without generating an excessive underutilization of equipment and a large stock of produce and in-process inventories may be quite relevant for the comparative assessment of the organizational efficiency of firms. In the stable oligopolistic markets for which fairly standardized products are supplied, "short-run" market demands may be reasonably predictable. Under such a situation a short-run production plan may be fixed firmly for a certain period of time, based on the management's prior knowledge of market demands. The whole production process may be divided into a series of specialized functions, each standardized, and each work unit may be required to perform exclusively the specific jobs dictated by the prior plan. Ex post adaptation to actual market conditions may be accomplished through the adjustment of product and in-process inventories. Under the

---

4. These studies were conducted prior to the early 1980s and surveyed in Cole and Yakushiji (1984). Cusamano (1985) provides a more careful estimate of Japanese producers' comparative performance within the framework of accounting.

said market condition, such internal coordination—the *H-mode*—may be able to exploit the informational efficiency of hierarchical coordination and economies of specialization.[5]

The efficiency of the H-mode of coordination may become problematical, however, when diverse consumers' tastes come to demand a variety of products, when demands shift in a volatile fashion from one variety to another, and when the need to deliver ordered products without delay becomes imperative for gaining a competitive edge. How have Japanese auto producers responded to these challenges and consequently gained competitive advantage? In the concrete case of a representative auto producer, manufacturing coordination takes place roughly as follows:

The central production planning office drafts the quarterly and monthly production plans for each factory, based on its market demand forecasts, and presents corresponding procurement plans to outside suppliers. These prior plans provide only a general guideline, however. The integrated production-delivery plan for a ten-day period is prepared by the commodity-flow office on the basis of orders from regional and overseas dealers. In response to this plan, the engineering office of each factory prepares a sequence of daily production schedules. The daily schedule is then adjusted two days prior to actual production in response to actual customers' orders transmitted from dealers to the factory through the on-line network system (the "daily adjustments"). On the final assembly line, wagons, two-door hatchbacks, and four-door sedans with red, beige, and white bodies; with left-hand (for export) and right-hand (for domestic) steering wheels; with a variety of transmissions, engines, and options; are rolled out seemingly at random. Actually the sequence of production of varieties of cars is scheduled to minimize inventory and to respond to the daily customers' orders with the maximum flexibility.

The supply schedule of parts is fine-tuned according to daily production scheduling through the famed *kanban* system.[6] In this system neighboring shops (or the prime manufacturer and the supplier) are connected directly with each other through the chain-linked circulation of *kanban* (a taglike card). Downstream shops, several times a day, issue order forms called *kanban* to the immediate upstream shops (or the supplier) for the provision of particular numbers of parts of various types at a particular time. These *kanban* in turn are returned to the original issuer as a check on the implementation of downstream orders. The periodical automatized chain-linked

---

5. For a discussion of efficiency of hierarchical coordination, see Williamson (1985, ch. 9), and Aoki (1988a, ch. 2.2).
6. Monden (1983) and Abegglen and Stalk (1985, ch. 5).

circulation of the *kanban* is known to be effective for fine-tuning the prior supply plan, while reducing the time and effort needed for intershop communications and negotiations without hierarchical intervention by the production planning office and the procurement office.

The firm I described produces about 20,000 kinds of cars, distinguished by the ways various features are combined, and about 50 percent of total cars sold are produced at the rate of fewer than fifty vehicles per kind per month. Currently the number of vehicles produced according to actual customer's orders at dealers is about 35 percent of total production (approximately 6,000 vehicles per working day), and these vehicles are delivered to customers 8 to 12 days after they are ordered by customers (2 to 3 days for production scheduling, 2 days for manufacturing, 2 to 3 days for delivery, and 2 to 4 days for holidays). Ater the centralized indicative monthly plan has been formulated, actual production, parts supply, and delivery are coordinated in a horizontal manner, with the decisive lead emanating from the customer end. The computer network system of this auto firm is akin to the airline reservation system, but it distinguishes itself by integrating the manufacturing process involving thousands of steps and parts into the system.

Quality Control—A Steel Industry Case

The traditional steel manufacturing method was composed of a sequence of mutually disjointed work processes, such as the blast furnace process, the open hearth process, ingot making, slabbing, rolling, heat treatment, and plating. If products are standardized and sold for mass markets, such disjointedly sequential processes may be effectively integrated by the H-mode of coordination. One of the most important characteristics of process innovation by leading Japanese steel manufacturers in the last two or three decades has been, however, to transform the traditional steel making processes into a continuous operation by the introduction of such techniques as continuous casting, continuous rolling, and continuous annealing to obtain savings of energy, time, transportation costs and in-process inventory. Meanwhile demands by auto manufacturers, electrical and other machinery makers, and construction contractors have become increasingly diverse and specific so that integrated steel plants today produce varieties of final products in small and medium batches in response to actual and anticipated orders, though not for anonymous markets. Under such technical and market conditions the flexible computerized production control system becomes imperative for transforming actual orders into continuous process control. This seems to be clear. However, in order for continuous processes to be workable, horizontal coordination among related processes also seems to be essential. Let us illustrate this from the quality control point of view.

Consider, for example, the related processes of casting and rolling. In the Western plant linkage is patterned after the H-mode. That is, the engineer at the quality control office sets engineering specifications for each process (e.g., a mineral composition for the casting process and heating temperature for the rolling process) according to his prior engineering knowledge. Each process manager is required to implement the directive and is relieved of responsibility if he realizes the given target within a certain error margin. On the other hand, the engineer would not step into the workshop. For continuous processes there may well be a quality defect problem that can be detected only at the end of the rolling process, but that originates from a scar of the equipment at the congealing step of the casting process. Who can discover this problem, pinpoint its source, and institute a remedy to prevent its recurrence? If the engineers isolate themselves from workshops and if process control is segmented and relegated to each process manager, it is indeed difficult to cope with such problems.

At a representative Japanese plant, an "integrated engineering control room" exists side by side with the engineering office for each workshop. They are not hierarchically ordered in terms of status. In fact there is often a rotation of personnel between the two to facilitate knowledge sharing among them and discourage the development of shop-centered interests. The integrated control room and the workshop office are differentiated only by primary responsibility. That is, the integrated engineering control room is responsible for locating and solving "cross-shop" problems through discussion and bargaining with offices in charge of individual workshops. In the actual solution of cross-shop problems the control room acts like a coordinator at the same horizontal level with the workshops. The organizational device is said to be one of central foci of recent technical assistance by Japanese steel manufacturers to American and other steel manufacturers.

Product Development

The development of any new product proceeds in a hierarchical order: It starts with the basic conceptualization of the new product and its analytic design and proceeds to the successive phases of detailed design; prototype fabrication, testing and redesign; mass production and shipping; and marketing. Such development processes may be also characterized by various feedback loops. The first conceptualization of a new product may arise from recognition of a potential market opportunity prompted by marketing activity. Engineering experience at the testing phase and service experience at the after-sales maintenance phase may be fed into the redesign phase. These features may be thought of as universal phenomena.[7] Yet there seems to be a subtle difference between representative Western manufacturers and Japanese manufacturers in the ways that feedback mechanisms are utilized.[8]

In the case of a representative American computer manufacturer, each developmental phase is made clearly distinct in such a way that the transition from one phase to the next is subject to a strict independent phase review. The phase review is carried out from the viewpoint of engineering as well as business (cost, marketability, etc.). It is therefore conducted by a group of people drawn from various internal divisions, such as the manufacturing division, the patent section, the sales and services engineering division. If a development project at one stage does not pass the review, it cannot normally proceed to the next stage. It may happen that representatives from the manufacturing plant participate in the early design phase, but in such a case the internal transfer payment for participating personnel is to be made from the development department to the plant, and the independence of each phase is kept clear. The feedback loop for redesign is also formalized. If some engineering change occurs at the factory level, this information is fed back to the design department, which formally redrafts the design accordingly and files the revised design into the 'corporate development and production record system' so that the same updated engineering specification is automatically available to all factories and service and maintenance divisions all over the world.

At representative Japanese manufacturers as well, phase-review systems of various kinds are normally instituted. But the transition from one phase to the next is in general more flexible, and different phases are actually intermeshed and overlapped. For example, there is more interaction between design engineers and plant engineers at the early phase of design, and it is often difficult to say where the phase of prototype fabrication and testing actually starts. Very often the design laboratory is located at the site of the plant, and there is even a rotation of engineers between the

7. For a model of innovation incorporating the feedback mechanism, see Klein and Rosenberg (1986). For an application of this model (the "chain-linked" model) to the U.S.-Japan comparison, see Aoki and Rosenberg (1989).
8. Aoki and Rosenberg (1989) and Imai, Nonaka, and Takeuchi (1985).

design laboratory and the plant engineering office, which facilitates informal information sharing between the two. Also the engineer who has been responsible for the design of a new product, but who possibly has passed the peak of his productivity in design and development, may be transferred to a plant as a line manager responsible for the manufacturing phase of the new product (Westney and Sakakibara 1985). This practice motivates the design engineer to be very attentive to suggestions and opinions from the plant level in order to avoid the embarrassment he would face if engineering problems occur at the manufacturing phase because of a design flaw.

In the case of one auto manufacturer, the development team is called the SED team, which is composed of members from the sales, manufacturing, engineering, and development divisions. This cross-disciplinary team is organized at a very early phase of product development and carries out development processes to the very end as a group. In other words, feedback loops are internalized within the team. As much as possible cross-jurisdictional problems are discussed and solved collectively at every phase of development. A developed project is proposed for the formal phase review by executive managers, who are also drawn from SED divisions, only if the plan is adequately matured. By contrast with the Western manufacturer's case described above, the Japanese review committee is said not to exercise a decisive autonomous judgment. Without any value judgment at this point, one could say that feedback loops of development processes or, more generally speaking, horizontal coordination among various organizational units, are more intense, and yet they tend to be more informal (undocumented) in the Japanese case.

## 2.2   Theory and Interpretations

The preceding examples of industrial practices in Japan suggest that the coordination mode that operates within representative Japanese firms differs from the traditional modeling of organizational hierarchies—the H-mode. Let us now try to identify the fundamental differences between the two modes by focusing on a few important factors and examine how the relative cost efficiencies of the two can differ in various environments. In doing this, one is bound to commit the sin of oversimplification. But the point here is to make it clear that the cost function of the firm is not exogenously and solely determined by an engineer's blueprint; it also depends on organizational and human factors. I will therefore venture to offer a sharp theoretical formulation of nonhierarchical coordination and then interpret its performance characteristics in the context of the Japanese economy.

The H-mode has two essential features: (1) the hierarchical separation between planning and implemental operation and (2) the emphasis on the economies of specialization. That is, planning, such as for production scheduling, manufacturing process control, and commodity development is entrusted to an office at the top level of each function (the production planning office, the engineering office, the development laboratory, etc.) which is supposed to have specialized prior knowledge (on markets, engineering know-how, etc.). Let us call this planning *prior planning*. Prior planning is fixed for a certain period of time and implemented by operating units of the lower levels (e.g., workshops or plant), each of which is assigned a hierarchically decomposed special operational function. Any random event during the implementation period may be coped with by a priori devices (e.g., buffer inventories, troubleshooting specialists such as snaggers and mechanics), and new knowledge that emerges may be used only for the next round of planning by the higher office.

Consider an alternative mode reflecting aspects of Japanese firms—let us call it the *J-mode*, which has two main features: (1) the horizontal coordination among operating units based on (2) the sharing of ex post on-site information (learned results). That is, prior planning sets only the indicative framework of operation. As new information becomes available to operating units during the implementation period (e.g., customers' orders at dealers, quality defect problems that become apparent at a workshop, or engineering problems associated with development of a new product that become evident only at the plant site), prior plans may be modified. But, for on-site information to be utilized in a way that is consistent with the organizational goal, adaptation must be coordinated among interrelated operating units.

In the J-mode, on-site information may be better utilized for the realization of organizational goals (more formally, one may say that the J-mode can generate information value by the use of ex post information). Such a gain of course is not costless. In the J-mode, economies of specialization of operational activities are sacrificed, since some portion of time and effort of the operating units needs to be diverted for acquiring new information (i.e., learning) as well as for communicating and bargaining with each other for coordination. Such costs may be reduced by the development of information technology: hardware, software, and humanware. Therefore the comparative advantage of the H-mode and the J-mode depends on such factors as the learning ability of personnel, the ease of communication among operating units, and the degree of economies of specialization with regard to the variety and volatility of market demand.[9] Aoki and Itoh examined the advantages and disadvantages of the two modes and came up with the following noteworthy proposition: When environments for planning (e.g., markets, engineering process, and development opportunity) are stable, learning at the operational level may not add much information value to prior planning, and the sacrifice of economies of specialization in operational activities may not be worthwhile. On the other hand, if environments are extremely volatile or uncertain, decentralized adaptation to environmental changes may yield highly unstable results. In both these two contrasting cases the H-mode may be superior in achieving the organizational goal. In the intermediate situation, however, where external environments are continually changing but not too drastically, the J-mode is superior. In this case the information value created by learning and horizontal coordination at the operational level may more than compensate for the loss of efficiency due to the sacrifice of operational specialization.

The result is consistent with the often-stated suggestion that the hierarchical mode of coordination based on a highly developed specialization scheme, which prevailed in the American steel and auto industries until the late 1960s, lost its advantage in the face of product variation and weakening oligopolistic control.[10] Economies of specialization may be exploited more favorably for the stable and large-scale production of standardized commodities but not for the small- and medium-batch production of varieties of products in a high-volume assembly process where thousands of independent steps must be coordinated. These markets are precisely the ones where Japanese manufacturers exhibit strong competitive capabilities; however, "in simpler processes, such as a foundry, where perhaps thirty operational steps are required, the Japanese advantage is slight, and sometimes nonexistent."[11]

These propositions are consistent with the observation that Japanese manufacturers have shown relative strength in process innovation, as exemplified in the steel industry, to which intense interactions between engineers in the development laboratory and engineers, and even workers, at the factory site may contribute.[12] On the other hand, Japanese manufacturers have not shown a conspicuous advantage in highly uncertain innovations involving new conceptualizations of market potential and highly specialized scientific approaches. Nor have they acquired a competitive

---

9. Aoki (1986, 1989) and Itoh (1987); see also Cremer (1989).
10. Piore and Sabel (1984).
11. Abegglen and Stalk (1985, 61).
12. Mansfield (1988).

edge in industries where there is customized production of newly designed products, such as in the aerospace industry.[13]

It is obvious that greater efficacy of communications and learning at the operational level tends to favor the J-mode relative to the H-mode in a large, and perhaps growing, sector of industry. It is interesting to note, in this connection, that the J-mode of horizontal coordination based on shared learning at the factory site has emerged and developed in the last two decades or so by relying on highly qualified and diligent blue-collar workers who have formed the core of the work team. They were mainly recruited directly out of high schools in the 1950s and early 1960s when the share of male persons who found employment at age 15 right after junior high school was still as high as 45 to 25 percent depending on business cycle conditions (currently less than 4 percent). Now that the economic obstacles for qualified and motivated youths to advance to higher education have been virtually removed, a serious challenge facing representative manufacturing firms in Japan today is to recruit highly qualified blue-collar workers.

The J-mode as practiced by Japanese firms has one feature in common with advanced Western firms as exemplified by the American computer manufacturer described in the third example of section 2.1, that is, *knowledge sharing* among various organizational units. The subtle difference is, however, that in the case of the American manufacturer, knowledge sharing is formally instituted based on explicit documentation through the computerized network system and other technological means. In the Japanese case, by contrast, knowledge sharing and the horizontal coordination based on it are often informal and based on verbal communications (even tacit understanding), although here too there is increasing use of the computer network system as indicated by the integrated marketing-manufacturing network system of the auto manufacturer described in the first example. Such undocumented communications may generate information value by the finer use of on-site information that is too subtle or cumbersome to document usefully. But the efficacy of face-to-face communications is limited by geographical proximity. (t may be recalled that the research laboratories of Japanese manufacturers are often located at the factory site. The need for geographical proximity may explain why there is also such a high concentration of commercial and financial business activity in Tokyo.) Also the ethnic homogeneity of the Japanese domestic factory may have been a crucial factor for the development and effectiveness of the J-mode.[14]

---

13. Mowery and Rosenberg (1985).
14. Aoki (1988a, ch. 7).

Further the dual functions of performing an operating task and of learning, communicating, and bargaining, both of which contribute to smooth horizontal coordination, may require intense effort on the part of blue-collar workers. It is clear that all these factors are now subject to serious challenge. On the one hand, Japanese firms are expanding their activities globally to an ever increasing degree and, on the other hand, their ability to recruit qualified blue-collar workers willing to carry out intense work on the shop floor is becoming problematical as a result of recently acquired affluence.

## 2.3    The Hierarchy of Ranks

Having examined the coordination mode of the Japanese firm, I now turn to its incentive system to show how the characteristics of these two aspects of Japanese firms are related to each other. I will begin by listing some factors required for the efficient and effective operation of the J-mode that may have important bearings on the nature of the incentive system at Japanese firms.

1. In the H-mode, operating tasks are separated from the coordinating task and divided into specific functions. Operating skills valued in this mode are therefore specialized skills. In the J-mode, however, operating units are expected to be engaged in mutually coordinating their tasks as well. Exclusive attention to the efficient performance of a particular operating task in isolation may not contribute to overall efficiency (i.e., the generation of information value made possible through efficient horizontal coordination based on information sharing) and may not be appreciated much. In addition to skills in particular operating tasks, the ability to communicate and work together with peers and others with different functions is required. (Recall the role of the engineer in the integrated process control office in the steel industry in the second example of section 2.2.)

2. As suggested by the automobile industry example in the previous section, smooth adaptation of production scheduling to emergent customer demands through horizontal coordination requires each operating unit to be capable of responding to needed changes quickly (e.g., in jigs and tools) and of coping independently with somewhat unusual problems (e.g., breakdown of a machine, quality defect of an in-process product). Otherwise, smooth operation may be disrupted. Workers in the final assembly line are entitled to stop the line whenever they see problems that would justify doing so. The problem is handled on the spot, possibly with the help of

neighboring workers, team leaders, foremen, and so on, but not by calling in outside specialists such as mechanists. The integration of operating skill with autonomous problem-solving capability can be ensured only when the worker has a good understanding of the relevant work process as a whole, rather than only a certain aspect of it. Such general understanding in turn may be nurtured by making the worker familiar with many related aspects of the work process. This is a point that Koike has rightly emphasized in a series of influential papers.[15]

3. In the steel industry and product development examples and in the last section, it was pointed out that the practice of job rotation of engineers among different engineering offices, as well as between engineering jobs and supervisory jobs at the factory, facilitates the knowledge sharing needed for horizontal coordination among different phases of engineering and development processes. For similar and other purposes, white-collar workers on the lifetime career track (and sometimes even blue-collar workers) are rotated among various jobs in different offices and workshops every few years. Such rotation familiarizes workers with various jobs and enhances their ability to process and communicate information needed for the efficient operation of the J-mode. Regular rotation also prevents workers from identifying strongly with specific jobs, workshops, plants, and offices so that the development and assertion of local interests inconsistent with the organizational goals are restrained.

These factors point to two important needs: first, the design of incentives that are not tightly related to a specific job category but that motivate wide-ranging job experience among employees, and, second, the development of a personnel office that administers such incentives and is also responsible for personnel posting, including interjurisdictional rotations, with an eye to the firm's long-run organizational goals.

As for the first, Japanese firms have developed rank hierarchies as a primary incentive device, which Aoki describes in some detail.[16] The essential idea may be summarized as follows: There are usually separate rank hierarchies for blue-collar workers, white-collar workers, and engineers, as well as one for the supervisory and managerial employees above them. Each rank carries a certain level of pay but not a specific job. Therefore employees in the same rank may be doing different jobs. For instance, an engineer at the integrated process control office, an engineer at development laboratory, and an engineer at the plant site may well be in the same

---

15. Koike (1984, 1988, 1989).
16. (1988a, ch. 2); also see Dore (1973) for a classical description.

rank and receive identical pay (possibly with minor allowances for particular jobs). New entrants to the firm who are just out of school are placed at appropriate ranks in the nonmanagerial rank hierarchies determined by their years of education.

After entry at an identical starting point for a certain educational credential, employees compete for promotion in rank throughout their careers. The criteria for promotion are years of service and merit, with the latter not specifically related to particular jobs but to broadly defined problem-solving abilities, communication skills, and so on. The speed of promotion for all employees is the same early in their careers, however, as young employees are considered to be in training and their aptitude for the firm's specific implementation of the J-mode is being tested. Differences in speed of promotion among employees becomes more apparent, however, in mid-career (e.g., after employees reach their mid thirties). So the fast flyer among blue-collar workers may reach the top rank in his late thirties (and proceed to supervisory ranks afterward), while the slow mover may reach the top rank only a year before mandatory retirement at age sixty. Promotion criteria become stricter particularly for the white-collar employees as their careers advance. If an employee does not exhibit continual progress, he or she may be separated in mid to late career, although an honorable exit is usually arranged by the employing firm by posting the employee to a less promising quasi-outside job at a minor subsidiary or other related firm. Thus the mystifying notion of lifetime employment and the seniority system tells only half of the truth. Also relevant is the fact that in the late 1980s, the personnel departments of some large Japanese firms began official recruiting of midcareer specialists and skilled workers from other firms as the shortage of such staff became more pronounced.

The ways in which rank hierarchy works as an incentive, that is, the ways in which it copes with the problems of moral hazard (the possibility of employees' shirking in the absence of proper monitoring), adverse selection (the difficulty of hiring the right workers, whose qualifications cannot be known with certainty prior to employment), and the provision of motivation for wide-ranging firm-specific learning and teamwork can be rigorously analyzed in the light of recent development of the incentive literature, and the theories proposed may be tested.[17] From the theoretical point of view, one point should be stressed here: The existence of a credible threat of discharge when the employee does not meet the criteria for continual

---

17. See Aoki (1988a, ch. 3) for the theoretical analysis of Japanese employment practices and the relevant literature.

promotion plays an important role in enabling the rank hierarchy to operate as an effective incentive to curb shirking. A discharge in midcareer may point to some negative attributes of the discharged so that he or she may not be able to gain equivalent rank outside, when information about him or her is not perfect. So an employee must compare short-run gains from shirking with potential losses in wealth due to discharge and consequent demotion. As stated above, lifetime employment and seniority advancement are not automatic. Otherwise, they would not be effective as incentives.

Theoretical analysis shows, however, that actual dismissal as a disciplinary measure seldom needs to be observed, insofar as the rank-hierarchy system operates well as an effective monitoring mechanism.[18] Also the possibility of promotion gives employees a positive incentive to learn within the context of their employing firms, and the potential loss of seniority and of retirement compensation related to duration of employment discourages the midcareer exit of trained employees. As a result the duration of employment tends to be relatively long for Japanese workers.[19] But how much of the seniority rise in employee's income is due to learning achievement and consequent productivity increase (which is explained by human capital theory) and how much to bonding for diligence (which is explained by monitoring theory) is still to be empirically settled.

To administer rank hierarchies, Japanese firms have developed the personnel department as an important institution. This department has full control of the recruitment of new employees for career tracks out of school, designs and runs rank hierarchies (pay scale and promotion criteria), and rotates white-collar workers with an eye to the wider interests of the organization. (The rotation of blue-collar workers may be delegated to a subsection of a personnel department at the plant level.) Since the personnel department potentially has excessive power because of its control of promotion and rotation, managers of the department are usually themselves subject to rotation. To avoid demoralizing employees by unfair treatment, the criteria for promotion and rotation are designed to be as objective as possible. Also the supervisory assessment of an employee by multiple supervisors through the rotation of the employee and supervisors may make actual personnel decisions consistent with "public opinion" within the firm. Yet mistakes and personal complaints, reasonable and unreasonable, are unavoidable. Since protest by exit is costly, the enter-

---

18. See, for example, MacLeod and Malcomson (1986).
19. See, for example, Hashimoto and Raisian (1985); Mincer and Higuchi (1988).

prise union, the institution through which employees can voice their complaints and grievances, has developed as a counterpart to the personnel department.

The enterprise union covers all regular employees, blue-collar and white. It does not negotiate about the wage rate for each job category; it does negotiate about the base pay for the bottom rank, pay differentials among ranks, and the admissible range regarding the speed of promotion. Within the negotiated agreement, however, the personnel department has discretion over the ranking and job assignments of employees. One of the important roles of the enterprise union is to absorb employees' grievances about personnel decisions and to monitor the fairness of the personnel administration of the firm. It is not accidental that unions take an enterprise-based form at Japanese firms rather than that of industrial or craft unionism as in those economies where workers' careers are more oriented to a broader market rather than to the individual firm.[20]

Thus there seems to be an interesting asymmetry between typical Western firms and typical Japanese firms regarding ways that incentive and coordination modes are interrelated. In the Japanese firm, rank hierarchy is used as a primary incentive device, while the coordination mode is less hierarchical. In contrast, the Western firm combines a relatively more hierarchical approach to coordination with the relatively decentralized market approach to incentives (i.e., clear employment contracts relating specific jobs to competitive wages may be written). In the Japanese firm management may feel secure in delegating tasks of coordination to lower levels where relevant on-site information is available, because employees are aware that they are being evaluated by their own long-term contributions to organizational goals. Thus they are induced to comply with management authority without explicit hierarchical direction over daily operation. On the other hand, in the societal environment where more individualistic values prevail, management authority is not automatically assured within the firm organization and needs to be asserted by a contractually agreed hierarchical structure of decision making.

Keeping in mind that the alleged asymmetry is an oversimplified stylization,[21] let us dare to summarize it in the following manner:

---

20. Aoki (1984a, 3); Koike (1984); and Shirai (1984).
21. Organizational practices usually attributed to "Japanese management" such as lifetime employment (actually long-term employment), internal career advancement based on seniority and merit, the rotation of personnel over jobs and broader job assignment, and bonuses—have for quite some time also been widely observed in the personnel administration of white-collar employees of many "well-run" Western firms (e.g., Foulkes 1980). Koike(1984) has described the position of blue-collar workers in Japanese firms, albeit somewhat controversially, as "the white collarization of blue-collar workers."

THE FIRST DUALITY PRINCIPLE   For firms to be internally integrative and organizationally effective, either their coordination or their incentive mode
needs to be hierarchical, but not both.

Comparatively speaking, Japanese firms tend to be less hierarchical in
the coordination mode, while they rely upon rank hierarchies in their incentive system.

## 2.4   Bank-Oriented Financial Control

In this section I take up the financial aspect of Japanese firms and examine
its characteristics. I argue that there is a close and logical symmetry between the internal organizational aspect and the financial control aspect of
Japanese firms, and I summarize this symmetry as the "second duality
principle." As regards the financial control aspect, I need to explain the
following two stylized facts. I regard the two as parts of a unified and
consistent system, even if they do not appear to be necessarily consistent
internally and mutually from the orthodox neoclassical (contractual) view
of financial control.[22]

1.  In Japan, banks (city banks, trust banks, local banks, etc.—each specialized in different business activities subject to regulation and administrative
guidance by the Ministry of Finance) are allowed to hold stocks of nonfinancial companies up to the maximum of 5 percent of the shares of each
stock. Financial institutions as a whole (including insurance companies) own
about 40 percent of the total stock outstanding of listed companies, but
there is usually one or a few influential city banks for each listed company
that own up to, or close to, the maximum. There is also one city bank for
each company among its major stockholders, called the *main bank*, which
has the closest tie in terms of cash management, as well as short-term (and
long-term) credits. The main bank plays the role of manager of a loan
consortium when a group of banks extends major long-term credit to the
company, and it is responsible for closely monitoring the business affairs
of the company. If the company suffers a business crisis, the main bank
assumes major responsibility for various rescue operations, which include
the rescheduling of loan payments, emergency loans, advice for the liquidation of some assets, the facilitation of business opportunities, the supply of
management resources, and, finally, reorganization to secure the claims of

---

22. For detailed data supporting the stylized facts summarized here, consult Aoki (1988a,
ch. 4).

the consortium.[23] In the normal course of events, however, the main bank exercises explicit control neither in the selection of management nor in corporate policymaking. Well-run companies that incur little or no debt from banks appear to be virtually free from banks' intervention, and their managements enjoy the highest degree of autonomy.[24]

2. Because a large proportion of the equities held by banks and other corporate entities are extremely stable, the managements of Japanese firms are insulated from takeover raids through the open market. Individual stockholders, who own only about 30 percent of outstanding total equities of listed companies, do not have any effective voice in the corporate governance structure. As long as a company is well run, top management is selected by the outgoing president (or chairman) from among the firm's own managerial corps. Thus top management is considered to be the highest rank for the career advancement of employees. From this observation, some authors suggest that Japanese firms are run virtually in the interests of employees subject to some degree of financial constraint.[25] At the same time, however, individual stockholders have enjoyed the high annual after-tax real market rate of returns to stockholding of 11.7 percent (the standard error 18.5 percent) over the period 1963 to 1986.[26] The economic interests of individual stockholders do not seem to be entirely neglected at least ex post.

Thus there seem to be paradoxes. On the one hand, banks are major stockholders of companies. But banks do not appear to exercise vertical control over management of these companies, and they remain as silent business partners in good profit states. Their power becomes visible only in bad states. On the other hand, even though the individual stockholders have only apparently weak control over firms, banks are de facto benefici-

---

23. Sheard (1989).
24. For instance, 15 percent of the stock of Toyota Motor Corporation is owned by three city banks. Tokai, Sakura, and Sanwa, but there is no collusion on the part of these banks to influence the corporate direction and management selection by Toyota. They do, however, woo Toyota management competitively for commercial dealings.
25. See for example, Abegglen and Stalk (1985) and Komiya (1987, 1989).
26. For a more detailed, firm-based estimate of the market rate of stockholding, see Ando and Auerbach (1988). Taking into account both taxes and risk premia, Bernheim and Shoven (1989) attempt to estimate the cost of capital for Japanese firms. Whether the ex ante cost of capital facing Japanese firms is relatively lower or higher than the American counterpart has not been empirically settled yet and is still controversial despite an often-made allegation that the cost is relatively lower (e.g., Hatsopoulos, Krugman, and Summers 1988). See Aoki (1988a, 112–13) for a criticism of the casual comparison of costs of capital between different economies based on raw data unadjusted for different tax and accounting conventions. See Aoki (1988a, 113–16).

aries of Japanese firms. These are paradoxes only from the viewpoint of orthodox financial theory in which stockholders are assumed (or at least ought) to control management through the corporate governance structure as well as the threat of market discipline (i.e., takeover raids). But this does not mean that Japanese firms are completely free of financial control (monitoring).

First, let us note that main bank's control manifests itself in bad profit states. If the profit of a company starts to decline, the main bank is able to detect the problem at a rather early stage through information gained from the management of commercial accounts, short-term credits, long-term personal contacts with top management of the company and its business partners, and so on, because of its special position.[27] Tacit and explicit pressure for the internal overhaul of management would be initiated in exchange for various types of rescue operations, as noted before. If bad states continue, the main bank may decide to take over management through the governance structure of the company (stockholder's meeting, board of directors). Recent experiences indicate, however, that banks do not change the fundamental nature of internal management; rather they hand over top management after recuperation to internally promoted employees.[28]

It is because of this possibility of bank takeover that I have adopted a definition of the main bank that focuses on its role as a major stockholder as well as a main lender (or manager of a loan consortium). I would argue that although in the normal state bank control is not visible, the potential threat of bank takeover may play an important monitoring function when the financial system is viewed as a whole. A recent contribution by Aghion and Bolton (1988) is suggestive in this regard. Aghion and Bolton argue that the essence of debt contracts lies neither in its return characteristics (e.g., fixed-interest claims combined with bankruptcy risk) nor in defining a liquidation point, but in the following arrangement regarding the transfer of control: As long as good profit states continue, the outside investor (bank) does not intervene and inside management continues to manage; otherwise the outside investor (bank) takes over management and reorganizes. Within the specific context of their model, they showed that such a

---

27. In the bank-oriented system in Japan, a single bank (the main bank) monitors the company closely as the major cash manager-creditor-stockholder so that it is in a position to detect a problem early. In contrast, at the time of near bankruptcy of Chrysler, about 400 banks had extended credit to Chrysler, and no bank was aware of the magnitude of the problem until the real crisis became evident.
28. See Pascale and Rohlen (1983) for an interesting case study of the bank takeover of Mazda.

financial system can achieve ex ante Pareto superior outcome under certain conditions. The external investor with control rights may be excessively risk prone in good profit states, while inside management may be excessively wasteful in bad states by trying to survive at the creditors' expense.

Needless to say, the Japanese situation is much more complicated than the Aghion-Bolton model. Also Aghion and Bolton's analytical result does not imply that bank-oriented financial control is always efficient. But one cannot deny that in Japanese practice there is a close positive correlation between the degree of management freedom from bank control and the level of corporate profits. Because internal management naturally abhors external interference by the main bank, and bank control is a humiliating blow to the failed manager, management aspires to pursue high profits. It may thus be considered that corporate ranking by profit is an effective discipline exercised over the apparently autonomous management of Japanese firms, even though its form is different from that envisioned in the orthodox Anglo-American financial literature (hierarchical control of stockholders through the corporate governance structure combined with market-oriented incentive contracting for managers and the threat of takeover.[29] This observation suggests that the nature of the financial control over Japanese firms is symmetric to that of the internal control within them: There is no clear hierarchical division between corporate control and managerial operation. Financial control by bank cum stockholders concerning corporate direction is exercised only in a business crisis. Otherwise corporate decision is delegated entirely to management on site. Management, however, is indirectly disciplined through competition over ranking, this time, ranking of firms by corporate profits. A question may then be raised: Is there any logical reason for the said symmetry—weak-decision

---

29. It is doubtless true that North American managers are potentially more vulnerable to takeover raids. There are, however, some interesting developments that may suggest a convergent phenomenon. First, the growth of institutional stockholding, such as by pension funds in the United States, tends to stabilize a large proportion of the ownership of major firms' equities. As a result a closer relationship between management and major institutional investors based on the sharing of business information may emerge. Also in the United States the spread of leveraged buyouts has brought in many of the features associated with bank-oriented financial contracting, such as high debt ratio and combined debt and equity holdings (strip financing). In the case of a management-leveraged buyout, management becomes more insulated from possible raids by outsiders but vulnerable to banks' controls when the firm's performance deteriorates (Berglof 1989). Whether these phenomena are temporary or not (except for the growth of pension funds and its implications) is not yet clear, but together with increasing reliance of Japanese firms on bond financing abroad, the distinction between the bank-oriented system and the market-oriented financial system is becoming somewhat blurred.

hierarchy cum incentive-ranking hierarchy (WDIR) both in the internal and financial aspects? In other words, can a WDIR-type internal structure be combined effectively with a non-WDIR-type financial system as envisioned in the orthodox finance literature?

First, note that for horizontal coordination within internal organization to operate more effectively (in the sense of being able to achieve organizational goals), management decision needs to be continually adapted in response to on-site information available at all levels of the functional hierarchy. Further, organizational goals themselves may need to be adjusted in response to the employees' voice. In this way a sense of joint effort is created so that employees' active cooperation in horizontal coordination may be elicited. This amounts to a set of mutual vertical commitments in which management recognizes the interests of employees, and in return employees exert greater effort. Commenting on my previous work (Aoki 1986) Leibenstein wrote: "We are likely to find that a high degree of mutual vertical commitment creates a sense of common objectives and a concern for the results beyond one's own job, which in turn is likely to support horizontal coordination on production goals.... Thus while I agree with Aoki on the importance of horizontal cooperation I would argue that where horizontal cooperation on production goals flourishes it is likely to be a consequence of a high degree of mutual vertical commitments" (p. 170).

Toward the end of the next section I inquire more precisely into the logical structure of the mutual vertical commitments which can yield a Pareto-superior outcome for financial and employees' interests. Anticipating that, I only maintain here that the sharing of knowledge, as well as the partial identification of interests, across various levels of internal organization is essential for facilitating vertical interactions, especially for management to absorb information and demands at the lower level, for corporate decision making. The internal selection of management through promotional ranking may serve as an effective mechanism by which such knowledge sharing and interest identification are nurtured on the basis of the sharing of experiences. Further, rank hierarchy as an incentive device becomes fully operative only if the internal promotion ladder for employees extends as high as the top executive position. And the autonomy of internal management from external financial interests is guaranteed under the WDIR-type financial control as long as the profit state is satisfactory.

From the perspective of incentive as well, the WDIR symmetry seems to be logical. Under an employment contract established in the context of a rank hierarchy, operating employees tend to be associated with a particular firm on a more or less permanent basis because midcareer mobility (exit) may be costly.[30] Their lifetime wealth is at stake with the employing firm in the form of future claims for seniority payments and retirement compensations, and this wealth is not salable. Opportunities for risk diversification are thus limited. There needs to be a mechanism, therefore, that insures employees to some degree against firm-specific risk. Because of the stable concentration of stockholding, as well as continual information flow between firms and banks in the context of the WDIR financial system, the reorganization of a troubled firm by the main bank may occur sooner than under the market-oriented financial system, and this may mitigate the risk of bankruptcy.[31] In fact the bankruptcy of companies associated with a reputable main bank rarely occurs in Japan. Horiuchi, Parker, and Fukuda (1988) tried to refute empirically the insurance hypothesis regarding the main bank. But the function of a monitor and that of an insurer against bankruptcy risk by the main bank are not necessarily mutually exclusive. At the time of the rescue operation, the main bank normally bears more than proportional costs in comparison to other members of the consortium, and this may be explained by the supposition that the main bank's reputation as a good and responsible monitor is at stake.[32] On the other hand, managers and operating employees are relatively mobile across firms under Western-type employment contracting, but well-developed securities markets can provide an efficient mechanism through which individual wealth-risk is diversified and thereby reduced. Therefore I claim the following:

THE SECOND DUALITY PRINCIPLE    The internal organization and financial control of the Japanese firm are dually characterized by weak-decision hierarchy and incentive-ranking hierarchy. This duality is not accidental.

## 2.5   Dual Control over Corporate Management Decisions

In this section I discuss questions concerning the goals and purposes of Japanese management. We have seen in the last section that Japanese management is relatively independent of external financial control in making corporate decisions. This freedom, however, exists only so long as a satisfactory state of profits is maintained. Should that state be seriously compromised, the external power of the main bank, which stands in the background, will be exercised. This substantial, if constrained, freedom

---

30. Hashimoto and Raisian (1985) and Mincer and Higuchi (1988).
31. Berglof (1989).
32. Aoki (1988a, 142–49, 232–33).

of Japanese management poses a question: Is the conventional profit-maximizing objective itself routinely qualified by an admixture of other goals? Does it apply only as a subsidiary constraint on the pursuit of other goals? Some influential economists argue in that way. For example, Komiya advances the hypothesis that a Japanese firm "chooses the amount of output and the amounts of labor and capital inputs so as to maximize income per employee ... after the payment of a fixed share of profits to stockholders."[33] Such a presumption essentially boils down to the model of a worker-controlled firm that postulates the maximization of income per worker since the profit motive is assumed not to have any direct impact on the decisions of corporate management. I predict, however, that it will be difficult to sustain such a hypothesis, if its implications for corporate behavior are empirically tested. For example, the hypothesis implies that to protect the interests of incumbent employees the growth rate of the worker-controlled firm would be slower than that of a profit-maximizing firm (Atkinson 1973), an unlikely situation in Japanese firms.

On the other hand, there are reasons to believe that employees as a group constitute assets specific and internal to the firm. We have seen that Japanese firms rely upon a system of horizontal coordination in which employees at the operational level actively participate. Also I have argued that the information-processing and communicative abilities of participating employees are nurtured largely through learning by doing in the context of a firm-specific coordination network. Such abilities cannot be acquired in ready-made form prior to membership in the network, and their values cannot be thoroughly realized in isolation from it. In other words, skills effective for the creation of information value in the context of horizontal coordination may not be classifiable along well-defined job categories, for which market contracts transferable between firms can be unambiguously written. One may reason then that employees of Japanese firms as a group become assets specific to the internal network and that rewards for them are internally determinable (subject to possible external constraints) and payable out of the value generated by the network net of costs due to the training of employees, the sacrifice of economies of specialization, and so on.

If so, however, the following hypothetical question may be raised: Why do employees not purchase the physical assets necessary to maintain the network through debts and replicate the network, guaranteeing to themselves its whole value? In short, why would an employee-controlled firm

---

33. Komiya (1989, 115).

not be created? This question arises not only from intellectual curiosity alone, for some authors do argue that Japanese firms are in effect managed on behalf of their employees. Yet there are reasons that make it difficult for employees to control their firms explicitly and entirely. One is the obvious limitation of the availability of finance for the purpose of creating the employee-controlled firm. It may be recalled that monitoring by the main bank is particularly effective because of its dual position as a major creditor and a main stockholder. But, since potential creditors are excluded from equity ownership of the employee-controlled firm, they may not feel as secure in providing credit and reluctant to do so.

Further, to convince all employees to move to the new "clone" firm, they must agree on how to divide up the value appropriated by the firm. This division involves costs of collective choice which may be prohibitively high, specifically when the employees are not homogeneous. Also Mailath and Postlewaite (1988) have argued that if there are intangible gains that employees get from the firm (as distinguished from the network as such) and that they cannot each verify, they may be induced to exaggerate their reservation wages (i.e., the wage at which they would move to the proposed clone firm) and that an attempt to induce truthful revelation may make a proposal for a new viable employee-controlled firm untenable. This would be especially true when the size of the network becomes very large. Such private reservation wages, for example, may take the following forms. The performances of employees of the Japanese firm are evaluated and rewarded in the long run by the elaborate and admittedly impartial personnel administration system crystallized in the hierarchy of ranks, and this may provide to workers the long-run security and the sense of fair treatment they desire. It does not seem obvious, however, how the egalitarian idea of employee-controlled firm and the centralized management of hierarchy of ranks can be made mutually compatible. Also the loss of the main bank's services in monitoring management may impose costs of monitoring management on each employee in terms of time, effort, and resources.

The discussion in the preceding two paragraphs is admittedly hypothetical, but it may help us understand that the impact of financial control over Japanese firms cannot be neglected entirely even if employees are network-specific assets. A portion of the value created by the network thus accrues to financial investors who supply finance and monitor management. On the other hand, if employees' reward cannot be entirely determined by external market competition, but is negotiated internally, employees too would be interested in how corporate decisions are made. Corporate decisions would have an impact on workers' short-term and long-term positions in the rank hierarchies that define their lifetime earnings. Employees are not only interested, they are also able to exercise influence on corporate decisions. When employees are promoted to be executive managers, their motives may well remain mixed and contain a carry-over from their longer careers as employees in the lower ranks. It is true that, as executive managers, they must give attention to profit making in order to maintain their own position and autonomy. Yet they may retain a degree of identification with the interests of employees and a degree of freedom to support them.

For financial interests as well, it may be reasonable to leave open the possibility of mutually beneficial exchange between the levels of employees' earnings and effort, on the one hand, and the direction of corporate decision making, on the other. For example, employees may be willing to trade off current earnings and expend more effort for higher job security, which may also raise the profit level. Further such exchange may help preserve the network-specific assets as well, which would be mutually beneficial in the long run. Therefore we propose the following hypothesis, making its behavioral implications subject to future empirical testing:

THE THIRD DUALITY PRINCIPLE    The corporate management decisions of Japanese firms are subject to the dual control (influence) of financial interests (ownership) and employees' interests rather than to unilateral control in the interests of ownership.

It may be noted that this proposition departs not only from the usual neoclassical presupposition but also from the "share system" view of Weitzman, although Weitzman claims that the Japanese economy is "the only industrial economy in the world with anything remotely resembling a share system."[34] The essential difference lies in the fact that in the model I propose not only distributive shares but also corporate decision making is implicitly or explicitly subject to sharing. In Weitzman's theoretical design only the share parameter defining the division of value-added between profit and workers' earnings is subject to bilateral agreement. After such agreement corporate decision making, such as on the size of employment, is the prerogative of management who are driven exclusively by the profit motive. If the marginal return from a worker is diminishing, yet the share parameter is fixed ex ante at less than one, income per worker is ever diminishing as the size of employment increases. On the other hand, when marginal returns are positive, management is induced to expand the size of

---

34. Weitzman, (1984, 76).

employment. I find it unrealistic to imagine that unions (at least the Japanese enterprise union) fail to recognize the subsequent outcome of agreeing with the Weitzman's share contract, namely that they lose control over remuneration per worker. I would maintain that the hypothesis of dual control by financial and employees' interests over corporate decision making is a more reasonable one, once the network specificity of employees' skills is accepted.

Questions to be asked next are as follows: How do firms behave under dual control? Is there any qualitative or quantitative difference between the implications of dual control and unilateral ownership control in how firms are run? How is dual control exercised? What role do management and employees each play?

First, we note that employees as a group can withdraw cooperation in horizontal coordination if they feel that they are not treated fairly by management in pecuniary rewards and corporate decision making. Similarly the main bank as the major creditor cum stockholder can threaten management with the discipline of bank takeover if a sufficient level of profits over time is not assured.[35] Since management's social prestige and autonomy are enhanced if the managed firm stands higher in corporate profit ranking, we may suppose that the distribution of a firm's revenue between employees' earnings and profits reflects either the relative bargaining power of the enterprise union vis-à-vis management acting in the interests of profits or the notion of fairness held by management.[36] Further let us imagine that management strikes a balance between employees' interests and financial interests in making corporate policy. Finally, suppose that to the degree that employees trust management corporate policy making to be fair, they supply more effort in operating activities and horizontal coordination than would be expected under the competitive wage system (i.e., more effort that maximizing individual labor surplus

---

35. Strictly speaking, there is the question of whether there is any conflict of interest between the main bank as a creditor cum stockholder and the individual stockholders. This problem is investigated in Aoki (Investors 1988a, 127–38) within the framework of a miniature general financial equilibrium model incorporating features of taxes and financial regulation in Japan. This analysis indicates that the bank prefers its portfolio company to rely more on debt financing than on the equity financing of individual stockholders and that the conflict has been resolved in favor of the bank, although less so since the mid-1970s.

36. If the management's notion of fairness is represented by Nash's formulation of symmetry in his axiomatic approach to bargaining (Nash 1950), on one hand, and if the relative bargaining power of the union is measured in terms of "boldness" as formulated in cooperative game theory, on the other hand, the distributive outcomes predicted by the two approaches and identical (see Aoki 1984a, ch. 5).

obtained by equating the marginal value disutility of effort with the wage rate).

Such mutual commitments by management and the employees are expected to yield a Pareto-superior outcome under the assumption of network specificity of human assets.[37] The following are some of their behavioral implications in which the stockholder-controlled firm refers to a firm that maximizes the stock value (the present value of a stream of future profits) of the firm under the competitive wage system:

1. The dually controlled firm pursues a higher growth rate (or somewhat more loosely speaking, tends to have a longer horizon) in investment decision making than the stockholder-controlled firm facing the same level of employees' current earnings, because the former takes into account employees' extra benefits from the growth of the firm in the form of enhanced future promotion possibilities in their rank hierarchies.[38]

2. The dually controlled firm sets the amount of employment at the level at which the marginal value product of an additional worker is equal to a worker's earnings minus the marginal rate of an implicit unemployment insurance premium. Thus, if the employees' fear of unemployment is positive, the dually controlled firm provides a higher degree of job security than the stockholder-controlled firm.[39]

3. To protect the interests of incumbent employees, the dually controlled firm tends to limit the expansion of the work force relative to the growth

---

37. Let us imagine as a thought experiment that management formulates corporate policy by weighting the policy optimal to the representative employee and the policy optimal to long-run profit making (i.e., the present value of the future stream of profits), with weights being given by each distributive share in firm-specific quasi rent. I call this policy making the "weighting rule" (Aoki 1984a, 74–80). Further assume that the empoloyees supply the level of effort that maximizes "collective" value surplus by equating the marginal value utility of effort with the marginal value product (not the wage rate). When the utility function of both the profit claimant and the representative employee are of the "constant pure boldness type" in the sense defined in Aoki (1984a, 74–77), this idealized constellation of mutual commitments will yield a generalized Nash bargaining solution, with weights given by distributive shares (see Aoki 1984a, ch. 6, 1988a, ch. 5, for a proof). As is well known, the Nash bargaining solution is the only one outcome that satisfies the set of axioms that John Nash (1950) imposed on the efficient and "fair" (symmetric) arbitration to fulfill. Also a recent development in game theory shows that under certain conditions an equilibrium of a noncooperative two-person bargaining game—known as the "perfect subgame equilibrium"—exhibits qualitatively equivalent characteristics with the generalized Nash bargaining solution (Binmore, Rubinstein, and Wilinsky 1986). Although the idealized construct given above may appear arbitrary at first, its behavioral implications may well stand up to variant institutional assumption.
38. Aoki (1988a, 164–66).
39. Aoki (1988a, 174–76).

of value added by spinning off relatively labor-intensive activities to relatively lower-wage subsidiaries or outside suppliers,[40] as well as leaning more toward capital-intensive technology than the stockholder-controlled firm.[41]

4. If the implicit unemployment insurance premium payable by employees is high, the dually controlled firm chooses work sharing rather than layoffs as a first response to bad business conditions.[42]

5. The dually controlled firm seeks innovative opportunities by developing an in-house knowledge base rather than pursuing breakthrough innovation requiring an entirely new organization of its research and development team.[43]

Theoretically speaking, the dually controlled firm may be viewed as a mixture of the conventional neoclassical model (the N-model) of the stockholder-controlled firm, and the model of the worker-controlled firm (the W-model) in the manner of Domar-Ward.[44] It is well known that the worker-controlled firm tends to limit the size of the labor force in order to increase the probability of job security in comparison to the conventional N-model.[45] The behavioral characteristics of the W-model may help us understand propositions 2 through 4 intuitively. Proposition 1 appears to run counter to this characteristic, but note that this proposition is stated in comparison to a firm that chooses a growth rate solely to maximize its stock price after having made its wage bargain. Efficiency requires the conjoint decision of wage rate *and* growth rate when employees become assets internal to the network, because employees may be willing to forgo the current earnings level for future benefits made possible by promotion in the rank hierarchy. Proposition 5 may be understood by considering that engineers and researchers who have firm-specific knowledge are constituent members of the dually controlled firm.

The characterizations above may seem to imply that employees are the only beneficiaries of the dually controlled firm. But this is not so. Since employees in the dually controlled firm may be induced to trade off the level of current earnings, make investment in training, and commit to the

---

40. Differential earnings between the parent firm and its satellite firms are substantial, but it should be noted that the use of a lower wage is only one aspect of subcontracting among many others.
41. Aoki (1988a, 166–74) and Miyazaki (1984).
42. Aoki (1988a, 176–81).
43. Aoki (1988a, 237–52) and Aoki and Rosenberg (1989).
44. Aoki (1984a, ch. 5).
45. Miyazaki (1984).

higher level of effort for those benefits indicated above, the profit level is expected to rise as well. In other words, once employees become network-specific assets, mutual commitments of employees and management would yield a Pareto-superior outcome.

## 2.6 Concluding Remarks

In this chapter I have described a model of a Japanese firm based on stylized facts, which are summarized in the three duality principles. This model—the J-model—is in many respects different from models of the firm constructed by Western economists. Archibald described the current state of the theory of the firm in his contribution to *The New Palgrave: A Dictionary of Economics*: "It is doubtful if there is yet general agreement among economists on the subject matter designated by 'theory of the firm,' on, that is, the scope and purpose of the part of economics so titled."[46] It would be fair to say, however, that agency theory is currently one of the most influential theories on the firm, especially among Anglo-American theoretical economists.

According to this theory, the firm is conceived as a "nexus of (agency) contracts."[47] In an agency contract the entity called the "principal" delegates decision making for realizing its own objective to the agent who may have superior on-site information but different preferences. The principal tries to control the latter's action by the design of an appropriate incentive contract. The ultimate principal of the firm is its owner, or the stockholders in the context of the modern corporate firm, and its agent is management. Management is then conceived to operate hierarchically through a chain of incentive contracts, with management of the higher level acting as the surrogate for the ultimate principal and that of the lower level as the agents of higher-level management. At the bottom of the hierarchy, management controls operating employees through incentive contracts.

An agency contract may be written in many ways, but its design is conditioned by outside markets in one important way: The principal cannot induce the agent to enter a contractual relation unless the principal guarantees the agent at least the level of its reservation utility determined by outside opportunities. Finally, the stockholders' rights to control management are market transferable so that the "bidding" among investors will

---

46. Archibald (1987, 357).
47. Jensen Meckling (1976).

ultimately lead to the maximization of firm's value subject to the inevitable costs incurred in the chain of agency contracts (the agency loss).

The characteristics of the agency model of the firm are (1) hierarchical decomposition of control originating at stockholders (H-mode), (2) market-conditioned incentive contracting, and (3) the control of the management decision according to the value maximization criterion. Clear differences are evident when they are compared with the three duality principles for the J-model. Why are there differences? Is it because the J-model is culturally unique and useful only as a tool for a microanalytic understanding of the Japanese economy?

One of the reasons why many Anglo-American economists are comfortable with the agency model as *the* model of the firm, and why I am presenting the J-model as a tool for understanding the workings of the Japanese economy, is doubtless that there *are* differences in the ways that firms are run in the West and in Japan and that the models reflect some aspects of those real differences. But are these differences absolute? Are they more important than the possible commonality that may not be taken into account by either of the models? If there is a convergent trend between the West and Japan, does it not mean that the J-model and the agency model represent only prototypes to be absorbed into a more general hybrid model of the firm?

The primitive comparative analysis of the H-mode versus the J-mode of coordination which I summarized at the begining of the chapter indicates that the relative efficiency of these two prototype models depends on various environmental parameters such as defining the nature and volatility of consumer demands, the degree of market concentration, the technology involved in the production process, and possibly government regulation. Therefore, if only efficiency mattered (and if relevant government regulations were alike across national economies), we would observe different coordination patterns across markets. Despite the increasing globalization of markets, the fact that we have been observing a relatively similar coordination mode within each economy, but relatively dissimilar patterns in the West and Japan, may have to do with historical, cultural, and regulation factors. As indicated just before the description of the first duality principle, the maintenance of organizational integrity in the context of individualistic values in the West (particularly in North America) may have necessitated contractual agreement on the more hierarchical structuring of internal coordination. On the other hand, in Japan, respect for differentiated status by attributes (sex, age, seniority, family background, etc.) and level of training has been a dominant traditional social value. A superior in Japan may therefore be more comfortable in delegating actual decision making to his subordinate. Also within a small group, horizontal coordination rather than clear job demarcation tends to emerge spontaneously in Japan, possibly because of the collective memory of the traditional agrarian customs and values.[48]

Having admitted that there are some cultural and historical traits in the ways that firms operate in each economy and that the efficiency criterion is not the only factor shaping the ways that firms are run, however, I would maintain that there is an important element of conscious design in viable business organizations. For example, small group dynamism per se, to which cultural anthropologists attribute the role of a driving force in Japanese organization (e.g., Nakane 1970), cannot be effective in the context of large organizations. A coherent, self-centered group may develop and assert its own interests at the sacrifice of organization goals. Managements of Japanese firms have taken pains to combat such tendencies by consciously designing intergroup coordinational mechanisms (the *kanban* system is but one example), shifting the emphasis from seniority to merit acquired by experience as a promotion criterion. They have transformed the seniority-oriented rank hierarchies into forms compatible with an organizationwide competitive drive, and so on. The sharing of rents and the commitment to employees' interests in corporate policymaking are no longer considered an expression of paternalistic benevolence of the management or owner, but they can be regarded as a means to elicit employees' cooperation and diligence. Many elements of the J-model should now be regarded as serious objects of economic analysis, particularly in view of Japanese industrial and technological challenges on the global scale.

As indicated in preceding sections, the relative merits of horizontal versus hierarchical coordination, market-oriented incentive contracting versus rank hierarchy, bank-oriented versus market-oriented financial control, are not yet so clear-cut, and comparative analysis dealing with such issues has only just begun. Meanwhile there is a greater tendency toward a convergence of organizational form and practice because of the strong force of natural selection operating through international market competition and because of deregulation within and across national boundaries.[49] Phenomena similar to some aspects of the J-model have emerged in the West

---

48. Aoki (1988b).
49. See notes 3 and 7 for details on this trend.

spontaneously or as a result of conscious design, while some elements of the agency and other contractual modeling are becoming ever more visible in Japan. From this angle the J-model may provide a new analytical insight into the working of newly emergent—or latent—phenomena in the Western economy. Similarly the agency model may be helpful for understanding some aspects of Japanese organization. But the J-model is perhaps fated to be subsumed in the future under the yet to be developed general theory of the firm, and so is the agency mode.

# 3

# The "Human-Capital-ism" of the Japanese Firm as an Integrated System

Hiroyuki Itami

How can we characterize the essential nature of the Japanese firm? We do need, of course, careful empirical and theoretical clarification of its individual characteristics. But these fragmented, analytical level studies are not enough. A holistic understanding of the Japanese enterprise as an integrated system, as a gestalt which lends meaning to its constituent parts, is also necessary. Which comes first? It is naive to assume that a mere accumulation of particulars can depict the whole, and it would equally be a mistake to maintain that "in the beginning was the whole". How one manages the interaction between the two is obviously a basic methodological problem on which each researcher must make up his own mind.

My own stance in this particular chapter is this: Having in previous work developed my understanding of individual features of the Japanese firm to a fair degree, I think the time has come to take my courage in both hands and attempt to establish a holistic picture. In the belief that there is a need for more debate on this question of the relationship between the particular and the general, I propose to offer an overall framework for what seems to me a plausible characterization of the essential elements of the Japanese enterprise system. Obviously I would not wish to claim that this is the only such possible characterization. There are, and should be, others quite compatible with it that take off from a different starting point, and perhaps others that are incompatible and serve to promote competing points of view. If this chapter can be a stimulus to such a debate, it will have done its work.

## 3.1 The Three Elements of an Enterprise System

The activity of an enterprise results from the participation of a large number of people. Shareholders and banks provide capital. The people who work in it provide their knowledge, their skills, their energies, their labor.

From this collectivity of people emerges the organization of the enterprise. Such enterprises are connected in the market through cooperation and the division of labor. The entire complex is conceptualized as an enterprise system. A good way of thinking out the principles on which this system is structured is to consider its orientation in terms of three points: (1) The concept of the firm, to whom does it belong? (2) Concepts of sharing, who does what and who gets what? (3) The conception of the market, what are the relations between firms?

The first is the most fundamental: the conception of the nature of the firm. The main participants in the enterprise are (1) the providers of capital, (2) the managers, and (3) the workers. Which one owns the firm? It is the answer to that question which constitutes what I call the conception of the firm. The cooperative interaction of these groups constitutes the total activity of the firm. Nevertheless, within the firm the questions of how managers relate to workers, and how individuals relate to other individuals are not just of who owns the firm, but of the patterns of division of responsibilities and rewards which I call "sharing." By what principles those patterns are formed is the basic determinant of the internal structure of the firm. "Sharing" in this sense has three elements: the basic inputs for the firm's activities, the outputs, and the decision-making process that relates the two. How are these divided among the participants in the firm's activities?

The firm's most basic input is information. The technology a firm uses is an obvious example. How that knowledge is divided is an example of input sharing. With the information at its disposal the firm buys resources from the market and provides goods and services, which it then sells. Its output is the value it adds. The division of this value added among the wages and bonuses received by the workers, the dividends and interest payments to those who provide capital, and the rewards to managers is output sharing. The production of that value added on the basis of the information input constitutes the process of decision making. How in practice the power, in all the multiple decisions that have to be taken, is distributed or held in common is the question of decision sharing.

The third conceptual element of the system concerns the nature of the market, which determines the relationships between firms. In a market economy it is through the division of labor and the possibilities of cooperation provided by the market that firms are able to produce goods and services. "Relationships between firms" means both the pattern of division of labor between buyers and sellers in the market and the nature of the transactions between them. It is in the market, in these transactions, that the "enterprise system" as a global whole takes shape. What kinds of transactions, based on what principles, are pervasive within the economy or are taken for granted, constitutes what I call the "concept of the market."

## 3.2   Characteristics of the Japanese Enterprise System

With respect to each of these three concepts I would maintain that postwar Japan has created an enterprise system that is substantially different from the typical (or perhaps one should say "textbook") picture of the capitalist enterprise system. A simple stylization of the difference is to be found in table 3.1.

The American system is probably closest to the classical model. To be sure, I am not suggesting that all Japanese enterprises have the characteristics listed in the table, nor that all American firms are purely "capitalist," but that the overall differences between Japanese and American firms can be characterized in this manner. (There are of course many ways of defining capitalism as a system. In what follows I will use "capitalism" in a classical and somewhat narrow sense in order to bring out more clearly the special characteristics of the Japanese system. As will become clear, I consider Japan's market system to be somewhat different from "capitalism," but this is by no means to deny that it is a market or free economy.)

## 3.3   Employee Sovereignty

By "employee sovereignty" I mean that the firm belongs to the people who have committed themselves to it and worked in it for long periods. They are the holders of "sovereign power." In other words, they are the people who have the right to make the decisions of basic importance to the firm, and they have priority rights in the distribution of the economic products of the firm's activities. (There may be readers who will object to the use of a word with such strong overtones as "sovereignty" in this connection. I do not intend to imply that employees are the sole possessors of

**Table 3.1**
Characteristics of the Japanese enterprise system

|  | Japanese enterprise system | Classical capitalist enterprise |
| --- | --- | --- |
| Enterprise concept | Employee sovereignty | Shareholder sovereignty |
| Sharing concept | Diffused sharing | Unidimensional sharing |
| Market concept | Organized markets | Free markets |

rights in the firm, nor that employees have something like a one-man-one-vote equality of power. It is just a shorthand expression designed to capture what people mean when they say the firm belongs to the people who work in it, and I use it because I cannot think of a suitable alternative. What it means in precise detail will become clear in what follows.)

It is usual in the classical form of capitalism to think of those who have provided the risk capital, the shareholders, as the possessors of sovereign power. Stockholder sovereignty—"the firm belongs to the stockholders"—is the normal perception in American society. In Japan, however, especially in the big firms, if you were to ask "who exactly does the firm belong to?" some employees would say "the shareholders," but most would say "it's our firm." By "employees" in this context I mean managers as well as white- and blue-collar workers, that is to say, all who have committed their working lives to the firm. It is worth noting that the Japanese word for "employees" ( *jugyoin* ) includes top managers too.

To say that employees are the holders of sovereign power is to speak *de facto*. *De jure*, the Japanese Commercial Code also makes the shareholders the owners of the firm. But this formal position is not reflected in practice; many features of the behavior of enterprises are understandable only on the assumption that the firm belongs to the employees rather than to the shareholders. Typical of such actions, for instance, is the fact that firms seek to maintain employment even at the expense of a dividend cut, or the fact that a takeover attempt is likely to be fought off by the combined action of managers and the union. Only when legal ownership of the firm is in question are shareholders on center-stage.

As I noted earlier, not every employee is equally a holder of sovereign power. There is a group of what one might call "core employees" with a long-term commitment who are the real "owners," or "sovereigns." The dividing line between them and the rest is not easy to draw, but part-time workers and most women workers do not belong to the core group. Those who do are people who see their employment not just as a matter of contracting to provide certain labor services for a certain wage. They have a sense of becoming a member, a sense of identification with the firm which is at the core of the idea of "working *in* a firm."

All this is not to say that the actions of the firm always and exclusively give priority to the welfare of the employees, nor that the "logic of capital" does not apply at all. That phrase has two general meanings. One is "the logic of the capitalist," the notion that firms are operated for the profit of their owners. The second is simply "the pursuit of profit," irrespective of whom the pursuit might benefit.

An employee-sovereign firm is certainly not free from "the logic of capital" in that latter sense, however little priority it might give to "the logic of capitalists." However, to speak of the pursuit of profit for the collectivity of employees as "the logic of capital" might well invite misunderstanding, and I will avoid the phrase henceforth. I will return to this question below, since the compatibility of the profit principle and employee sovereignty is no always well understood.

## 3.4   Diffused Sharing

In the classical, textbook form the entrepreneur—possessor of market and technical information—is the owner of the firm, takes all the decisions and, after paying wages etc. at market rates, takes all the rest of the value added. There is a correspondence in the three patterns of sharing—information, value-added, and decision-making power—all concentrated in the same individual. Let us call this the "classical unitary pattern," both in the sense that there is a correspondence in the three dimensions and that these dimensions involve very few individuals. Many American firms are close to this pattern. Put simply, in a unitary pattern, a small number of people with ability and access to information, monopolise the power to make decisions and take the lion's share of the proceeds. Top-down, centralized management, very large salary differences, differences of treatment in the workplace which amount to a distinction of status between managers and workers—many American firms approximate this unitary, concentrated pattern.

By contrast, in Japanese firms, first, the three patterns of sharing do not necessarily correspond; for example, the persons with the greatest decision-making power do not necessarily receive the highest rewards. And the sharing itself shows a more equal, less skewed, distribution; for example, the president's salary is a much lower multiple of that of a newly recruited worker. By "diffuse sharing" pattern, then, I mean both of these characteristics—relatively equal distributions and a lower correlation between distributions.

The low level of concentration of salaries in Japanese firms has various manifestations, not just in the minimization of differentials by rank. For example, in manufacturing, the salary levels of technologists working alongside blue-collar workers, are generally lower than those of their university contemporaries employed in white-collar jobs in banks and trading companies. This results from a concern not to let the differentials between white- and blue-collar workers within the firm get too big.

Japanese management style is often said to be of the "bottom-up" variety, meaning that there is a great deal of de facto delegation of decision-making power. As frequent discussion of the problems of sectionalism suggest, decision-making power tends to be spread around the organization, with top management performing arbitrating functions, rarely taking the lead in decision-making in any of the divisions.

However, as Aoki (1986) has pointed out, there is one exception to this diffusion of decision-making power; personnel decisions are far more centralised in Japanese than in American firms. One rarely finds an American equivalent of a Japanese firm's headquarters Personnel Office. In the United States, personnel decisions depend on department heads; your boss is your personnel officer. In Japan, although department heads contribute personnel evaluations, theirs is not the only input the personnel office receives, and generally departmental heads have no power over job reshuffles.

As for information sharing there is much evidence that technical knowledge is not highly concentrated: the fact that shop-floor workers are the repositories of a good deal of the technical knowledge the firm uses, or that they contribute to improvements in process technology, or that a large number of engineers work on the shop floor, or that the technical competence available on the shop floor is large relative to that available off it. In American and European firms engineers have a larger share and those on the shop floor a smaller share of the firm's stock of technological knowledge. What applies in the sphere of technology applies elsewhere too; information of all kinds gets widely diffused—among the various divisions, and also to all ranks of the hierarchy—in Japanese firms.

## 3.5   An Organized Market

The picture of the competitive market which emerges from most economic textbooks is an extreme caricature of the concept of the free market in classical capitalism. In pure free-market transactions, buyers and sellers of equal wealth negotiate with many potential partners until they find the most profitable deal, transaction by transaction. There is freedom to exit and freedom to enter at any time. Hence the fact that one has hitherto been dealing with A is no reason for not switching to B if it offers cheaper supplies. Let us call markets characterized by such transactions "free markets" (the textbooks' perfectly competitive markets being a special case within the category).

For such markets to function properly, there needs to be a large number of (actual or potential) buyers and sellers; in fact the more the better. Fixed trading relations are seen as an undesirable loss of freedom; it is expected that one should always be seeking out new potential partners. Such, indeed, is the American concept of a market.

But in no way do the market transactions among Japanese firms represent a thorough application of these principles of the free market. Once transactions are begun, they frequently become long-standing relationships. Trading partners tend to become fixed; their number does not much increase, rather the emphasis is on developing a high degree of cooperation within a limited number of stable long-term relationships.

We might call this an "organized market"; it represents the penetration of the principles of organization and community into the concept of the free market as opposed to structuring trading relationships with sole reagard to short-term economic calculations.

Perhaps the most fundamental principle of "organization" is the cooperation of likeminded persons in the pursuit of common goals, and the construction of authority relations to further those purposes. In a market penetrated by the principles of organization, the fixing of the terms of trade between those involved in long-term continual trading relationships is not based on each side's attempts to maximize its own profits but on the principle of "maximizing common interest." The final adjustment of separate interests involves the application of something like authority. Buyer and seller, who in the textbooks are seen as having opposing interests, instead, enter into a relation of long-term cooperation.

Of course not all Japanese markets are "organized"; for some commodities market partners are constantly changing. Even in organized markets economic calculations do, in the last analysis, come into play; firms are not in business to set up friendship clubs. But Japanese firms are clearly positively disposed (though the tendency is not confined to Japan) to introduce "organization" elements into their market transactions. The most typical manifestation of that disposition is in the *keiretsu* relationships between the "parent firms" and their suppliers or their distribution network, but it applies more widely and is not confined to *keiretsu* ties.

### 3.6    The Economic Rationality of the Japanese Enterprise System

The Japanese enterprise system, with all its characteristics just described, has a high degree of economic rationality. That is why it has persisted and that is why it has made a fundamental contribution to Japan's postwar growth. That rationality resides in the system's superiority in the following four respects: participation, cooperation, long-term vision, and informational efficiency. Whether in each of these respects the system has overwhelming comparative advantage as compared with classical capitalism, I do not know, but at least one can assert that it is capable of exceptional levels of performance.

## 3.7   The Rationality of Employee Sovereignty

There are basically two kinds of arguments involved in demonstrating the economic rationality of any kind of social arrangement. One concerns economic efficiency, the other social acceptability—the likelihood that, like ideas of fairness, the arrangement will be widely accepted. Employee sovereignty scores on both counts. The economic efficiency of the Japanese system rests on two of its aspects: the coincidence of interests, and informational efficiency in decision making.

By coincidence of interests I mean the coincidence between employees' own personal goals and the goals of the organization itself. To do one's best for the firm, to take the trouble to get the right decisions for the firm is, ultimately, to do the best for oneself. Under shareholder sovereignty where people are paid to promote the interests of the owner's capital, there is always the possibility of a clash of interests, and incentive systems have to be devised to motivate effort. Even under employee sovereignty, incentive systems are necessary to concretely express the notion that employees are the ultimate beneficiaries, but there is a big difference between that and having to overcome a situation defined as a fundamental opposition of interests. Where there is coincidence of interests, in the first place, people are much more willing to make the effort. It is not just a matter of doing what you are told, and only that, but of seeking to participate positively in the work of the organization.

Second, people are more likely to take decisions based on their perceptions of the interests of the firm over the long term. They are less likely to look to short-term advantage, or to assume that what's good for their own work section is all that matters; they know that if they do take a parochial view, they themselves might be affected by the consequences in the long run.

Third, this comprehensive and long-term view facilitates the accumulation of skills as a team. People are keen enough to make the immediate sacrifice of time and effort for long-term gains, and *who* gets the training becomes less important if the team is likely to stay together.

Employee sovereignty also promotes informational efficiency. The information necessary to make key decisions—in what direction should the firm seek new markets, what direction should its new acquisition of technology take, what should guide its investment policy—is information about the real nature, the concrete details, of the firm's hidden assets. That knowledge is most likely to be held by the people who do their daily work in the firm and have some sense of shop-floor realities.

Regarding the economic efficiency of employee sovereignty, the question of control naturally arises. What constraints prevent abuse of that sovereignty, prevent mismanagement and eventual loss of efficiency as employees pursue a narrow definition of self-interest, or prevent them sacrificing the interests of other stakeholders, notably the providers of capital? First, the most important constraint is market competition. Firms driven by employee egoism risk losing their place in the market and becoming bankrupt. The ferocity of what is often called "excessive competition" in Japan therein serves a useful function. Second, there are the constraints exercised by the providers of capital. Banks are very important in this, but so are the shareholders, in spite of—or perhaps even more because of—employee sovereignty.

As for the social acceptability of employee sovereignty—the other qualification for the claim to economic rationality—it can be explained as resting on two criteria. The first is from the size of the essential contribution, the provision of the most important and scarce resource by the people who commit their lives long-term to the firm. The second is from the size of the risk burden they assume; theirs would be the greatest loss from any decline or collapse of the firm.

Is there an argument as to whether shareholders or employees provide the most scarce and essential resource? Whatever may have been the case in times when capital accumulation was low, at the birth of the joint-stock company in the nineteenth century, today there can be no doubt that skilled and committed manpower is less easily obtained than money.

People will respond differently to this question depending on their basic assumptions about the core nature of the modern enterprise. My view is that what most characterizes a firm's identity and determines how it can survive in the economy is its technology, and its people who are the bearers and creators of technology. If the people, the essential resource, are of high quality, the money will come to them. Good people are scarcer than money and that is why I would say that the shareholders do not make the essential contribution.

As for risk, shareholders who stand, albeit with limited liability, to lose all their money would seem to bear a large risk. But given today's stock market institutions, it is a much smaller risk than that of the committed employee. If the firm goes into decline, shareholders can sell their shares and be compensated for their erstwhile participation in the firm. The employee cannot withdraw so easily, and there is no market to give compensation for all the time and energy an employee has invested in the firm. Apart from transferable experience and ability, the employee has nothing left, only the option of seeking another job. Moreover investors can diversify their portfolios and spread their risks; the employee, given the very nature of work and commitment, cannot. In these ways, ironically, it is the institution of the stock market that gives a legitimacy to and creates conditions for Japan's employee sovereignty.

These two principles—the essentiality of contribution and size of risk burden—underpin another feature—that not all those working in the firm are equally sovereign employees. These principles can be used to draw the line between those who are "core members" of the firm and those who are more peripheral, such as part-time workers, and the "office ladies" who work only for a few years before marriage.

They also explain why, in many small and medium firms, the owner-manager has an overwhelming share of sovereign power—what one might call a polar case of employee,[1] or at least firm-member, sovereignty. Of all his firm's core members, the owner-manager is the one on whose contribution and on whose bearing of risk the firm overwhelmingly depends, to whose entrepreneurship often the firm owes its very creation. Owners frequently put up their own personal property as collateral for loans, or give personal guarantees, taking on personal risks of unlimited liability.

These two features socially justify the fact that the owner-manager possesses a dominant share of sovereign power, rather than the fact that he probably owns a large share of the equity capital. His capital ownership can be seen as the formal expression, a symbolic recognition, of the essentiality of his contribution and the importance of his assumption of the risk. As this example shows, "employee sovereignty" does not mean equal sovereignty. Employee sovereignty means that sovereign power is graduated according to commitment and the resources that employees bring to the firm.

### 3.8 The Profit Principle and the Rights of Shareholders

"Employee sovereignty" may suggest that the management is altruistically concerned only with the welfare of the people working in the firm, but that is not necessarily or usually the case. The profit principle still works, and

---

1. The term translated in this chapter as "employee" (*jugyoin*) suggests in its characters "those engaged in work." It is in this sense that it can be used to refer to owner-managers.

the shareholders get their returns. The system would not be economically rational otherwise.

To be sure, Japanese firms pursue profit. To be more precise, they pursue not profit as economists usually define it but the value added that can provide the basis for long-term job stability, and for a style of management that provides for the long-term provision of meaningful and satisfying work for the employees. Thus it is not "profits in the long-term"but "total value added in the long term," even though people conventionally talk about long-term profits. Therefore it is not the pursuit of profits in the classical sense of resources available for distribution to shareholders.

Employee sovereignty does not imply that the maximization of wages in the short term becomes the objective. It means that it is the body of employees who decide how the enterprise acts, and it is that body that has priority claim to the proceeds of its actions. Those proceeds are multi-dimensional: cash reward, the satisfaction gained from the work itself, and social satisfaction derived from participating in the society of the work-place. All these rewards depend on the firm making money—on its creating value added.

The interests of shareholders cannot be ignored, however. Dividends have been low in Japan, but capital gains have been high. It is well known that, taking the two together, shareholders have received high returns. This is not, however, evidence of "shareholder sovereignty"; it just happens that hitherto firms have provided considerable rewards even to their second-priority stakeholders.

I hope that I have made it clear that the profit principle—given its definition, as above, in accord with the actual realities—does not imply shareholder sovereignty, nor is it incompatible with employee sovereignty. It is widely accepted that wages in Japan encompass a share of profits. Interpretations of that statement vary. I would say that it is a reflection of employee sovereignty. Masahiko Aoki interprets it in terms of an employee/shareholder shared sovereignty, or dualism. According to his interpretation, it is shareholder power that provides the profit principle and employee power that provides the concern with immediate wages and welfare. I think it is more consonant with the realities of Japan to think of employee power as exercised to achieve—in appropriate balance—both welfare and profit, profit being defined as above.

### 3.9   The Economic Rationality of Distributed Sharing

The influence on the structure of the enterprise of the sharing patterns on our three dimensions—value added, decision making, and information—

has to be considered in the light of the fact that the firm is at one and the same time the locus of economic activity, and a social structure that is created when people work together, spend time together.

If one asks about the effect of sharing on economic activity, clearly one has to look at the effects on the quality and efficiency of decision making and on the willingness to put effort into work. If one is concerned with the effect on social structure, one asks how the sharing patterns affect the quality of life on the shop floor; how they satisfy the need for social recognition or self-fulfillment or other social needs. To be sure, the ultimate purpose of the firm is economic activity, but a single-minded concentration on economic efficiency can make it impossible to sustain the firm in a social sense, so ultimately economic efficiency itself is lost.

I use the term "distributed sharing" in two senses. First, on the three dimensions of value added, decision-making power, and information, there is no concentration in the hands of a small number of people. Second, the pattern of distribution on those three dimensions is by no means identical or interconnected. The nonconcentrated distribution of value added enhances a sense of fairness, inhibits the development of stratification in the workplace, and so makes the firm a more pleasant place to work in and stimulates the desire to participate. Both the criteria of social acceptability and of economic efficiency are satisfied.

The distribution of decision-making power, apart from being socially acceptable on the grounds of both avoiding the concentration of power and inhibiting the stratification in the workplace, has two advantages. The first relates to informational efficiency; if decisions are taken close to the point of production, there is a greater chance that they are taken by people with the best information. The second advantage is the flexibility of a self-governing system. If subunits of the system have greater freedom of action, the system as a whole has greater flexibility, and risks can be hedged. Again, shared decision making enhances the willingness to participate and speeds the execution of decisions; employees both understand decisions better and have a stronger will to carry them out than if they receive them as orders handed down by someone else.

The most important aspect of information sharing is possession in common; information is shared by the top and the bottom of the organization, thanks not only to the existence of upward flows but also to the frequency of opportunities for downward flows. It is also shared horizontally, between different divisions. This sharing of information surely has a beneficial effect in promoting the will to participate and in raising the quality and efficiency of decision making. At the same time the wide distribution of information makes it possible for people to think in terms of the whole and not solely in terms of the work for which they are personally responsible. The minimization of information gaps also reduces tendencies towards stratification in the workplace.

My point about the noncoincidence of sharing patterns relates specifically to the subtle variations in the distribution of shares in value added and that of shares in power. If one person receives relatively more money and another relatively more substantial power in decision making, each can have his or her own source of satisfaction, and a sense of fairness prevails. Social harmony in the workplace is more easily attained than if a limited number of people monopolize all three—money, authority, and information.

A typical example of this is found in the actual operations of the *nenko* (seniority-plus merit) system in the best Japanese firms. If the *nenko* system used to allocate status and salary is to a certain degree dictated by a cultural tradition of respect for elders, the distribution of power can nevertheless be made subtly to diverge from the distribution of status and salary so that younger persons with real ability can have effective decision-making authority. The best firms certainly do not allow the distribution of status, salary, authority, and information to be determined solely by *nenko*; that would soon lower the quality and efficiency of decision making and lead to failure in market competition. Nor, on the other hand, do they allow that distribution to be determined solely by the criterion of ability; that would bring the danger of a disruption of social harmony and failure to function efficiently as a group. Hence with noncoinciding distributions, young people are rewarded by the quality of their work content, older people by status and salary. Here again, the essential point is the generation of a sense of fairness; everybody has his own flower, nobody monopolizes the bouquet.

There is a limit to the extent to which there can be divergence between the distribution of information and the distribution of decision-making authority. Decision makers need information. The Japanese pattern of noncoincidence here lies in the much wider spread of information, well beyond those who need it for the decisions they have to take.

The desire to acquire information and skills can be autonomous, as when an engineer seeks to deepen his or her mastery of a technology. For many, that enlarged share of the firm's stock of technological knowledge can compensate for lesser shares of money reward or decision-making power—again a possible source of greater overall satisfaction from the noncoincidence of sharing patterns. Answers to the question "Why do people work?" are multiple. The dimensions of the sharing—money, information, decision-making power—are equally dimensions of human needs. Noncoincident distributions can maximize overall satisfaction and induce a greater sense of fairness.

### 3.10   The Economic Rationality of the Organized Market

Here again the first ground for arguing the rationality case is the low degree of noncoincidence of interest. If one sees a trading relationship as certain to last a long time, one is less likely to behave opportunistically and more likely to see advantage in cooperative behavior and a fair distribution of profit between buyer and seller. One is spared all the expense of energy in mutual suspicion and maneuvering to make sure that one is not done down. Cooperation springs from the coincidence of interests.

The cooperation in question becomes a kind of integrated federation of buyer and sellers to maximize the "federal profit" in competition with other federations in the market. Such cooperation is not likely to last long if the distribution of federal profits is not a fair one.

Coincidence of interests may also generate a long-term perspective; both parties can think ahead—in the matter of investment, for instance—without fear of being left high and dry. And precisely because the perspective is long-term, neither party has to balance and close the books on every transaction. Short-term losses or gains that occur when some unforeseen contingency arises are perceived as "loans" and "debts" that can be sorted out in the long term. The transaction efficiency of being satisfied with a long-term balancing of accounts and not insisting on immediate renegotiation of contracts is considerable.

From this combination of the long-term view and cooperativeness there can develop joint R&D projects, long-term investment geared to the partner's particular needs, long-term production plans, flexible responses to unforeseen emergencies, and so on. The incentives for such behavior are lacking in a pure free market; the risks arising from uncertainty as to a trading partner's future decisions are too great. The advantages of reducing that uncertainty and promoting trust are considerable, not least in improving the returns on investments, economics of scale, and the ability to respond to shocks.

There is also, in an organized market, a greater efficiency in the buyer–seller transmission, and accumulation, of information. Information networks become stabilized with continued use over time; each partner builds up its store of information about the other, and cooperative relations that facilitate communication develop. The high degree of coincidence of interest also promotes a high level of mutual disclosure.

This makes it easier for each to understand and predict the needs of the other, and to get to know each other's strengths and weaknesses. That in turn makes it easier to develop new products or new techniques adapted to what the partner wants, to know its production plans and stock situation. An organized market reduces the need to build stocks, either because of uncertainty or for speculative reasons.

By "efficiency in the accumulation of information," I mean the accumulation of technology and know-how, and the accumulation of knowledge about trading partners. Trading partners can share technology, with each taking responsibility for developing one aspect of a new product or process. Sellers often teach technology to their buyers, so trading partners can help each other to acquire technology and provide feedback that leads to improvements. They can stimulate each other's accumulation of technological information. This accumulation in the marketplace is unlikely to happen when trading partners are frequently changing.

## 3.11   Conclusion

There is one common thread running through the above discussion of employee sovereignty, diffused sharing and organized markets. To give employees, or suppliers, the incentive to participate cooperatively, to prompt them to take a long-term view and to accumulate and use technology efficiently, an essential prerequisite is to create stable networks of interpersonal relationships and to give careful thought to the structuring of such relationships and the flow of information within them.

This emphasis on creating interpersonal networks may be contrasted with the classical capitalist enterprise system in which the economic system is held together through the cash nexus. It is a capitalism in which human, not material resources, are the capital base; hence, my title "human capitalism." Those who provide that human capital base are the sovereigns, not those who provide the money. Diffuse sharing patterns depend on a recognition of the importance of personal relationships, of the fact that the firm is also a social unit, not just an instrument for pursuing the monetary logic of economic efficiency. By contrast, a stereotypical American firm is merely the place where one plays out one's economic life. Monetary indicators of ranking govern the organization's structure of personal relations; it is a money-centered rather than a people-centered pattern of sharing.

Likewise, in the organized market, the formation of organized networks of firms has its origin in the personal relationships among people within which communications flow and trust is built. Thus the "capital as people (Japan) versus capital as material resources (America)" distinction pervades all three dimensions—the definition of the firm, its internal structure, and the relations between firms.

This characterization of the Japanese firm may well be criticized as appearing overharmonious. Of course the Japanese enterprise system is not all a tale of sweetness and light. There are conflicts, contradictions, irrationality, and discrimination in the Japanese system, but underlying these shady aspects, I believe, are the basic characteristics as I have described them. When I speak of "human-capital-ism" I do not mean to assert that Japan's is not a market or a free economy; it is one development within the broad spectrum of capitalism. Capitalism is a powerful concept. Nevertheless, the actions of firms are the actions of people. It is people who participate, cooperate, exchange, and accumulate information. Money does not create or accumulate information; it is only a signal and a medium for these activities.

There is a certain plausibility in the proposition that you get a more efficient economic system when money rather than human linkages are at the basis of the organization. Money is more quantifiable and more homogeneous than people. It is, one might say, the central insight of classical capitalism.

But is it always true, always the only possibility, if it can be shown that there are various ways to secure the exchange and accumulation of information among heterogeneous actors at low cost? The "human-capital-ism" paradigm, I would suggest, casts doubt on our traditional assumptions. It certainly demands a fundamental rethinking of any attempt to understand the Japanese enterprise using the paradigm of the neoclassical theory of the firm.

# 4 The Provision of Resources and Barriers to Exit

Tadao Kagono and
Takao Kobayashi

There is a distinctive way of doing business in Japanese industrial society. It is a method whereby resources that cannot be freely traded in the market are provided on a mutual basis. Barriers to exit from these relations are then constructed, and within those barriers competitive trading takes place. This method of trading is encountered in various sectors of the economy. A typical case is the invisible investment made by employees in their firms, which goes a long way to explain employees' sense of identification with the firm (especially in large firms), the sense of ownership found amongst employees and managers, the control of the firm by employees and managers, the firm's growth orientation, and so on; all the distinctive characteristics of the Japanese firm.

Resource provision of this sort exists, too, where transactions occur between the owner of an SME (small- or medium-sized firm) and his own firm, between a given company and its subcontracting firms, and between a manufacturing maker and its distributors. For example, the owner of an SME supplies resources to the firm in the form of money capital. Unlike the average shareholder in a large, quoted company, he cannot freely realize this money capital, except, usually, by signing away the entire enterprise. In which case there is no guarantee that the value of his invested capital would be appropriately assessed. Furthermore owners of this kind often give their own personal guarantee in respect of the money the firm borrows, which is a futher constraint on their ability to sell. Similarly a subcontracting firm that deals only with a single customer company is likely to develop capabilities that are specific to its customer; for example, the techniques and skills appropriate for dealing with that customer, an organizational configuration specialized in the direction of production as opposed to sales, and a system of management geared to that customer's production system. It is possible that the value of these techniques and skills, organizational configuration and management system, will not realize the same returns if the firm were to deal with another firm or with the market at large. They may even disadvantage it in transactions with other firms. These capacities too are resources that are undervalued by the market.

In this chapter we will explain the particular characteristics of a variety of such transactions that take place in Japan's business world. We refer to the planning philosophy behind such transactions as "the logic of commitment," and in a concluding section we will examine the respective strengths and weaknesses of Japanese and American firms by comparing this logic to the logic that applies to trade in America, the logic of exit.

### 4.1    The Relationship between Employees and Firms: Paradoxes

Before entering the discussion proper, let us look at a paradox to be found in the relationship in Japan between employees and their firms. Among the particular characteristics of Japanese firms, the one that has come to be cited most often is the employees' sense of unity, of sharing a common fate. There is an intimate link between what are popularly known as the Three Sacred Treasures of Japanese employment practices—namely lifetime employment, the seniority-merit wage system, and enterprise-based unions—and this feeling of unity. Metaphors such as family community, clan, "house," village, or *iemoto* have come to be used to refer to these peculiarly Japanese features. There is almost a consensus that, leaving aside the subtle differences among firms, there is a long-term relationship based on a sense of identification with the firm that transcends the short-term employment contract. The ideas evoked by these metaphors include the positive enjoyment of a sense of belonging, the sharing of gains and losses, unity, mutual help, loyalty to the firm, and diligence. Certainly we cannot deny these aspects of the Japanese firm (or at least of many firms). However, should we think that these are the only characteristics of Japanese firms, we would be wrong. The facts are at variance with the reality of how firms operate.

First, although employees of Japanese firms may feel at one with and loyalty toward their firms, they may also feel a great deal of dissatisfaction toward them. Many surveys have shown that Japanese workers' satisfaction with their firm, their work and their superiors is low in comparison with their European and American counterparts (Smith and Misumi 1988). Dissatisfaction within the young managerial stratum is especially pronounced; the degree of satisfaction within Japanese firms is more or less commensurate with age. Strangely, dissatisfaction of this kind coexists with unity, loyalty, and diligence. Moreover, on occasion, the energy put into attempts to eradicate such dissasfaction has become the springboard for the growth of the firm. This is one paradox.

Another reason why metaphors of community do not fit too well is to be seen in fierce internal competition. The more prestigious the company, the more apparent is internal competition and the more it actually occurs. Such competition is useful in the formation of skills that promote the development of the firm. But how can solidarity, togetherness, and fierce internal competition coexist? We have to conclude that this is another paradox.

Why have such paradoxes arisen? The key to answering this question lies in examining in detail the transaction relations between the firm and its employees.

## 4.2 The Supply of Resources: Resource Provision by Employees

Employees in Japan contribute resources to firms. Broadly speaking, we can divide their resource contribution into two categories. The first is invisible investment; the second, the nonapparent provision of resources that arises when skills unique to the firm are cultivated.

As for the first, consider the system of lifetime employment and wage payment primarily according to seniority developed in the postwar years. By "lifetime employment" we mean that recruits employed on graduation from school or university are employed until retirement, and by "wage payment primarily according to seniority" we mean the system whereby wages are determined primarily on the basis of the number of years of service with the firm, though also by a variety of other factors—for example, performance, qualifications, acquired skills, and worker grade. In recent years the weight accorded to these latter factors has increased. Even so there is a strong seniority element involved in the actual evaluation of qualifications or worker grades, so the influence of the seniority element remains large. Seniority wage payments and lifetime employment are the two sides of the same coin. The firm has to guarantee employees' livelihoods in order to keep them in the firm until retirement. A seniority-based payment system premised upon a livelihood-safeguarding guarantee achieves this better than one which pays directly in accordance with the employee's current contribution to the firm.

Here we are not concerned here with why or how the two systems of payment by seniority and lifetime employment came about. The purpose of this chapter is to discuss the significance they carry for employees and firms—employees' invisible investment. Under a system of seniority wage payments, wages rise more or less with little variation in accordance with years of service. The degree to which employees contribute to the firm (the marginal productivity of labor) also varies with age. There are no definitive data on how that contribution varies in correspondence with age, and indeed it is questionable whether the measurement of an isolated individual's contribution is possible. However, in general terms it is reasonable to consider that the contribution by age varies according to the following pattern.

First, by working in the firm, an employee will develop a variety of skills. It is to be expected that the degree to which the employee contributes to the firm will be in proportion to the skills that he or she has developed. If we assume that skills follow a general learning curve, productivity will rise as years of service increase, but the rate at which it will rise will gradually decrease. On the other hand, if we assume that there is a given rate of technological progress, skills will also become out-of-date. When the rate at which skills increase in accordance with years of service falls below a given rate, the rate at which they become obsolete becomes greater than the rate at which they increase, and productivity begins to decline. In figure 4.1 we represent productivity by a gently sloping curve in the shape of an upturned U with a peak at a given age. Where the peak occurs will probably differ from individual to individual, and may depend on job function. However, we can probably accept as a general rule that there is no simple correspondence between the increases in wages that go with an increase in years of service and increases in productivity.

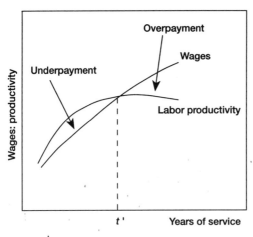

**Figure 4.1**
Wages and productivity

If wages rise at a uniform rate while the rate of contribution reaches a peak at a given age, then we can regard the system of wage payment as producing an exchange relationship between the employee and the firm that is unbalanced at any particular time but balanced out over a lifetime. The diagram shows that, apart from the very early stages of service, the employee is paid less than his or her rate of contribution up to a given age $t'$. Thereafter the employee receives wage payments that exceed his rate of contribution. The employee is underpaid during the first half of the term of employment, and thereafter is overpaid.

Hidden within this temporal imbalance, the underpayment during the first half-term of service can be regarded as the employee's investment in the firm. This investment reaches a peak where the curves depicting the rate of contribution and the wage cross. Thereafter, the employee begins to receive a return on his or her investment.

"Invisible" Investment

An employee's investment is "invisible" in two senses. First, no shares are issued that correspond with it, and second, there is no account in the books that corresponds to it. It is the undistributed surplus produced by the employee's underpayment (and as we will explain later, a surplus can easily arise when a firm is growing at a rapid rate), and it is appropriated as capital reserve—in other words, legally as shareholders' equity. In addition such investment has a particular characteristic. At first glance it resembles an employee share ownership system or a stock option scheme. However, it cannot be freely transferred to a third party, as it could (sometimes with restrictions depending on the share distribution scheme) if shares were issued, making it possible to quit the company in midcareer with little loss. The Japanese employee's returns on invisible investment are lost to the employee if he or she quits the company midway through the period of service. The return is absolutely zero. In this sense the invisible investment becomes a barrier to exit.

This invisible investment also differs from a share distribution scheme in that the returns depend not only on the performance of the company as a whole, but also on the efforts of the individual and the extent to which these are rewarded with promotion. By dint of effort and over a long period winning out in the continuous competition for promotion, an individual can increase his or her return. This return is a reflection of both group and individual effort. So far, then, we have demonstrated the first property of invisible investment: namely, the way it acts as a barrier to exit.

The Formation of Firm-Specific Skills

The same applies to the second resource that employees provide to the firm—the formation of skills that are specific to that firm. Firm-specific techniques, knowing how to work in cooperation with particular colleagues, knowledge of the firm, forming a network of personal relations— these are significant resources as long as the employee continues to work for the firm, but they are not valued by other firms.

Skills are acquired automatically through learning by experience. However, the tempo of acquisition is not even. Innate learning potential may be involved, but more important, the acquisition of skills is a function of the time and effort (mental energy) invested by the individual. However, the return on this invested resource can only be secured by continuing to work for the particular firm. Workers may also acquire skills that are commonly valued by other firms and not specific to the firm in question. These can therefore be priced fairly in the market. It sometimes happens too that the owner of an SME sends his son to work for a large firm. This suits the large firm since the firm-specific skill resources he acquires are useful to the large firm in subsequent dealings after he takes over the small firm. The value to the small firm lies in its future owner's acquiring general as well as those firm-specific skills. But apart from these special circumstances, firm-specific skill resources are not necessarily fully and properly valued in the general labor market.

## 4.3   Barriers to Exit

The way in which underpayment of wages in the early years of service and the acquisition of firm-specific skills create barriers to exit is obvious. These exit barriers perform several important functions for the firm as an organizational entity. The first is the incentive function whereby the interests of the firm and the interests of the individual are linked. Unable easily to exit, people can only protect their interests by working to ensure that the firm prospers. There are also personal incentives since the size of their future return depends on the extent to which they achieve promotion. This is a function of effort.

Second, exit barriers function to spur efforts to recover from a crisis. The collapse of the firm makes it impossible to recover any return on the resources supplied. The interlinking of interests means that when crisis looms, efforts are redoubled. The option of leaving the sinking ship is not freely available, either to the crew or the captain. This sense of sharing in a common destiny also is a source of the captain's authority and the legitimacy of his orders, a point to which we will return.

The third function is the advantage that the firm can derive directly from the resources supplied. When the numbers of younger employees and older employees balance out, the underpayment of wages to younger employees is canceled out by the overpayment to older employees. However, when a firm is growing and younger employees predominate, the underpayment of wages becomes relatively the larger. These surplus profits can be used as a source of capital for growth. Similarly the accumulation of firm-specific skill resources raises productivity.

The fourth function of such barriers to exit is that of protecting the profits of other, passive participants such as the shareholders of large quoted companies who are not subject to barriers to exit. In terms of our ship metaphor they are the crew who *can* leave the ship, knowing that everything is entrusted to a captain who cannot leave. It is a little like the partnerships and other types of companies that existed before the appearance of the joint stock company. Passive participants with limited liability were prepared to entrust control to those with unlimited liability. When such a mechanism for the protection of their interests exists, passive participants are likely to regard the power wielded by participants who face barriers to exit as justified. The investment of resources that constitute a barrier to exit provides a justification for the exercise of powers of control.

The fifth function is that firms are able to exercise rather a large amount of power over their employees. The power that a given person $X$ has over another person $Y$ is in proportion to the extent that $Y$ depends on $X$ for resources. The degree of resource dependency is determined by how important to $Y$ the resources are and by the possibility of being able to furnish them from elsewhere (Emerson 1962). Because employees are dependent on the firm for the return on the resources they have supplied, the firm is able to exercise rather more degree of power over them compared to employees for whom exit is freely available. Of course this relative power will be offset by the dependency of the firm on the employee.

Inducement to Participate

Looked at in simple terms, it is not advantageous from the point of view of employees to provide resources in this way and constrain their options. The greater the effort put into providing resources, the higher become the barriers to exit. Why, then, do people participate in this system? Unless there are inducements that justify the sacrifice, the system is unlikely to survive for long. What are they?

First, there is an immediate inducement at the point of joining. Large enterprises in Japan have paid higher wages than small- and medium-sized firms. The second inducement is the promotion and evaluation system in firms. As we have already stated, the return on invisible investment is not paid in uniform fashion to all employees. The magnitude of the return depends on the degree to which promotion has been achieved. The majority of large firms in Japan open up promotion opportunities to as broad a class of employees as possible. Of course there is a risk, even for employees who contribute greatly to the firm and build up their skills that they will not see their efforts recognized and repaid. To reduce this risk, large Japanese firms have constructed detailed, long-term systems of employee evaluation. The premium wages may also induce people to take a gamble on this risk.

Another condition has to be met for this sytem to continue in the long term. The firms that adopt it have to be effective. If they were not and they were to lose out in competition in the market, the mechanism would be unlikely to last long. However, the mechanism itself carries the advantage of inducing people to maximize their contributions, and so helps to provide the efficiency that makes possible the premium wages.

On the other hand, the system requires sacrifice if it is to be maintained, chiefly in the form of restraint on the freedom of the individual. Had people assigned greater value to freedom, especially the freedom to change jobs, than to the benefits they receive from it, it is unlikely that the system would have come about. This sense of constrained freedom—"I'd like to quit but I can't"—probably explains the curious paradox referred to at the outset of this chapter. In sum, though, one can assume that the sacrifices bring net benefits to both firms and their employees.

Barriers to Exit and the Nature of Transactions

Transaction practices whereby the transacting parties both enjoy advantages from raising barriers to exit are not confined to those between employees and firms. They are also found elsewhere in the Japanese business world. The employment system we have described is not something constructed on the basis of a blueprint. Rather, it was a natural development. But within this process there was hidden a logic that might be described as a tacit design or blueprint. We refer to this as "the logic of commitment." What we imply by that term is that the efficiency of transactions is increased by raising barriers to exit from the transaction relation, and by thereby stimulating competition within the relationship. This blueprint applies widely, for example, in the transaction relationships between manu-facturers/assemblers and the companies supplying their parts, between makers and distributors, in the financial transactions between banks and nonbank industrial and commercial enterprises, and in the pattern of cross-shareholding among firms.

Manufacturers/assemblers in Japan have constructed a unique mecha-nism whereby they supply the parts they need from specified (subcontract-ing) firms (Itami et al. 1988). Most subcontracting firms deal only with a single manufacturer/assembler, and they formulate manufacturing and managerial arrangements appropriate to those dealings. These manufactur-ing and managerial arrangements cannot easily be transferred to transac-tions with another manufacturer/assembler. The cost of transfer is very high. This is a barrier to exit for the subcontractor. On the other hand, manufacturers/assemblers too face exit barriers in the form of unwritten, social rules such that prevent them from ceasing to deal with their normal subcontractors at will. But why has this unfree method of dealing come about?

A similar relationship exists between manufacturing firms and distribu-tors. In a number of fields such as foodstuffs, alcoholic beverages, machin-ery, or electrical goods, manufacturers have constructed arrangements that confine their dealings to designated wholesalers. Likewise the wholesalers are accustomed to dealing only with specific manufacturers. Transacting in this way is sometimes stipulated in the contract; in other cases it is the customary practice through tacit agreement. Sometimes wholesalers are unable to perform their primary function of providing a complete assort-ment of goods and thereby reducing trading costs, something often char-acterized as a source of inefficiency in the Japanese distributive sector. Why is it that nonetheless, these sorts of barriers to exit were created?

Most of Japan's SMEs have the legal form of joint-stock companies, but they are not always treated as such by the banks. When lending to SMEs, banks are accustomed to demanding the personal guarantee of the manager (in almost all cases the owner) as well as security. In other words, the manager as an individual bears unlimited liability for the debts of the firm, which raises barriers against his exit. Cross-shareholding among large firms is similar. Mutual equity ownership involves a tacit understanding that each party will not dispose of these shares on the market. They cannot exit to realize the investments they have made.

These transaction practices have frequently been branded as pre-modern and inefficient. However, the "logic of commitment" enables us to under-stand the rationality of such practices. We have already described the benefits that accrue through the mutual construction of barriers to exit in the case of firms and their employees. Here we will discuss them in a rather more general way.

First, barriers to exit bring out psychological energy that stimulates the development and growth of the parties to the transactions. When both parties depend on a given, limited area of transactions, the development of each depends on that of the other. Barriers to exit for each of them is the incentive to cooperation. The distributor will cooperate—indeed has to cooperate—in the development of the manufacturer, as will the subcontractor.

The second advantage is the incentive to forestall potential disasters before they happen. By constructing barriers to exit, and establishing mutual dependence, the parties come to take a great risk, the greatest risk of all being the collapse of the trading relationship. Hence the incentive to be on the look out for looming crises and to cooperate to avoid them, and the incentive to avoid decisive confrontations over the distribution of benefits and resources. Only thus can they avoid losing the resources they have contributed to the relationship.

The third advantage lies in the stimulation of internal competition. When exit is free, it is possible to negotiate on the basis of opportunities and advantages that exist elsewhere. A manager who is highly thought of in another firm and who can transfer freely to that firm, can negotiate his own remuneration on the basis of that evaluation. But where this is not possible, he can only rely on comparisons made within his organization. Thus internal competition is stimulated. Similarly large manufacturers may source the same parts from a number of subcontractors and so stimulate competition among them. Similar arrangements are also found in the distribution sector.

The fourth benefit is the anticipated consonance of interests that promotes the delegation of the power to make decisions affecting the fate of the group to people with a large resource commitment to it—similar, as already noted, to the principle of unlimited partnerships and other forms of organization where the profits of the investor are protected by entrusting the actual power of management to members of the organization who have unlimited liability for it. This probably underlies banks' requirement of personal guarantees from the managers of SMEs.

## 4.4   Freedom and Commitment

At the opposite extreme from the "logic of commitment" stands "the logic of exit" which recognizes and protects the interests of the parties involved by allowing the freedom both of participation and of exit. If the Japanese business world stresses the former, the American business world stresses the latter. Nowhere has this appeared more plainly than in the differences in the practical workings of the joint-stock company system in Japan and the United States. A comparison should help to illuminate the strengths and weaknesses of the two systems.

A number of Japan's first rank quoted companies are controlled by members of the founding family. Toyota Motors, Sanyo Electric, Wacoal, and Yamaha are typical examples. The family forms the nucleus of the management group, though it does not necessarily hold a controlling proportion of the shares in their firms: The mechanism of mutual cross-shareholding allows managerial control or employee control irrespective of capital ownership. This family control is not regarded as unfair. Why should this be so? One interpretation is that managers from the founding family are regarded as representatives of the employees. But the important justification for their control lies in the resources they provide to the firm. In principle they can sell their shares in the market, but it is easy to imagine what would happen if they attempt to do so. The interests of many people are protected by entrusting decision-making power to those who have a large commitment. This logic of commitment holds in both family firms and management controlled firms.

Compare this with, at the other end of the spectrum, the American firm. Since the second half of the 1960s the American firm has operated according to the logic of exit. One factor that can be adduced as a reason for the decline in the competitive position of American firms is the existence of a variety of systemic conditions that restrain long-term investment. Among these, the pressure for short-term returns stemming from the stock market can be said to exert an especially serious influence (Kagono et al. 1983). In recent times there has even appeared a movement that aims to eliminate the influence of shareholders; and in some states, such as Delaware, an attempt to embody this in legislation is being advanced.

As far as the legal system known as the joint-stock company is concerned, that shareholders should exert control over the running of their firm is unproblematic. However, in practice this has produced problems in the running of firms. Why should this be so? We need to examine the system through which shareholders express their views, and the effect that this has on the running of firms. The reality of company governance in large firms in the United States underwent a rapid change from the mid 1960's. The ruling convention up to that point was managerial control which was fostered by two conditions. The first was the dispersion of share ownership, which made it difficult for individual shareholders to excercise any control over the choice of managers, or to influence the policies of the firm by the exercise of "voice" except by the prohibitively costly method of assembling letters of proxy for voting at the general shareholders meeting.

The second condition was the difference in the information available to shareholders and managers which, given the complexity of modern business and the high level of ability required to master it, made it difficult for shareholders to formulate policies for the firm or to find substitute managers if they were dissatisfied with the incumbents. Two circumstances changed this; the shareholders' exercise of the option of exit, and the discovery of the expedients of buy-out and take-over.

Managements that behave in a way prejudicial to the interests of the shareholder come to face the danger of losing their positions as a result of buy-outs and take-overs. Shareholders who are dissatisfied with the incumbent management reveal their intentions not by "voice" but by selling their shares. This brings about a decline in share prices. A fall in share prices represents an opportunity to secure a large profit by buying-out the firm when its share prices are low and installing a management that will protect the interests of the new shareholders. Hence a management team that wishes to maintain its own position will employ a management policy that will avoid a shareholder withdrawal of the kind that will produce a fall in the firm's share prices.

In the second half of the 1960s, when American firms began to change the principles according to which they behaved, the new configuration of the firm known as the conglomerate began to appear. When the device of forming conglomerates through company buy-outs became widespread, shareholder withdrawal came to exert a powerful influence on the management of companies. Also important was the systematization and standardization of knowledge relating to business management, and in addition, the spread of educational organizations giving instruction in this knowledge. This made the organizing of alternative management groups easier and increased the relative strength of the shareholders.

The consequences for management were profound. Firms became extremely vulnerable to the decisions of shareholders with low barriers to exit, particularly to the small shareholder and the institutional investor who were not suppliers of firm-specific resources. Shareholders also had a strong influence over the determination of share prices. To avoid take-overs—in other words, to curb a fall in share prices—firms had to be run in accordance with the inclinations of shareholders who were more interested in the returns to be derived from the shares they owned than in the long-term development of the firm. Second, the change had an impact on managerial mentality. With the increasing threat of take-overs through the securities market, and especially hostile take-overs, the position of managers became insecure. To cope with this insecurity, managers had always to act so as to maintain their reputation outside the firm for which they worked. In other words, they had to act so as to be able themselves to choose the "exit" option. For that reason they had to preserve the universality—the general applicability—of their own capabilities and to avoid any specialized iden- tification with skills specific to their firm that would weaken their position. This further lowered their commitment.

This lowering of the commitment of managers has ramifications too for the supervisors and employees who work under them. When the position of managers is vulnerable and their commitment low, the position of em- ployees and supervisors is also weak. To protect themselves, they too have to preserve the possibility of exit. To do this, they must not specialize in such a way that their abilities match only the requirements of their present firm. Thus the way the typical American company works prompts all par- ticipants to protect their own positions and interests by preserving their "exit" options. This option of exit confers a large measure of freedom, but it also lowers the commitment of individual participants toward their firms.

## 4.5 Conclusion

There is clearly a difference between the logic of commitment and the logic of exit. It provides a key to understanding the behavior of Japanese firms and a variety of phenomena within the firm, as well as to understanding the differences between the American and Japanese corporate systems with their respective strengths and weaknesses. But there is no simple answer to the question of which is the better system, or which will come to predomi- nate in the future in the United States and Japan. We wish here to avoid a clear-cut conclusion; indeed we confess that we do not know. However, we are able to cite certain factors that would seem to have a bearing on the judgment, and on contemporary signs of change.

The American system has begun to provoke debate even within the United States. The debate about who really owns firms has come to be associated in particular with the question of mergers and acquisitions, and a movement has arisen in some states for the limitation of shareholder power. Further, among those firms trying to attract first class MBAs, most consultancy firms have recently opted for a partnership form of organization rather than the joint-stock form. Again, leveraged buy-outs by managers perform the function of raising managers' commitment to their firm. These suggest that a trend toward the logic of commitment is occurring in the United States.

Conversely, a movement in Japan toward freer exit is becoming noticeable. Factors inducing this change from the logic of commitment toward the logic of free exit are the rise of interfirm mobility among technologists, the flattening of the wage–length-of-service curve, the trend toward mergers and acquisitions, changes in the value systems of the young, the internationalization of the activities of firms, and the freeing and internationalizing of the stock market.

Of course, ideological choices are the product not merely of trends in society but also of individual choices and the processes of natural selection resulting from competition. However, the preceding list does give us an idea of the basic problem that the modern firm as an organization is facing, namely the reconciliation of the freedom of the individual with the development of the organization as an entity. The end result we do not know, but it will certainly be a central question for the future world of business.

# II

# Intercorporate Relations

# 5    Interfirm Relations and Long-Term Continuous Trading

Motoshige Ito

The so-called "Japanese pattern" of interfirm relations is in fact not unique to Japan but exists also in Western corporate societies. However, for reasons that will become apparent in this chapter, that pattern of relations may be thought to be more conspicuous in Japan than elsewhere. Automobile component suppliers, for example, do not merely manufacture components according to the specifications provided by car manufacturers. In the process of supplying components, a variety of other things are also exchanged in a complex manner—technical information, financial assistance, and personnel (Itami 1988). Similar multiplex relationships are also found between banks and client firms—relationships which go beyond the mere borrowing and lending of money—and also in the distribution sector.

Distribution is commonly very fragmented. There are cases of highly vertically integrated distribution channels from production to consumption depending on the type of product and the mode of retailing, but these are relatively rare. In the more common fragmented system, relations between manufacturers and their numerous wholesalers are not merely a matter of receiving orders for goods and transporting them. The distribution system has various other economic functions such as the collection and processing of information, the adjustment of delivery dates, financial transactions, and the spreading of risks associated with inventory holding and unsold goods. The nature of interfirm relations is of central importance to the capacity of a distribution system to fulfill these functions. They involve a variety of interesting features, such as mutual shareholding and exchange of personnel, and complex modes of payment, such as rebate and discount systems.

To understand these interfirm relations, let us ask under what circumstances the straightforward market exchange of goods and services may

---

1. The contents of this chapter overlap with Ito and Matsui (1989), to which frequent references are made.

not be adequate. The first is when firms can engage in monopolistic behavior. The argument that subcontracting relationships in such industries as automobiles are created by the assembler firm in order to exploit its subcontractors adopts this explanation. A similar line of argument applies to *keiretsu* groups in distribution that are said to exist in order for manufacturers to maintain monopolistic prices. This perspective on interfirm relations shapes one large category of research in Japan. It is also deeply rooted in the thinking behind the antimonopoly policy in the United States. Thus the following assertion by Coase (1972):

One important result of this preoccupation with the monopoly problem is that if an economist finds something—a business practice of one sort or other—that he does not understand, he looks for a monopoly explanation. What people do not normally do is inquire whether it may not be the case that the practice in question is a necessary element in bringing about a competitive situation. (pp. 67–68)

One cannot deny that certain aspects of interfirm relations involve monopolistic behavior, and they are important. But my space in this book is limited, and there is already a good deal of research in this area. I think, as Coase does, that the alternative perspective (to be elaborated below) is more important. That other perspective may be summarized as follows: long-term continuous trading relationships without explicit contracts can contribute to efficiency by avoiding market failures due to imperfect information or uncertainty and by altering the incentives of firms engaged in trading.

## 5.1 Simple Exchange and Interfirm Trading

Market exchange is a mechanism that sustains the social division of labor in contemporary economies. The conceptualization of market exchange in its pure form in economic theory is that the goods exchanged are highly standardized and that there is no great asymmetry in information concerning the goods between the buyer and the seller (not necessarily perfect information—approximately equally imperfect information is also possible; see Akerlof 1970). It follows that once prices are established, exchanges may proceed in straightforward fashion.

However, these assumptions clearly do not hold in the real world. Components supplied by automotive parts manufacturers to car assemblers may be customized products, or even if the parts themselves are not custom-made, they often require customer-specific investment if one takes account of various services which accompany product development and delivery.

Such investment is often not easily diverted to some other purpose. Moreover, from a car manufacturer's viewpoint, once it has decided to purchase a component from a particular supplier, it may be difficult to switch to another supplier immediately if an existing supplier fails to deliver. Consequently a car manufacturer and its parts suppliers may enter into long-term trading relationships.

Even in such a relationship, if two firms can sign and execute a perfect contract, it is possible to realize a situation basically identical to simple exchange. If the parts supplier has numerous potential customers, and the manufacturer many willing suppliers, there can be tough competition up to the contracting stage. Once trading partners forge an exchange contract, it is then just a matter of trading according to the contract. Of course, various elements of uncertainty may enter into this. But there is no problem as long as contracts cover all future contingencies and to the extent that parties fulfill the contract faithfully. This is the world of "contingent contracts" as portrayed by Arrow and Debreu.

But in the real world it is difficult to establish a perfect contingent contract, never mind execute it. When two firms intend to trade over a relatively long-term period, it is practically impossible to capture all the contingencies that may occur after the contract is signed. The alternative, of signing a contract that does not seek to cover contingencies and simply binds the parts manufacturer to supply a certain quantity of components at a fixed price, and the car manufacturer to accept delivery under whatever circumstances, is equally unacceptable. Companies, particularly those that are risk averse, do not wish to be tied to such a simple exchange contract when rapid new product development and frequent design changes are predicted and when there are large elements of uncertainty in market trends associated with exchange rates and business cycles.

The enforcement of such a contract poses other problems. Severe penalties for breaking contract can be specified, but this can lead to challenges and the need for a third-party institution such as a court of law to monitor whether the contract has been broken. Here again problems arise because it is difficult for a court to judge accurately whether the contract has indeed been broken. For instance, if the car manufacturer refuses to accept delivery due to an alleged violation of the contract in component design or structure, it may not be easy for the court to judge the highly detailed and technical factors that have to be taken into account in deciding which side has broken contract. Such court proceedings inevitably take a long time and can be very costly not only in court fees but also in production delays—costly both to the firm and to the economy as a whole (see Hart and Homstrom 1987).

In short, where there is uncertainty and firms seek to maximize their own interests, it is unlikely that a maximization of joint benefit will be achieved. The concept of "nonappropriable quasi-rent" developed by Klein et al. (1979) is relevant here. For example, let us assume that a parts supplier has just made an investment specific to a particular car manufacturer and would incur considerable losses if it were to try to use this equipment to manufacture components for a different customer. Suppose that the car manufacturer threatens to break off the trading relationship unless prices are greatly reduced. The parts supplier would have no choice but to give in to this tough demand. Nonappropriable quasi-rent is the quasi-rent that is lost when a trading partner terminates the contract.

Such nonappropriable quasi-rent will increase when a firm develops a long-term trading relationship with a particular partner, which involves customer-specific investment. The maintenance of satisfactory long-term trading relationships requires some way of reducing the likelihood that the vulnerability of firms in such a position will be taken advantage of.

One consequence of this condition not being met may be a distortion of the pattern of investment. If the car manufacturer cannot be trusted to maintain long-term trading, the component supplier might hesitate to undertake specific investment in equipment or know-how. It would prefer to make investment into general equipment or accumulate general technological know-how, which may not be optimal either from the point of view of car manufacturers, or of suppliers whose trading opportunities may thereby be narrowed.

The above discussion of the difficulties involved in conducting long-term trading under conditions of uncertainty simply on the basis of a contract has concentrated on vertical interfirm relations, but similar problems occur in the context of horizontal exchange relations between firms, as for example when two firms attempt to establish some form of joint venture. How are such problems resolved in the real world?

One solution is to internalize exchanges within one firm through vertical integration. GM's acquisition of Fisher Bodies, according to Klein et al., was precisely for this reason. In an integrated firm the self-interest of people in the components division relates to that of those in the car assembly division in a rather different way from when they trade as independent companies. But it is clear that integration is not a panacea. If it were, the economy would consist of nothing but giant integrated companies. The problems that sometimes make integration worse than trading between independent companies have not been made very clear (though Grossman and Hart 1986 offer an interesting theoretical analysis) and I do not propose to take the discussion of the integration alternative further here.

Instead, I want to look at another solution, namely to resolve the problems in trading discussed above by modifying exchange methods and trading relationships. Mutual share-holding, personnel exchange, and complex pricing methods may be understood in this light.

## 5.2   Theories of Long-Term Continuous Trading

Game theorists have shown how repeated games differ from one-off games (Rubinstein 1979; Axelrod 1981). In one-off games players seeking to maximize self-interest do not necessarily seek the maximization of joint benefits. But in repeated games, if players make cooperative choices (which might not maximize self-interest for any play taken alone), as long as the other does the same and cooperation ceases only when the expectation of cooperation is betrayed, a cooperative equilibrium is produced.

This helps our understanding of real world phenomena. An automotive parts manufacturer dealing with an assembler does not act solely on the basis of self-interest in the current transaction but takes also into account the effect on future transactions, and the greater the benefits from future trading at stake, the more likely the manufacturer is to do so. Likewise the assembler customer also takes the effect on future transactions into account, not only considering how much it needs the particular supplier but also the reputation effect. If the assembler behaves in a manner which is considered a betrayal, it will lose the trust of the suppliers of other components.

If, as suggested, cooperation is likely to be generated naturally, then there is no need for a detailed written contract when what is expected to be a long-term trading relation is initiated. The contract may specify certain things, but more important is the "implicit contract" to discuss matters in a cooperative spirit when circumstances change.

It is of considerable significance that the period in which such cooperative relations were developed in Japan was a period of rapid economic growth. When company sales and industrial output are growing, opportunities for future profit become all the more important and are likely to outweigh the possible temporary profit from betrayal. This may be why the diffusion of Japanese trading norms such as subcontracting relations, the Japanese employment system and distribution *keiretsu* occurred during the rapid growth period (see also Klein et al. 1979).

As explained above, the fact that trading tends to be prolonged does not merely increase the likelihood of cooperative relations emerging. Other features also arise, such as the accumulation and joint ownership of information, the diversification of payment modes, and changes in incentives for competition. I will consider these in turn.

First, the accumulation and joint ownership of information: Through continued trading, partners accumulate information on each other's technology and environment, and come to own it jointly, and the longer the relation continues the more this is so. Toyota Motors is said to have implemented just-in-time (*kanban*) methods within its factory first before spreading the practice to affiliated components firms. It was the latter's familiarity with the fundamental features of this production system that made this spreading possible in a way that mere use of written manuals or short-term exchange of information would not have achieved. The game theory notion of "focal point" (see Schelling 1971; Kreps 1986) relates to this joint ownership of information.

There is another aspect of information accumulation, namely the avoidance of moral hazard through long-term performance appraisal. To explain this, I first consider the example of insurance for traffic accidents. Traffic accidents may occur due either to drivers' carelessness or to bad luck. Since it is often difficult to distinguish the precise cause, insurance is paid out regardless of why the accidents occurred. Moral hazard refers to the possibility that some drivers, reassured by the fact that they are insured, may not pay the attention necessary to prevent accidents, for instance through regular maintenance of their cars. They may also drive recklessly. Consequently as accidents increase, insurance premia rise, and drivers end up worse off for being insured. If all drivers acted more carefully, accidents would decline, and premia would also fall. But since there is no impact if just one driver pays more attention, many drivers tend to act negligently. One way of dealing with the problem of moral hazard is to incorporate a merit system into the insurance premia schedule. Premia may be lowered for drivers who do not cause accidents, and raised for those who are accident prone. Since the element of bad luck ought to be randomly distributed, it may be judged over large numbers that long-run accident-prone drivers must drive recklessly. Each driver's incentive to drive safely is enhanced by such an insurance premium system, which in turn leads to a reduction in accidents and a lowering of premia.

Similarly the method of appraising performance from a long-term perspective is very important for interfirm relations. For instance, if the car manufacturer appraises the parts supplier not on the basis of its short-term efforts for product improvement but on the basis of fairly long-term performance, then it can evaluate accurately the supplier's capability in product development and effort expended on it, and the random luck element that attends all development work is eliminated. In long-term interfirm relations in Japan, there is a tendency to appraise suppliers from such a long-term perspective. In activities that tend to give uncertain rewards to effort, such as product and quality improvement and cost reduction, the accumulation of information necessary for such long-term appraisal is very important.

The second point concerns the diversification of payment methods. It becomes unnecessary to have precise payment arrangements every time exchange occurs if it is premised on long-term continuous trading. It suffices that payments work out satisfactorily over a whole series of exchanges.

This flexibility of payment methods may also act as a form of risk sharing between trading agents. Let us assume that one firm is risk averse and the other firm is less risk averse because it has alternative methods of avoiding risk. The latter may bear a larger share of business cycle risks. If a parts supplier is more risk averse than its customer, a car manufacturer, the latter may agree to purchase a certain quantity of parts, or make a payment equivalent to such purchase, regardless of business conditions, thereby bearing the full burden of risk. The supplier may, in return, be able to hold component prices low. Then in effect the supplier is purchasing an insurance policy from the car manufacturer. The corresponding risk premium is reflected in a low component price. (For a theoretical analysis, see Azariadis 1975 and Baily 1977.) The mode of risk sharing is more complex in the real world, but the basic principle is that explained above.

Flexibility in the mode of trading may also be used as a mechanism for creating incentives to cooperate. If it is possible to delay payments or to make advance payments, a firm may offer a "hostage" to its trading partner. Incentives to cooperate result from this "hostage" mechanism, a point to which I will return.

The nature of competitive relations changes also as trading becomes long term. External competitive pressures are weakened in a continuous trading relationship in which a firm restricts itself to trading with only a small number of partners. There is little of the textbook "market competition" that exists when a car manufacturer draws up a specification and circulates it to all possible component suppliers, looking for the one offering the best terms. When it opts for maintaining long-term relations with a selected few suppliers, it is hard for new entrants to break in. Such limits to market competition are widespread—in retail and distribution, for example, and also where internal labour markets limit competition from outside. (For a detailed development of the argument, see Ito and Matsui 1989.) Such limits to competition constitute a serious problem of long-term continuous trading relationships.

That is not to say that there are no competitive mechanisms in continuous trading relations; indeed the forms of competition in such relationships may in some circumstances even be more desirable. Competition among a restricted number of agents is more severe than competition among a large number of unidentified agents. Ito and Matsui (1989) speak of "face to face competition," and describe some of its features as follows.

First, it has the character of a rank-order tournament, which may well involve fiercer competition than competition between a large number of unidentified agents, though we need to clarify the terms of competition and find some way of measuring the severity of competition before saying so confidently. (These are theoretical questions that are on this author's agenda for future research.)

The second feature is that in the process of competition, rivals keenly observe each others' characteristics, and this strengthens the will to compete. Particularly important is observation of rivals' inputs. In long-term competition inputs are accumulated at each step, and it is the cumulation of steps that ultimately determines the final performance outcome. It is quite conceivable that competition becomes more severe when rivals can observe each others' circumstances than if they are blind as to each others' conditions at each step.

The third feature corresponds to the comparison of "exit" and "voice" mechanisms as elaborated by Hirschman (1970). If restaurants' customers simply exit and start going to another restaurant when they are dissatisfied with the quality of the food, one might end up with a low-quality equilibrium. If, on the other hand, they use voice—complain about the quality of the food, with the threat of exit if quality does not improve—there is more likely to be a general raising of standards. In long-term trading relations, customers use voice.

The fourth feature of competition in long-term continuous trading relationships is what Itami has called "controlled competition" (Itami et al. 1988). The buyer can exercise better control over the terms of competition among suppliers. Competition in market exchange is primarily over price. It is difficult for a buyer that is interested in the long-term improvement of quality to induce competition in those terms because quality of performance is hard to guarantee ex ante. But in long-term trading relationships it can; decisions about the next contract can depend on performance in the last.

## 5.3 Mechanisms Supporting the Implicit Contract

It will have become apparent from the preceding explanation that functions unattainable in simple one-off exchanges come into operation by prolonging trading relations. But how are such long-term continuous trading relationships sustained when there are incentives to make greater profits from breaking out of such relations? The answer is that firms are operating in an environment in which breaking off would count as a "betrayal" which, through its reputation effect, would curtail opportunities for future business. Firms operate in communities where social sanctions work.

Research in the Philippines by Ootsuka et al. (1987) is of interest in this regard. In the suburbs of Manila, landlords let land to peasants on fixed rent leases—as Jeepney owners rent their vehicles to drivers. By contrast, sharecropping is more common in the countryside. Fixed rent leases in which all fruits of labor at the margin accrue to the workers provide stronger work incentives, while sharecropping shares risks, including the owner's risks. Why is sharecropping common in rural areas but not in the outskirts of Manila? In the countryside, personal relations are strong, and local communities sanction peasants who do not work conscientiously. Japanese firms for the most part operate within business communities that have the same effect.

If such are the noneconomic factors that support long-term continuous trading, there are also economic factors at work. When trading volumes are expanding, the opportunity cost of breaking away from existing trading relations is large. The fact that so-called Japanese-style interfirm relations became reinforced during the rapid growth period may be due to this factor, though one has to consider also that growth brings new opportunities for forging new relationships that can compensate for the loss of existing ones.

A second factor supporting long-term continuous trading is the underdevelopment of external markets. For example, if banks and firms are locked into the "internal markets" of long-term trading relationships, "external" financial markets such as stock markets may not develop. Where internal markets are strong, external markets are weak, and vice versa (see Ito and Matsui 1989).

The third economic factor supporting long-term continuous trading is what Williamson (1983) has called the mechanism of "hostages"; for example, the customer-specific investment that a parts supplier might make can only be fully amortized by continuing the relation with a particular customer. This reassures the customer of the supplier's commitment and helps to maintain the relationship, but it can also lead to *shitauke ijime*—bullying of subcontractors. The customer may take advantage of the hostage-offering parts supplier by pressing for a revision of trading terms. Consequently the hostage mechanism works better if both parties put forward hostages. Effectively, in the case of big automobile companies, the hostage at stake is its reputation for fair dealing.

Hostages take a variety of forms. Besides visible forms such as capital equipment, human capital and technological know-how may also be customer-specific and lacking in general applicability. Also, if a variety of goods are traded, and if ceasing to trade in one good leads to terminating all other deals, then the hostage mechanism operates. For example, in a creditor-debtor relationship between a bank and its client firm, which also involves exchange of information and human resources, ending the credit relationship would also lose valuable supplementary services. Long-term trading relationships do tend to develop this multiplexity.

Payment arrangements may also involve hostages. Payments due in the future may be lost when trading is terminated. A car manufacturer may bear part of the cost of investment by a supplier and not get its money back if trade is discontinued. The point to be emphasized is that offering a hostage does not necessarily put a firm at a disadvantage. It offers a "credible commitment" to the relationship, to use the terminology of game theory, and can thereby reinforce the commitment of the other party.

## 5.4 Conclusion

To summarize, this chapter has analyzed long-term trading relationships as they have developed in Japan as a means of dealing with externalities among firms. Our theory of long-term continuous trading holds that it becomes easier to maintain cooperative relations as trading becomes prolonged, and as trading becomes prolonged, it becomes possible to accumulate and jointly own information. The particular forms of competition under long-term continuous trading also have useful functions.

The perspective offered here—that trading partners seek mechanisms to act cooperatively when trading is so complex that the terms and conditions of trading cannot be fully specified by contracts (i.e., when trading cannot but be through implicit contracts)—does seem to offer an explanation of phenomena characteristic of the Japanese business world. However, long-term continuous trading is only one such mechanism. Among other mechanisms for maintaining cooperation one thinks first of mutual or cross-share-holding. But there are also, for example, exchanges of personnel, relations mediated by a common main bank or shared membership in an industry association. These are topics for future research.

# 6         Enterprise Groups

## Kenichi Imai

Many people associate Japan's so-called enterprise groups with *zaibatsu* descendants such as Mitsui, Mitsubishi, and Sumitomo, and the peculiar group-oriented behavior of Japanese companies. Indeed *zaibatsu* were a powerful economic force that helped Japanese capitalism "take off" during the Meiji era, and for more than a hundred years they and their descendants have made an enormous impact on the Japanese economic system. Even today interest is sufficient to ensure the annual publication of *Industrial Groupings in Japan* in both Japanese and English (by Toyo Keizai and Dodwell Marketing Consultants, respectively). What exactly constitutes an enterprise group, however, is far from clear, and views are often colored by preconceived notions. This is particularly true for those who see enterprise groups as a major source of corporate power and monopolistic vice.

One line of enquiry is the historical role that *zaibatsu* have played, and how they gave rise to today's enterprise groups. Why, indeed, do enterprise groups still exist today? I have attempted to address these issues elsewhere.[1] Enterprise group theory has also been criticized by Miwa (1988), and I will not deal with it directly in this chapter. Another way to approach enterprise groups is through markets and hierarchies analysis. Sustained interfirm relationships have become an important factor in the behavior of firms in the contemporary economy. It is essential for corporate management to expand its horizons and include relations with other firms when establishing the "boundaries" of the firm. From such a perspective a study of enterprise groups may provide fresh insights into the behavior and definition of the modern firm. This is the approach used in this chapter, with historical issues being referred to where appropriate.

The following section provides a general overview of how enterprise groups have been analyzed in conventional economics. We will see that

---

1. Imai (1986a, 1987–88), and a revised version forthcoming in *The Political Economy of Japan*, vol. 3.

this approach is no longer realistic or appropriate. In section 6.2 a framework for understanding contemporary enterprise groups is given. Finally, section 6.3 categorizes and examines enterprise groups through case studies.

## 6.1 Frameworks of Analysis

Interlinked Oligopolistic Groups

It was not until economics began showing interest in corporate power and problems of monopoly that enterprise groups began to attract attention. These studies had as their origin the classic analysis of finance capital groups by Hilferding in the 1910s, and ran through Sweezy's (1953) "Interest Groups in the American Economy." These works tried to assess the extent of power possessed by "interlinked oligopolistic groups." Monopoly and oligopoly were becoming a social issue in both America and Europe, and large corporations attracted attention not only from academe but also from the general public. Such works were linked to an analysis of ownership and debated the separation of corporate ownership and management, as presented by Berle and Means (1932).

This line of enquiry has been inherited by social scientists. A broad sociological perspective is needed when looking at problems such as corporate power, and levels of analysis range from corporate organization to interfirm relationships and include social backgrounds and class. Important empirical works have looked at statistics on interlocking directorships that link corporations. Recently statistical network analysis has been used, and social scientists in America and Europe have accumulated considerable data on this subject (see also Ueda 1983).

As the risk of oversimplification, the results of such studies show a long term trend in all countries from strong intercorporate linkage to more flexible arrangements, with a decline in the influence of interlinked groups. Studies of monopoly show a declining trend, and it is no wonder that the level of interest in these issues has declined gradually also. It would seem that such analyses are coming to the end of their usefulness. To gain fresh insight, it is important to look at how enterprise groups have changed along with changes in the economic environment (see Imai 1987–88).

Markets and Hierarchies

From the above perspective, companies try to expand their sphere of influence, directly or indirectly to boost their power. On the other hand, in corporate theory from Coase through Williamson, corporate boundaries are determined by efficiency. In other words, companies decide, according to their assessment of transactional costs, whether they should procure goods and services from the markets or produce them internally, and this determines their boundaries. More generally, in many cases where market transaction costs are high, it is because of market failures,[2] and to save on such costs means to respond to market failures. Transactions within companies give rise to certain organizational failures, however; thus companies determine their corporate boundaries by weighing the costs and benefits of these two ways—markets and hierarchies—of acquiring goods and services (Imai, Itami, and Koike 1982).

Also, if the firm determines its corporate boundaries from the viewpoint of transactional efficiency, sharp divisions need not be drawn between the inside and outside. A middle transactional ground can exist between markets and hierarchies (see Williamson 1975). Thus enterprise groups can be defined as an institutional invention to cope with both market failures and internal organization failures (Imai 1976; Goto 1982).

Transaction cost analysis has provided a fresh perspective for trying to understand corporations. As critics have pointed out, however, transaction costs can be illustrated by examples but are difficult to define clearly, and the theory lacks conclusive empirical substantiation. What is more, it tends to be static, treating the firm as an entity selecting the most appropriate alternative from market and internal possibilities. In a dynamic economy the mode of transaction is continually reformulated. Transaction cost analysis can provide post facto explanations, but it is a poor tool for discussing what directions corporations should move in.

To avoid these problems, attention must be paid not only to the negative aspects of institutional arrangements, such as market and hierarchy failures, but also to how the merits of markets and internal organization actually emerge. Chandler (1988), for instance, attaches great importance to coordination through internal organization in explaining why vertical integration came to be so prevalent among major American firms. At the same time he notes Williamson's transaction cost theory and explains the emergence of enterprise groups as follows: The reason administrative coordination by large firms, as opposed to "interagency organization" such as cartels or syndicates of Europe, became widespread in the United States was due to both technical and geographical conditions of the country during

---

2. Sometimes the efficiency of the nonmarket organization is higher, whether or not there are market failures, such as ownership of country/summer houses or mining development.

the 1890s, when dispersed markets were becoming unified and vertical integration by firms with central offices established economies of scale. At the same time, economies of speed were established, with the rapid growth of distribution networks creating entry barriers and conferring advantage on vertically integrated corporations. The reason for the American firm's preference for vertical integration was the clear advantage it gave the firm in the U.S. market at that time.

It may be argued that other patterns persisted in Europe because there was a history of legal arrangements between firms that lowered transaction costs, whereas these costs were higher in the United States, and anti-monopoly law was treated differently. This still does not explain why vertically integrated American firms dominated world markets. Chandler stresses economic efficiency, expressed as "economies of speed", or speed from production through to distribution. His argument, I believe, captures the essence of how the firm determines its boundaries. Under the market conditions of that time, the coordination of raw materials procurement through manufacturing to sales by large vertically integrated companies not only established economies of scale but enabled rapid adaptation to environmental change. This became the source of their overwhelming competitive advantage at the time.

Clearly, then, to analyze the dynamics of enterprise groups from the perspective of markets and hierarchies, we need to grasp the failures and successes of both simultaneously, and realize that the choice of utilizing either markets or hierarchies is shaped by given economic conditions. I will later analyze enterprise groups from a perspective similar to that of Chandler, but under today's technological and market conditions. Under these conditions Japanese-style vertical integration that penetrates both markets and hierarchies has gained the edge in terms of economies of speed.[3]

## 6.2   Current Issues: From Enterprise Groups to Enterprise Networks

Enterprise Tasks

Before discussing enterprise groups, it is useful to review the tasks enterprises perform as organizations. If an enterprise consists of individuals with

---

3. Recent network theory has developed along these lines. In their studies of economic networks sociologists have attempted statistical analyses of corporate power expansion, as can be seen in articles of the journal *Social Network*. Of course there are other kinds of networks besides economic ones. For an overview of network analysis, see Imai (1986b).

different motives but who contribute to common economic objectives and gain compensation for this, the main tasks are the establishment of the following:

1. The scope of decision making as a coherent body; the sphere of main activities.

2. Means to acquire necessary inputs, especially capital and labor.

3. Means of providing incentives.

4. Procedures for coordinating, controlling, and evaluating the tasks of individual members.

5. Procedures for distributing resources and profits.

6. Ways to process information.

7. Means of solving short- and long-term problems, learning from them, and accumulating the knowledge learned.

The structure of the enterprise's organization (including group formation), or what Williamson calls "governance structure," is determined by which of these tasks the enterprise emphasizes. As Chandler demonstrated, for example, if task 4 (task coordination, control, and evaluation) and task 5 (distribution procedures) are emphasized, and the advantages of speed of coordination through internal commands are stressed, the basic organizational form will be a vertically integrated hierarchy. Because the efficiency of the firm hinges heavily on the efforts of managers' steering activities at the central office, it is critical to provide them with incentives to elicit their maximum contribution. This system worked well during the early stages of American industrial development, when market conditions favored mass production and mass sales. Task coordination is important under today's technology and market conditions too, but fundamental conditions affecting it have changed.

Changes in the Function of Coordination

Under today's technology and market conditions there is no reason why coordination from production to distribution—to which Chandler pays special attention—is always most efficient when placed within the boundaries of the corporation. The situation differs from industry to industry, but it is feasible for independent firms to coordinate efficiently through the use of communication network links. Thus task scheduling and coordination is no longer part of the essence of individual corporate activities. What is important for today's firms is the ability to grasp subtle market changes through direct contact with the marketplace and to feed this information into production, marketing and research and development (R&D) in order to promote product development and improved sales and marketing. Here task coordination is necessary, and it is handled not through authority or orders but through negotiation, persuasion, and leadership. In other words, coordination takes place through interaction.

### Need for "Place"

A common "place" is crucial for interaction. This is a different concept from that transaction costs. Interaction can easily be carried out in internal organizations, and in the market through sustained relationships. Another such interaction "place" is Silicon Valley, where universities and high-technology firms are located in close geographical proximity.

The strengths and weaknesses of "places" naturally depend upon what is being attempted through the interactions. Internal organization is advantageous because it provides not only a physical place for information exchange but also common "interpretation systems" that are created within enterprises. It has shortcomings, however. A limited number of people share the "place," and information generated through interaction tends to become homogenized. On the other hand, an entrepreneur trying to create a "place" for interaction in the marketplace will also face obstacles, such as the high investment of time and psychological effort. Time is critical to the enterprise, and time spent in creating and sustaining groups or networks can be considerable. Such interaction, however, can expand or contract flexibly to accommodate various members, enhancing the prospects of new solutions arising from the negotiations and confrontations. Clearly groups and networks do not have formal authority to resolve disputes and cannot function through orders. If they cannot solve problems creatively, they will lose their raison d'être.

The second point is the ability to cope with unexpected events. These can occur at various stages from design through supply of the finished product. When confronted by unexpected events, people within an organization often go out of their way to cope with problems, and they can often succeed, thanks to a shared sense of responsibility generated by peer pressure. However, when people belonging to different organizations collaborate, they often have to put other work first. They may not have the time and energy to get the job done, and they may fail to overcome critical points even if they have a sense of responsibility. Those within an organization are willing to put themselves out because their efforts will be recognized, which acts as an incentive.

That is not to say that there cannot be incentives for coping with unexpected situations, except in internal organizations. In factories where standards for effort appraisal are clear, internal evaluation systems function well. For other functions such as R&D and marketing, where there is continuous interaction with people from the outside and the line between organization and group becomes blurred, there are few standard jobs. It is one unexpected situation after another. Thus it is difficult to devise standards for evaluation. If the evaluation is done by organizational superiors, they may see only one side of a person's work. Even then, evaluating the worker's effort must be carried out through interaction. And in fact the reputation of the specialist worker does get established by peer group opinion. If such interactive evaluation patterns can be established, even groups and networks can provide incentives for coping with unexpected situations.

As Blau's (1964) theory of social exchange and power explains, social interaction appraisals are made according to contributions that everyone can recognize, and power accrues from this. If that power is consumed for personal purposes, it simply means that a person's ability is recognized. However, if it is used for the improvement and vitalization of a "place," it provides leadership. In other words, authority emerges spontaneously, and when it is recognized by others, it becomes approved authority, which can promote work performance.

Such leadership can be established not only within an enterprise but among individuals across corporate boundaries. It can stop at promoting friendly interaction or become a strong driving force. Measures are needed within groups or networks in order to create and sustain the driving force necessary to complete a job. A good example of such measures would be where the core enterprise of an enterprise group assumes the responsibility to monitor interaction in order to identify leadership, allocate financial resources, and officially assign members to the project. To create a framework that can generate a driving force, such a core is vital.

Enterprise, Enterprise Group, and Enterprise Network

I turn now to the distinctions among enterprise, enterprise group, and enterprise network, with particular attention to the processes by which the boundaries of the firm are enlarged. In economics the firm is treated as a single management and decision-making entity or range in which activities are controlled. This range must be considered carefully in specific cases, but as a first approximation one might define the business organization as a single accounting center not consolidated with others. "Enterprise group" is a group of enterprises with interfirm linkages in the form of interlocking directorships or a certain level of cross-shareholding, and cooperative activities. "Enterprise network" refers to a substantial linkage between enterprises through information sharing and interaction between people, whether or not they are institutionally linked.

The formation of an enterprise group or network involves enterprises expanding their boundaries and forming a "place" for interaction. There are three important considerations:

1. Most important to the modern enterprise is not the repeated performance of tasks; rather, it is the establishment of a constant innovation process, together with the creation of information and search for new business contexts through interaction. Shareholders have little influence over this process. Where holdings are concentrated, they may control top personnel appointments, but rarely do they use that power except in times of crisis. Their influence is generally confined to matters of corporate finances, again because finance can become critical in moments of crisis. Shareholders have even less influence over the process of innovation through interaction under the sort of "constellation of interests" (Scott 1985) created by a wide dispersion of shareownership or by cross-holdings. Hence declining importance is attached to "securing authority over management" by acquiring a majority of shares. Indeed ownership is influential only in times of crisis. Task coordination can be carried out with delegated authority, and the ownership itself does not provide leverage to expand the boundaries of the enterprise or enterprise group.

2. Another important factor in the preference for internal organization as the locus of interaction is the speed of response to competition. The frontiers of modern competition lie in the making of a flexible supply system that can meet the challenges of world markets where product life cycles are short, through continual technological innovation in combining products, software, and services. What shapes this frontier of competition is the kind of dynamic competition where time and timing are important. The speed of interaction between production and marketing, or research and development, and the speed of interaction between an enterprise and its various suppliers are decisive. Enterprises like Hitachi, NEC, Toshiba, and Matsushita are at the forefront of international competition because they have internal organizations that can rapidly carry out these different interactions. They constitute a "core," as will be explained later. The need for interaction speed is not identical in all fields and at all times. Therefore

internal organizations (cores) with fast interactions and networks with slower interactions are complementary, and boundaries can change flexibly. What is critical for today's competitive strategies is the ability to manage the locus for interactions. This ability, it should be noted, is fundamentally different from the imperative coordination of tasks or the minimization of transaction costs.

3. A final important determinant of interenterprise links is the locus of value added. This will influence whether the linkage takes the form of merger, joint venture, joint R&D or licensing. In semiconductors, for instance, the choice between holding equipment to make products that use semiconductors (cospecialized assets) and actually producing right through to the finished product, on the one hand, or doing this as a joint venture, on the other, is strongly influenced by where value added can be obtained. Under today's competitive conditions it may be more advantageous to hold such equipment internally, especially when taking the speed of adjustment into consideration. Competitive advantage here is thus tipping toward vertically integrated Japanese enterprises. In the fashion industry, in contrast, flexible links between producers and retailers are the source of value added. Since the locus of value-added creation is not determined, there are various forms of linkage such as joint ventures, joint development, and licensing.

With these arguments in mind, let us proceed to the case studies. Enterprise groups are divided into four categories: *zaibatsu*-type enterprise groups, enterprise groups among independent firms, "fission"-type enterprise groups, and enterprise networks.

## 6.3   Four Types of Enterprise Groups

*Zaibatsu*-Type Enterprise Groups (and the Other Three Major Groups)

Pre-war industrial organization in Japan was characterized by the *zaibatsu*-type corporate connections. The *zaibatsu*, in particular Mitsui, Mitsubishi, and Sumitomo, were giant conglomerates under the control of family-dominated holding companies, centered in giant banks and trading companies, with the majority of major companies in the main industrial areas under their influence. In terms of relative size in the national economy they were without parallel in the world. Domination of Japanese industry by a limited number of *zaibatsu* is a thing of the past, however. Interest is now focused on how the *zaibatsu* changed and developed into today's enterprise groups and networks (figure 6.1).

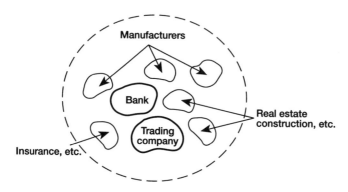

**Figure 6.1**
Enterprise groups (*zaibatsu* type)

Enterprise groups organized around former *zaibatsu* have the following characteristics:

1. Although there are no central headquarters as in the former *zaibatsu*, the main enterprises exchange information regularly through the presidents' councils and other means.

2. Member enterprises maintain long-term and large-scale cross-shareholding. Members of the presidents' councils thus are major shareholders in other member firms.

3. Major banks are at the core of financial transactions, providing loans to group enterprises and often appointing directors to them.

4. At the center of commercial transactions are large trading companies. Diverse transactions are conducted among group enterprises that call for cross-shareholding and the appointment of directors.

5. Top-rated enterprises in major industrial fields belong to the enterprise groups of *zaibatsu* origin.

The three enterprise groups with the above characteristics are Mitsui, Mitsubishi, and Sumitomo. (The pre-war Big Four included Yasuda, whose operations were mostly limited to financial business, and whose base in industry was weak.) Three other groups—Fuyo, Sanwa, and Dai-ichi Kangin (DKB)—are often included in the present day Big Six, but they are centred around banks and are quite different in nature from the three former *zaibatsu* groups. The Mitsubishi and Sanwa groups are compared in table 6.1. The Mitsubishi group normally has only one top-ranked enterprise in each industry. In the Sanwa group a number of firms from the same industry, including some in direct competition, belong to the presidents'

**Table 6.1**
Comparison of former *zaibatsu* with bank-centered enterprise groups

|  | Mitsubishi group | Sanwa Group |
|---|---|---|
| Banks | Mitsubishi Bank | Sanwa Bank |
| Insurance | Mitsubishi Trust & Banking | Toyo Trust |
|  | Meiji Seimei | Nihon Seimei |
|  | Tokio Marine & Fire Insurance |  |
| Trading | Mitsubishi Corp | Nichimen |
|  |  | Nissho-Iwai |
|  |  | Iwatani Int'l |
| Construction | Mitsubishi Construction | Ohbayashi Corp. |
|  |  | Toyo Const.n |
|  |  | Sekisui House |
| Food | Kirin Brewery | Ito Ham Foods, Suntory |
| Textiles | Mitsubishi Rayon | Unitika |
|  |  | Teijin |
| Pulp-paper | Mitsubishi Paper Mills | — |
| Chemicals | Mitsubishi Kasei | Tokuyama Soda |
|  | Mitsubishi Gas Chemical | Sekisui Chemical |
|  | Mitsubishi Petrochemical | Ube Industries |
|  | Mitsubishi Plastics | Hitachi Chemical |
|  | Mitsubishi Monsanto Kasei | Tanabe Seiyaku |
|  |  | Fujisawa Pharmaceuticals |
|  |  | Kansai Paint |
| Oil | Mitsubishi Oil | Cosmo Oil (Maruzen) |
| Rubber | — | Toyo Tire and Rubber |
| Glass | Asahi Glass | Osaka Cement |
|  | Mitsubishi Mining & Cement |  |
| Steel | Mitsubishi Steel Mfg | Kobe Steel |
|  |  | Nisshin Steel |
|  |  | Nakayama Steel Works |
|  |  | Hitachi Metals |
| Nonferrous metals | Mitsubishi Metal | Hitachi Cable |
|  | Mitsubishi Aluminium |  |
| Machinery | Mitsubishi Kakoki | NTT Toyo Bearing |
| Electric | Mitsubishi Electric | Hitachi Ltd. |
|  |  | Iwatsu Electric |
|  |  | Sharp Corp. |
|  |  | Kyocera Corp. |
|  |  | Nitto Electric Industrial |
| Transportation | Mitsubishi Heavy Industries | Hitachi Zosen |
| machinery | Mitsubishi Motors | Shin Meiwa Industry |
|  |  | Daihatsu Motor |
| Precision instruments | Nikon | — |
| Retail | — | Takashimaya |
| Financial | — | Orient Corp. |

**Table 6.1** (Cont.)

|  | Mitsubishi group | Sanwa Group |
|---|---|---|
| Real estate | Mitsubishi Estate | — |
| Transport/ communications | Nippon Yusen Mitsubishi Warehouse | Hankyu Corp. Nippon Express Yamashita Shin-Nihon |
| Mutual equity ownership among member firms[a] | 30.6% | 16.0% |

Sources: Toyo Keizai Shimposha, *Nihon no Kigyo Gurupu* (Japan's Enterprise Groups); Fair Trade Commission, *Nihon no Kigyo Shudan* (Japan's Enterprise Groups).
a. These two figures were tallied by dividing the number of shares mutually owned by firms belonging to the president's councils by the entire number of outstanding shares issued by these firms.

council. Powerful enterprises such as Nissho Iwai, Hitachi Ltd., and Kobe Steel belong to both the Sanwa and DKB groups. Another notable difference, shown at the bottom of the table, is a 30.6% cross-shareholding ratio for the Mitsubishi group versus 16.0% for the Sanwa group. Clearly the three bank groups should be treated differently from the three former *zaibatsu* groups.

From an economic perspective, these enterprise groups are characterized by multifaceted interfirm relations, and their constituents are interlinked even though they lack strong central authority. Whether or not they function as an entity, however, is a difficult question. The cooperation of Mitsubishi group enterprises in buying back Mitsubishi Oil shares from Getty Oil and the absorption of employees of group enterprises in structurally depressed industries by enterprises in expanding sectors are indeed examples of united group action.

In day-to-day activities, however, transactions with group enterprises are only carried out if they are financially advantageous. Statements and survey responses[4] of group officials to this effect should be treated with caution of course, but if they *did* favor intragroup transactions irrespective of economic merit, they would soon find themselves declining in the face of today's stiff competition and threats from new entrants. In fact, as shown in table 6.2, group enterprises carry out more transactions with *other* group enterprises than within their own group. The main reason for a high proportion of stable transactions within enterprise groups is low transaction

---

4. Fair Trade Commission (1980) *Rokudai kigyo shudan no jittai* (State of the Six Major Enterprise Groups).

**Table 6.2**
Joint business agreements inside and outside groups, 1980 (unit: cases)

|  | Intragroup cases | Intergroup cases | Other outside cases |
|---|---|---|---|
| Mitsui | 7.2 | 11.8 | 52.7 |
| Mitsubishi | 9.1 | 7.1 | 36.9 |
| Sumitomo | 9.4 | 17.3 | 64.7 |
| Fuyo | 2.7 | 6.3 | 27.7 |
| Sanwa | 1.9 | 6.2 | 29.0 |
| Dai-Ichi | 2.0 | 7.5 | 24.3 |

Source: Fair Trade Commission.

costs stemming from long relational histories, which enables information to be transmitted simply and accurately. Cooperation within groups is fostered by trust relations stemming from these long-term relationships. Also, particularly when expanding overseas, the brand names of old *zaibatsu* enterprises are advantageous.

Independent Enterprise Groups

There is no definition for independent enterprise groups. Generally speaking, they are not diversified like enterprise groups of *zaibatsu* origin. They are built around large, powerful enterprises such as Hitachi, Matsushita, and Toyota. The 1988 edition of *Kigyo Keiretsu Soran* (Enterprise *Keiretsu* Conspectus) lists 28 such groups, including some that also belong to former *zaibatsu* groups (see figure 6.2 and table 6.3).[5]

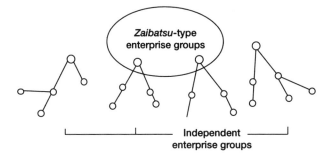

**Figure 6.2**
Independent enterprise groups

5. Sakamoto and Shimotani (1987) have attempted a positive economic analysis of independent enterprise groups.

**Table 6.3**
Independent enterprise groups

| Enterprise group | Enterprise group |
| --- | --- |
| Ajinomoto | Matsushita Electric Industrial |
| Toray | Sony |
| Asahi Chemical Industry | Mitsubishi Heavy Industries |
| Sumitomo Chemical | Nissan Motor |
| Mitsubishi Chemical | Toyota Motor |
| Shinetsu Chemical | Honda Motor |
| Nippon Steel | Mitsui and Co. |
| NKK | Mitsubishi Corp. |
| Sumitomo Metal | Daiei |
| Kobe Steel | Ito-Yokado |
| Hitachi Ltd. | Nomura Securities |
| Toshiba Corp. | Seibu-Saison |
| NEC | Tokyu |
| Fuji Electric-Fujitsu | NTT |

Source: Toyo Keizai Shimposha, *Kigyo Keiretsu Soran* (Enterprise Group Conspectus), 1988.

Because independent enterprise groups have historically been formed around powerful enterprises, they have diverse characteristics that defy rigid classification. The following general characteristics, however, may be observed:

1. Groups where enterprises have separated from the parent and grown into major semi-independent enterprises themselves, with their own subsidiaries and affiliates linked to them by operational ties. Group enterprises are diverse, covering several industries. Example: the Hitachi group.

2. Groups whose enterprises have their origins as business departments of the parent firm and have grown to have their own subsidiaries, all under the umbrella of the parent company. The group expands in the same product areas. Example: the Matsushita group.

3. Groups whose parent company unifies multiple layers of subcontractors in vertical production relationships. Example: the Toyota group.

4. Groups whose production subsidiaries are organized by region, and various subsidiaries and affiliates established in new fields. Example: the NEC group.

5. Groups led by a powerful founder or owner-manager. Example: the Seibu (railways) group.

Descriptions of the Hitachi and NEC groups may help to clarify the nature of the independent enterprise groups.

*The Hitachi Group*

Historically speaking, the Hitachi group has come to be composed of the following three subgroups: (1) major enterprises such as Hitachi Cable, Hitachi Metals, Hitachi Chemical, and Hitachi Construction Machinery that have been separated from Hitachi Ltd. and no longer fall into the category of subsidiaries but are independent firms in both name and reality, (2) enterprises integrated into the *keiretsu* through business expansion involving tie-ups, acquisition, and new start-ups such as Babcock Hitachi, Kokusai Electric, Hitachi Maxell, Horiba Ltd. and Hitachi Information Network, (3) troubled firms rescued through equity participation by Hitachi Ltd. such as Shin-Showa Industry, Takico, Nihon Columbia, Japan Servo, and Hitachi Denshi.

The Hitachi group has 46 consolidated and 522 unconsolidated subsidiaries. Along with Matsushita, it is the biggest independent corporate group. It includes a wide range of manufacturing industries, from raw materials to manufacturing of heavy electric goods, home appliances, semiconductors, electronic-communication equipment, industrial machinery and machine tools, and service activities such as software for information processing products, and marketing.

Unlike the groups of *zaibatsu* origin, there is no central group bank. Its main banks are Fuji and DKD, but the proportion of Sanwa Bank loans is also high. Consequently, Hitachi Ltd. belongs to three presidents' councils; the Fuyo-kai (Fuji Bank group), Sansui-kai (Sanwa Bank group), and Sankin-kai (DKB group).

One characteristic of the Hitachi group is that it is not strongly controlled by Hitachi Ltd. Rather, it is a diverse, loosely linked group in which quasi-independent specialized enterprises are connected through business, vertically from the supply and procurement of raw materials to sales and marketing, horizontally through cooperating in different fields, and through R&D cutting across all areas (figure 6.3). An enterprise group like Hitachi respects the autonomy of member firms, but it is also capable of rapid product innovation—from design through marketing and servicing—and process innovation—through linkage with equipment suppliers, and efficient in-group coordination before starting a new venture.

*The NEC Group*

The consolidated and unconsolidated subsidiaries of the unique NEC group are shown in figure 6.4. The group has 23 independently incorporated manufacturing subsidiaries such as Tohoku (northeast) NEC and Kagoshima NEC, which are clearly situated in the divisional organization. These

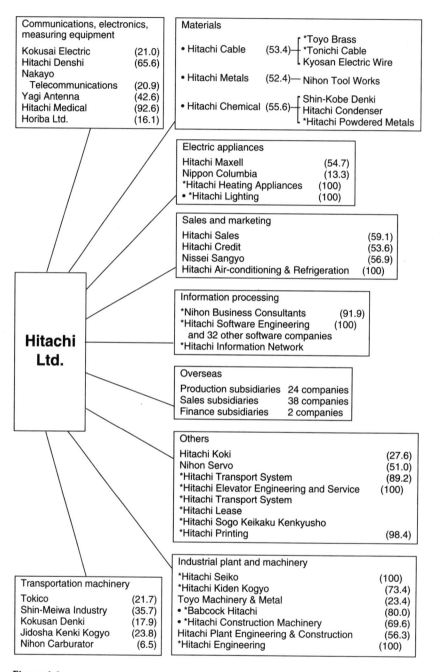

**Figure 6.3**
Major Hitachi group firms by industry. The *bullets* indicate companies separated from Hitachi Ltd., and the *asterisks* nonlisted companies; Hitachi Ltd.'s equity is given in parentheses.

## Consolidated

**Production subsidiaries**

*Telecommunications equipment*

Tohoku, Yonezawa, Miyagi, Fukishima, Saitama, Shizuoka, Hyogo (= seven regional NEC companies); NEC Radio Electronics; NEC America; NEC Australia

*Computers and other electronics equipment*

Ibaragi, Gunma, Niigata (= three regional NEC companies); NEC Software; NEC San-ei; NEC Information Systems (USA)

*Electronic devices*

Yamagata, Akita, Toyama, Fukui, Kansai, Yamaguchi, Kyushu, Fukuoka, Kumamoto, Oita, Kagoshima (= 11 regional NEC companies); NEC Electronics (USA); NEC Singapore; NEC Malaysia; NEC Ireland; NEC Semiconductors (UK)

*Home electronics, etc.*

NEC Nagano, NEC Home Electronics, Japan Aviation Electronics Inc., Ando Electric, Nippon Avionics

**Sales/service companies**

NEC Field Service, NEC Toshiba Information

System, NEC Information Service, NEC Engineering, NEC Warehouse & Distribution, NEC Factory Engineering, NEC System Integration & Construction, NEC Electronics (Germany), NEC Industries (USA)

**Software companies**

NEC software companies in Hokkaido, Tohoku, Nigata, Nagano, Hokuriku, Shizuoka, Chubu, Kansai, Kobe, Okayama, Chugoku, Shikoku, Kyushu, Okinawa

## NEC Corp.

**Engineering companies**

NEC Denpa Kiki Engineering, NEC Robot Engineering, NEC Environmental Engineering, NEC Yubin Engineering, NEC Marine Engineering, NEC Laser Kiki Engineering, NEC Electric Power Engineering, NEC Cable Media Engineering

*Related companies*

NEC Glass, Nitsuko Corp., Anritsu, Toyo Communications Equipment, Tohoku Communications Equipment, Tohoku Metal Industries, Nihon Denki Seiki, NEC Kosan, NEC Lease, Sumitomo 3M, Hakodate NEC Sales, and others

## Unconsolidated

*Computers, communications*

NEC Computer Systems, NEC Business Systems, NEC Office Systems, NEC Electric Communications Systems, NEC Telecommunications Systems

*Sales and marketing*

NEC Techno Marketing, NEC Boeki Gyomu, NEC Market Development, Hokkaido NEC Sales, Chubu NEC Sales, Shikoku NEC Sales, Kochi NEC Sales, Kyushu NEC Sales, Okinawa NEC Sales, NEC Product Lease, NEC Distribution Center, NEC Product Service, NEC Canada, and 27 other overseas companies

*Manufacturing*

NEC Data Terminals, Showa Koki Seizo, Anten Kogyo, NEC Shinku Glass, Tama Electric, Niigata Seiwa Denki, Oitama Denshi, Nichiden Kikai, NEC Light, Nisshin Denshi, Fuji Kogyo, Shinshu Koku Denshi, Hirosaki Koku Denshi

*Others*

NEC Design Center, NEC Culture Center, and others

**Figure 6.4**
The NEC group according to NEC securities' reports

subsidiaries are independent joint-stock companies, but their stock is 100% NEC-owned and their personnel affairs come under the control of NEC's personnel department. These subsidiaries therefore should be considered as being within the borders of the NEC Corp.

These production subsidiaries have been incorporated by region for management reasons. NEC's production system became too unwieldy during the mid to late 1960s, and fundamental reform had to be carried out to ensure improved management. Also the difficulty of recruiting young workers for the main factories in the capital (Keihin) region led the company to establish regional mass production factories where workers were still available (with the Keihin factories becoming technology and management centers). By turning these into independent companies, slightly lower wages than at headquarters could be paid. Some authority was delegated, but key personnel, finance, and R&D functions were retained by the headquarters. Thus the reforms responded to the need for decentralization.

Another characteristic of the NEC group is that software and engineering have been largely separated into independent enterprises that, unlike the production subsidiaries, can operate relatively free from headquarters control, even in personnel matters and R&D. Since software and engineering are critical to NEC's corporate strategy, key areas have been retained internally. However, software and engineering rely on advanced, specialized capabilities, and are not suited to simple control. Engineers are expected to accumulate knowledge resources by working on projects with other firms and interacting with other groups. Thus core functions are retained, but other activities are left to independent enterprises developing on their own. In the case of makers of important production equipment such as Ando Electric and Anritsu, NEC owns shares, has directors on their boards, and generally maintains close relations with them.

The NEC group may be represented as in figure 6.5. It is, in sum, a group in which there is a gigantic core with subgroups of strongly and weakly linked related enterprises.

"Fission"-Type Enterprise Groups

Unlike an enterprise group such as NEC, "fission"-type groups do not have a core organization with a unifying function. They set up independent subsidiaries to meet particular business opportunities and the only unifying force is information exchange and some coordination between the

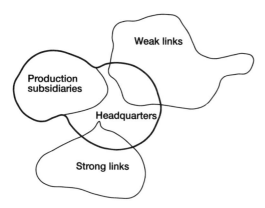

**Figure 6.5**
A conceptual diagram of the NEC group

independent enterprises. "Fission" here means the separation of business divisions or sections into autonomous enterprises (see figure 6.6).

Maekawa Ltd. is a noteworthy example of this type of group.[6] Its strategy is to set up independent enterprises and delegate authority to them based on the smallest unit of management of between 5 and 150 people. Maekawa Ltd. started out as a firm specializing in the development of refrigerator and cooling-plant technology, and is now a world leader in industrial refrigeration engineering. In 1989 the group had 73 independent companies by region and 21 by business, as well as 6 affiliates.

Characteristic of the group is the idea that each company is its own center, as opposed to being a spin-off from a core. There is a fundamental difference between the concept represented in figure 6.6 and that of figure 6.5. First, although NEC's production subsidiaries are independently incorporated, production plans and capital investment are decided by headquarters. In Maekawa, by contrast, not only production plans but also capital

---

6. No doubt economists are divided as to whether the group should be viewed as companies that have become independent from Maekawa Ltd. (as the present president conceives it) or as a company with a high degree of decentralization. Legally the companies are independent and pay taxes independently, but the individual companies pay 3 percent of their sales turnover to Maekawa Ltd., they can receive finance at the official rate plus 1 percent, and Maekawa owns equity (which varies in amount) in the individual companies, and the latter attempt to pay 20 percent dividends to Maekawa Ltd. The individual companies can recruit their own staff, but all new graduates are recruited by Maekawa Ltd., which sends them to the companies. The companies pay ¥500,000 per person for recruiting costs.

This is like an internal transfer, in the traditional sense, and the group might be best considered as one company. But, as I have argued, the fact that important decisions are left up to individual companies makes it more appropriate to view it as a network. I prefer to regard it as a new type of network with information bonding with the main company.

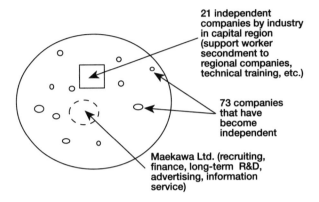

**Figure 6.6**
The "fission"-type Maekawa group

investment is decided autonomously by individual companies, which are free to go outside the group to borrow funds. Personnel appointments to top posts of the individual companies are decided following consultation among those companies, and Maekawa Ltd. merely makes the announcement. Patented know-how is mostly under the control of Maekawa Ltd. headquarters, but individual companies are now also obtaining patents.

Workers do move between the companies, but this is decided according to the wishes of the individuals concerned and consultations between the companies themselves, and not by the headquarters' personnel department. Headquarters does the recruiting of new college graduates for member companies, which pay a fee for the service, but it does not have the usual headquarters function of personnel management. The only headquarters functions, besides recruiting new college graduates, are finance and long-term R&D. The number of people at the headquarters has gradually declined, and now stands at 30 to 40 out of a total group work force of 1,400.

The "fission" management system has been adopted in the belief that decision making should be carried out at the localized level directly connected to operating in the market. This belief and its connection to group organization is expressed by the president, Masao Maekawa: "We take an independent company approach. What is important is the relation between the individual and the whole. Each company strives to have its own character, but the more clearly defined that character becomes, the clearer it becomes that it is part of the whole, and that it must collaborate with other group members which have other characters. When the company pursues its own path, it naturally realizes its relation to the whole" (sixtieth anniversary publication).[7]

The previous section noted the importance of maintaining a "place" for interaction, and argued that the coordination of interaction depends on the conditions of a given industry. With custom order production where close interaction with users is necessary, network-style interaction between "the individual and the whole" as noted above is possible. On the other hand, a business like NEC necessitates a vertically integrated organization with a core because of its production system, and for economies of speed.

Enterprise Networks

An enterprise network does not have formal capital or personnel links between the individual enterprises. Enterprises are linked, but without a core enterprise or a core from which companies can be spun off. The reason the word "network" is used is to emphasize the fact that interenterprise linkage does not necessarily hinge on capital and personnel relationships, and because the technical means of linkage is very often through communication networks.

The example shown in figure 6.7 is a network for the supply of daily use goods. In addition new types of networks such as the pharmaceutical sales Pharma and the Community Network Ltd. are emerging.[8] Networks have a fundamental weakness in their ability to respond to unexpected events, but this weakness can be compensated through the leadership of a key

---

7. The Taiyo Industries Group is similar in a number of respects to the Maekawa Group. It began in 1947 as Taiyo Painting, branched out into press work, and from these bases spun off companies in electronics equipment, printed circuit boards, condensers, information systems, and so on. With the concept that "spin-offs create founders" promising employees from the "parent" company are selected as presidents of the new enterprises; as "founders" they are free to build the companies according to their own discretion. The new companies have general affairs, personnel, and accounting functions. In some cases they have further spun off "grandchild" companies.

To signify their independence, the 24 companies in the inner circle of figure 6.8 below have completely different names. The outer circle contains derivative support companies. In effect, this is a "fission-type" group of SMEs; the individual companies are independent but rely on each other without difficult problems like centralized R&D. Shares are not held by the owner but by group companies.

8. Community Network (CN) is a successful network of living and information service-related companies. The core (Big Holiday, Jet Tours, etc.) travel company has developed a VAN (value-added network) with the JR-affiliate VAN company Transnet and the enterprise brings together 27 companies in travel, ticket sales, sports service facilities, banking and insurance. Participants are not connected vertically as "parent," "child," and "grandchild" companies but horizontally.

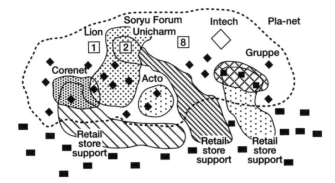

**Figure 6.7**
A simplified enterprise network of daily goods industries. The *open diamond* represents the VAN company, and the *open boxes* represent the manufacturers, the *filled-in boxes* the retail stores, and the *filled-in diamonds* the wholesalers. The network can be very diverse; it can incorporate wholesalers and retailers from other areas, as well as other network companies providing hardware and communication systems.

enterprise, which can provide an effective "place" for the interaction and business development of the others. (A more detailed discussion of network organization has been given elsewhere [Imai and Kaneko 1988] and will not be repeated here.)

Such pure networks are of great interest, but it goes without saying that few enterprises and their groups constitute a single pure type. My four types—*zaibatsu*, independent, fission, and network—are only a useful classification device and many leading groups combine features of more than one type. For instance, a vertically integrated organization can be the core, and other parts can utilize the merits of decentralized decision making through "fission" or networks. Or when small enterprises form a network they may also establish a core to enhance information exchange, cope with unexpected situations and support financing efforts. The mix depends on the situation and industry, and none has a decisive intrinsic advantage but depends on the forces of centralization and decentralization in a competitive environment. Today's enterprise groups and networks are in this sense hybrids, with the form determined by technology and market conditions.

## 6.4   Conclusion

The arguments presented in this chapter may be summarized as follows:

1. Debates about enterprise groups from an economic perspective began, historically speaking, with problems of corporate power and monopoly.

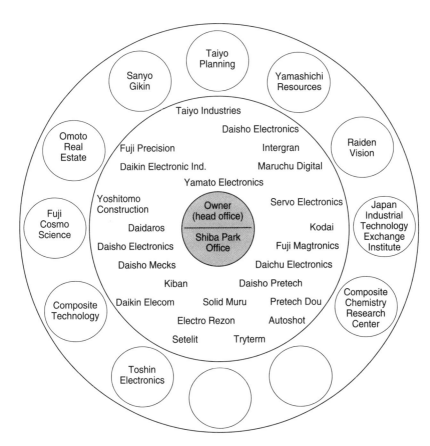

**Figure 6.8**
Taiyo Industries group (as of January 1986). Source: Sakai (1986).

**Community Network Ltd.**

**Figure 6.9**
Community Network Ltd. Source: Ihara and Okada (1988).

They were concerned with socioeconomic power of interlinked oligopolistic enterprise groups. This line of enquiry, however, has exhausted its historical role.

2. The starting point for the modern framework of analysis is transaction cost economics. Monopoly analysis sees the firm as striving to increase its influence by directly and indirectly expanding its boundaries, while in transaction cost analysis the firm decides its boundaries from the perspective of efficiency. However, this approach tends to be static in that the most appropriate organizational form is supposedly decided from existing market and intrafirm transaction possibilities.

3. To overcome this shortcoming, the transaction mode must be viewed as not merely existing in a dynamic economy but as continually shaping and reshaping the respective merits of markets and hierarchies. The critical task for the modern firm is to create information through human interaction, find new business contexts, and establish a process for cumulative innovation. The choice between market and hierarchy is thus decided from the perspective of how to coordinate such interaction. Specifically, internal organization is designed to foster speed of interaction between R&D, production and marketing, while links with outside firms foster interaction and information absorption.

4. Japan's enterprise groups can be classed into four categories: enterprise groups of *zaibatsu* origin, independent enterprise groups, "fission"-type enterprise groups, and enterprise networks. As for the first, the debate over whether a few large *zaibatsu* dominate Japanese industry is a thing of the past, and the subject of present interest is how *zaibatsu* evolved into today's enterprise groups and networks. Independent enterprise groups have a wide diversity, ranging from groups of enterprises split off from parent companies to vertical subcontracting groups. Generally speaking internal and external organization is combined in an attempt to generate the respective merits mentioned above. Recently a number of groups have appeared, formed either by fission or by the coming together of independent firms, with no core and a division of labor determined by the nature of the business. These networks, which may have no formal capital or personnel links, are of increasing importance.

The fourfold classification, however, is only a typological device. The multilayered enterprise groups of today's Japan frequently combine elements of more than one type.

# 7        Subcontracting Relationships: The Automobile Industry

## Yoshiro Miwa

This chapter looks at the mechanisms behind the remarkable success of the Japanese automobile industry. A great deal of attention has been directed toward Japan's economic growth and industrial success, which is seen as owing much to the fabrication and assembly industries. A chief exemplar of this is the automobile industry. Hence, by analyzing the mechanisms for success in this industry, we may be able better to understand the central mechanisms of rapid growth in the whole Japanese economy. The rising interest in Japanese subcontracting (or buyer-supplier) relationships,[1] the subject of this chapter, testifies to their importance as a key element in that success.[2]

While opinions are divided on specific details of the success of the Japanese automobile industry, there is general consensus that besides satisfying basic consumer demands in developed countries, its products have a low defect rate, low gasoline consumption, and relatively low prices compared

---

This chapter is based on a paper presented to the second conference on "The Subcontracting System and Small- and Medium-Sized Enterprises (SMEs)". The second and main section of the original has been substantially shortened, with the principal conclusions presented. See Miwa (1988) or the revised Miwa (1989b) for further discussion. I am very gratful for the helpful comments of Kenichi Imai in preparing this paper.
1. As discussed elsewhere (1989a), there is a large gap between the overriding image of Japan's SMEs and reality. Further the terms "subcontracting relations" and "subcontracting system" evoke an image of strong large firms and weak SMEs (1989b). Because this general image does not reflect reality, the use of these terms in this chapter may create some confusion. They have been retained, however, in preference to alternatives such as "specialized relationship."

I do not mean to assert that subcontracting relationships in the automobile industry are representative of Japanese subcontracting relationships in general, and neither is this chapter a "general theory" of subcontracting relations.

2. According to Nakamura (1985, 90): "Today the subcontracting system is being reassessed as one foundation for the supremacy of Japanese industry, and for the good communication it provides between enterprises on the basis of an advanced social division of labour."

to competing products with similar features. Although an industrial and technological base had been developing since the pre-war period, there were critical problems in quality and productivity when production began in the postwar passenger car industry.[3] From these early conditions the success of the industry was its achievement of high productivity and high quality within a short period and a rapid increase in the volume of production. How was this success realized? What role did various economic actors play? What kind of interaction was there between the economic actors? There are questions this chapter will attempt to answer.

The basis for the expansion of the Japanese fabrication and assembly industries as represented by automobiles was the steady accumulation of small innovations. Two criteria were critical: sustained creative application by a large number of related economic actors (not necessarily part of the same firm), and careful cultivation of an effective mutual understanding among the actors about how their creative efforts are to be coordinated.

For those readers used to equilibrium analysis it may be difficult to fully appreciate the importance of the creation and maintenance of a system for lowering costs and improving quality through the mutual transfer of finely tuned skills and know-how accumulated by each economic actor. Section 7.1 therefore looks at the success of the industry and the challenges it faced, while section 7.2 moves on to an analysis of subcontracting relationships, the primary concern of this chapter. The key questions are: Why did enterprises in subcontracting relationships demonstrate creativity? Why did they continue to make commitments that required substantial time before results (profits) could be realized? What did the "parent" assembler companies do to engender such creativity and commitment. In short, what kind of "incentive systems" support subcontracting relationships?

In section 7.2 I briefly describe the inability of the conventional view to answer these questions, before proceeding to sections 7.3 and 7.4, which form the core of this chapter. Section 7.3 examines the "incentive system" that brought about the continued participation and active involvement by so many firms in these relationships. This incentive system had to include measures to create and sustain long-term relationships isolated from market

---

3. The comment by Bank of Japan President Ichimata is representative of those after the war who thought a passenger car industry was a lost cause: "It makes no sense to foster a car industry in Japan. Because we live in an era of an international division of labor, we can rely on the United States."

   The number of foreign cars sold in Japan between 1951 and 1953 was 30,463, or 64 percent of the total domestic supply of passenger cars. Marked differences between foreign and domestic cars existed in performance, style, and price (Miwa 1976, 348–49).

transactions. Section 7.4 looks at such measures, and section 7.5 offers some concluding observations.

I would like to offer the following caveats:

1. Effectiveness in achieving the intent of a subcontracting relationship by the participating firms is not the same in all cases. For the purpose of exposition, section 7.1 refers mainly to the Toyota group, which is said to have the strongest relationships. From section 7.2 on I examine control mechanisms of subcontracting in the whole Japanese automobile industry; thus the term "assembler" refers to the average Japanese assembler.

2. No assessment is made of why Toyota relationships are stronger than other Japanese assemblers, or why Japanese assemblers as a whole have been more successful in constructing efficient subcontracting relationships than assemblers in other countries.

3. Such questions as why the system of subcontracting was chosen over internal production, or why present locations were chosen are not considered.[4]

4. The discussion focuses on assemblers and those who supply parts to them. Among parts suppliers, it considers parts processing companies, and not off-the-shelf suppliers of unit parts (vendors), because the relationship is more intimate, and closer to the typical image of subcontractors in the automobile industry.[5]

5. I do not consider overall reasons for the success of Japan's automobile industry; rather, I focus on the functioning of one important cause of this success. I do not assert, however, that this is *the* sole or most important reason for the success.

6. This chapter does not present a clear hypothesis with data to support it. It attempts to gather and interpret fragmented information and to present a view very different from the one that has been widely held.

---

4. Of course to merely assert that it was rational does not answer the question. It is not easy—today at least—to find reasons why Toyota-style subcontracting relations were not a rational choice for other domestic and foreign assemblers too.

5. This difference is especially notable in the case of a latecomer assembler, who can nevertheless utilize the parts supplied by a vendor to more established assemblers.

The ratio of raw materials, parts purchased from vendors and subcontracted parts is 10, 60, and 30 percent, respectively (*Nihon no jidosha buhin sangyo* [JAPI], 1984, 106). Vendors make long-term arrangements with subcontractors, as well, and with mechanisms similar to those developed between assemblers and subcontractors. Thus the overall industry figure for subcontracting is higher than 30 percent. Of course in many cases the relationship between assemblers and vendors is identical to that between assemblers and subcontractors.

## 7.1  Industrial Success and Its Challenges

Success of the Industry

For those familiar only with the Japanese automobile industry today, it may not be easy to envision the conditions that led to its success. In January 1955 "a vehicle that was really worthy of the name 'passenger car' —the Crown,"[6] was unveiled. Production of passenger cars for all of Japan in that year was 20,000 vehicles; by 1968 it had reached 2,000,000, a 100-fold increase. In 1961 10,000 passenger cars were exported from Japan. This figure climbed to 100,000 in 1965 and 1 million in 1971. By 1976 more than half the automobiles produced in Japan were exported.[7]

When Japan began full production of passenger cars, its productivity was markedly lower than that of other countries. Starting with measures to limit imports through foreign currency controls, various policies were implemented to protect domestic producers. While the domestic market was protected from foreign competition,[8] in export markets Japanese assemblers had to overcome the low reputation of new entrants. Because of the rapid increases in the volume of production, however, productivity rose within a short period from an extremely low level to one that enabled Japan to compete successfully in international markets. Production and productivity grew rapidly in all countries during this period, forcing Japanese firms to increase their efficiency at an even faster pace.

The rapid increase in the export of Japanese passenger cars was based on relatively low prices and high quality. Compared with conditions in the industry when it first began to grow, around 1960, this reflected a dramatic improvement within a short period.[9] Automobiles are made up of around 20,000 parts of 5,000 different types, produced by large numbers of enterprises. Thus the dramatic improvement in the quality of the final product meant significant and simultaneous increases in the quality of parts, mate-

6. Toyota Eiji (1985, 172).
7. For a summary of the growth process, see, for example, Itami et al. (1988, vol. 1).
8. Assembled passenger car imports were liberalized in October 1965. As a result of the Kennedy Round negotiations in June 1967, it decided that customs tariffs for small passenger cars would be lowered from 40 to 30 percent by 1972.
9. Toyota, a symbol of industrial success, made a successful bid for U.S. Army Procurement Agency (APA) special procurements in 1959. To meet the APA's stringent quality requirements, Toyota was forced to pay close attention to the quality and performance of parts from its subcontractors. Differences in conceptualization and execution of quality control in each factory created problems for the setting and realization of quality standards. The quality committee established by Toyota in 1953 had still not produced sufficient results. For details on developments in this period, see Wada (1984).

rial for parts, machine tools and other production equipment. During these years Japan faced a chronic shortage of foreign currency, and many materials, machines, and parts had to be produced domestically. From related industries such as tires, bearings, glass, steel, and machine tools to the in-house presses and machining work, quality levels were raised all round.[10]

## Impediments to Industrial Success

What problems did assemblers (and their groups of related firms) have to solve to bring about increased productivity and improved quality? Production of the vast range of parts necessary for automobile production was dispersed among many enterprises.[11] These enterprises had to establish and maintain good communication by exchanging information, achieving mutual understanding, and coordinating interests. Such information was important for raising the technological level of individual firms, which started from a low base.

The automobile industry has a number of distinctive characteristics. It is a mass production industry, an assembly industry using a vast array of parts. Precision and durability requirements are high, and there is a need for continuous improvement. In the beginning it was not simply a matter of selecting the best firms with which to build relationships. A complete reform of management thinking and execution was called for, from production and quality to labor affairs, accounting, stocks, and raw materials. Would-be suppliers could not easily meet the demands.[12]

Close, cooperative, long-term relationships were developed between assemblers and subcontractors. That its competitors generally conceded Toyota's superiority in building relations with subcontractors is an indication of the nature of the problems that had to be overcome. For example, improving tools and dies and the efficient use of equipment were targeted

---

10. Production volume and quality of passenger cars is said to be a barometer that shows the technological level, productive level, and overall economic power of a country. Japan's overall economic power increased dramatically in an extremely short period.

11. The number of firms with direct and indirect trading relationships with a single finished car maker exceeds 40,000 (*Bungyo kozo jittai chosa*, SME Agency, 1977).

12. Even if subcontractors could meet production requirements, it was not always easy to meet delivery schedules, a prerequisite for an efficient production system. Simultaneously they had to satisfy productivity, quality, performance, price, and development requirements. The history of the Japanese automobile industry is one of diversification into an increasing number of car types and options, with stricter schedules and a constant battle against increases in production and inventory costs.

to reduce fixed equipment, and hence total, costs. Toyota and its subcontractors are still admired for the levels they reached, levels that were continually raised.[13] It was extremely difficult and time-consuming to raise the level of all firms from a low technological base, establish close, cooperative relations between those firms, and to use this to rapidly improve productivity and quality (see Miwa 1989b).

## 7.2   The Success Mechanism in the Automobile Industry: Preliminary Considerations

Let us move on to examine the role individual firms played in improving productivity and quality once production of automobiles began to increase. This did not come about of its own accord. What mechanisms supported subcontracting relationships? To begin with, the following three points should be made:

1. The heretofore dominant view of subcontracting, which uses as key terms "exploitation," "shock absorbers," and "dependency" does not yield a satisfactory explanation.

2. The influence of "parent" companies (through the devices of personnel exchange, capital investment, advance payments, supply of raw materials, technology guidance, lending equipment and machine tools, bank loans, etc.) cannot be considered the main cause.

---

13. The senior managing director and head of the purchasing department of Mazda made the following comment: "The development of efficient methods is the goal in production from now. Dies, jigs, and so on, are critical. We need to be able to make them cheaply and change them quickly. The contrast between Toyota and the rest is one of night and day. Toyota companies have made great efforts to use equipment efficiently and decrease fixed costs" (JAPI 1985, 79).

   Insight into these efforts can be gained from the comments of R. Kojima, president of Kojima Press and chairman of the Tokai Kyohokai (an organization of Toyota subcontractors):

When talking about Toyota's production system, the popular term *kanban* comes to mind. The *kanban* system aims at "what I want, in the amount I want, when I want it" and it has at last become possible to realize this. It is a prerequisite that all supplies obtained through the *kanban* system be of good quality. (If bad parts come in, the assembly line will stop. If we consider the large number of parts involved and the entire assembly line is stopped, "what I want in the amount I want" is no longer a desirable goal.) Because this is a prerequisite, all parts are assumed to be of high quality, and inspection of delivered parts disappears. It is impossible to eliminate this step without good technological support, however, and it requires two, even three, years to accomplish the production of high-quality parts without defects. (ibid., 162–63; paraphrased)

3. Policies for rationalization and cost reduction in parts supplier firms tended to rely on independent decisions rather than on the strong influence of "parent" companies.[14]

With these points in mind, let us investigate the mechanism that maintains subcontracting relationships in the Japanese automobile industry.

## 7.3   "Incentive" Systems

Rationalization and modernization are principles pursued zealously by assemblers, vendors, and subcontractors, with the result that parts suppliers are more self-motivated than directed by assemblers. Building cooperative relationships between companies to increase productivity and improve quality was extremely difficult and required a great deal of time to cultivate as noted earlier. Historically assemblers themselves were not fully aware of the importance of continuous improvement at first, and it took some time for the awareness to penetrate all divisions of their own companies. There was no grand scheme of overall concrete plan; relationships were forged and modified through repeated reexamination and trial and error.

To examine the mechanism that supports subcontracting relationships between assemblers and parts suppliers we must investigate both what the economic actors did and the "incentive" system that led them to behave as they did, in the formative phase and the subsequent expansion phase.

The Formative Phase

In the early stages it was difficult for subcontractors to understand what was expected of them. Assemblers had to show subcontractors the nature of the industry, the role they were expected to play. Several things had to be done quickly: The conditions and standards subcontractors had to meet needed clear delineation (through the assignment of immediate goals), subcontractors had to be offered incentives to start and continue participation; and they needed assistance in order to reach the goals.

---

14. On the role of suppliers associations, see Miwa (1989b). Even if parent companies had a strong influence, careful examination of the attendant "responsibility" would reveal limitations to this. For example, N. Yasusada, president of Akebono brakes and chairman of the Japan Auto Parts Industries Association commented on whether assemblers ask suppliers to follow them to North America: "They do not ask, because it would be seen as a guarantee. If the parts makers do go, the makers will welcome it, but they do not say they will buy the parts" (JAPI 1987, 57).

Participation required a change in managers' attitudes, and a considerable investment of time and energy. Workers had to be employed and trained, and capital investment made. The role of assemblers in this period was to offer repeated, clear guidance to their subcontractors so that they could meet the necessary standards in quantity, quality, and delivery dates.

Incentive System in the Formative Phase

The abilities (or "skills") acquired by the subcontractors while under the guidance of assemblers can be divided into two categories: skills specific to an assembler that would lose their economic value if the relationship with that assembler were broken off or significantly reduced, and general skills that would retain their economic value even if the relationship were not maintained. A comparison of the formative and expansion phases shows that the importance of general skills was proportionately higher in the earlier period.

As it develops, with these skills a subcontractor gains a general manufacturing capability which makes it attractive to other assemblers or even firms in other fabrication and assembly industries (even if the relationship with the assembler *is* maintained).

By contrast, the more skilled a subcontractor becomes, the more an assembler suffers if that subcontractor breaks off the relationship. The assembler in this position faces several alternatives: nurture the skills of another subcontractor to fit its needs, seek a substitute subcontractor, or internalize production. The costs incurred by an assembler when relations with a subcontractor are broken depend on the direct costs incurred until a substitute source of supply is secured and the extent of the impact on its entire production system during the transition period. The greater the dependence on the subcontractor for specific parts, the greater the cost.

Hence an assembler must first of all consider carefully whether or not to become involved with a subcontracting firm. Having decided to do so, it has to work at maintaining a mutual relationship with it (i.e., minimize the risk of its "escaping" to a competing assembler). And, third, it has to encourage the subcontractors continually work at developing their capabilities.

The most important precondition in establishing such a relationship is to persuade the subcontractor that it will be profitable to participate. To do this, (1) the assembler should belong to an industry that has good prospects, (2) the assembler must have strong prospects within that industry, (3) the subcontractor should not feel trapped in a disadvantageous position by agreeing to participate (the pre-agreed transaction conditions—for example,

price, quantity, delivery date, and term of contract—should not be changed
unilaterally by the assembler), and (4) the assembler must give appropriate
guidance and assistance to the subcontractor.[15]

In the formative phase of the mass production system in the automobile
industry, the prospects for the industry, and for individual firms in it, were
by no means clear, so assemblers had to work even harder at conditions 3
and 4. Subcontractors were in an advantageous position. Response to the
assemblers' demands had to be carried out in steps, and a subcontractor
could choose whether or not to advance to the next step. Further, if the
subcontractor chose to withdraw part way through, not all of the skills
it had accumulated became worthless, for the importance of assembler-
specific skills was relatively small at this stage. If a relationship was terminated, the loss for the assembler was larger than for the subcontractor.

The Expansion Phase

Once a subcontractors had been persuaded to become part of an assembler's specialized production system and developed minimum qualifications
in order to assume responsibility for some part of the process, the assembler next had to ensure that it could keep pace with expanding output and
improving quality. Specific requests were made of subcontractors: active
expansion of capital investment and employment in order to increase the
scale of production, larger and more modern equipment to increase productivity and precision, synchronization and standardization of the production
system and specialization of equipment.

Satisfying the assembler's requests required a subcontractor to commit
substantial energy, time, and capital over a long period, and the requests
were achieved step by step. In this respect conditions had not changed
from the earlier formative phase. However, when we consider the increased
scale of the demands and the increased importance of assembler-specific
skills (which become useless if the relationship is broken off), especially
through synchronization and standardization, it is clear the subcontractor's
commitment to the transaction relationship had deepened.

The assembler had to do the following: ensure that the subcontractor did
not become uneasy about increasing its commitment, ascertain what was

---

15. It is not easy for an assembler to acquire and maintain the confidence of its subcontractors. For example, when Mitsubishi set up its mass production facility in Mizushima, a major
problem was eliminating the strong distrust of "parent" companies that was held by SMEs
as a result of being squeezed out when the market for three-wheel trucks, their product until
that time, slumped in 1958–59. See Takizawa (1966, 16–17).

necessary to ensure the efficiency of the overall production system and guide subcontractors accordingly, and provide subcontractors with incentives to do this.

## Incentive System in the Expansion Phase

As subcontractors developed skills under the guidance of an assembler, the proportion of skills specific to that assembler steadily increased. At the same time the damage suffered by the assembler—the losses until an alternative supply source was found, and impact on the entire production system—if the subcontracting relationship was ended was higher than in the formative phase. The higher the subcontractor's skill level, the greater the proportion of assembler-specific skills and the greater the dependency of the assembler on the subcontractor.

Under these conditions there had to be incentives to ensure the continued participation and commitment of a subcontractor. First, rules had to make it clear that the assembler would bear or share risks.[16] For example, the assembler specifies a certain sum in "die compensation"—to be paid if a last-minute design change makes a die useless—sometimes amounting to several hundred million yen (JAPI 1986, 98). These guarantees are transaction specific, but the convention that such guarantees are offered is part of the overall incentive system.[17] A second incentive—to the assembler—for maintaining the relationship was Williamson's (1983) hostage effect—the fact that the costs of ending the transaction relationship were extremely high. Third, because each assembler had relationships with many subcontractors, its actions toward a particular subcontractor were determined by careful consideration of the influence of those actions on its other subcontractors. The wider context thus circumscribed the actions of the assembler and increased the costs of terminating the relationship with a specific subcontractor.[18] In a sense the entire production system was a hostage (see Williamson 1983, again, and, on reputation, Kreps 1984).

---

16. Up to ¥100 million is paid in compensation to subcontractors for late design modifications by the assembler that require, for instance, changes in dies. See JAPI (1986, 98) for Nissan's case.

17. If we apply this to the hostage ($h$) in Williamson's (1983) model, $\alpha = 0$ because for the subcontractor the value is 0.

18. Again using Williamson's model, if subcontractors are identical such that breaking a relationship with one of them causes a chain reaction among $n$ firms, the cost for the hostage becomes $nh$. Moreover, because the number of firms that can substitute for the subcontractor decreases over time, the expense to the assembler of finding an alternative may be even greater than $nh$. See Kreps (1984) for a discussion of reputation.

A fourth incentive factor was that from the time an assembler first sought to recruit a particular subcontractor, it had to offer the subcontractor the promise that the relationship would be long-lasting and that it would not endanger the relationship by acting opportunistically for short-term advantage.[19]

These are the considerations that condition a subcontractor's decision whether, how far, and under what circumstances to respond to an assembler's request for commitment (and condition the means by which the assembler can be sure that the commitment is real and effective). The relation develops by stages. The stages are not clearly separated; they may be marked by a specific upgrading of the assembler's guarantees. But more important is the gradual deepening of a "friendly" division of labor.

## 7.4    The Success Mechanism and Controversies Surrounding It

Policies for Productivity Improvement

If committed relationships are established and the subcontractor is threatened neither by the assembler buying in the spot market nor by in-house manufacturing, how is it that the subcontractor does not just enjoy its security and relax? Productivity improvement is the combined result of multiple policies:

1. *Competition still an effective stimulus.* Assembler's networks are likely to contain several other firms that can perform the work as well as, or nearly as well as, any particular subcontractor. And there is always the possibility of in-house manufacturing. Subcontractors who perform badly can be replaced, and the disruption caused thereby minimized, if the replacement is sufficiently well planned ahead of time. Assemblers do also double or triple source, and they vary the proportions of orders according to subcontractors' performance.

2. *Countermeasures to prevent inefficiency.* An assembler can reduce its expenditure by setting targets and insisting that subcontractors meet them, by

---

19. This can be even more clearly shown in the relationship with vendors. For example, according to a managing director of Nissan:

We say that we buy technology, not parts from our suppliers. We buy goods that are the outcome of technology. We make contracts to buy parts with the assumption that the supplier will add new technology and produce the parts more economically using new ideas and methods if we incorporate a similar part into our next model. Thus we do not only buy current parts. We make contracts that include anticipation of tomorrow's technological developments. (JAPI 1986, 87).

providing guidance on reducing inefficiency based on their detailed knowledge of the subcontractors' work processes.

3. *Guidance for systemwide improvements.* The assembler can give a subcontractor guidance for improvements in a wide variety of areas, such as selection of raw materials, necessary jigs, tools and machines, work methods, and employee training. Communication channels with subcontractors providing information on the effective use of the latest machinery, and the like.

4. *Stimulating subcontractors' resourcefulness.* Advances in the production technology of the automobile industry are based on an accumulation of individual, small improvements, the product of workers' concern to improve efficiency and quality. Subcontractors and their workers have an important role to play in this, and assemblers offer incentives to mobilize their involvement.

5. *Efficiency increases in the overall system.* Improvements in the assembler's production system can lead to throughput standardization and more efficient use of subcontractors' equipment. Standardization of parts can raise order volumes and subcontractor productivity, for instance. Combined, such policies complement the incentive system discussed above and raise the productivity of the overall system.

Note that, the competition factor apart, all of these mechanisms require close collaboration between assembler and contractor.

Long-Term Trading Relations?

My description of "security mechanisms," as that of incentives in section 7.4, assumes that the transaction relationship between assembler and contractor is long term, or that the subcontractor either perceives the relationship in that way or is confident that the assembler is treating it as a long-term relationship. On the other hand, I have just argued that the system of competition plays an important role in the long term as a means of improving productivity. Here I briefly explore the logical relationship and balance between the two and examine the meaning of "long term."

There are a number of circumstances in which an assembler might wish to reduce or suspend a trading relationship with a subcontractor if the security mechanisms discussed above are absent. These circumstances include low efficiency on the part of the subcontracting firm, R&D results lower than initially anticipated, a change in the production system or in raw materials (e.g., from steel to plastic) rendering a subcontractor's product no longer useful, a business slump that forces the assembler to lower production levels and to internalize some operations to maintain its employment level, and withdrawal by the assembler from a particular industrial field (or the closing of a particular factory). What "security mechanisms" imply is that a'subcontractor knows that the assembler has to be prepared to bear considerable expense to reduce or suspend the transaction relationship and that therefore, even in the conditions just described, it will not readily break it off.

The strength of subcontracting relations of course varies; here we have discussed relations in which the connections are strong. The assembler ranks its subcontractors on the basis of their importance, and for example, when reductions in the total volume of orders are unavoidable, those with high ranking suffer lower reductions. In this sense the subcontracting relationship provides the overall system with a degree of flexibility; what constrains the assembler's degrees of freedom is that it must act in accordance with what is clearly understood to be the "importance ranking" of it subcontractors—though this is often wholly implicit, except when made explicit by, for instance, admission to the Kyōryokukai, the key suppliers' association.

As mentioned earlier, if an assembler wants to suspend or reduce its transactions with a subcontractor it must assess whether its action will be seen as justified by all of the firms with which it deals (i.e., seen as genuinely necessary or unavoidable). If not, it will generate mistrust among other firms and suffer heavy long-term loss. The same conditions apply to the apportionment of increases in orders. The assembler must be cognizant at all times of the need to appear fair to its subcontractors.

Increasing internal production to maintain employment levels in the face of declining orders, closing a specific plant without a persuasive explanation, or withdrawing from a specific business field; if the decision appears arbitrary, and taken without concern for others, all these actions can have severe long-term consequences. And it is a matter not only of what is done but also of how. Assemblers must notify their subcontractors as far as possible in advance to allow them time to react, and sometimes give them assistance in coping with the difficulties the change imposes on them.

Even if a subcontractor does not think at the outset that a trading relationship will be suspended without reason, it does not know how the volume of orders from the assembler will change. The subcontractor recognizes that increases in the volume of orders, profitability, and its own position within the assembler's group of firms depend largely on its own achievements.

A group of firms maintaining a subcontracting relationship is an organic, united body with mutual dependencies and influences whose parts the firm at the center (the assembler) cannot shuffle around at will without taking account of the opinions of other participants—unless the firm is closing down (and it cannot even do that free from pressure from the banks or from government).

## 7.5  Conclusion

Ten years before the start of the passenger car industry in Japan, Hayek (1945, 524–25) wrote:

> If we agree that the economic problem of society is mainly one of rapid adaptation to changes in the particular circumstances of time and place, it would seem to follow that the ultimate decisions must be left to the people who are familiar with these circumstances, who know directly of the relevant changes of the resources immediately available to meet them.... We must solve it by some form of decentralization. But this answers only part of our problem. We need decentralization because only thus can we ensure that the knowledge of the particular circumstances of time and place will be promptly used. But the "man on the spot" cannot decide solely on the basis of his limited but intimate knowledge of the facts of his immediate surroundings. There still remains the problem of communicating to him such further information as he needs to fit his decisions into the whole pattern of changes of the larger economic system.

Examination of the mechanism maintaining subcontracting relations— one of the most important reasons for the success of the Japanese automobile industry—reminds us of Hayek's thinking. The economic problem he depicted was also the challenge of the efficient production of passenger cars made up of 20,000 parts in 5,000 categories.

The Japanese automobile industry started from a low technological level and had to simultaneously raise its productivity and quality dramatically. With few exceptions, long-term, close relationships with many firms (i.e., subcontracting relations) were chosen over extensive internal production and heavy reliance on market transactions, and with great success.

Those managers and firms with the capacity and desire to become "men on the spot" made full use of their ingenuity, and "information" was continuously generated and transmitted for such "men on the spot" to reconcile their decision making with the overall production system. These were the aims to which the assemblers (and the groups of firms with which they had cooperative relations) aspired, and which they realized. The continual process requires close cooperation over a long period of time, and the skill with which the individual assemblers executed it has been a major factor in their performance.[20]

---

20. When product cycles become as short as they have recently, product development is also normally carried out cooperatively among a number of firms. The skill with which these relations are handled can decide the life and death of an enterprise.

# III

Enterprise Behavior

# 8

# Organizational Structure and Behavior in Research and Development

Ryuhei Wakasugi

Research and development (R&D) in Japanese firms is often portrayed as significantly different from those of European and U.S. firms. This perception is embodied in the frequent assertions that Japanese firms allocate a low proportion of their people and financial resources to basic R&D and that they tend to depend on foreign countries for basic research, while they channel most of their budgets and their best people into development and applications tied directly to commercialization. A similar assertion is that technology development in Japanese firms produces results that are imitative or incremental rather than creative and pathbreaking, and that even in recently emerging areas of advanced technology, these traits are not changing to any significant degree.[1]

Two kinds of data are used to support the assertions that Japanese firms specialize more in the application and development stages of R&D than their U.S. and European counterparts. The first concerns the most critical element of R&D: capable people. Japanese firms employ large numbers of engineering graduates in their engineering-oriented R&D but bring in relatively few science graduates whose role is so important in basic research. A comparison of the number of university graduates and degree holders[2] from science and engineering departments in Japan and the United States (table 8.1) clearly shows the very high proportion accounted for in Japan by engineering departments. In consequence the supply of engineering graduates to the labor markets has grown more rapidly than that of science graduates, and this aspect of the supply of human resources has greatly influenced the R&D activities of Japanese firms.

---

1. See, for example, Mansfield (1988) and Rosenberg and Steinmuller (1988).
2. For Japan, the distinction between graduates and degree-holders is a necessary one, particularly in engineering: universities grant doctorates to people who submit advanced research done outside the university, usually in industrial settings, to fulfill the degree requirements.

**Table 8.1**
Educational background of R&D personnel in selected countries

| Country | Year | Science degree | | | Engineering degree | | |
|---|---|---|---|---|---|---|---|
| | | Bachelor | Master | Ph.D. | Bachelor | Master | Ph.D. |
| Japan | 1977 | 10,234 | 1,663 | 717 | 69,221 | 6,925 | 1,079 |
| | 1984 | 12,698 | 4,361 | 2,485 | 71,396 | 18,868 | 2,223 |
| United | 1975 | 88,990 | 17,560 | 8,040 | 53,520 | 18,400 | 3,130 |
| States | 1980 | 78,246 | 13,829 | 7,587 | 90,121 | 20,927 | 2,813 |
| Britain | 1974 | 11,878 | 1,719 | 2,241 | 6,897 | 2,092 | 1,043 |
| | 1981 | 20,151 | 5,056 | | 14,616 | 3,416 | |
| West | 1974 | 5,839 | | 2,258 | 20,972 | | 801 |
| Germany | 1982 | 6,387 | | 2,427 | 6,551 | | 919 |

Source: Ministry of Education, *Kyoiku Shihyo no Kokusai Hikaku* (International Comparison of Education Indicators), 1978, 1985.

The second kind of datum used to support the general image of Japan's R&D as essentially imitative concerns the use made of technology that has been generated elsewhere. The amount of technology imported by Japanese firms from European and U.S. companies remains high even today. On the other hand, the number of patent applications from Japanese firms— not only in Japan but also in the United States—has grown enormously in recent years. Nevertheless, these two sets of factors, the supply of technical graduates and the flow of trade in fundamental technologies, are taken as evidence that the most vigorous R&D activities of Japanese firms are tied to commercialization.

To date, research on the relatively low basic expenditures of Japanese firms and their growing expenditures on the application and development stages has stopped at demonstrating the differences between Japanese firms and their U.S. and European counterparts. Little has been done to try to explain, in economic terms, the underlying reasons. The purpose of this chapter is to raise some questions about the commonly drawn contrast between Japanese and Western firms and to reexamine the structure of R&D in Japanese companies. It goes without saying that the structure and behavior of the firm is influenced by the social and economic conditions around it. This analysis therefore extends beyond the firm itself to examine conditions in the external environment.

Section 8.1 discusses technological backwardness and the structure of the social system as factors producing distinctive features in Japanese firm-level R&D. Section 8.2 lays out some of the characteristic organizational principles in the R&D divisions of Japanese firms by which the allocation of

R&D funding and the distinctive career paths of researchers have been managed and that have in turn given rise to unique structures and processes in Japanese R&D. Section 8.3 shows that the Japanese industrial R&D system is not solely a product of firm-level behavior but has also been influenced by government R&D policies. Section 8.4 disusses the functions performed by cooperative research in supporting the R&D systems of Japanese firms. Finally, the last section discusses the potential limitations that the current structures and processes of R&D divisions impose on the efforts of Japanese companies to increase the creativity of their R&D.

## 8.1   The External Environment and Characteristics of R&D

Japanese firms in the past have originated relatively few new product concepts. Far more commonly, they have demonstrated an outstanding capacity to absorb and impove something whose basic product concept has already been developed somewhere outside the firm. The mindset underlying this behavior is an orientation toward improving products to fit the needs of users in the market and devising ways to realize greater efficiencies in the manufacturing process. In these repects Japanese companies have exhibited outstanding capabilities. They have invested their financial and human resources in technology development that enables them to absorb technology from overseas very rapidly, to improve on it, to generate additional technical innovations for commercialization, and to achieve success in competition in the marketplace.[3] Yet even today, the extent to which Japanese companies depend on foreign technology is high: In the very advanced technology fields a considerable amount of technology continues to be imported.

The traditional explanation for this dependency has been the technological backwardness of Japanese firms compared to their Western counterparts. Being technologically backward, they had not developed the stock of technology to enable them to develop products independently. The disparity in technology levels compared with Western firms produced a backlog of exploitable technology that Japanese firms came to use aggressively. But rather than viewing the technology gap as a disparity between firms, we should see it as a difference in the technology level of entire nations.[4]

---

3. See Rosenberg and Steinmuller (1988).
4. See Ohkawa and Rosovsky (1981).

**Table 8.2**
R&D investment and technology imports in (¥billion, %)

| Year | R&D investment (a) | Technology imports (b) | b/a |
|---|---|---|---|
| 1971 | 895 | 134.5 | 15.02 |
| 1975 | 1,684.8 | 169.1 | 10.04 |
| 1980 | 3,142.3 | 239.5 | 7.62 |
| 1985 | 5,939.9 | 293.2 | 4.94 |

Source: Office of the Prime Minister, *Kagaku Gijutsu Kenkyu Chosa Hokoku* (Science and Technology Research Survey Report).

As table 8.2 shows, in the 1970s the amount that Japanese firms paid for technology imports was a relatively large proportion of their total R&D expenditures. Even today the greater part of their technology imports involves bringing in the technological knowledge of U.S. and European firms.

Since Japanese firms conducted R&D on the same technologies already existing overseas, they could not attain the profits accruing to the first comers, and the costs were extremely high. On the other hand, to the extent that firms can absorb them, technology imports provide technical knowledge with a certainty and predictability not matched by autonomous research. Studying success already achieved is the most efficient method of technological learning. Moreover Japanese firms are also equipped with the necessary conditions for actively using technology imports. The educational system provides an abundant supply of human resources with the capacity to learn from and absorb the best of foreign technical knowledge. This supply of human resources makes it possible for companies to import technology, to carry out incremental R&D and modify it to suit their production lines, and to manufacture higher quality products. Nevertheless, an explanation that builds only on a theory of technological backwardness will not hold up for the recent R&D patterns of Japanese firms: In many fields Japanese companies have drawn even with or surpassed their Western counterparts in terms of technological level.

Developing countries have always depended on the technological knowledge of more advanced countries. At one time U.S. firms depended on European technology; today the developing countries of Asia are heavily dependent on the technological knowledge of U.S. and Japanese firms. One interpretation of this phenomenon is that it indicates a sequential broadening of the R&D system: Only when applied and developmental technology has been accumulated does R&D begin to extend into basic research. Thus, according to Itami (1987):

Original and advanced technology is like the tip of an iceberg, of which the underlying mass is production technology, applied technology, the capacity for improvement, and the detailed know-how accumulated in the workplace. To date, much of Japan's stock of technology has involved building up the iceberg below the waterline. Just as the size of the iceberg's tip is determined by its mass below the water, unless you first build up the stock of technology produced by "sweat-stained workers," you cannot develop the technology of the white-coated scientists.

However, although the technology level of Japanese companies has risen and their technology stock deepened, a "natural"extension into basic R&D has not really occurred. Recent increases in R&D spending by Japanese firms have been dramatic, but it is difficult to assert convincingly that the focus of that spending has shifted to basic research. At most we can identify "targeted basic research"—a concept midway between basic research and established technology development for manufacturing—but that is as far as the enhanced R&D expenditures seem to go.

## Social Conditions

In addition to differing technology levels, another viewpoint contends that compared to the United States and Europe, Japanese society is poorly disposed to value originality and has a social environment that strongly supports the adoption of external models.[5] Where the most advantageous strategy is absorbing externally derived technology, the process works most smoothly when the rights to technology are kept as vague as possible, and therefore the society's protection of technology of necessity remains at a fairly low level. Because technical information is externally derived, and to the extent that systemic conditions allowing high monopoly profits from technical information are absent, the rate of profit from technology remains low. In such cases no one is willing to invest financial and human resources in creative R&D.

A number of technical processes are required before the ideas generated from research and development become concrete commercial products. Ultimately profits may be produced beyond those that accrue from the creation of original ideas. Moreover, the closer the commercialization phase, the greater is the potential of generating monopoly profits though these technical processes. In other words, the economic value of technical processes can be greater than that of creative ideas. It is hardly surprising

---

5. See, for example, the article entitled, "An American Views Japan's Copycat Culture" in the *Wall Street Journal*, July 15, 1988.

then that firms would specialize in R&D focused on processes that generate high profits and eschew basic R&D that generates original ideas.

This tendency is enhanced when the social system is organized to encourage technology followership. Japan's patent system is one example. Long after Japan's patent system was established (in the Meiji period), formal product patents were not recognized; the legal system did not recognize intellectual property in ideas for products. Indeed such patents have only been granted since 1975. Instead of developing original product ideas, it was more advantageous for firms to do research on how to manufacture products efficiently, and Japan maintained a system that recognized property rights in production techniques (the "utility model"system) even if it did not recognize "newness" in inventions.

The hallmark of Japanese firms has therefore been that instead of investing their financial and human resources in basic research fields, they have put most of their resources into the commercialization phases. A convincing case can be made that this trait has been shaped by material and social conditions, supported by the economic principle that firms will decide how to allocate R&D resources according to the rates of return on R&D.[6]

The Followership Explanation

If the distinctive characteristics of R&D in Japanese firms were determined only by the relatively low level of technology of past years and by a social system and environment that made the adoption of externally generated technology models acceptable, we would expect Japanese R&D activities to come to resemble those of U.S. and European firms as those conditions changed over time.

As previously stated, the technology level of Japanese firms is approaching that of their Western counterparts. Indeed the amounts of money invested in R&D are comparable to Western firms, and Japanese firms now have an advantage in terms of product development. The notion that Japanese firms have no surplus to allocate to basic research because their

---

6. Mansfield (1988) distinguished between basic and applied R&D activities and measured the rates of return on R&D expenditures in each stage. According to his study, in contrast to the high rates of return on basic research in U.S. firms, Japanese firms enjoyed high returns on applied research. Based on his measurements, he concluded that U.S. firms excel in basic research and Japanese firms in applied R&D. If we concede, provisionally, that there are large differences in rates of return between basic and applied R&D, however, we would expect that in the future each side would reallocate financial and human resources, equalizing the two. We would expect the subsequent rates of return to become equal, in accordance with the allocation of R&D resources.

expenditures on R&D are low overall is no longer convincing.[7] And over a decade has passed since Japan's patent system was revised to recognize product patents. Yet although these objective conditions under which Japanese companies operate no longer differ significantly from those of U.S. and European firms, the distinctive features of R&D in Japanese firms have not changed very much. Even today Japanese R&D continues to focus on product development to meet market needs and to import basic technology from abroad. The traditional explanations for the engineering-based, commercialization-oriented R&D of Japanese firms are no longer acceptable.

To develop a more convincing theory, let us therefore turn our attention to the structure and principles of conduct of R&D divisions within Japan's firms and the modes of activity of those engaged in R&D.

## 8.2 The Structure and Norms of the R&D Division

Structural Linkages within the Firm

The division charged with the responsibility for research and development stands with the manufacturing divisions that actually make the products and the marketing and sales divisions that sell them as the key functional units within the firm. The content of R&D is influenced by the relationships the R&D division maintains with the other functional divisions and by the role it is expected to play within the firm as a whole.

A firm's R&D division does not simply try to maximize its own direct earnings through royalties on its patents and revenues from the applications of its technical know-how; it also aims to cooperate with other divisions and maximize the total sales and profits of the firm as a whole. Like other divisions, R&D is integrated into the goals that more or less unify the entire firm, and compared to U.S. and European firms, in Japanese firms the linkages that the R&D division maintains with manufacturing and sales are close. It goes without saying that the R&D division is expected to develop new products and generate new technology. The R&D divisions of Japanese firms not only work independently to achieve these goals, they also engage in dense information exchange with related business divisions to develop systems that can achieve their targets as efficiently as possible.

---

7. National statistics indicate that the ratio of R&D spending to total sales for Japanese firms differs little from that of U.S. and European companies. For example, the average ratios for manufacturing firms were 2.9 percent in Japan (1986), 2.6 percent for the United States (1984), 3.2 percent for West Germany (1983), and 3.4 percent for France (1982).

| All industries (N = 384) (includes "others") | Researchers (46.9%) | Business departments (40.4%) | Production departments (2.1%) | Other (10.0%) |
|---|---|---|---|---|
| Machines (109) | (44.0%) | (44.0%) | (0.9%) | (11.0%) |
| Electric/Electronics (65) | (49.2%) | (44.6%) | (6.2%) | (6.2%) |
| Chemicals (63) | (44.4%) | (46.0%) | (9.5%) | (9.5%) |
| Metal (29) | (31.0%) | (62.1%) | (6.9%) | (6.9%) |
| Public (37) | (55.6%) | (29.6%) | (14.8%) | (14.8%) |
| Construction (48) | (47.9%) | (27.1%) | (10.4%) | (14.6%) |

**Figure 8.1**
R&D project proposals. Source: Sakakura (1988).

| All industries (N = 385) (includes "others") | Within R&D (43.9%) | Within overall organization (34.5%) | Seed (creating) (10.9%) | Seed (raising) (7.0%) | Other (3.6%) |
|---|---|---|---|---|---|
| Machines (110) | (36.4%) | (35.5%) | (12.7%) | (11.8%) | (3.6%) |
| Electric/Electronics (65) | (36.2%) | (33.8%) | (13.8%) | (4.6%) | (1.5%) |
| Chemicals (63) | (36.5%) | (42.9%) | (14.3%) | (4.8%) | (1.6%) |
| Metal (29) | (37.9%) | (51.7%) | (3.4%) | (3.4%) | (3.4%) |
| Public (28) | (75.0%) | (75.0%) | (3.6%) | (3.6%) | (3.6%) |
| Construction (48) | (43.8%) | (41.7%) | (6.3%) | (4.2%) | (4.2%) |

**Figure 8.2**
R&D needs. Source: Sakakura (1988).

The depth of the structural relationship between R&D and the other functions is attested to by questionnaire data on the initiative of various divisions in the selection of research projects. Sakakura (1988) found that 40 percent of the proposals for R&D projects in the companies in his sample were generated by business divisions, compared with 47 percent proposed by the researchers themselves (figure 8.1). The same study found that only 44 percent of the projects were driven by the needs of the R&D division itself; the rest reflected the needs of the company as a whole (figure 8.2). In addition a study by Mansfield (1988) found that in U.S. firms many of the R&D projects were decided on the initiative of the R&D division, whereas in Japan more were undertaken on the initiative of manufacturing or sales divisions (table 8.3).

Flexible Allocation of R&D Funding

Close interrelationships between R&D and the business divisions are sup- ported by the system of R&D fund allocation, which clearly reflects the

**Table 8.3**
Sources of R&D projects in Japan and the United States, 1985 (in %)

| Industry/ country | Percentage of R&D projects suggested by | | | |
|---|---|---|---|---|
| | R&D | Marketing | Production | Customers |
| **Total** | | | | |
| Japan | 47 | 18 | 15 | 15 |
| United States | 58 | 21 | 9 | 9 |
| **Chemicals** | | | | |
| Japan | 49 | 23 | 15 | 3 |
| United States | 45 | 25 | 14 | 8 |
| **Electrical** | | | | |
| Japan | 47 | 21 | 5 | 27 |
| United States | 90 | 7 | 1 | 1 |
| **General machinery** | | | | |
| Japan | 44 | 22 | 11 | 20 |
| United States | 56 | 21 | 4 | 18 |
| **Autos, instruments** | | | | |
| Japan | 48 | 8 | 26 | 13 |
| United States | 51 | 25 | 12 | 11 |

Source: Mansfield (1988).
Note: Sample size included 100 firms: 26 in chemicals, 20 in electric machines, 26 in general machines, 28 in transport and precision machines.

strategic intent of the manufacturing and marketing organization. Within the firm, expenditures on R&D are often classified into three categories: the R&D division's regular operating expenses, each business division's regular expenditure on product development, and the expenditures of the firm as a whole for the product development on which the long-term strategy is built. The first category—R&D operating expenses—is capital allocated by the R&D division autonomously, through its own internal decision-making processes, but this constitutes less than half the total company R&D funding. In decisions about other R&D expenditures, the strategic intent of other divisions—for example, business divisions and corporate headquarters—has a strong influence.

For this reason it is difficult to segment the structures of R&D and other divisions. The framework makes it easy for R&D funding to go primarily to activities that have a clear and concrete goal and topic, as in applied research and product development. It is a framework in which R&D funding is not rigidly assigned to the R&D division but instead is allocated flexibly and responsively in order to meet efficiently the needs of the business divisions and the headquarters, according to the firm's situation. As a result, however, the allocation of funds to basic research, which requires a lengthy time frame, may not be regarded as important.

Under this system the R&D division adopts tactics to increase the amount of its autonomously controlled R&D funding. But this involves expanding even further the R&D funding for applied research and product development. If the outputs of R&D enable the production division to realize greater production efficiencies, and the development of superior products enables the sales division to succeed in attracting more customers, the activities of the R&D division will be highly valued by other divisions. If those activities are a major support for the business divisions, greater funding may well be made available to the R&D division. Allocation of the firm's limited human and financial resources to the R&D division depends on how much it contributes to the earnings of the firm as a whole, or how much it is expected to contribute in the future.

To obtain more resources, the R&D division must therefore contribute more to other divisions. In other words, it must be sensitive to the demands that the business divisions and the headquarters make on it. As a result more and more resources may be allocated to applied research and product development, and less to basic R&D.

Career Paths of Researchers

The human resources that maintain the R&D divisions of Japanese firms are very flexibly distributed within the firm. As one observer indicates, whereas in Western firms outstanding technical graduates are seldom assigned in large numbers to the production floor, Japanese firms place a very strong emphasis on the base-level arena of activity.[8] The primacy of the *genba*—usually meaning the production floor, but literally meaning the place where the real work is done—is a principle that is also applied in R&D.

For those engaged in R&D in Japanese firms there is a clear pattern of job rotation, as follows:

First, from entry into the company through their twenties, they pass through an educational period in R&D support work (stage 1 of the career); in the first half of their thirties they grow into the tasks of the individual technologist (stage 2). From around age thirty-five to around forty, they become administrators in the first line of the R&D division in such roles as project leader, normally at the level of section head (*kacho*: stage 3). Thereafter they move away from direct R&D activities into administrative work (stage 4).[9]

8. See Moriguchi (1978).
9. For studies providing data on these patterns, see Japan Productivity Center (1985, 1987, 1988).

In stage 4 the researchers move away from the main locus of research activity, not only into R&D administration, for they might be assigned to production, product management, operations, or marketing. Staying in the R&D division throughout one's career does not equal advancement; outstanding technical people are moved into production, planning, and sales divisions to open paths for them to higher managerial status.

In addition administrators in stage 3 are sometimes assigned to production or marketing divisions. Even those still actively engaged in R&D are sometimes moved to other divisions; they experience a "spiral staircase" process of advancement that provides those who begin their employment in R&D opportunities to gain a range of information about decision making for the organization as a whole and about product planning, production, marketing, and so on.

In contrast, U.S. and European firms provide two kinds of career paths for their researchers. Researchers may continue doing research throughout their careers, or the firm may provide choices for them to move into administration or some other division, with the researchers themselves making the choice. One of the distinctive features of Japanese firms is that they have not institutionalized career paths solely within R&D.[10]

There are two explanations for the Japanese pattern. First is the low mobility across firms of those employed in R&D in Japan. To date, there is no labor market through which R&D employees move between firms in search of the locus of activity for which they are best suited. As a substitute for an external labor market, building a system that puts those employed in R&D into the most suitable workplace within the company is a rational way to raise R&D efficiency.

According to a study by the Nihon Seisansei Honbu (Japan Productivity Center 1985), R&D researchers reach their peak of productivity between the ages of 35 and 40. However, their salaries continue to rise thereafter, and this creates a gap between the actual contribution of middle-aged and older employees to R&D and the salaries they are paid. To fill that gap, moving researchers whose productivity has fallen to other business divisions is economically rational, and this is done in many Japanese firms.[11]

In contrast, Western firms provide an autonomous career path for researchers, who can choose to be employed consistently in R&D and not to

10. Tracking the career paths of researchers in certain large Japanese firms has shown that only 1 in 6 of the laboratory heads had experience only in the R&D division compared with only 8 of 21 midlevel research managers. Many had accumulated experience in such divisions as production and sales. Similar results can be seen in the career paths of many other researchers, indicating that this is a fairly general pattern.
11. Kao, for instance, openly places an upper ceiling of 40 years of age on its researchers.

be posted to a variety of functions through job rotation. Where they cannot be maintained in a research role in their firm, they can move to another firm or research institution. This makes possible an entire career path as a researcher.

The second explanation as to why a consistent research career path has not been institutionalized in Japanese firms, and why a management mode that confers high status on the research career path has not been adopted, is the way R&D is evaluated within the company. To date, basic research has not been seen to contribute significantly to company profits; it has been more advantageous to use fundamental research results from outside sources—foreign firms and foreign research institutions. The fact that the impetus within the firm to confer high status on the basic researcher is so weak has generated the distinctive career paths of the researchers in Japanese firms.

Distinctive Features of Career Paths and R&D

The Japanese career path makes it possible to maintain the close relationship between R&D and the business divisions, and it is a causal factor behind the dramatic rise in the efficiency of applied research and product development and the specialization of the R&D activities of Japanese firms in these fields. The fact that those employed in R&D in Japanese firms have virtually no option but to climb the "spiral staircase" career path promotes information sharing between R&D and the sales and production divisions, and raises the capacity for cooperation and shared problem-solving across divisions.

Given this kind of career path, there is no advantage to R&D employees in remaining solely in the R&D division. Indeed experience in many divisions is advantageous. Whatever the field, decisions about R&D strategy are generated by negotiations in the middle management class of stages 3 and 4. Because the future career paths of these middle managers lead into areas where they will personally be managing specific products—production management, product planning, and sales—they are naturally very eager to improve performance in ways that gain favorable evaluations from these areas of the company. Over and above the advantages to their own careers, a strong awareness that such improvement is important also comes into play. As a result those employed in R&D pay attention to what transpires in the market and in the production process and to what this requires of the R&D division.

Interdivisional R&D cooperation with such career paths avoids information blockages acorss organizational units and makes for efficient operations. Nonaka (chapter 11), for instance, describes a system of product development whereby the project team incorporates talented people from R&D and the business divisions to achieve development targets in a very short time frame. Statistical data show that the time from the inception of R&D to its completion is shorter in Japanese than in U.S. and European firms.[12] This could only be achieved through close relationships generated by job rotation.

Where the R&D division boasts a complete career path, as in U.S. and European firms, the researcher can accumulate R&D information over the long term, internal turnover is low, and there is considerable potential for raising the efficiency of basic research. However, horizontal contacts between R&D and other business divisions are limited, and the exchange of information between these divisions is low. As a result there is a tendency for R&D divisions to generate their R&D strategy independently.

The R&D strategy of the Japanese firm is not one in which product design reflects strong initiative from the R&D division, which is then passed along to production and sales; most R&D targets incorporate information from sales and marketing, and from the production process. R&D strategies are market oriented and strongly reflect the requirements of the production floor. Thus R&D is not of the "technology push" type but more a function of "demand pull."

### 8.3    R&D and the Impact of Public Policy

In the United States and Europe, between 20 percent and 30 percent of corporate R&D expenditure derives from the government; in the case of Japanese firms the level of government support amounts to only 2 percent.[13] This difference has probably exerted a considerable influence on the R&D systems of Japanese and Western firms. When funding is supplied by the firms themselves, they seek to generate profits from their research projects. But projects funded by the government are not necessarily linked

---

12. See Nonaka's chapter in this volume. According to a study by America's NSF (1976), the time from start of R&D to finished product is reported as 7.4 years in the United States, 6.7 in the United Kingdom, 5.6 in West Germany, and 7.3 in France compared to 3.5 in Japan.

13. The government share of the R&D expenditures of firms is 34.5 percent in the United States (1986), 17.4 percent in West Germany (1988), 23.2 percent in Britain (1985), and 22.4 percent in France. In contrast, Japan at 1.8 percent (1986) is exceptionally low. This pattern has been maintained over many years.

to commercialization or expected to increase profits. If more R&D funding had been provided for Japanese firms by the government, it may have been allocated to basic research rather than applied research and product development. In addition, because government R&D funding is given directly to the R&D division of a firm, it raises that division's status vis-à-vis the other divisions.

Japanese firms do receive favorable tax treatment for their R&D expenditure. The contribution made by these tax breaks is relatively high in Japan, compared to the role of direct government R&D subsidies. Government R&D policy in Japan is thereby tilted toward encouraging the disbursement of R&D funding based on the profit motives of the firm.[14]

## 8.4 Collaborative R&D

Supplementing Basic Research

It is very difficult to prevent R&D output from diffusing to third parties that have not incurred the associated R&D costs. A firm that develops an innovation can only capture a part of the profits that accrue from it. In consequence overall spending on R&D may be discouraged. Public policies can be adopted to avoid this shortfall through, for example, supplementing low profit rates with tax breaks and subsidies. At the same time steps can be taken to disseminate the results of R&D as widely as possible.

A contrasting approach is to build a system that protects the profits earned by the output of R&D as much as possible, recognizes patent rights on a broad scale, and encourages R&D expenditures through private initiative. However, this approach is not without its problems. As Brown (1984) indicates, it is extremely difficult to monitor with any certainty whether taxes and subsidies play any direct role in increasing R&D expenditures and thereby to decide on the appropriate levels for tax breaks and subsidies. On the other hand, if action is taken to limit the external economic effects of the output of R&D and to have profits return as much as possible to the innovating firm, the danger of monopoly arises.

If the economic externalities of technical information cannot be avoided, collaborative R&D can attempt to gather in advance several firms that appear to be capable of profiting from the innovation, in order to share the burden of costs and to internalize the so-called externalities. Because the

---

14. See Wakasugi (1986) for a detailed discussion of the influence on firms of contract research funding, R&D subsidies, favorable tax treatment, and government R&D funding.

participants collectively share the required R&D costs, the cost to any one firm ends up being lower. If the attempt succeeds, it offers an effective measure for avoiding the inadequate funding of R&D. However, the externalities of technical information vary greatly, depending on the content of the information. Institutionalizing collaborative research does not generate widespread externalities from the technical information that such research produces; the externalities are narrowly focused, limited to the firms that have participated in the joint R&D.

Originally collaborative R&D was developed in Britain and Germany and was emulated by Japan. However, a larger number of Japanese firms have succeeded in carrying out collaborative R&D than in the original countries. Joint computer-related R&D projects on VLSI, optoelectronics, the fifth-generation computer, and so on have performed quite well. Collaborative R&D has made a considerable contribution to raising the technological level of Japanese firms and generating innovation.

Japan's Antimonopoly Law has been quite tolerant of cooperative behavior in R&D. In addition the Japanese government has given positive encouragement to the implementation of collaborative R&D by providing subsidies to cooperative projects. Currently, however, the environment for U.S. and European firms has converged on both these dimensions, so it is impossible to explain the extent of collaborative R&D of Japanese firms solely on the basis of law and policy.

Collaborative R&D is itself relatively small in scale: It does not occupy a major position in the overall R&D activities of the firm. However, collaborative R&D is closely connected to the distinctive features of R&D in Japanese firms.[15] Collaborative R&D projects are not engineering-based technology developments that serve as essential elements of commercialization, nor are they centered on R&D to generate a specific product. Rather, they focus on the development of new technology and generic technologies, avoiding firm-specific technologies of product development and the production line.

In the joint R&D for very high performance computers, some of the research targets have been generic technologies in basic system design for high speed and high capacity computers, and the semiconductor logic circuits they require, and the development of generic technologies for the manufacture of memory devices; in the VLSI consortium, electron beam technology for the manufacture of semiconductor elements and generic

---

15. We will defer a detailed analysis of collaborative R&D to another occasion; here we will discuss only its relationship with the R&D organization of the firm. For a theoretical analysis, see Ito et al. (1988); for an empirical analysis, see Wakasugi (1988a, 1988b, 1988c).

technologies in large aperture single crystal growing; in cooperative research in optoelectronics, the development of materials needed in the manufacture of integrated circuits. This is neither pure basic research nor the establishment of specific product concepts, but rather middle ground between the two: generic technologies that must be worked out if the firm is to undertake commercialization. These activities also engender a shared awareness of technological issues among the firms that participate in collaborative R&D.

The level of competition among firms varies according to the arena of R&D. Because success or failure in the stage of R&D into which Japanese firms put most of their resources—R&D for commercialization—directly affects the performance of the firm, competition across companies here is fierce, and there is little ground for cooperation. In contrast, interfirm competition is not that intense at the stage of generic technologies, where the firms' input of money and people is relatively small. The scope for cooperation among firms on common technological problems is greater as the linkage with commercialization-focused R&D attenuates. To the extent that Japanese firms concentrate their allocation of financial and human resources for R&D on commercialization, their resource allocation to basic research remains relatively low, a condition under which collaborative R&D is relatively easy to establish. The fact that Japanese firms frequently engage in collaborative R&D is compatible with the fact that, compared to their U.S. and European counterparts, they have to supplement the R&D activities within the firm at the pre-commercialization stages.

Mobility of Researchers and Collaborative R&D[16]

The career path by which capable people who pass through the research track in the R&D division then advance into production, product planning, and sales divisions produces an invaluable asset for the firm: people who have a diversified knowledge of products. R&D employees who have experience in a number of areas are highly valued within the organization, and from the viewpoint of the firm, having a large number of such employees is essential for generating success in business. If people like this leave the firm, their individual value declines, and the firm loses an important assets; a disadvantage for both sides. To retain the great strength such people pro-

---

16. The following discussion draws on interviews with researchers in collaborative R&D; these interviews were conducted in the context of a research group in collaborative R&D of which the author was a member.

vide, especially in R&D close to commercialization, job rotation functions to keep them within the firm.

However, it is difficult to expect this kind of employee to succeed in basic research. Furthermore, as was pointed out above, Japanese firms have not institutionalized a separate career path to compensate for this aspect of organization. Given that they are unable to produce people suited to basic research within the firm, Japanese companies might find it necessary to bring in people with the required technical expertise from outside the firm. However, in today's R&D organization, bringing outsiders into the R&D division invites various problems: Not only are the individuals concerned not always treated well, but the practice makes it difficult to maintain job rotation within the firm.

Personnel engaged in collaborative research projects are all seconded from the companies concerned. When the project ends, they return to their respective firms. If the time frame of the project is quite long, they are replaced after three to four years by other researchers on secondment from the same company. For the firm, collaborative R&D does not interfere with internal job rotation patterns, and it makes it possible to conduct R&D beyond the boundaries of the firm.

Personnel dispatched to collaborative R&D projects often have unique talents, but some have become disengaged from the traditional mobility track. Such people may contribute outstanding research in collaborative projects, which are key contact points with the external environment. Secondment to collaborative R&D projects has been implemented in the context of the distinctive career path for researchers in Japanese firms.

The secondment of researchers is one means by which firms gain technical information. For the seconded researcher, sending back as much information on the project as possible is seen as an indicator of loyalty to the company and affects how the company evaluates his or her performance. The fact that the researchers return to their companies once the project is completed means that their technical information is transferred back to their firms. In this way collaborative research compensates for the rigidities of the internal job rotation system and the lack of interfirm mobility. In U.S. and European firms, where many able researchers change employers, collaborative R&D that requires the secondment of researchers would not have quite the same meaning.

## 8.5    Conclusion

Japanese firms have come to engage in vigorous R&D activity, but that activity has a distinctive pattern: The firms bring in basic research and technology and focus their own efforts on engineering-based technical innovations closely related to the stages of applied research and commercialization. The distinctive features of R&D in Japanese firms cannot be completely explained by technology followership—that is, by the economic advantages of incremental improvement over the development of original ideas, and by a social system organized to satisfy the requirements of followership. I have advanced the theory that the structure and activity of R&D organization are also significant.

Let me reiterate the points made so far. I have indicated that a distinctive feature of the R&D divisions of Japanese firms is that they do not strive for autonomy but instead have very close relationships with the other divisions, and together with them aim to maximize the profits of the firm as a whole. This was explained by two factors. First is the existence of a system whereby R&D funding is allocated not by the autonomous decisions of the R&D division but by flexible responses to the wishes of other divisions and the corporate headquarters. Second is the existence of a distinctive career path, whereby R&D employees are not permanently assigned to the R&D division but are subsequently posted to other divisions to rise through the "spiral staircase." These people are especially important in making R&D in Japanese firms so distinctive. As a consequence of these patterns, Japanese R&D is extremely efficient at applied research and product development and is increasingly slanted toward these areas; on the other hand, the allocation of researchers and resources to basic research remains low. The fact that compared to other countries, the government's support for R&D expenditures is relatively low and the weight of tax breaks (compared to direct subsidies) relatively large has influenced the structure of R&D within Japanese firms. Furthermore the fact that in Japan collaborative research in pre-commercialization areas is undertaken with considerable frequency signifies that there are many areas in which firms must compensate for the lack of interfirm mobility among researchers and supplement their own R&D.

However, given that R&D in Japanese firms is centered on applied research and product development, it is quite possible that these distinctive features of structure and behavior will become obstacles when firms move toward more basic research. Given that researchers reach their peak of productivity around the age of 40, but their salary levels continue to rise, offering research opportunities to young researchers and instituting job rotation beyond R&D to older researchers is a rational choice. On the other hand, basic research differs from research for product development: Success comes only by accumulating long-term research activities with an extended time horizon. This kind of research activity is difficult to carry out unless the R&D division strengthens its autonomy vis-à-vis other divisions and develops continuous research career paths within the firm.

Recently a number of firms have attempted to create such career paths, and little by little change is coming. By introducing foreigners into their R&D divisions and internationalizing their R&D facilities, Japanese firms are feeling their way toward a diversification of their internal systems. However, it will probably take a considerably long time before they really institutionalize career paths exclusively in research.

In cases where this career path is consolidated, the relationship between the researcher and the firm will change, and this will in turn bring about further changes. Researchers will become involved in R&D according to their own interests, and they will move across firms in search of a more favorable research environment. It is possible that it will become more difficult to accumulate technical knowledge within the organization and that the productivity of R&D for the firm as a whole will fall. When the two different career paths are institutionalized within Japanese firms, the structures and behavior that gave rise to the distinctive features of their R&D will begin to change. In that case differences in output and productivity between the R&D system closely linked to the production and marketing divisions and the system with a high level of autonomy will become a new topic for investigation.

# 9

# Profitability and Competitiveness

## Hiroyuki Odagiri

This chapter uses 1964 to 1982 data on large Japanese manufacturing companies to consider trends in profitability, how the level of profitability and the interfirm variance in profit rates compare with those in the United States and Britain, and what relationship corporate profits have to market structure and corporate strategies. Section 9.1 compares average levels of profitability and the interfirm variance in profit rates using data on 376 Japanese corporations, 413 U.S. corporations, and 243 British corporations. The results show that the profitability of Japanese corporations is low. Section 9.2 considers whether these are truly low levels of profitability in an economic sense or whether they are a superficial phenomenon due to the differences between accounting and true profitability. Section 9.3 looks at the implications for market competition, and in section 9.4, regression analysis is used to analyze the relationship between variation in individual Japanese corporations' profitability and growth rates, on the one hand, and variables representing market structure and corporate strategy, on the other. Section 9.5 presents concluding observations.

## 9.1 International Comparison of Profitability

Of the 458 manufacturing companies listed on the first section of the Tokyo Stock Exchange at the end of 1964, 399 companies were still listed on one of Japan's 8 stock exchanges at the end of 1982. Thus the survival rate was 87 percent. Of the 59 delisted companies, 41 were delisted due to mergers, 8 either went bankrupt or applied the Company Rehabilitation Law,[1] and 10 were delisted for other reasons. Accordingly the survival rate

In writing this chapter, I received many useful suggestions from Mamoru Aoyama and also comments from Ryutaro Komiya. I have cited conclusions from analysis carried out jointly with Hideki Yamawaki, and use British data from J. Cubbin and P. Geroski. I would like to express my deep gratitude to them.
1. These eight companies include companies such as Sanyo Special Steel Co. which suc-

reached 87 percent (339/458). By industry, the survival rate ranges from 50 percent for shipping to 100 percent for pharmaceutical and rubber products, with a median of more than 90 percent. If shipping, pulp and paper (73 percent), and steel (73 percent) are omitted, less than 10 percent of the companies went out of existence due to merger or bankruptcy.[2]

In this Japan differs greatly from the United States and Britain. According to Kuehn (1975), the survival rate of 3,566 British companies over the 13-year period from 1957 to 1969 was only 51 percent. According to Mueller (1986), the survival rate of 1,000 American companies over the 23-year period from 1950 to 1972 was 58 percent. Most of the U.S. and British companies disappeared through mergers and acquisitions (M&A). The high survival rate of Japanese companies appear to be due to the low level of M&A activity in Japan.[3]

Of the surviving 399 companies, 23 carried out major mergers; the sample used here consists of the remaining 376.[4] The ratio of after-tax profits to total assets is used as the measure of profitability.[5] To observe changes in the level of average profitability, the average profitability of the 376 companies for each year has been calculated and the secular changes graphed (figure 9.1). The average profitability of the 413 U.S. and 243

---

ceeded in rebuilding and was relisted on the stock exchange after application of the Company Rehabilitation Law.

2. Even if one looks at the 900 companies including the Tokyo Stock Exchange's Second Section, the survival rate is still 85 percent. It is unlikely then that the below-mentioned differences between Japanese and U.S. companies are due to the difference in the number of companies or the sample's bias toward large companies.

3. Elsewhere I have analyzed 243 instances of M&A of Japanese companies by Japanese companies and found a the strong relationship between the low level of M&A and internal labor market practices (Odagiri and Hase 1989).

4. The criteria used for major mergers are that capital increased by more than 30 percent or that tangible fixed assets increased by more than 100 percent. Each merger was individually checked, and some discretion was used in categorizing it. Since most of these were so-called mergers on equal terms, it was necessary to calculate the pre-merger sales and profits of both companies in order to maintain the continuity of postmerger data. In most cases these date were not available, so the companies were eliminated from the sample.

5. Total assets include liabilities, hence profit rate figures will be affected by methods of capital procurement. To avoid this, profit plus interest paid (recurring profit + interest paid − corporate tax) is used as the numerator. Return on net worth is often used in addition to return on assets as a measure of profitability. Return on sales, which is computed before capital expenses are deducted, is inappropriate since it is affected by the industry's capital intensiveness. Return on net worth (the ratio of after-interest profit to net worth) was not used for the following reason: When a corporation enters a market, it estimates the profitability it can achieve from the necessary investment (whether the capital is obtained from equity or from debt), and it will only enter the market if profitability exceeds the cost of capital obtained by the optimal method. Accordingly it appears that when corporations enter a maket, what concerns them is return on overall assets.

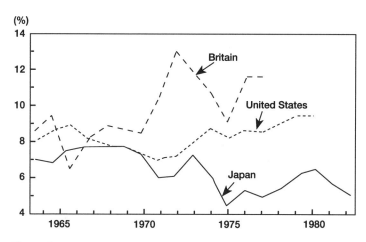

**Figure 9.1**
Average after-tax return on assets in manufacturing

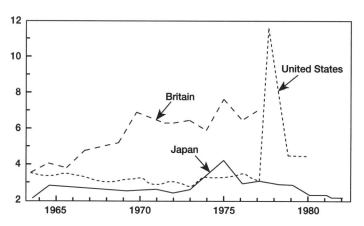

**Figure 9.2**
Standard deviation of profitability among corporations

British companies has also been graphed, but the data limit the figures for the United States to the years 1964 to 1980 and for Britain to 1964 to 1977.

According to figure 9.1, with the exception of Britain in 1966 and Japan in 1969, British companies consistently had the highest average profitability, followed by the United States, while Japan had the lowest. Over the period 1964 to 1980, the United States averaged 8.3 percent while Japan averaged 6.4 percent, a difference of almost 2 percent. Moreover this difference increased after the first oil crisis (1973–74). In fact after 1970 the profitability of U.S. companies showed a rising trend, while that of Japan fell. However, Japan's profitability gradually recovered after hitting a low point in 1975.

Next, in figure 9.2, standard deviations are plotted to allow us to look at the interfirm dispersion in each year's profitability. U.S. companies' standard deviations are higher than those of Japan, with the exceptions of 1975, and the two years 1974 and 1977 in which Japanese and the U.S. trends are almost the same. In 1975 profitability in Japan hit its lowest point due to the recession following the first oil crisis (see figure 9.1), and there were many bankruptcies such as Kojin in that year, which pushed Japan's standard deviation upward. With these exceptions the U.S. standard deviation of corporate profitability exceeds Japan's. (The reason for the unusual rise in the United States in 1978 is unclear.) The gap with Britain is even greater. The British standard deviation greatly exceeds that of the United States and Japan for the years 1964 to 1977 for which data were collected. The significance of this is considered in a later section.

Interestingly, when the correlation between average profitability and standard deviation is analyzed on a time series, in Janpan there is a negative correlation, $r = -0.48$ for 1964–82, whereas in the United States $r = 0.46$ for 1964–80 (if 1978 is omitted, $r = 0.78$) and in Britain $r = 0.10$, both positive correlations. Thus in good years, when average profitability is high, the variation in profitability among Japanese companies tends to decrease, while it tends to increase among U.S. and British companies. This is in line with the discovery of Qualls (1979) and Domowitz et al. (1986), that in the United States the effect of market concentration on price cost margins increases in periods of prosperity, and it seems to contradict the work of Wachtel and Adelsheim (1977), that to the extent that an industry is highly concentrated cost margin rates are raised in recessions. In Japan, Odagiri and Yamashita (1987) did not find a clear correlation between degree of concentration and margin rate and changes in the economy, so it is difficult to explain the above-mentioned negative correlation between distribution of corporate profitability and average profitability as a function of changes in market concentration.

## 9.2 Is Profitability of Japanese Corporations Truly Low?

As the previous section clearly showed, at least on the basis of accounting reports, average profitability of Japanese corporations is lower than that of U.S. corporations. There is a need to examine more carefully, however, if Japanese corporations' profitability is truly low.

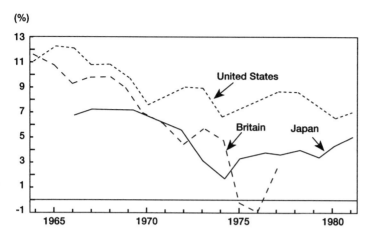

**Figure 9.3**
Real pretax return on assets for nonfinancial companies

First, since the book value of total assets is, as a rule, based on value at the time of acquisition, there is a possibility that in a period of intense inflation such as that following the first oil crisis, total assets may be understated and profitability overstated relative to total assets. It is also possible that, due to differences in the assessment of book value, international comparisons may not be accurate. To adjust for this, an international group led by Holland (1984) tried to revalue total assets at market prices and recalculate actual profits. The estimated values are shown in figure 9.3. Profits are defined as in the previous section, except that they are pretax, while total assets are valued at market value, and inventory is revalued due to price increases.[6] Also the calculation uses nonfinancial companies (except in Britain where it is manufacturing companies), so the number of companies is greater and coverage is broader than in the preceding section's analysis.

Comparison with figure 9.1 reveals a major difference. U.S. and British corporate profitability, rather than showing an upward trend, has declined.

6. They calculated actual profitability according to various definitions. Here the above-mentioned definition of profitability is used, since it fits most closely with this chapter's concept of profitability. They refer to this in their notation as ROCw (BT). After-tax profitability also is calculated for Japan and the United States, but the discussion that follows in this chapter is limited to before tax. Also Japanese profitability is calculated using the ratio of each period's profits to the preceding period's total assets. This differs from the analysis of the United States and Britain, and from the analysis of the preceding section. As a result Japan's actual profitability may register slightly higher.

Since the oil crisis, a gap between the United States and Japan in terms of profitability on market-valued assets has existed, but it is smaller than for book-valued assets. This can be attributed to the sustained inflation experienced by the United States and Britain in the latter half of the 1970s.

Another difference from figure 9.1 is that the United States and Britain reverse positions, with the United States showing the highest levels of profitability. However, there is no change in Japan's position as the least profitable (with the exception of Britain in the 1970s). Accordingly it is clear that Japan's low level of profitability in figure 9.1 cannot be explained by the difference between book and market values. In fact it is in Japan where book values based on historical acquisition costs are most common[7] and where the gap between acquisition cost and market value is the greatest. Consequently Japan's relative profitability ranking would if anything fall if recalculated on the basis of market value.

Second, the following differences in accounting rules pertain among Japan, the United States and Britain:[8] (1) In the case of depreciation Japan generally uses the fixed rate method, while the United States and Britain use the straight-line method. As a result, as long as a company grows, in Japan its expenses will appear higher and its profitability lower. (2) In inventory valuation Japanese corporations generally use average valuation, while American companies are divided between the FIFO (first in, first out) and LIFO (last in, first out) methods. Since the United States uses both FIFO and LIFO, it is difficult to say whether Japan or the United States would show higher profitability.[9] (3) Start-up costs and bond-issuing costs are treated as current expenses in Japan, while in the United States they are amortized over several years. Periods in which such expenses are rising, would tend to understate Japanese corporations' profitability.

Accordingly differences 1 and 3 would understate the profitability of Japanese corporations. However, detailed internal documents are needed to adjust for these differences, and it is very difficult to do. Choi et al. (1983) did it for 10 Japanese corporations and concluded that the profitability of Japanese corporations remained below that of American corporations even after these adjustments.

---

7. Mergers and corporate acquisitions are more common in the United States and Britain, and when these occur, corporate assets may be revalued. Also current cost accounting— which values assets at market values—has been general practice in Britain.
8. See Barrett et al. (1974), Choi et al. (1983), Nobes and Parker (1985), and Wakasugi et al. (1988, ch. 3).
9. This description relies on Wakasugi et al. (1988). Choi et al. (1983) use FIFO for the United States, in which case when inflation is higher there, United States corporations' profitability will also appear higher.

Third, profitability is affected by differences in corporate practices between Japan and the United States, as in the following four examples: (1) In Japan the reserve for employees' retirement allowances is included in liabilities as unpaid employee remuneration. U.S. corporations do not have this system. Pensions are dealt with in a separate account and do not appear as a corporate liability. This reserve would increase total assets for Japanese companies, and consequently depress returns on those assets. (2) Corporate loans for housing are common in Japan. These loans are treated as assets, like deposits, and thus raise the assets of Japanese corporations. (3) Transactions among corporations on an accounts receivable and accounts payable basis are said to be more common in Japan. This raises both assets and liabilities. (4) American corporations are said to use much off balance sheet financing. For example, when new machinery is needed, if the corporation buys it becomes an asset, while if it leases it, assets do not increase. To the extent such leases are used in the United States, assets will appear lower.

Fourth, the profitability of Japanese corporations is based on the books of the single corporation, while U.S. and British corporations use consolidated accounting. In the past few years Japanese corporations have also had to prepare consolidated accounts, so it is possible to compare unconsolidated and consolidated statements. Profits appear to increase more than assets when accounts are consolidated; accordingly returns on total assets appear higher when calculated using consolidated results.

Finally, and related to the gap between book and market value which was mentioned in point 1, profits in corporate reports does not include capital gains from holding assets. Particularly in Japan, where land and stock prices have risen so remarkably, such capital gains are very large. However, it is unclear whether corporate managers view this as an actual form of profit. Of course, if one views the corporation as belonging to the shareholders, it makes little difference whether one views land and stocks as belonging to the shareholders or to the corporation; both shareholders and managers will view these as profits. However, where the corporation is not necessarily viewed as belonging to the shareholders—as in Japan—and where assets are held in perpetuity for the survival of the company, these capital gains are seldom realized, so it is reasonable to assume that they are not treated as profits from corporate activity. Mitsubishi Estate Co.'s large land holdings in Tokyo's Marunouchi district are frequently cited as an example of this. In stocks too, particularly within enterprise groups that engage in cross-shareholding, this tendency is strong. It is doubtful that Japan's corporations consider capital gains from asset holdings when they think about profitability.

Wakasugi et al. in the above-cited Holland (1984) attempt to calculate a rate of real profitability that takes into account capital gains from holding land, equipment, and inventory as well as capital losses from holding liquid assets. The results are not conclusive; estimates of the extra profitability from asset holdings range from 0.9 to 8.7 percent over the period 1966 to 1981.[10]

The analysis above illustrates the difficulty of performing international comparisons of profitability. Section 9.1 of this chapter showed that Japanese corporations' profitability is low as measured by return on total assets. However, this section showed that most differences between Japanese and U.S. (or British) accounting understate Japanese profitability. It is difficult to speculate to what degree Japanese corporations' profitability would be raised by adjusting for these differences, but from the various analyses it appears that it would be insufficient to bridge the 2 percentage profitability gap with United States, or the more than 3 percentage gap with British, corporations.[11]

## 9.3 Market Competition and Profitability

Let us now consider the relationship between market competition and corporate profitability. According to microeconomic theory, when market entry is completely free and profits exist, corporations will enter the market, and over the long term, excess profits will sink to zero. Since excess profit is profit minus the opportunity cost of capital, this is the same as saying that zero excess profits exist when profits equal the cost of capital. If there are no barriers to entry in all markets, then as long as profitability is calculated correctly, the profitability of all corporations must be equal (condition A) and profitability equals the cost of capital (condition B).

When testing this prosposition using actual data, we must confront the problem that a long-term equilibrium may not exist. For this reason the author, with Yamawaki, has estimated long-term profitability rates from corporate time series data and analyzed whether differences among corporations persist (Odagiri and Yamawaki 1986, 1990). When the average

---

10. The difference arises according to whether assets are revalued based on price changes during the period, since profitability is calculated on the basis of the previous period's assets (see note 6).

11. The detailed data required to make adjustments on these points make international comparisons virtually impossible. Choi et al. (1983) and Ando and Auerbach (1988) have made partial adjustments. According to the former the difference between Japan and America is virtually unchanged ( Japan is lower), while Japan's lower level becomes more apparent with adjustment according to the latter.

profitability of all the companies is subtracted from the rate of profitability of each individual company, the result may be considered normalized or excess profits. Next the long-term level is estimated using a self-regression (partially adjusted) model from the normalized profitability time series. This is represented as $\pi_p$ or long-term profit. If the profitability rate calculated on the basis of accounting reports is correct, and if there are no barriers to entry (barriers to new corporations entering the market) or movement (barriers to corporations within the market moving from one position or strategy group to another), then $\pi_p$ of all corporations must equal zero.

The estimation results show that of 376 companies, 62 (16.5 percent) had a significantly positive (10 percent level two-tailed test) $\pi_p$ and 56 (14.9 percent) significantly negative. For two-thirds of the corporations the hypothesis of only average long-term profitability could not be dismissed. However, $\pi_p$ has a positive correlation ($r = 0.30$) with the profitability of each corporation in its initial period (average of 1964 and 1965). In other words, there was a tendency for corporations with initially high profitability to have high long-term profitability over the following 19 years. Thus there was continuity in profitability differentials.

Let us compare Japanese–American profitability differentials on three points. First, the correlation between $\pi_p$ and initial profitability is also positive ($r = 0.28$) in the United States, so this characteristic is shared by both Japan and the United States. Second, in the U.S. $\pi_p$ was significantly positive in 66 (16.0 percent) of 413 corporations and significantly negative in 137 (33.2 percent). Thus in about half of the cases there was a significant deviation from zero, a higher percentage than in Japan. Corporate differentials in long-term profitability are statistically more notable in the United States. Third, the standard deviation of $\pi_p$ among corporations is 1.55 in Japan and 5.21 in the United States, so the United States comes out much higher than Japan (the average value is approximately zero in both cases). The broad distribution of profitability among American corporations is not due to instability in individual corporation's profitability from year to year, but rather over time there are large and stable differences among corporations.

What do these differences between Japan and the United States mean? There are two reasons why $\pi_p$ may not be zero: (1) the difference between the accounting and economic definition of profitability and (2) barriers to entry and movement. If the corporate differential of $\pi_p$ is greater in the United States, one of these two must also be greater. The more natural hypothesis would be that the differential comes from barriers to entry and movement. This is because the sample is distributed among various industries in the manufacturing sector, and there are likely to be variations in the barriers in different industries. Even if differences in accounting could explain differences in average profitability between Japan and the United States, they can hardly explain differences within the same country.

Moreover the high degree of internalization of markets for labor and management in Japanese corporations is frequently mentioned in other chapters of this book. Since the external market for management ability, training, and know-how has not developed, it is likely that these qualities are undervalued in (accounting) remuneration relative to productive marginal value. This means that accounting profitability becomes separated from economic profitability and may be overvalued. Not only does management ability and accumulated know-how differ between companies, but the degree of separation also differs. This suggests that the disparity in accounting profitability among corporations should be greater in Japan. It supports our estimate that the equalization of profitability rates among companies (condition A at the beginning of this section) is more evident in Japan.

International comparisons of condition B, the equilibration of profitability and the cost of capital, are more difficult. First, there is the problem of international differences in accounting practices, as seen in the preceding section. Even if accounting rules differ among countries, if they are applied similarly within a country, there are few problems in international comparisons of distributions of profitability among corporations. However, differences in accounting rules will have a great impact on comparisons of profitability *levels*. It is also difficult to make international comparisons of the cost of capital. The cost of capital is the expense added per one unit of capital procured, and may be thought of as the interest rate for procurement through debt, or of the opportunity cost borne by shareholders for procurement through equity. Considering that internal retention reduces dividends, the profit rate attained from reinvesting what would originally have been shareholder dividends may be viewed as opportunity costs, or the cost of capital. Thus profit rate—return on equity—is the expected return on one unit of capital reinvested in a corporation's stock, which is an appropriate measure.

It is well known that the return on equity of Japanese corporations was (and is) higher than for American corporations.[12] On the other hand, the

---

12. Baldwin (1986) argues that the rate of return on equity is higher in Japan because risk is higher and that there is no gap between Japan and the United States if one takes the risk premium into account. However, many argue that the rate of return on Japanese equity is higher even when risk is taken into account (e.g., Solnik 1988, table 2.5).

gap between the interest rate paid on debt between the two countries is small. From this it would appear that while the cost of capital in Japan may be high, it certainly is not low. However, when we consider that not only is the interest rate paid on debt low (ignoring risk differences) in both Japan and the United States but that Japanese corporations rely more heavily on debt financing,[13] if a weighted average is calculated from the ratio of rates of return on equity and debt interest rates in overall finance, it is possible that Japan would come out with a lower cost of capital.[14] It is therefore difficult to determine whether Japan or the United States has a higher cost of capital. Holland et al. (1984) estimate the cost of capital in Japan (6.0 percent) to be slightly higher than in Britain (5.4 percent), but lower than in the United States (7.5 percent). However, the method of estimation differs by country, so there are questions about the comparability of the data.

As can be seen from the preceding arguments, it is difficult to compare the degree to which the conditions for long-term equilibria are realized. Although it is possible to surmise that profit equalization among corporations is better established in Japan than in the United States (condition A), it is difficult to make international comparisons on the equilibrium between profitability and cost of capital (condition B).

### 9.4 Regression Analysis of Profitability and Growth

Let us finally consider the relationship between corporate profitability and growth rate of sales, on the one hand, and market structure and corporate strategy, on the other, and make use of regression analysis to do so.

The normalized long-term profitability rate $\pi_p$ which was defined in section 9.3 will be used to represent profitability, while $G$, the growth rate of sales for the period 1964–82, will represent the growth rate. There are other rates, such as the growth rate of total assets, that can be used to represent growth. However, since the growth rate of sales is most important to corporate managers, and since there would not be much difference in results whichever rate is used, we will use only the growth rate of sales. Since this is a nominal growth rate of sales, it is influenced by inflation. The price effect is one reason why the nominal growth rate of industrial ship-

---

13. It isn't clear whether a gap in the ratio of debt would remain if the accounting differences, and so on, mentioned in section 9.2 were taken into account (see Kuroda and Oritani 1979).

14. See Weston and Copeland (1986) for the use of a weighted average as the cost of capital.

**Table 9.1**
Regression results on profitability and growth rates

| Dependent variables | Explanatory variables | | | | | | |
|---|---|---|---|---|---|---|---|
| | Constants | IG | AD | CR | MS | DS | $\bar{R}^2$ |
| $\pi_p$ | −2.353[a] | 0.066 | 0.167[a] | 0.019[b] | | 0.0073[c] | 0.145 |
| | (3.305) | (1.457) | (2.633) | (2.551) | | (1.777) | |
| $\pi_p$ | −2.169[a] | 0.083[c] | 0.096 | | 0.036[a] | 0.0056 | 0.175 |
| | (3.486) | (1.765) | (1.352) | | (3.290) | (1.312) | |
| G | 4.848[a] | 0.534[a] | −0.011 | 0.0064 | | 0.029[a] | 0.412 |
| | (4.774) | (8.252) | (0.122) | (0.622) | | (4.936) | |
| G | 4.928[a] | 0.532[a] | 0.070 | | 0.0080 | 0.026[a] | 0.434 |
| | (5.486) | (7.809) | (0.684) | | (0.501) | (4.247) | |

Note: Parentheses enclose the $t$-statistic (absolute value). The sample size is 100 for CR and 88 for MS.
a. Significant at 1 percent level of confidence in a two-tail test.
b. Significant at 5 percent level of confidence in a two-tail test.
c. Significant at 10 percent level of confidence in a two-tail test.

ments shows a strong (positive) effect on $G$. $\pi_p$ is used as the indicator of profitability because it has the advantage of eliminating distortions from excess profits (or excess losses) due to short-term disequilibria. The following five variables are used as explanatory variables (the source of the data is given in parentheses):

CR = concentration rate of four firms, 1964 (*Kosei torihiki iinkai*),

MS = market share, 1964 (*Toyo keizai tokei geppo*),

AD = ratio of advertising expenses to sales, 1965 (*Sangyo renkanhyo*),

IG = growth rate of industrial shipments, 1964−82 (*Kogyo tokei hyo*),

DS = diversification (into other industries) index, 1964−82 (*Kaisha nenkan*).

(The index DS = $100 \times (X_{1964} - X_{1982})/X_{1964}$, (where $X_t$ = the share of the main division in total sales in year $t$.)

It is necessary to point out that these data are incomplete in many ways: First, CR data are for only 100 companies, and MS for 88. Second, each company is treated as belonging to a particular industry, and aside from DS, the data relate to that industry. Thus errors in measurement may occur when that industry does not represent a large proportion of the company's business. Companies in which diversification has made it difficult to select the main industry, such as textile companies, have been eliminated from the sample.

Third, in addition to advertising, R&D is an important variable indicating market structure, but it is not used because often data on R&D can be imprecise or impossible to obtain. Instead, in this analysis DS is used to represent corporate strategy. Considering the importance of product and business composition strategies to corporations, DS is likely to be a good indicator of such strategy. It refers to a higher-level corporate strategy than pricing, advertising, and R&D on existing products, and cannot be decentralized, even in a divisional structure.[15]

Fourth, the analysis is carried out using the least squares method, so there is a danger in drawing conclusions about cause and effect from the results. Values for CR, MS, and AD are used around the starting point of 1964 in an attempt to avoid reverse cause and effect relationships (from profitability to market structure) from time differences.

With these caveats in mind, let us look at the results of figure 9.1. There are six principal findings : (1) $\pi_p$ is most strongly explained by CR and MS. Of the two, MS shows the strongest explanatory power. (2) AD also has a positive effect on $\pi_p$. (3) DS has a positive effect on $\pi_p$, but its significance is weak. As for G, (4) IG has the strongest explanatory power. (5) DS is also positive, with the strongest explanatory power after IG. (6) AD, CR, and MS are not statistically significant.

These findings suggest that market structure variables such as market concentration, market share, and industry advertising intensity (which show the extent of barriers to entry and product differentiation) mainly contribute to long-term profitability, while diversification (leaving the main industry), the key corporate strategy, mainly contributes to corporate growth. However, the degree of concentration rather than market share best explains profitability, and individual company characteristics are more important than overall industry characteristics.

These results suggest two conclusions about Japanese industrial organization and corporate behavior. First, if we look at corporate results in terms of profitability, it is useful to take an industrial organization approach that emphasizes structural variables such as market share and advertising. The traditional view is that the higher the market share, the greater is the concentration, and that the more differentiation through advertising, the

---

15. There is a negative correlation between DS and IG ($r = -0.61$), which shows that the more a corporation's industry is declining, the stronger the incentive to leave the main line of business. Even if diversification is a common corporate strategy, the strategic necessity varies by industry. According to regression analysis, when DS and IG are combined as the explanatory variable, the DS coefficient controls the industrial growth rate IG, and it is possible to see the influence of diversification.

more competition is lost and monopolistic profits exist and persist. However, it is dangerous to specify cause and effect relationships in this way. Demsetz's (1973) view that efficient corporations simultaneously have high market share and high profits certainly has merit.

Second, corporations appear to diversify more for growth than for profit. Marris (1964) and others have emphasized diversification as a primary means of achieving corporate growth. This applies to large Japanese corporations as well. In fact Yoshihara et al. (1981) shows that diversification has a significant positive correlation with growth, but an insignificant (negative) correlation with profitability. Their analysis of diversifying from main industries concurs very closely with the the results of this chapter. Of course, even if the relationship with profitability is negative, it is possible that growth through diversification will raise future profits and share prices, and thus contribute to shareholder profits.

## 9.5 Conclusion

The main points of this chapter were as follows:

1. Trends in the average profitability of Japanese corporations and their standard deviation using a comparatively large sample of 376 companies over the 19-year period from 1964 to 1982 were compared with U.S. and British corporations. The results show that on average American profitability is higher than Japanese profitability and that the differential between companies is also higher in the United States.

2. However, it is possible that because of difference in accounting methods, the profitability of Japanese companies, as shown in public account, is more understated relative to real profitability than is true for United States and British companies.

3. The relationship of this international comparison to competition was considered. If accounting profitability represents economic profitability and no barriers to entry or movement exist, profitability among corporations should equalize (condition A) and it should equal the cost of capital (condition B). The findings of point 1 above suggest that condition A is more established in Japan. It is difficult to reach conclusions about condition B because it is not easy to compare the cost of capital in Japan and the United States, and because of the problems in international comparisons of profitability levels (point 2).

4. A regression analysis of Japanese corporations' long-term profitability rates and rates of sales growth was carried out. It showed that the higher

the market share, the higher is the long-term profitability; on the other hand, corporate growth rate is largely related to the growth rate of the industry to which the corporation belongs and by diversification, and it is not influenced by market structure. But a lack of data makes it unclear as to how far the results of this regression analysis can be generalized. Hence the main contribution of this analysis is to stress the value of combining an industrial organization approach (emphasizing market structure) and a management strategy approach to analyze corporate behavior and results.

# 10        Plant and Equipment Investment

Yoshiyasu Ono and
Hiroshi Yoshikawa

In this chapter we study the particular features of movements in plant and equipment (fixed) investment and examine how such features have arisen. Section 10.1 begins with an overview of fixed investment during the period 1960 to 1988. In both the rapid growth period and subsequently, Japan's rate of investment was noticeably higher than that of other countries. During the "slow growth" period since the 1970s the average rate of investment actually exceeded that of the rapid growth period in real terms. In section 10.2 we analyze the factors behind the high level of investment for each of these periods from a macroeconomic perspective. In section 10.3 we consider whether the characteristics of the Japanese firm discussed previously actually encouraged this high level of investment. To the extent that a long-term vision for investment decisions, a positive attitude toward new technology from workers employed long term, and high worker morale are truly features of the Japanese company, we can say that they are also factors promoting high levels of investment.

## 10.1   Japan's Plant and Equipment Investment

Japan's rapid postwar economic growth was generated by the vigorous fixed capital investment of private firms. Greatly contributing to increases in effective demand, this investment also expanded the productive capacity of the Japanese economy. Since most new technology was embodied in capital goods, the investment was also very important for advances in technology. We will use the investment rate (investment as a proportion of GNP) in order to compare the experience of Japan's fixed investment

The authors would like to thank Ryutaro Komiya, Kenichi Imai, Tadanori Nishiyama, Ryushi Iwata, and Michio Nitta for their valuable comments during the preparation of this chapter.

**Table 10.1**
GNP and private business fixed investment selected countries in 1988 (in $100 million; %)

|  | Japan | United States | West Germany | France |
|---|---|---|---|---|
| Business fixed investment (BFI) | 4,980 | 4,884 | 1,477 | 1,053 |
| Increase in BFI since 1987 (%) | 28.2 | 9.3 | 11.1 | 13.5 |
| BFI as a share of GNP (%) | 17.4 | 10.0 | 12.2 | 11.1 |

Source: National income statistics for each country.
Note: BFI and GNP in nominal values; share of GDP is used for France.

trends with those of other countries. As shown in table 10.1, Japan's investment rate is conspicuously high. In 1988, when the exchange rate reached 128 yen to the dollar, Japan's business fixed investment surpassed that of the United States in absolute terms. Although we have used 1988 figures in table 10.1, we can also see the high rate of Japanese investment using a time series. We compare only Japan with the United States. Figure 10.1 shows both countries' private business investment as a proportion of GNP (in both nominal and real values). In both nominal and real terms Japan has had a higher investment rate than the United States for the past 30 years.

Looking at the corresponding profit rates ($P/K$ in figure 10.2), Japan's profit rates are, along with the U.S. rates, among the highest in developed countries.[1] At the end of the 1960s and especially after the first oil shock, however, they show a rapid decline. Still the share of profits in value added ($P/Y$ in figure 10.2) remains the highest of all the countries considered. Computing the capital/value-added ratios ($K/Y$), the United States, Britain, and West Germany had rates of about 0.7, 1.7, and 1.4 respectively, but Japan's rate increased from 1.3 in the rapid growth period to 2.0 in the 1970s. The drop in Japanese profit rates after the 1960s was brought on

1. International comparison of profit rates is a delicate matter, and for details of these estimates, refer to Hill (1979). Within Japan those based on the Ministry of Finance's *Corporate Statistics* on those based on the New SNA's *National Economic Estimates* show quite different movements. In the former, book value assets tend to be undervalued because of the depreciation measure used, and consequently the profit rate estimates are relatively high. In the New SNA figures assets are valued close to market value, and the unincorporated sector is included in operating surplus figures. For both of these profit rate measures, see Yoshikawa and Takeuchi (1989, fig. 6).

In Hill's (1979) estimates used in figure 10.2, Japanese interest rates are higher than U.S. rates, but with simple gross captial or sales profit rate comparisons from the *Corporate Statistics*, Japanese rates are much lower. The profit rates in figure 10.2 are calculated as net operating surplus divided by the capital stock and value added. In the *Corporate Statistics*, however, profit rates are computed as after-tax profits divided by either gross captial (net worth + liabilities) or sales (not value-added). Here, with Hill, we take Japanese profit rates as being high.

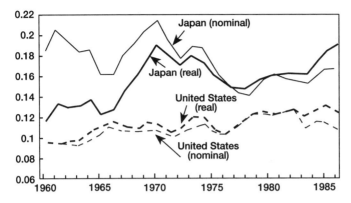

**Figure 10.1**
Fixed business investments/GNP for the private sector according to national income statistics. Source: Hill (1979).

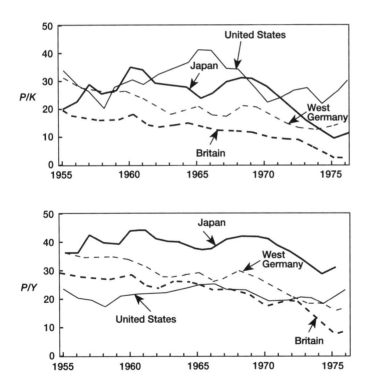

**Figure 10.2**
Profit rates. Source: Hill (1979).

**Table 10.2**
U.S. and Japanese investment averages and standard deviations (in %)

| | Japan | | | United States | | |
|---|---|---|---|---|---|---|
| | Average | Standard deviation | Coefficient of variation | Average | Standard deviation | Coefficient of variation |
| Nominal | | | | | | |
| 1960–86 | 17.0 | 2.0 | 0.118 | 10.5 | 0.9 | 0.086 |
| 1960–73 | 18.5 | 1.5 | 0.081 | 10.0 | 0.6 | 0.060 |
| 1974–86 | 15.5 | 1.1 | 0.071 | 11.1 | 0.7 | 0.063 |
| Real | | | | | | |
| 1960–86 | 15.3 | 2.1 | 0.137 | 11.0 | 0.9 | 0.082 |
| 1960–73 | 14.7 | 2.4 | 0.163 | 10.5 | 0.7 | 0.067 |
| 1974–86 | 16.0 | 1.2 | 0.075 | 11.6 | 0.7 | 0.060 |

both by the increase in the capital/value-added ratio and by the fall in the share of value added assigned to profits.

Looking next at movements in fixed investment as a share of GNP during the postwar period, we see in the standard deviations of table 10.2 that movements in the Japanese rate of investment are considerably higher than those of the United States.

From figure 10.1 it is clear that the investment rate differs considerably depending on whether the base is measured in nominal or real terms. Both series peak in 1970, but while the nominal series investment rate for 1961 approaches that of 1970, the real series is much lower. As a result the trough in 1965 is shallower in the real series than in the nominal. The difference between these two series at the beginning of the 1960s illustrates that in this period the value of investment goods was relatively high in comparison with the GNP deflator. In passing we note that in the United States there is virtually no separation between the nominal and real values.

In contrast to the 1960s, the real investment rate is higher than the nominal rate in the 1980s. If we divide the sample into two periods around 1973, the nominal investment rate falls after 1973 in comparison with its average value in the high-growth period (table 10.2), while the real rate rises. More specifically, after the common peak in 1970 both the nominal and real investment rates fall until 1977–78, and then the real series shows a remarkable recovery, reaching the level of 1970 in 1986–87. The real series indicates that the post-1970s investment rate is higher than that of the high-growth period. Comparison between the two investment rates also shows that the relative value of investment goods fell substantially over this period.

Again using 1973 as a dividing point, we can examine the coefficient of variation of the investment rate (table 10.2) and see that since the 1970s the investment rate has become much more stable. This is especially noticeable in the real series. This change is not seen in the United States.

Summing up our observations so far, the Japanese business fixed investment rate has been high in comparison with other developed countries, and the coefficient of variation in the investment rate is also high. Comparing the period after the first oil shock with the rapid growth period, investment in real terms has risen slightly, while the coefficient of variation has fallen sharply. In the 1980s we observe the continuing rapid fall in the relative value of investment goods.

## 10.2 Macroeconomic Background

In this section we will explain these movements in Japanese corporate fixed investment from a macroeconomic point of view. For ease of exposition we have divided the period into the rapid growth period and the post oil shock period as in the previous section.

The exceedingly low level of the capital stock at the beginning of the high-growth period as well as the large-scale introduction of new technology from the United States are important factors in the high rate of investment during the rapid growth period, but we believe that the most important factor was the high rate of growth in effective domestic demand.[2] Of course investment itself is one component of domestic demand, but it is the rapid growth in the demand for a wide range of consumer goods, especially durables, that lies behind the high levels of investment. Behind the rapid growth in demand for consumer goods were such factors as (1) a rapid increase in the number of households (exceeding the rate of population increase) created by the migration accompanying urbanization and industrialization and (2) technological innovation and increased labor

---

2. There has been much debate over the role played by external demand (exports) during the rapid growth period. Exports were naturally important in the sense that they financed the imports of essential raw materials, but it would not be appropriate to say that exports led domestic growth during the rapid growth period. For example, the correlation between the index of industrial production and exports (using quarterly data) for 1960 (III) to 1971 (IV) is −0.41, for 1972 (I)−1985 (IV) is +0.56. Again, looking at the contribution of external demand to real GNP growth, we find that it is −8.3 percent on average during 1963−73, +17.8 percent during 1976−84, and finally +40.2 percent during 1980−84. (Exports during the rapid growth period, however, sustained the economy in bad times through "export drives.") It is only since the latter half of the 1970s that external demand actually pulled economic growth.

productivity, leading to increased incomes *and* lower costs so that consumer durables became more affordable.

This macroeconomic mechanism was evident during the rapid growth period, but we should also note that the investment movements of many industries were synchronized. The correlation coefficients of industry rates of change in investment are mostly positive (Yoshikawa and Ohtake 1987). This high degree of correlation in investment provides a good explanation for the high volatility of investment rates mentioned in the previous section.

This mechanism promoting rapid growth ceased to function after 1970, principally because of the rise in ownership of consumer durables produced with preexisting technology, as well as the drying up of the pool of surplus population of rural villages. The turning point preceded the first oil shock and was brought on by changes in domestic economic conditions.

Despite the fact that the real GNP growth rate fell from 10 percent in the rapid growth period to 4 percent from the mid-1970s, the investment rate measured in real terms barely fell at all. The principal factors explaining this are (1) energy- and labor-saving investment induced by the increase in labor and energy costs,[3] (2) technological innovation based on microprocessor technology in the 1980s, and (3) the large drop in the relative price of investment goods over this period, as explained in the previous section.

Looking at movements in investment by industry from the 1970s, we see that in contrast to the rapid growth period they are fairly desynchronized. In most cases the interindustry correlation coefficients are zero or negative. This indicates that investment in any given industry was more strongly influenced by industry-specific microeconomic factors than by the macroeconomy. Desynchronization also leads to the stabilization of macroeconomic investment rates.

We have now explained some of the stylized facts about fixed investment from the macroeconomic perspective. Macroeconomic mechanisms existed in the rapid growth period to give rise to a rapid growth in— primarily domestic—effective demand. This is the principal factor behind high levels of investment in the first period. This mechanism disappeared after the early 1970s but the rise in the real price of factors of production, the fall in the real price of investment goods, and technological innovation centering on semiconductors kept the levels of investment high.

---

3. Rises in real wages or in the cost of energy induce an increase in investment as changes in factor prices shift the equilibrium to a more capital-intensive point along the production isoquant (see Yoshikawa and Takeuchi 1989).

## 10.3   Microeconomic Factors in High Levels of Investment

Compared to American firms, Japanese firms are characterized by greater managerial control (shareholders' rights to manage are only nominal), and related to this, a distinctive employment system. Many studies have indicated that in Japanese firms, the formal corporate system with shareholder control should not taken at face value (Nishiyama 1981, 1983; Aoki 1984; Komiya 1988a, b). According to Nishiyama (1981), for example, in most cases the wishes of managers take precedence, even over the wishes of the principal shareholder. Rather than being simple representatives of the interests of shareholders, managers act instead as representatives of the interests of the employees. They will fight off "threats" from people cornering their company stocks as in the cases of Takashimaya stocks cornered by Daiei's Nakauchi Isao, Miyaji Steel Works stock by the Seibi Group, and Katakura Industries Stock by Wang Zeng Xiang, a Hong-Kong businessman (ibid.). A recent example is the strong resistance T. Boone Pickens met with from the management of Koito Manufacturing when he acquired their company's stock, leading him to ask "What *is* a stockholder in Japan, anyway?" (*Nihon Keizai Shinbun*, April 8, 1989). Even in the selection of top management, the views of the managers carry more weight than those of the shareholders. As examples Nishiyama cites the shares of the Kawakami family failing to secure control at Japan Musical Instruments, and more recently those of the Anzai family failing to secure the company presidency at Tokyo Gas. Such thoroughgoing separation of ownership and control allows managers to aim for the long run development of the company rather than short term dividends, while at the same time it complements the long-term employment system. For individual workers as well, the firm is not simply a place to sell labor services; rather, it is thought of as the foundation for their lives, and the firm's development is seen as being tied up with their own betterment.[4] Finally, the firm's own objective is not the simple maximization of stock value, since it also takes account of the payment levels for the workers. We will now take a critical look at each of these points in turn from the standpoint of various microeconomic theories and consider whether they give rise to high levels of investment.

---

4. As Matsumoto (1983, 213) explains, "Japanese people generally do not have the sense that labor is something 'sold' to a firm, but rather think of work as something that one actively 'contributes.'" This in turn gives workers a long-run perspective that raises motivation and fosters a positive attitude toward the introduction of new technology.

The Long-Term View and High Levels of Investment

It is often said that Japanese firms take a long-term view in comparison with those in other countries. The Nikkei Newspaper's *Nihon no Kaisha* (The Japanese Company), for instance, argues as follows:

A characteristic feature of Japanese executive directors is that they are young and not owners of the company. This opens the way for a long-term perspective that favors growth through sales expansion rather than profit maximization. This long-term orientation originated with the onset of the era of the salaried director and the management specialist. It corresponded with the need for redevelopment of the Japanese economy from the ground up after the Second World War, and laid the basis for subsequent transition from postwar recovery to rapid growth.

Of course this long-term orientation does not mean that the short-term view is absent in Japanese companies, nor that Japanese companies pursue expansion with complete disregard for profits. It is clear, however, that in comparison with the American firm's profit-oriented management, Japanese companies aim for long-run growth. A questionnaire-based survey of Japanese and U.S. companies by Kagono et al. (1983, 28) found that "in comparison with Japanese firms, American firms show great agility in making acquisitions and withdrawing from loss-making activities. Their strategy is to raise the efficiency of resource allocation in the short run rather than saving resources over the long run." Using a similar survey, the Research Committee into Company Activities (1988) found a significant difference between Japanese and US companies with respect to new business ventures. Figure 10.3 illustrates the long-term strategic stance of Japanese firms, and the demand for high dividends by stockholders of American firms which leads to managerial concern with cash flow in the short run. Cognizant of this, then U.S. Treasury Secretary James Brady examined the possibility of corrective policies through the tax system (*Japan Economic Journal*, January 4, 1989).

Nevertheless, if we assume that capital markets are perfectly competitive in the sense that every firm can borrow any amount at the going interest rate, then even if stockholders take a short-term view placing emphasis on dividends, it is still possible for the firm to both invest for the long-term and pay high dividends by borrowing on the capital market to compensate for the lower cash flow that the increase in investment causes over the short run. Accordingly the claim that high dividends interfere with investment assumes that capital markets are imperfect, and that through limitations on borrowing or new stock issues it is not possible to fund both dividends and investment. This does not seem, however, to have been

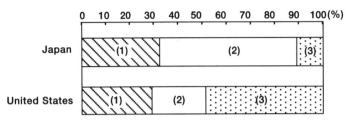

(1) Will start new business as long as there is no prospect
of medium- to long-term losses
(2) Will start new business as long as the medium- to
long-term rate of return is at least as high as company
average
(3) Will start new business if the rate of return is above
average from the very start

**Figure 10.3**
Attitudes toward new business ventures and profitability. Source: Research Committee into
Company Activities (1988).

thoroughly looked into by those who argue that institutional investors'
concern with high dividends impedes investment.

For there to be no contradiction between the shareholder taking a short-
term view and the firm making investments using a long-term view, we
must assume perfect foresight in addition to perfect capital markets mentioned earlier. This of course is unrealistic. Only management can be well
informed on such matters as the actual form of labor-management relations and personnal decisions, new product development, the rationalization and diversification of products, complex accounting procedures, and
active marketing in a volatile environment. On the basis of this knowledge
they, the managers, draw up a consistent managment plan for a set planning period and this gives the firm its character, its identity. It is an over
simplification to say that American managers forced to heed the wishes of
shareholders with short-term concerns must therefore take a short planning
period. The difference in planning period is, rather, a difference in style of
entrepreneurship.

The longer the planning period, the longer the assessment period for
future profitability of an investment and, it may be argued, the more this
raises profitability and promotes investment. Accordingly the probability
increases of carrying out fixed investment that requires a long period to be
profitable. This is one factor enabling the pursuit of investment in basic
research or in mass production for overseas markets (assuming that marketing abroad requires a longer planning horizon than domestic marketing).

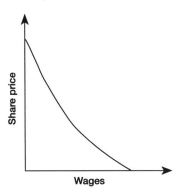

**Figure 10.4**
Share price and wages curve

It is difficult to show empirically that Japanese firms have longer planning periods than firms of other countries, although there is much circumstantial evidence. Here we have been referring to the characteristics of the average Japanese firm. Naturally there are many exceptions among individual firms. For example, it is well known that Dupont and IBM put great effort into basic research for products that are planned for the distant future. In the paper industry Canadian and Swedish firms plant trees looking 100 and 200 years into the future, whereas Japanese firms tend to be interested only in buying timber where it is available now.

Differences in Corporate Objectives

Next we ask whether we can explain differences in the investment rate from differences in corporate objectives, originating in differences between owner-controlled and manager-controlled firms. In the usual theory of the firm, the optimal choice is an investment plan that yields the maximum value, taking wage rates as set externally. Figure 10.4 (from Aoki 1984, 125) depicts a downward-sloping share-price/wage frontier given by optimal investment strategies. The curve indicates the highest achievable combinations of stock prices and wages for a given firm. The level of investment will be lower to the extent that the firm favors the interests of the worker, and that it chooses a point with a higher wage rate. The higher a firm weighs workers' interests, the lower the level of investment will be. If Japanese firms are labor-controlled in this sense, then their investment rates ought to be low. There is no explanation here for high levels of investment.

Perhaps the answer is that managerial control and the long-term employment system in Japanese firms serve to raise efficiency in production, investment, and use of labor, rather than to alter the firms' objectives. We examine this possibility next.

## The Cost of Adjusting Investment

The long-term empolyment system is another characteristic of Japanese firms, with low interfirm and high intrafirm mobility for both blue-collar and white-collar workers (Koike 1981, 35–38). In contrast to the job-specific form of employment where one chooses an occupation and assumes the costs of learning the necessary skills oneself, in Japan occupations are not thought of so rigidly, and adjustments are made through on-the-job training (OJT). The fact that business schools are not regarded as highly as in the United States, and that many Japanese business school students are sent by their companies, is a reflection of this. In the United States, where the improvement of work-related skills is viewed as the individual's responsibility, the business school functions as an important means of making oneself more salable in the executive market. In reality business school graduates tend to jump to high positions, but in Japan academic qualifications tend to have little direct connection to one's work and are taken as an indicator of latent ability. Work ability is thought to come from experience and education (including OJT) within the firm. Since the business school is not a substitute for education within the firm, its importance is not as great.

Furthermore, owing to high occupational mobility within the firm, employees' sense of identity with the firm is stronger, and present jobs are relatively less important to their sense of self, given that they might be doing a very different job in the future. The response to the question "What do you do?" is usually "I work for Company X" rather than "I am an (engineer)."

Even if an occupation is eliminated through the introduction of new technology, workers engaged in the occupation will not become unemployed as a direct consequence. Through job rotation and OJT they will be able to keep their jobs. As a result workers come to think of the betterment of their own lives as being directly tied up with the company's development. In the owner-controlled firm, on the other hand, the worker is seen as separate from the firm, selling labor to it on the basis of a contract. As agents of the owner's interests, managers will likely deem it advantageous to fire unnecessary workers and hire new workers who have the necessary skills, rather than retraining workers who may then move to another firm immediately after learning the new skills. It is only natural that workers resist the introduction of new technologies that may lead to their dismissal.

Investment aimed at improving production efficiency has thus tended to proceed relatively smoothly in Japan in comparison with the West. For example, automation in newspaper printing was accepted relatively smoothly at all of Japan's newspapers, while in Britain there were lengthy strikes by the typesetters, as at *The Times*. Adjustment costs of investment are therefore lower in Japan, and when the adjustment costs are lower, levels of investment will be higher.

## Competition within the Firm and Incentives

As argued above, in Japan workers tend to aim for the development of the enterprise. This is encouraged by competition among workers within the firm, generated by the *nenko* wage and promotion system. In the past it was thought that the *nenko* system paid wages for long tenure regardless of ability and effort. Recognition has spread, however, that it does in fact provide incentives and promotes the most competent: "The *nenko* wage system is definitely not a standard seniority system (with the exception of the immediate postwar period), and merit raises are incorporated.... Where job evaluations are incorporated into the system, in reality individual wages are determined by individuals' abilities and achievements" (Sekiya 1974, 38–88).

Payments according to age or seniority are only one part of the actual wages. Components are not always explicit, and performance evaluations enter into the calculation (Koike 1981, 55). In addition to high motivation from the lifetime employment and *nenko* wage and promotion systems, "Japanese-style" management is also said to foster greater competition than is found even in "competitive" U.S. society (Iwata 1977, 145–46). This kind of competition system has been established for certain white-collar workers in the West.[5] In most unionized U.S. workplaces, however, pay for job content is the general rule and wages for different jobs are set horizontally across workplaces in a setting of industrial and occupational unionism. Promotion to higher-paid jobs is based on seniority at the workplace. By contrast, an outstanding characteristic of the Japanese workplace

---

5. Ishida (1988, 21), for instance, reports that in Britain the salaries of the managerial class are greatly influenced by performance evaluations.

is that for both blue-collar and white-collar workers a competitive evaluation-based system has been established (Koike 1981). Accordingly, we can say that an effective incentive system for blue-collar workers has become a major feature of the Japanese firm.

Solow (1979) and others offer the theory of efficiency wages which focuses on how the wage system is used to raise the efficiency of labor. This theory hypothesizes that a worker's efficiency rises or falls with the level of wage payments. If one uses the wage that maximizes net profits (known as the efficiency wage), the marginal efficiency of capital will rise above that obtainable at any nonefficient wage rate. Since the marginal efficiency of capital and the optimal investment rate are positively related, the investment rate will also be maximized under a wage system that maximizes the marginal efficiency of capital. Since the efficiency wage is set at a higher level than the market wage, both wages and investment rates will then increase together. This result is opposite to that of the model mentioned earlier where the investment rate falls the more firms try to raise the level of workers' wages, and seems to be more in keeping with the features of the Japanese firm. It is unclear, however, whether existing theories of efficiency wages are actually applicable to Japanese firms.

Under the long-term employment system, both white- and blue-collar workers are concerned with maximizing their advancement within the firm. Evaluation results are particularly significant to workers of the same rank. Competition is mainly over relative wages, not the absolute amount of wages. This is not entirely in keeping with the efficiency wage theory where high wages in and of themselves elicit worker efficiency. Competition is maintained over a long period since the accumulation of even very small advantages over fellow workers is connected to advancement. A single success is not decisive, and the competition is repeated for each year's wage determination. Moreover in firms in which employees spend the better part of their waking lives, success in these competitions tends to go to people who are generally seen by their colleagues as all-around first-rate people. One's standing in the competition plays an important part in one's sense of self (see Iwata 1977).

Long-term competition that motivates workers may not be in strict accord with efficiency wage theory, but there is a definite accompanying rise in labor efficiency. The marginal productivity of capital is raised, making investment more profitable. As a result the investment levels are higher for any given interest rate.

In this chapter we have examined the microeconomic grounds for the high investment rate of Japanese firms. We identified three contributing factors: (1) a long-term view of investment decisions, (2) worker receptiveness to the introduction of new technology under a long-term employment system with high intrafirm mobility, and (3) high worker incentives. We also found that the tendency toward worker control and low dividend rates do not necessarily raise investment levels.

# 11      Product Development and Innovation

Ikujiro Nonaka

Innovation is a product of inevitability and chance, an outcome of continuity and discontinuity. It is not just produced from a planned distribution of resources with clearly defined targets: It often emerges discontinuously from chance or uncertain circumstances. Quite often information generated in product development leads to innovations not initially intended.

Most studies of innovation have focused on its continuity and inevitability, assuming a "problem-solving" or "information-processing" model (e.g., Allen 1966; Marquis 1969). According to these models the process of innovation starts with the setting of targets relating to the type and the standard of the product to be made, namely by defining the problem. Once the problem is set up, the most effective and efficient means is found to process and solve it. Innovation emerges from the processes of information processing and problem solving. According to this approach knowledge is retained by the problem solver who searches for related circumstances in order to obtain the necessary information. In finding a solution, the problem solver follows a well-defined algorithm (Simon 1979).

Such an information-processing perspective might explain the repetitive or routine aspects of organizational phenomena that are based on settled rules. However, it cannot explain new forms created from nonroutine (chaos) situations. It might provide a meaningful perspective from which to observe the process of innovation when chance and discontinuity are external to the organization and beyond its control. However, it is not adequate for capturing the dynamism of the innovation process in the Japanese case. This is because new problems tend to be generated from nonroutine (chaos) situations as innovation occurs. In other words, the notion of chaos is important in the *creation* of information or knowledge.

Innovation in Japanese enterprises can thus be explained more effectively by using a problem *formation* or information *creation* model rather than the traditional model of problem solving or information processing.

The former model not only enables us to understand the process of innovation more integratively, but it also makes it possible to develop new ways of managing innovation (see Nonaka 1989).

This chapter looks at problem formation and information creation features of innovation in Japanese enterprises. A key factor in explaining these characteristics is the concept of information redundancy. The chapter limits the discussion to product innovation at the establishment and the enterprise levels. Section 11.1 defines the concept of information redundancy, which derives from studies of product innovation. Section 11.2 shows how information redundancy is related to the innovation process. Section 11.3 points out problem areas in innovation brought about by information redundancy. Section 11.4 brings the discussion to a close with a look at theoretical implications of the concept.

## 11.1   Redundancy of Information

Innovation case studies cover a wide range of areas and extend across almost all the stages of the prototype life cycles.[1] They include such products as personal computers (introduction period), printers (introduction period), copiers (growth period), automobiles (maturity period), cameras (maturity period), and consumer electronics (maturity period). We use the concept of "information redundancy" to explain what appears to be the most common and fundamental factor of innovation observed across these cases. It refers to a situation in which individuals, groups, or organizations embrace information regarded as superfluous from the viewpoint of information-processing efficiency.[2]

However, from the qualitative perspective, extra information can enrich the application of information. It can help further to clarify the intent of a particular piece of information and at the same time broaden its scope of meaning. Information has two aspects, form and meaning. It is precisely because creation of the latter requires chaos that redundancy of information is important. The information-processing model basically sees "redundancy" as something that ought to be eliminated, but as far as the information and knowledge creation aspects of innovation are concerned, it is significant.

Information redundancy is not so much generated by structural or organizational factors such as by fuzzy job definitions but by human interactions (between individuals with diverse backgrounds). It is through

---

1. These are based on the author's own research, in addition to those quoted in Takeuchi and Nonaka (1986).
2. For example, Ashby (1955).

interaction with others that individuals, groups, or organizations embracing certain information are able to acquire various new information, and thus extend their activities beyond their specialist areas. We now turn to some illustrations of redundant information at different levels in the innovation process of Japanese enterprises.

Information Redundancy in Project Teams

Groups can generate more ideas and different ideas than individuals. This is particularly so when groups are composed of members with different job functions who think differently. That is why cross-sectional project teams are often used at the various phases of product innovation.

For example, in developing its "City" model, Honda formed a project team composed of members from research and development, production, sales, and marketing at the development phase. The project team analyzed the automobile market and the conditions of competition, and was able to set the target, the quantity of production, and the prices flexibly and promptly. Similarly, Matsushita Electric's project to commercialize an "automatic home bakery" involved members from sales and production departments besides those from development. The project team set the basic targets of design, quality, and cost reduction, and it was in the process of grappling with these issues that the team devised a revolutionary new method of baking bread.

Epson developed a representative group system that cut across departments, section, and teams to fully utilize the group dynamics of innovation. Different groups undertook the development of circuits, cases, operating system, and language for one type of machine. Naturally groups conflicted on specifications, cost, and delivery date. But Epson showed that problems can be solved through conflict and resolution. Self-expression can generate a sense of solidarity, which can help in surmounting obstacles. The EP101 dot-matrix printer was developed through confrontations among mixed teams.

As shown in table 11.1, project teams involved in product innovation are generally composed of 10 to 30 members. They are comprised of people with different backgrounds: research and development, planning, production, quality control, sales and marketing, and after-sales service. This is in line with existing studies that compare the degree of specialization of project teams in Japan with Europe and the United States. Clark, Chew, and Fujimoto (1987), for instance, clearly showed the low degree of specialization of the development teams in Japan. Table 11.2 shows that

**Table 11.1**
Background of team members involved in new product development

| Company | R&D | Production | Sales and marketing | Planning | Service | QC | Others | Total |
|---|---|---|---|---|---|---|---|---|
| | | Functional background | | | | | | |
| Fuji Xerox (FX3500) | 5 | 4 | 1 | 4 | 1 | 1 | 1 | 17 |
| Honda (City) | 18 | 6 | 4 | — | 1 | 1 | — | 30 |
| NEC (PC8000) | 5 | — | 2 | 2 | 2 | — | — | 11 |
| Epson 10 (EP-101) | 10 | 10 | — | — | — | — | — | 28 |
| Canon (AE-1) | 8 | 3 | 2 | 1 | — | — | 1 | 15 |
| Mazda (New RX7) | 13 | 6 | 7 | 1 | 1 | 1 | — | 29 |
| Matsushita Electric (Automatic home bakery) | 8 | 8 | 1 | 1 | 1 | 1 | — | 20 |

the average number of engineers involved in projects in Japan was 485, compared to 903 and 904 in the United States and Europe, respectively. A striking feature of the innovation projects in Japanese enterprises thus is diversity, and this is related to the "multiskilling" of team members.

Information Redundancy in Interdepartmental Development Process

Ideas generated in project teams through cross-sectional group dynamics are developed by production and marketing. Since innovation in Japanese enterprises cannot be understood as a fixed, clearly demarcated work-force responsibility, it is more appropriate to describe the process as shared, as a loosely connected and mutual overlapping activity that allows for flexibility in all its different phases. Each phase is distinct and yet loosely connected, which adds vitality to interphase interaction and promotes information sharing. The total process becomes a whole system sensitive to change.

For the FX3500, for example, Fuji Xerox shifted from the traditional NASA type of phased program planning (PPP) management to a *sashimi* process in which the different phases overlapped and progressed simultaneously (see figure 11.1). As a result what took 38 months under the previous

**Table 11.2**
Degree of project specialization: Average number of engineers

| Region | Number of engineers[a] | Number of projects |
|---|---|---|
| Japan | 485 | 11 |
| United States | 903 | 3 |
| Europe | 904 | 8 |

Source: Clark, Chew, and Fujimoto (1987).
a. Total number of engineers and technical support staff involved in the projects.

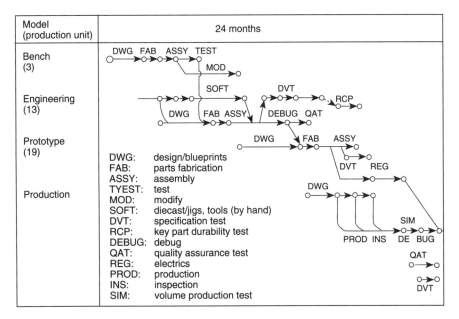

**Figure 11.1**
Development stages of Fuji Xerox FX3500. Source: Imai, Nonaka, and Takeuchi (1985).

sequential· development method was reduced to 24 months. The underlying reason is closely related to the frequency of human contact. Figure 11.2 illustrates the time distribution of the project members' daily work activities: Design and drawing constitute 39.7%, meetings and discussions 31.6%, information searching and editing 16.1%, and other activities 12.6%. The amount of time spent on human interaction constitutes up to one-third of the total daily working time. It would not be possible to conduct activities across the phase boundaries if they were isolated and the different functional areas highly specialized. It is only through close interaction among project members that such parallel development becomes possible.

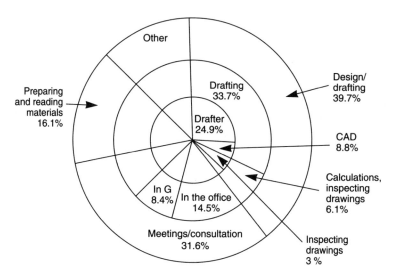

**Figure 11.2**
Percentage of time allocated to developers of FX3500. Source: Company engineers (19 in all) interviewed one month prior to completion.

The different phases in the development of Canon's Auto-Boy were similarly blurred. As one project member commented. "The desire to follow through one's own design to make sure it will turn out a truly good product persistently lingers in the mind of the designer. Those making the product want to absorb the designer's thinking, too, and try to understand why the product is designed a certain way. So instead of keeping to our own jobs, we invade each others' turf in a constructive way. This generates very positive effects." Canon did away with clear job distinctions, and although this brought about frequent conflicts, the loose coupling of the different phases ensured redundancy of information.

Information Redundancy in Interfirm Relationships

Shared labor between groups can also be observed in the organizational relationship of "parent" and affiliated companies. Affiliated companies are not isolated from the parent company, nor is the division of labor exclusive. Both are autonomous yet work in a tightly knit interdependent relationship.

In the early stages of developing the new RX7, design engineers from Mazda's head office carried out detailed consultation meetings on component parts with the staff of suppliers such as Hiroshima Aluminium, which supplies aluminium components for brakes. The engineer in charge of the project in Hiroshima Aluminium explained: "Although the design was meant to be a company secret not to be leaked out, we actually sat and worked together right from the beginning. In the past we somehow managed to make the products from the drawings given to us. This time people from the design and the production functions actually worked together. You might wonder why the Mazda people went as far as this. In fact it has proved extremely useful in bridging the gap which often exists between design and production. We cannot easily understand the logic behind the drawings. Drawings show shapes, they don't communicate the intentions behind them."

Fuji Xerox has also developed this type of relationship with its affiliated companies. According to the head of the design function in Fuji Xerox: "We ask our suppliers to come to our factory and start working with us as early in the development process as possible. The suppliers also don't mind our visiting their plants. This kind of mutual exchange and open sharing of information enhances flexibility. If we simply make an order when the drawings are completed, the buyer and the supplier are entirely separated from each other. However, if suppliers participate right from the beginning, even when you only order one single component, they can make the single part knowing how it fits into the whole product. Going one step further, if they are capable enough, they might bring forward several prototypes based on a rough sketch, and the designer simply approves them."

Fuji Xerox encourages members of the product development teams to drop in on their suppliers periodically. It further recommends that the vendors visit their subcontractors. Fuji Xerox thus is linked with its primary and secondary subcontractors in such a way that their interaction promotes information redundancy and enhances the flexibility of the whole process, which makes rapid product development possible.

Similarly a chief researcher at Honda recalls his experience in developing the City model: "During the peak period, I spent only about one-third of my time in the research laboratory and hardly any time at all at my own desk. I was either visiting the component manufacturers, or during the initial stage I had to go out and conduct market research."

**11.2   Potential Influence of Information Redundancy**

Looking at the process of innovation in Japanese enterprises from the stand point of groups, organizations, or networks of affiliated companies, the relationship governing the individuals with diverse backgrounds is not a tight, hierarchical one; rather, it is a loose relationship based on intimate mutual interaction. Such a loose relationship produces redundant information and provides each individual with extra information. In this unusual way information redundancy can give rise to innovation, and it can influence problem formation or information creation. In this section we focus on this aspect of innovation by looking at the potential influence of "information redundancy" on the organizing process of innovation.

## Promoting Mutual Exploration

As already discussed, information redundancy by individuals, groups, or organizations results in more information than required by each entity, but it promotes the creation process. When individuals share redundant information, it becomes possible for one party to penetrate the other's territory and identify the problem areas. As the suggestions are made by people of a different background and from a different perspective, they often bring about an awareness of new problems that might not otherwise have been noticed. If individuals only possess information specific to their own areas, it is not possible for them to "invade" others' territories and make suggestions. As new problems present themselves in an organizational process like innovation, it is necessary for the individuals to have more information and, more important, to share their insights.

The innovation process in Japanese enterprises is characterized by the phenomenon of "learning by intrusion"—individuals from different territories interact and learn from problems that arise. This distinctive feature is also manifest in the methodology of production techniques adopted by Japanese enterprises, as pointed out by Jaikumar and Bohn (1986). According to Jaikumar and Bohn, the characteristic feature of U.S. production techniques is a clear definition of basic manufacturing technology, workers' tasks, targets, and organizational environment, which are all seen as givens. That is to say, in U.S. enterprises, technology is assumed to be a predetermined factor, tasks are objectivized, and workers simply follow the known procedures. By contrast, in Japanese enterprises technology is regarded as an unknown, something embedded in the whole system which continually reveals itself in the process. It is a basic belief in Japanese enterprises that extraordinary situations are the very opportunities for learning (Koike 1988).

The identification of problems through information redundancy does not necessarily occur in a random manner. Solutions to each problem are fitted together into a meaningful set of information. Thus a linked spiral of

meaningful information eventually leads to a model concept. As noted by
H. Watanabe of Honda: "For the LPL [large project leader], once the concept is formed the work is half done." The final effect is a kind of "diffused
convergence."

## Redundancy of Potential Command

Because of information redundancy all the individuals are expected to raise
questions irrespective of the hierarchical relations. The person who has
acquired the most information and raised the most complex technical questions is the one who takes charge. MacCulloch (1965) described this as "the
principle of redundancy of potential command." The importance of the
separate parts is potentially equal, but depends on the importance of the
information that each is able to contribute to the total system. In other
words, under conditions of information redundancy, all contributors are
potential leaders. The person who produces the most important information is the leader, so the principle of hierarchy in which only those at the
top can be leaders loses its meaning. It is quite true that enterprises make
hierarchical distinctions between those at the top, middle and bottom, and
such a structure also exists in the relationships between the main company
and suppliers. From the viewpoint of problem identification, however, the
system does not necessarily correspond with the structural hierarchy.

Information redundancy therefore has important implications for the
structure of organizations. Innovative enterprises in Japan have developed
two parallel structural features. On the one hand, they are hierarchical, but
on the other, they have developed what Hedlund calls "heterarchical"
structures.[3] The identification of problems one after another and the continuous creation of information reflect the "heterarchical" aspect of the
organizations, but this is embedded in a formal hierarchy. The hierarchy
operates to process the emerging information efficiently. If such a hierarchy
did not exist, it would not be possible to utilize the information produced
in the process efficiently. As with information processing and information
creation, the relationship between hierarchy and heterarchy is complementary. When redundancy of information occurs, both the heterarchy and
hierarchy components interact to generate information. Compared with
a hierarchy which deals with given problems, greater efficiency can be

---

3. The meaning of "heterarchy" is not clear in Hedlund's (1986) study. It is used to refer to
"the existence of nonhierarchical type of organization." One special form is a holographic
system, whereby the individual parts acquire the information to reproduce the original
image of the whole.

**Table 11.3**
International comparison of lead times for automobiles

| Lead time (months) | Japan | United States | Europe | Total |
|---|---|---|---|---|
| Average | 42.6 | 61.9 | 62.6 | 54.2 |
| Minimum | 35.0 | 50.2 | 46.0 | 35.0 |
| Maximum | 51.0 | 77.0 | 97.0 | 97.0 |

Source: Clark, Chew, and Fujimoto (1987).

achieved through prior knowledge and understanding. Clark, Chew, and Fujimoto (1987) show that the time required for innovation is shorter in Japan than the United States (table 11.3). "Information redundancy" is a key concept for interpreting the characteristic features of innovation in Japanese enterprises and this efficiency.

## Trust and Self-control

Information redundancy among individuals, groups, and organizations increases the chance of establishing relationships based on trust. As individuals form close relationships and share information, they can more easily accept critical, probing questions without feeling threatened. This stimulates the desire to challenge ideas and thus forms a basis for creativity.

Trust is an important ingredient in any social system (Arrow 1974). It also affects innovation. If a relationship of trust does not exist, it is not possible for individuals to move beyond their own territories and interact extensively to form dynamic cooperative relationships and thus to exchange information continually.

The formation of trust relationships eliminates cheating or deception in information redundancy. Williamson (1974) argues that transactions within organizations reduce the risk of opportunism as compared with market transactions. The reason for this also lies in information redundancy within organizations. That is to say, redundancy of information encourages a relationship of trust through interactions and information sharing, and this reduces opportunism.

Information sharing gives each individual a role in the total system. Information redundancy also functions to direct individuals' thoughts and actions. The individuals are not isolated but are connected through their dependence on redundant information. Thus problems and information generated through information redundancy are controlled and this gives a general sense of direction.

## 11.3 Problem Areas

Although information redundancy promotes flexible and rapid innovation in Japanese enterprises, there are also some negative aspects that cannot be ignored.

Compromises in Group Thinking

Information redundancy sometimes promotes group thinking. On the one hand, it leads to flexible and rapid innovation, and yet on the other, it leads to compromises and failure to carry activities through to their conclusion. Trust and self-control can at times make individuals hesitate to do things that are out of the ordinary or to make creative suggestions. This is especially true when innovations are carried out by project teams or task forces facing a deadline. A. Yamanouchi, former director of Canon Development Center, made the following comment: "Project teams or task forces are excellent ways of organizing creative activities. But in most cases a deadline is fixed. This imposes limitations on the activities and directs them toward fixed targets. There has to be compromise at some point, and this means it is not possible to carry out thorough-going technological research."

Unlike the United States, Japanese enterprises cannot for the most part depend on in-depth scientific research. Depending on specialists would ultimately reduce self-expression in Japan and lock people into niches. As Argyris and Schon (1987) see it, in this "organizational learning" there can be single-loop learning but insufficient double-loop learning. Those who cannot question assumptions are only capable of factual knowledge (Bateson 1979). Innovations that undermine the accepted theories may therefore be rare.

High Cost and Human Fatigue

Repeated problems in innovation under conditions of information redundancy can be extremely costly, since everyone is pressed to solve each problem as it arises. Chief researcher Watanabe in charge of developing the Honda City commented on these costs: "No matter how unreasonable the demands are, we still have to carry on. Disputes occur here and there. As a result one can only sigh at the enormous money and energy wasted."

Information redundancy necessitates much social interaction, so when problems arise, all the members' efforts are held up. Inevitably there is fatigue. In the cases considered in this chapter, the average amount of overtime by design and development staff was over 100 hours per month in peak periods and roughly 50 hours in normal circumstances. Says Watanabe: "It's not so different from the Japanese army. I often wonder how on earth Japanese companies are able to beat the others. We sometimes feel as if we are defeated but carry on with mental strength." Those in charge of product development often complain about exhaustion. Excessive demands require intensive work not only of the organization but also of affiliated companies. A senior manager from an affiliated company made the following remark: "We often work frantically and not methodically. Whether it is the managers or whoever, we just carry on doing overtime. We don't follow any rules; we throw ourselves at it."

At the end of the day, the problems of high cost and human fatigue, which are inevitable outcomes of innovation based on information redundancy, have to be borne by the organization. The fact that the organizational conditions and the interorganization networks are able to bear these costs might explain why the Japanese innovation process works.

## 11.4   Conclusion: Some Theoretical Implications

This chapter has examined the concept of information redundancy as a fundamental element of the innovation process in Japanese enterprises. Innovations in Japanese enterprises cannot be understood from traditional problem-solving or information-processing perspectives. Rather, a problem *formation* or information *creation* model, which is closely related to the concept of information redundancy, is more appropriate. In this final section I will briefly summarize the arguments and discuss the theoretical implications of the concept of information redundancy.

Tightly knit interaction among individuals with different backgrounds can be readily observed in case studies of product innovation in Japanese enterprises. This occurs in project teams, in interdepartmental development activities, and also with affiliated companies. The sharing of extra information between individuals, departments, or organizations enables them to carry out a range of activities beyond their own specialist areas. This characteristic feature can be explained by the concept of information redundancy. Other features of Japanese enterprises such as the positive activities of mutual exploration, open command, relationships of trust, and self-control, and negative ones of the tendency to compromise in favor of group direction, human fatigue, and high costs, can all be accounted for by the concept of information redundancy as well. Information generation and problem creation are the most striking features of the Japanese innovation process brought about by information redundancy.

**Table 11.4**
Educational background and career history of the core members of the FX3500 development team

| Name | Level of education and area of specialization | Postentry career |
|---|---|---|
| H. Yoshida | Graduate—education | Technical service staff–personnel–product planning–program management |
| K. Fujita | Graduate—business administration | Marketing staff–product planning–program management |
| K. Suzuki | Graduate—mechanical engineering | Design–research–design |
| M. Kitajima | Graduate—electrical engineering | Technical service staff–quality control–production |

Morgan (1986) uses an analogy with the human brain to explain redundancy. But this brain metaphor as applied to organizational theory is limited to autonomous groups. In the case studies of this chapter, redundancy was characteristic of information itself which could be shared within and between organizations. The redundancy of information was found not only to be meaningful for small groups but also for large-scale formal organizations. In formal organizations the typical model is generally that of information processing based on hierarchical structure. Yet even in formal organizations information can be generated continually within hierarchies.[4]

There remains the question of how redundancy of information, which can be chaotic and sporadic, can be reconciled with an orderly system. Since innovation in Japanese enterprises is directed by clear-cut objectives, deadlines operate to focus problems and information. Likewise the special competitive conditions in Japanese enterprises call for a systematic approach. But, most important is the fact that Japanese enterprises consist of workers with multiple skills. As shown in table 11.4, the company members involved in the development of the Fuji Xerox FX3500 were competent in different fields, since they were experienced in different job functions. Such expertise facilitates the creation and processing of information and allows members to become involved at relatively high-level interaction. Ashby's "minimum effective diversity," which refers to the construction of information channels corresponding to the amount of information generated, was developed mainly from the perspective of formal information processing, but the concept can be extended to apply to the interpretation of information as well.

4. "Formal organization" is used here in contrast to "informal organization" or autonomous groups. It refers to formal structures and written rules.

# IV

Human Resources

# 12

# The Employment System and Human Resource Management

Kazutoshi Koshiro

In this chapter I analyze the evolution of labor market flexibility in large Japanese corporations after the first oil shock. First, I describe the main features of the employment system and the legislation on employment security. Next I measure the speed of employment adjustment during a period that includes the aftermath of the recession triggered by the appreciation of the yen in 1985–86. Compared with the aftermath of the first oil shock, employment adjustment loses speed while worker hours adjust to their optimal level within two years. I use case studies to indicate how the most representative large corporations coped with structural adjustment, taking into consideration measures such as reduction in the size of core employment, development of new lines of business, transfers, and other measures that increase employment flexibility. I then analyze wage flexibility and present some quantitative evidence on the relationship between bonuses, wage hikes, and profits. Having summarized the main points, I conclude that human resource management in large Japanese firms is guided by principles of the labor-managed firm. (This chapter does not deal with issues related to labor management in Japanese firms such as hiring, training, placement, promotion, and wage structure. For careers within firms, for instance, I refer the reader to Koike's paper [chapter 13].)

## 12.1 Main Features of the Japanese Employment System

A Survey of the Research

The traditional view of human resource management in Japanese firms was pioneered by Abegglen (1958), who noted *lifetime employment* and *pay according to age* as features peculiar to Japan. Added to these as the last of the "three sacred treasures" of Japanese industrial relations[1] was the

---

1. In a report by the OECD (1973).

*enterprise-based trade union.* The OECD report simplified for a foreign audience the leading view of "Japan as a special country" as expressed by Japanese sociologists (e.g., represented by Okochi 1952; Okochi, Ujihara, and Fujita 1959). Interestingly, this view was supported by the first empirical study after the Second World War which applied principles of American industrial sociology such as *dual loyalty.* Odaka (1958) concluded in this study that Japanese firms could be characterized as a *household management system.*

Criticism of the view of Japan as a special country, which emphasized the delays and distortions of Japan with respect to the European model of industrial development, was spurred on by joint research on contemporary Japan led by Jansen (1965). In the field of labor economics a major role was played by Kazuo Koike (1977), who did extensive empirical research on the comparative features of internal labor markets. At the same time the 1960s and the 1970s were dominated by the insights of Gary Becker (1964) and *human capital theory,* according to which long-term employment and wage structures could be explained as an extension of the neoclassical principle of marginal costs and benefits. Based on this theory was the comparative research on wage profiles in Japan and the United States pursued by Shimada (1974), which helped reduce the prominence of the traditional view of Japan as a special country.

Recent research in Japan has been dominated by the neoclassical and institutional schools, with empirical research devoted to clarifying both the labor market and human resource management in Japanese firms. Akira Ono (1981), for instance, stressed that interfirm mobility in Japanese firms is lower than in British and American firms and that job mobility based on wage differentials is hard to find. On the other hand, Shinotsuka and Ishihara's (1977) comparative study on the speed of employment adjustment after the first oil shock found that, when employment is considered, this speed in Japan is one-fourth that found in the United States, but when worker hours are considered, the difference between the two countries is marginal. This type of research applies to Japan the same economic principles applied to Western economies and identifies differences with different values of estimated parameters and with their significance. Obviously this analysis ignores legal constraints and social custom as important determinants of employment security.

The relatively good performance of the Japanese economy after the two oil shocks and its increased international competitiveness triggered by the microelectronics (ME) revolution has led a number of Western scholars to study extensively the reasons for this success, and in particular the special features of Japanese management and human resource development. Vogel (1979) and Ouchi (1981) stress the special features of Japanese management, a view pursued in Japan by Tsuda (1977) and Iwata (1977). On the other hand, Abernathy (1981), Drucker (1981), and Hayes (1981) use the insights of Leibenstein's "X-efficiency" theory (1976) to support the opposite view that one should focus on the "micro software" of management organization and labor relations. At the same time empirical research on internal labor markets and labor management in Japan was conducted by Dore (1973) and Puchick (1984). During the 1980s research was oriented to clarifying the differences in macroeconomic performance between Japan and Western economies. Prominent among these studies is the work by Weitzman (1984), who argued that the bonus system makes Japanese wages flexible enough to avoid the high unemployment which characterized Europe after the oil shocks. Weitzman's view is reflected by recent research conducted by the OECD (1986). Comparative research has also been undertaken at the Research Center on Labor Problems (Koshiro 1986) and for the International Symposium on Employment Security and Labor Market Flexibility (Koshiro 1989b).

Another feature of Japanese labor market flexibility that emerged after the oil shocks is the practice of dispatchment and transfers of employees, research on which has been done by Itami-Matsui (1985) and Nagano (1989). Extension of the concept of internal labor markets to the industrial group (what they called an "intermediate organization") was made by Imai, Itami, and Koike (1982).

The Main Issues

It cannot be denied that the Japanese employment system is based on the market mechanism, but there exist important historical, cultural and institutional factors that are special to Japan and that produce phenomena such as "organization orientation" and the system of "enterprise welfare" (see Dore 1973). Moreover, as explained in detail later on, the degree of employment security in the Japanese employment system is, from an international viewpoint, quite strong (see Sengenberger 1986).

This employment system was the by-product of an economy characterized, in its first stages of development, by scarcity of land and of natural resources, an abundant and unskilled labor force located on farms, and shortage of skilled labor. Given these conditions, the continual need to introduce new technologies led to education and training within the firm with a stable labor force. Long-term employment was thus necessary to increase the returns from an investment in human capital. The trade-off was obviously lack of flexibility to fluctuations in economic activity. This trade-off established the following policies:

1. Limitation of employment security to the core work force, with the creation of a peripheral and flexible work force composed of temporary workers, subcontractors, seasonal workers, part-timers, and dispatched employees.

2. Flexible utilization of the core work force by means of transfers, early retirement, and hiring of mobile workers.

3. Flexible use of working time.

4. Wage flexibility (in particular through the bonus system).

These policies were reinforced by the process of structural adjustment caused by the second oil shock and by the appreciation of the yen.

The Approach of Dore

The Japanese employment system is based on the application of human resource management inspired by the principles of the internal labor market and adjusted to the need to rapidly introduce new technologies typical of a late-industrialized country. It is important to stress that this pattern is not unique to Japan (see Koike 1977, 1981; Koike and Inoki 1987). It is also true, however, that there are several features peculiar to the Japanese employment system. Dore (1973), for instance, in his comparison of two British and two Japanese electrical engineering plants points out these differences between Japanese and British practices, which are quoted here in table 12.1.

It should be noted, however, that differences between the two countries are not absolute. For instance, interfirm mobility also exists in Japan and the wage system is not completely independent of labor market supply and demand. Moreover careers in medium and small enterprises were originally based on substantial mobility, and the phenomenon of divisions being spun off large corporations is quite common. In Japanese large firms there is a high standard of welfare provision, but pensions and medical care are based on social security. Nevertheless, as Dore indicates, the differences among the two employment systems are striking. Japan's system is "organization oriented," while Britain's is "market oriented." The Japanese system is a "welfare corporatist" rather than a patriarchal system. Japanese large corporations have applied to their employment system an organizational model considered in Europe suitable only for the army and the bureaucracy.

**Table 12.1**
Japanese employment system compared with British system

| Hitachi | English Electric |
|---|---|
| 1. Lifetime employment | Employment mobility |
| 2. Wage system based on seniority and merit rating | Wages and salaries based on the market |
| 3. Career system within the firm | External careers based on interfirm mobility |
| 4. Training within the firm | Job training through public agencies |
| 5. Enterprise union | Industrial and craft union |
| 6. High-level welfare within the firm | Reliance on social security |
| 7. Forges a personal identification with the firm | Greater identification with job, occupation, area, and class |

Source: Dore (1973).

Moreover the Japanese employment system, which underwent a social democratic revolution at the close of the Second World War, is from many points of view more advanced than the British system, and indeed superior to it from the basic standpoint of equality among employees, since there are very small differences between manual workers and staff. For instance, wages increase gradually in proportion to the changes in family living expenses not only for middle management but also for manual workers. In spite of being a "late-comer," the Japanese system has efficiently fitted its management to the demands of modern industry, whereas the British system shows signs of convergence toward this system. Others, apart from Dore, have pointed out that the utilization of labor in industrially advanced nations tends to converge to a common pattern. Kuwahara (1987, 1988), for instance, indicates the similarity between the "labor-managed model" of Japanese firms and the firms owned by employees (ESOP) in the United States.

The Practice of "Lifetime Employment" and the Legal Framework behind Employment Security

At the beginning of the 1970s an OECD research team visited Japan to search for written proof of the "lifetime employment system." This episode is quite revealing about the employment practices of large Japanese corporations. Labor contracts specifying lifetime employment do not in fact exist in Japan. Civil law forbids employment agreements longer than five years (Civil Law, Art. 626, par. 1) and the Labor Standards Law, as a rule, prohibits labor contracts exceeding one year in length (Labor Standards Law, Art. 14). What in Japan is commonly referred to as "lifetime employment," is, legally speaking, a "labor contract without provisions on employment length." As a rule, dismissal is not constrained. Freedom of dismissal is recognized as a civil law principle in Japan, as elsewhere, and any employment agreement without provisions on employment length can be canceled at any time with two weeks notice (Civil Law, Art. 627). The postwar Labor Standards Law did not go any further than to extend the dismissal notice term to 30 days.

The fact that the practice of so-called lifetime employment has largely became embedded in Japanese large corporations is due to the following circumstances:

1. Training of skilled workers within internal labor markets was an efficient way of importing and establishing modern technology so that a policy of stabilizing employment in the firm was adopted (see Hyodo 1971).

2. The large-scale personnel dismissals in the years after World War II led the Labor Courts to establish "principles regulating the right to dimiss" that require employers to specify "legitimate reasons for fair dismissal." As a consequence even in the case of redundancy, the employer was not allowed to enforce dismissals before undertaking to

a. prove the necessity of dismissing surplus workers,

b. make adequate efforts to transfer workers instead of dismissing them,

c. be fair in the selection of whom to discharge,

d. negotiate dismissals with the trade union, when this exists (Ariizumi 1963; Hanami 1979; Matsuda 1984, 1986).

3. Given the costly labor strikes experienced in the postwar period up to the early 1960s because of personnel cuts, firms were obliged to try to avoid dismissals in order to escape substantial loss, either economic or in social standing.

4. From 1960 on, the law concerning employment security was tightened. Article 21 of the Law on Employment Stabilization, enacted in 1966, forced employers to report in advance to the Offices for Employment Stabilization cases of mass dismissal (i.e., affecting more than 30 regular workers in a month; Regulations Relative to the Enforcement of the Law, Art. 8, par. 2). In 1975 the Employment Insurance Law helped to discourage the discharge of surplus employees by establishing a subsidy on employment maintenance to be paid to depressed firms. The law required as a condition for the payment of employment subsidies that the employer obtain the agreement either of the union representing more than half the employees or of a

worker representative in the absence of a union on measures such as temporary holidays, transfers, retraining periods, number of workers affected, and income compensation for these measures.

5. In 1977 the Special Law on Surplus Employment in Depressed Industries, later modified to become the Current Special Law on Depressed Firms and Depressed Areas (1983), established that employers in these industries must have approved, by the head of the local office for Employment Stabilization, any measures that they take for employment stability and the reemployment of workers affected by industrial restructuring. The head of the Employment Stabilization Office is entitled to reject the plans presented whenever s/he finds these measures inadequate (Art. 6).

Thus the practice of lifetime employment observed in large Japanese firms is not only a result of social custom but depends also on restrictions by law and legal practice.[2]

## 12.2   Employment Adjustment in a Period of Management Rationalization

Employment Changes after the First Oil Shock

The structure of employment in Japan has gone through three main changes since the first oil shock. First, manufacturing employment in the five years up to 1978 declined by more than 10 percent, only to recover (slowly) thereafter to the levels reached before the first oil shock. Second, in sharp contrast to the above, employment in the service sector increased by 60 percent from 1973 to 1988, and employment in the wholesale and retail trade sector also increased by 30 percent. Third, the employment share of big firms declined and the share of medium and small firms increased. As a consequence the share of employees protected by the "lifetime employment system" declined sharply.

With the exception of the government sector, the practice of "lifetime employment" is particularly widespread among the corporations listed in

---

2. The standard definition of lifetime employment (hiring from school, employment security in a depression, no interfirm mobility, and employment up to mandatory retirement; see *Economic Dictionary*, Tokyo Keizai Shinposha, vol. 2, 100–108) lacks precision. For instance, employment practices before the Second World War, when dismissal was not regulated, should be distinguished from employment security after the war when legal restrictions and collective action restrained dismissals. Distinction should also be made among stationary, growth, and recession models in the postwar period (Koshiro 1983a). For details on employment security in European and American firms, see Blanpain (1980), Daniel and Stilgoe (1978), Gutchess (1985), Lall (1985), Rosow and Zager (1984), and Sengenberger (1986).

**Table 12.2**
Employment changes in major Japanese corporations (in thousands; %)

| Year | Total employment (A) | Employees in the 895 firms listed in the first section of the Tokyo Stock Ex- change (B) | (B/A) |
|------|------|------|------|
| 1965 | 2,913 | 320.3 | 11.0 |
| 1970 | 3,340 | 371.5 | 11.1 |
| 1973 | 3,625 | 379.0 | 10.5 |
| 1974 | 3,638 | 381.1 | 10/5 |
| 1975 | 3,669 | 374.4 | 10/2 |
| 1979 | 3,896 | 339.3 | 8.7 |
| 1980 | 3,997 | 341.9 | 8.6 |
| 1982 | 4,125 | 348.7 | 8.5 |
| 1984 | 4,281 | 347.3 | 8.1 |
| 1985 | 4,328 | 348.3 | 8.0 |
| 1986 | 4,382 | 345.4 | 7.9 |

Sources: Office of the Prime Minister, *Labor Force Survey*, yearly average (ending in March of each year); *Japan Economic Journal* NEEDS. The data referring to end of year are excluded.

the first section of the Tokyo Stock Exchange. (Several firms listed in the second section and other stock exchanges, as well as unlisted publishing and insurance firms and a few unlisted famous companies, also follow this system.) Table 12.2 shows starting from 1965 the employment trend of 895 (out of a total of 1,134 firms in 1989) firms belonging to the first section of the Tokyo Stock Exchange. According to data collected by the *Japan Economic Journal* NEEDS company, employment reached 3,811,000 in 1974 and then declined up to 1979. A new peak was reached in 1982, followed by a decline up to 1984. The increase of employment in 1985 was more than compensated by the third decline in 15 years as a consequence of the appreciation of the yen. The share of workers employed in the 895 large companies over total employment declined steadily from 11 percent at the beginning of the 1970s to the 7 percent at the end of the 1980s.

Next table 12.3 compares the size of employment adjustment in the manufacturing sector on the three occasions when it occurred. The following three points should be noted:

1. The adjustment occurring after the first oil shock was the largest both for production and for employment.

2. After the second oil shock (and the ensuing worldwide recession) both production and labor inputs declined, but regular employment did not change.

**Table 12.3**
Comparison of three periods of employment adjustment (in %)

|                                                                      | First oil shock                              | Second oil shock                          | Yen application                              |
| -------------------------------------------------------------------- | -------------------------------------------- | ----------------------------------------- | -------------------------------------------- |
| Reduction in index of industrial production                          | January 1974– March 1975 15 months  − 20.2   | February 1980– May 1981 16 months  − 4.8  | October 1985– August 1986 10 months  − 2.7   |
| Reduction in index of regular employment in manufacturing            | May 1974–April 1979 36 months  − 11.6        | No reduction                              | September 1986– August 1987 12 months  − 2.0 |
| Reduction in labor inputs in manufacturing                           | October 1973– April 1975 19 months  − 18.6   | February 1980–July 1980 7 months  − 3.2   | September 1985– April 1987 20 months  − 4.1  |

Source: Economic Planning Agency, *Yearbook of Indicators of Economic Change.*

3. After the recession triggered by the appreciation of the yen in 1985, the decline in production was contained but regular employment declined because of structural adjustment. Thus the reduction in labor inputs was larger than after the second oil shock.

4. In all the three experiences the decline in factor inputs was larger than the decline in regular employment, which highlights the important role played by the adjustment of working hours.

5. The reduction in regular employment occurred with a time lag with respect to the decline in production and hours of labor. Thus the adjustment process was time-consuming. A graphic presentation of the adjustment process would show a gentle decline then rise of the former, with greater and more frequent fluctuations for the latter.

How was the observed reduction in employment accomplished? The social and legal constraints on the employment relationship explain why both individual and collective dismissals, which occurred frequently during the 1940s and 1950s, played almost no part in the adjustment process of the 1970s and 1980s. According to the *Survey on Labor Market Trends* published by the Ministry of Labor, employment adjustments occurring during the three recessions considered above were accomplished by the following means, ranked by relative importance:

1. Reduction of overtime and normal time.

2. Reduction/freezing of midcareer hirings.

3. Relocation and dispatchment.

4. Dismissal of temporary and part-time workers.

5. Temporary holidays.

6. Reduction/freezing of hirings of new graduates.

7. Anticipated retirement and dismissal.

This ranking changed little over the whole period considered (see *White Paper on Labor* 1983, 30, 1986, 24). Because of the careful policy of employment adjustment adopted by firms, labor conflicts related to rationalization did not occur with the exception of Sasebo Heavy Industries. Moreover, there have been no employers' actions subsequently invalidated by the labor courts (see Yasueda and Nishimura 1984; Yamaguchi 1984).

Speed of Employment Adjustment

Just after the first oil shock, a study by Shinozuka and Ishihara (1977) showed that the speed of employment adjustment in Japanese manufacturing (limited to firms with more than 30 employees) was 0.09 on a monthly basis during the period November 1973–March 1976. During the same period the speed of employment adjustment in the United States was 0.24, about three times larger than in Japan. On the other hand, if worker hours rather than employment are used, the speed of adjustment on a monthly basis rises to 0.39 in Japan compared to 0.43 in the United States, and the difference becomes insignificant.

After Shinozuka and Ishihara' seminal paper, a number of studies of employment adjustment followed (Muramatsu 1978; Shimada 1981; Yamamoto 1982; Ministry of Labor 1983; Koshiro 1983a; Seike 1983; Ohtake 1988). Since they use different data and techniques, which makes comparison difficult, I will focus in what follows only on the Solow-type partial adjustment model and convert the estimates on an annual basis.[3]

---

3. In the Solow-type partial adjustment model, actual employment $(L_t)$ and optimal employment $(L_{t^*})$ are related as

$$\left(\frac{L_t}{L_{t-1}}\right) = \left(\frac{L_{t^*}}{L_{t-1}}\right)_l,\tag{1}$$

where $l$ is the speed of employment adjustment. Optimal employment is given by

$$L_{t^*} = a_0 x_{t^1}^a \left(\frac{W}{P}\right)_{t^2}^{-a},$$

$$L_{t^*} = a_0 X_t \left(\frac{W}{P}\right)_t,\tag{2}$$

where $X_t$ is production and $(W/P)t$ is the real wage. Plugging (2) into (1) yields

$$L_t = c_0 X_t^{c_1} \left(\frac{W}{P}\right) t^{c_2} L_{t-1}^{c_3}\tag{3}$$

The 1973–76 monthly estimates by Shinozuka and Ishihara can be converted into annual estimates using the formula (4) in 3. The conversion yields a speed of adjustment for employment of 0.678. That is to say the adjustment of employment to its optimal level took about six years. In the case of worker hours the conversion to annual estimates yields 0.9973, which implies that full adjustment took place in one year or so. What happened subsequently in the light of the new legal restrictions and government policies affecting the ease of dismissal after 1976?

After the second oil shock the Ministry of Labor (1983) published a study based on a longer sample, extending on a quarterly basis from the first quarter of 1974 to the fourth quarter of 1982. The study uses data on the number of employees from the *Labor Force Survey* and fits the employment adjustment function used by Shinozuka and Ishihara. The main result is an estimated rate of employment adjustment of 0.39 on a quarterly basis, which is converted to 0.8615 on an annual basis. This rate implies that 98 percent of the total adjustment can be accomplished within two years. This is three times the rate found by Shinozuka and Ishihara. The difference between the two studies is partly a difference in the observation period, however. More important, Shinozuka and Ishihara had used the *Monthly Labor Survey*, which focuses on establishments with more than 30 employees and on regular workers. On the other hand, the study by the Ministry of Labor is based on the *Labor Force Survey* which includes small firms and temporary workers. This difference highlights how the rate of employment adjustment can decline if one focuses only on regular employees.

This point is affirmed by Koshiro (1983a). He uses the *Japan Economic Journal* NEEDS data on 580 companies listed in the first section of the Tokyo Stock Exchange for regular employees during 1972–81. Using the same partial adjustment, the rate is only 0.14. This is equivalent to 30 years of adjustment to the optimal employment level. Thus the numbers make it clear that the largest Japanese corporations practice the "lifetime employment system" for their regular employees.

It is important to note that the measurement of the employment adjustment rate described above is technically faulty. Equation (3) in note 3 is usually estimated by ordinary least squares, but since it includes Lt-1, the risk of an auto correlation cannot be ignored. This requires that the model

---

where $c_0 = a_0$, $c_1 = a_1 \cdot \lambda$, $c_2 = -a_2 \cdot \lambda$, $c_3 = (1-\lambda)$. Estimating (3) allows one to determine the value of $\lambda$. The conversion from monthly to annual data of the speed of employment adjustment is given by the following formula:

$$(1-(1-\lambda)^{12}).$$ (4)

**Table 12.4**
The employment adjustment function (monthly data) in manufacturing

| Dependent variable | Explanatory variables | | | | Employment adjustment | | $\bar{R}^2$ | D.W. | $\rho$ |
|---|---|---|---|---|---|---|---|---|---|
| | Constant | Production | Real wages | Previous month's figures | Speed $\lambda$ | Annual rate | | | |
| (1) Employees | 0.0314 (0.33) | 0.0182 (8.60) | −0.0187 (−5.79) | 0.9805 (202.5) | 0.0195 | 0.2106 | 0.9934 | 1.91 | 0.0987 (1.31) |
| (2)[a] Worker hours | 0.1801 (0.05) | 0.0683 (3.26) | −0.0341 (−2.20) | 0.8416 (20.55) | 0.1584 | 0.8737 | 0.9229 | 2.04 | 0.1432 (−1.71) |

Source: Economic Planning Agency (ed.) *Yearbook of Indicators of Economic Change*, September 1988. Used here are the index of industrial production, the index of regular employees in manufacturing, the index of manhours in manufacturing, the index of total wage payments and the index of wholesale prices.
a. The real wage is not adjusted by hours worked.

be handled by AR1 (first-order autoregressive model). Table 12.4 shows the estimates based on the data of manufacturing employment changes (limited to firms with more than 30 regular employees) for the period January 1973 to December 1987. The estimates are based on the AR1 technique and refer both to employment and to worker hours. Looking at the first row of the table we observe that (1) a 1 percent monthly change in industrial production produces on a 0.0182 percent variation in employment (2) a 1 percent monthly increase in the real wage reduces employment only by 0.0187 percent, and (3) the monthly speed of employment adjustment is only 0.0195, which is equivalent to 0.2106 on an annual basis. This implies that it takes 20 years to complete the adjustment process.

Focusing on row (2), on the other hand, and the trend in worker hours, observe that (1) both the output and the real wage elasticity of worker hours are much larger than those in row (1) and (2) the monthly speed of employment adjustment is 0.1584, eight times larger than the employment adjustment speed presented in row (1) and equivalent to 0.88 = 737 on a yearly basis. This implies that two years are enough for most of the adjustment to take place.

A comparison with the estimates by Shinozuka and Ishihara is difficult to accomplish because they use ordinary least squares. But one can safely say that compared with the period immediately after the first oil shock, the speed of employment adjustment has declined both for employment only and for worker hours. The reasons for this difference are both the greater speed and size of employment adjustment just after the first oil shock and the progressive difficulty in further employment cuts accompanied with legal and political restrictions on dismissals that followed the first burst of employment adjustment.

## 12.3  Active Human Resource Management in a Period of Employment Adjustment

In the previous section I looked at employment adjustment in Japanese firms as a passive response to an exogenous change in the level of economic activity. The response of firms was not limited, however, to a defensive reaction but involved also a positive policy of employment maintenance and expansion. In this section I consider a number of positive employment measures and evaluate the recent trend in human resource management by Japanese firms. The analysis is based on a survey I conducted in an earlier work (1988a). The measures considered are

1. entry into new lines of business,

2. establishment of subsidiary companies,

3. transfers of employees,

4. increasing importance of white-collar workers,

5. reduced importance of women among regular employees,

6. retirement, both early and at the mandatory age,

7. increased use of part-timers and dispatched workers.

Entry into New Lines of Business

Yoshihara et al. (1981) carried out an international comparison of diversification policy during the high growth era that showed Japanese firms to have a marked preference for sticking to their main line of business. The percentage of firms undertaking a diversification strategy in 1970 was 65 percent in the United States, 60 percent in Britain, 56 percent in West German, and only 47 percent (1973) in Japanese firms. According to a survey by Kagono et al. (1983), however, the difference between the United States and Japan has been reduced. A more recent trend noted by Yashiro (1986) is that of Japanese firms entering new fields of business through the creation of new subsidiaries.

My survey focuses on eight firms, which were studied after the exchange rate shock with the appreciation of the yen at the end of 1985. These firms are representative firms in steel, shipbuilding, chemical, precision instruments, car components, and communications equipment. All the firms considered in this study experienced, after the oil shocks, a significant reduction in their core businesses (see table 12.5). For example, for establishment Y of firm D, a typical case of a structurally depressed company in the shipbuilding industry, ships used to make up 60 percent of total sales. In 1980 the production of new ships was stopped, and the sale of equipment for the environment, bridges, and structures comprised more than half of total sales. On the other hand, in firm B in the chemical industry 60 to 70 percent of total sales were synthetic fibers which are now replaced by chemical resins and construction material, amounting to more than half of total sales. Firm E, which belongs to the expanding industry of car components, has reduced its production of oil seals from 70 percent to the current 40 percent and increased its output of plastic products for industrial use and electronic components. Firm G, which produces communications equipment, has reduced the share of its main business to 30 percent and replaced

**Table 12.5**
Development of new lines of business, with changes in the sales structure for the selected firms

| Name of product | 1965 | 1975 | 1985 | 1986 |
|---|---|---|---|---|
| **Firm A (heavy equipment)** | | | | |
| General equipment | 80.2 | 46.7 | 45.3 | 46.5 |
| Standard equipment | — | 17.5 | 34.8 | 26.0 |
| Ships | — | 35.8 | 19.8 | 27.5 |
| Mass production | 17.7 | — | — | — |
| **Firm B (chemicals)** | | | | |
| Resins | 7.4 | 8.7 | 31.5 | 28.1 |
| Textiles | 68.3 | 58.8 | 27.6 | 27.1 |
| Construction | 0.0 | 6.2 | 19.9 | 23.8 |
| Chemicals | 17.1 | 23.3 | 17.5 | 17.0 |
| **Firm C (steel)** | | | | |
| Steel products | — | 90.7 | 87.2 | 87.6 |
| Engineering | — | 5.9 | 9.9 | 10.3 |
| Chemicals | — | 0.9 | 1.6 | 1.3 |
| **Firm D (Plant Y) (heavy equipment)** | | | | |
| Environment equipment for the disposal of rubbish | 8.4 | 14.1 | 21.3 | 37.2 |
| Steel | 9.2 | 17.0 | 25.9 | 28.8 |
| Heavy electric equipment (turbines) | 21.9 | 27.3 | 28.1 | 25.5 |
| Ships (new ships up to 1980) | 60.5 | 42.8 | 14.6 | 6.6 |
| **Firm E (car components)** | | | | |
| Plastic for industrial use | — | — | 40.9 | 39.3 |
| Oil seals | 71.2 | 58.6 | 25.5 | 24.7 |
| Electronic components | — | — | 12.7 | 15.4 |
| **Firm F (precision instruments)** | | | | |
| Cameras | 60.8 | 66.6 | 49.2 | 53.7 |
| Semiconductors | 0.0 | 0.0 | 18.7 | 15.7 |
| Lenses for spectacles | 7.5 | 16.2 | 11.1 | 11.2 |
| **Firm G (communications equipment)** | | | | |
| Communications equipment | 68.6 | 51.2 | 35.8 | 31.3 |
| Electronic equipment and components | 20.0 | 40.0 | 19.6 | 18.8 |
| Computers | — | — | 40.4 | 45.0 |
| Home electronics | — | 9.0 | 7.4 | 4.9 |

Source: Koshiro et al. (1988a, 19).

it with computers and other electronic equipment. Firm F, a major camera producer, has reduced the share of its main product from about 70 percent to 50 percent and replaced it with an increasing share of semiconductors and lenses. Firm A, in the shipbuilding industry, increased its production of ships in the late 1970s mainly because of a merger with shipbuilder X at the beginning of the decade. Since the beginning of the 1980s, however, it has expanded its industrial equipment division.

One of the reasons for the drastic expansion of Japanese firms into new lines of business is their managerial and technical capability. Another reason is the "lifetime employment" practice. Entry into new lines of business has also been spurred on by the need to provide employment opportunities to regular employees. This has naturally meant transferring and retraining production workers. For instance, steelmaker C, after the recession triggered by the yen appreciation, closed down five blast furnaces at Muroran and Kamaishi and concentrated production in the Oita and Kimitsu plants. The company reached a peak of more than 82,000 employees in 1972 but had only 61,000 workers in 1987 (− 25 percent). By 1990 it is expected to have 19,000 surplus workers. According to its plan to cut steel production to 50 percent of total output, the company intends (with union consensus) to use 6,000 of its surplus employees in the electronics, information, and communication network business, to lose 9,000 workers by normal retirement and natural attrition, and to relocate the remaining surplus 4,000 workers to affiliated companies and to retraining schemes financed by government subsidies for employment adjustment.

The reason why Japanese large companies are able to retrain and relocate smoothly a large number of regular employees between plants and occupations without incurring substantial labor unrest is that the enterprise union gives the utmost importance to regular employees (i.e., union members) and to "good employment opportunities" for them. The reciprocal trust that characterizes Japanese industrial relations is not a sudden accomplishment but has developed since the first half of the 1960s.[4]

The Establishment of New Subsidiaries

Extensive use of affiliated subcontractors is peculiar to the assembler-dominated production that characterizes the electric, car, and precision instruments sectors. Compared with the United States, the degree of inter-

---

4. For discussion of the change in union strategies brought about by the prospect of the liberalization of trade and capital flows, see Koshiro (1983b).

nalization of industrial production is much lower in Japan (see Nakamura 1983). According to Imai, Itami, and Koike (1982), widespread use of sub-contractors and "intermediate organizations" by Japanese firms intensified after the oil shocks, when, for a number of reasons, firms spun off a number of subsidiaries.

According to this chapter's case studies, the phenomenon can be classified into the following five broad categories:

1. Entry into high- (expected) growth and high-risk sectors, such as electronics and information services.

2. Exploitation of local low-cost labor by setting up manufacturing plants of standardized production as separate firms.

3. Separation of simple industrial services, such as security, transportation, and maintenance.

4. Separation from the main body of the firm of services, such as travel agency, insurance, and banking, that treat employees as clients.

5. Separation of collateral lines of business, such as leisure centers, facilities for the elderly, training facilities, electronic sales, and worker dispatchment agencies.

Strategies 3, 4, and 5 acquired increasing importance as employment adjustment devices after the oil shocks and have become reservoirs of surplus employees. At the same time they have extended their business outside the sphere of the parent company.

Firm G, a leading firm in the computer and communications equipment sector, had 37,744 employees in 1988. To this can be added 55,148, if employees in 88 subsidiaries are taken into account. This means that 60.2 percent of total employment (94,892 workers) is covered by subsidiary companies, and this includes 5,053 workers (8.8 percent) dispatched from the parent firm. The subsidiaries are mostly provincial plants located all over the country from Hokkaido and Tohoku to Shikoku, Kyushu, and Okinawa.

Firm A, which operates in the car components business, entered new lines of business by setting up six subsidiaries (which employ 1,161 workers). It also transformed its manufacturing division into 12 affiliated companies, which operate as local subcontractors. The main purpose was to exploit lower labor costs in the countryside. The total number employed in these manufacturing companies is unknown. The six other subsidiaries were set up during the period 1960–79 to enter new lines of business such as electronics, nuclear power, and biochemistry.

Steelmaker *C* has 180 affiliated companies, about one-quarter of which were established after the first oil shock. More precisely, 18 new firms were set up in the late 1970s—early 1980s, and 25 new firms were established during the second half of the 1980s. As mentioned above, the parent company is planning to absorb surplus employees into new lines of business, including electronics, information, and communication networks and services. For this purpose the firm set up in June 1987 the multipurpose firm "C Business Promotion Ltd." (ten offices in the whole country) and established in April 1988 four firms operating in the information sector. Firm *C* has 62,000 employees. This number reaches 250,000, however, if we take into account the employees in affiliated and cooperating companies. Wages in subsidiary companies are on average 80 percent of the wages in the parent company.

In firm *D* in heavy engineering, one of its plants has its own six subsidiaries, in addition to the subsidiaries of the main firm. Firm *H*, established in 1961, is one of the six and does all the plant's drafting work and detail design, leaving to the parent plant only the more fundamental design work. This firm was established to create positions for employees of the parent firm who had reached mandatory retirement. More recently another of the six, firm *I* (machinery), was established in 1966 as a subcontractor to assemble equipment in the environmental control sector. The parent holds 50 percent of paid-in capital, and the employees number 30. Another example is firm *J* formed out of the transportation department (50 percent of capital held by the parent firm, 78 employees). Twenty-five percent of employees in firm *K* and 30 percent of firm *L* were transferred either temporarily or permanently from the parent firm.

In contrast with the pattern discussed so far, the establishment of subsidiaries by firm *F* has not been guided by employment adjustment reasons. Almost all the 24 national subsidiaries are 100 percent controlled dealers and manufacturing subsidiaries. Other subsidiaries acquired by merger include a manufacturer of lenses (1963) and a maker of camera bodies (1968). The firm also established "rest homes" for retired employees, an insurance firm, a travel agency, a land and home dealer, a transportation service, and a cleaning firm. Firm *F* adopted from the start a strategy of internalizing production for its main line of business (cameras). Starting in the second half of the 1960s, however, it has spun off its production lines into manufacturing subsidiaries. During the late 1970s the strategy evolved to limit the parent company to the function of technical center for the group. From 1980, however, the production and sales of a new product line, with equipment related to semiconductors, was completely internalized to speed up product development. Currently 80 percent is produced in-house.

Transfers

The strategy of slimming down the parent firm by setting up affiliated companies meant increasing the number of employees transferred out by the parent firm. The percentage of transferred employees is particularly high in structurally depressed industries such as textiles and shipbuilding. Structurally depressed firms are moving on a large scale into new lines of business, which suggests that more than 20 percent of total employment is being transferred to subsidiaries. Firm *A* (shipbuilding), firm *B* (textiles), plant *Y* of firm *D* (equipment for ships), belong to this class of firms; this trend has increased after the appreciation of the yen (table 12.6).[5] A similar trend can be observed for steelmaker *C*, which went through a structural crisis after the appreciation of the yen. In recent years this trend has extended to firms in growing industries. Examples are firm *E* (car components), firm *F* (precision instruments), firm *G* (computers, communications equipment). Nearly half of the 64,490 workers in the group controlled by firm *G*, for instance, are either employed by, or on transfer to, subsidiaries.

According to the *Survey on Labor Management* by the Ministry of Labor (January 1987), the total number of transferred workers is 570,000, which corresponds to 5.9 percent of all employees. This percentage rises to 7.6 in firms with more than 5,000 employees. With the exception of firm *F*, the companies considered in our case studies have a remarkably higher than average percentage of dispatched employees. Wages and labor conditions in affiliated companies are generally lower than in the parent firm. The parent firm is thus forced to subsidize the difference in wages to transferred employees (up to 30 to 40 percent of total wages); transfers are transformed, after a given period, from temporary to permanent. Generally speaking, workers over 55 years of age are transferred permanently and have to adjust to working conditions in their new firms.

Increase in the Share of Total Employment Covered by White-Collar Workers

As seen above in firms *E*, *F*, and *G*, the tendency to spin off the manufacturing division into separate subsidiaries has led to transformation of the

---

5. The usual distinction is between "temporary" and "permanent" transfer (*shukko*). The latter implies that the employment relationship with the parent firm is severed. The former maintains this employment relationship. Transfers are distinguished from dispatchments (*haken*) by agencies (e.g., secretaries who are employed *in order* to be dispatched). There are also cases of transfers from subsidiaries to parent firms for temporary support and training. See Sugeno (1985) for details.

**Table 12.6**
Transferred employees in some representative firms (recent trends)

| Company | Year | Employees[a] | Employees transferred out | Share of transferred employees |
|---|---|---|---|---|
| Firm A | 1982 | 10,880 | 1,382 | 12.7 |
|  | 1985 | 10,246 | 1,715 | 16.7 |
|  | 1986 | 7,837 | 1,773 | 22.6 |
| Firm B | 1969 | 23,756 | 4,990 | 21.0 |
|  | 1979 | 20,994 | 7,528 | 35.0 |
|  | 1986 | 20,617 | 5,044 | 24.5 |
| Firm C | 1982 | 69,100 | 3,700 | 5.4 |
|  | 1986 | 64,400 | 7,900 | 12.3 |
|  | 1987 | 61,600 | 9,100 | 14.8 |
| Plant Y of Firm D | 1982 | 3,701 | 158 | 4.3 |
|  | 1986 | 3,008 | 326 | 10.8 |
|  | 1987 | 3,310 | 930 | 28.1 |
| Firm E | 1955 | 3,334 | 284 | 8.5 |
|  | 1986 | 3,753 | 571 | 15.2 |
|  | 1987 | 3,817 | 608 | 15.9 |
| Firm F | 1982 | 6,421 | 222 | 3.5 |
|  | 1986 | 6,971 | 439 | 6.3 |
|  | 1987 | 6,868 | 535 | 7.8 |
| Firm G | 1984 | 34,950 | 2,703 | 7.7 |
|  | 1986 | 37,225 | 3,792 | 10.2 |
|  | 1987 | 36,722 | 4,336 | 11.8 |

Source: Koshiro et al. (1988a, 35).
a. Total on the books of the parent company.

parent firm into a technical and planning center. As a consequence the proportion of white-collar workers has increased in the surveyed firms; to as much as 60 to 80 percent in firms A, F, G, and D (plant Y). This tendency is encouraged also by the progress of automation and diversification into the service and high-tech sectors, a process accelerated by the oil shocks and the crisis triggered by the appreciation of the yen. Thus the tendency for production divisions to grow disproportionately during the 1960s and the 1970s has changed into the tendency to give a greater weight to planning, R&D, and sales divisions.

Decreasing Share of Women in Regular Employment

After the oil shocks there has been a remarkable overall increase in labor participation by women (especially part-timers). Since approval in 1985 of the Law on Equal Employment Opportunities for Men and Women, the percentage of firms hiring women for management and other jobs with career prospects has increased, but the percentage of women working as regular employees in auxiliary jobs and assembly lines has decreased quite dramatically. During the period of structural adjustment, women were separated first and tended to stay out of the labor force. The share of female labor declined from 24 percent in 1965 to 11 percent in 1986 in firm $B$ (textiles), from 43 percent in 1965 to 26 percent in 1987 in firm $E$ (car components), and from 31 percent to 12 percent during the same period in firm $F$ (cameras). In firm $G$ (computers) a decline from 30 percent in 1969 to 18 percent in 1979 was reversed and reached 25 percent as the firm expanded production of word processors and personal computers. In the two shipbuilders considered in this study, women make up less than 10 percent.

Retirement of Older Workers and Early Retirement

A remarkable recent change in the human resource management of Japanese firms is the treatment of older employees. Following the Law on Fair Labor Opportunities for the Elderly (1986), firms were encouraged to increase efforts to raise mandatory retirement to 60 years. In practice, companies are only gradually introducing the new system. The two oil shocks and the appreciation of the yen have made most firms wary of rapidly shifting mandatory retirement to 60.

For instance, in the case of shipbuilder $A$, the mandatory retirement age was gradually raised from 55 in 1974 to 58. After the first oil shock, however, it was agreed that all employees over 55 would retire, so the practical application of the new scheme was delayed. In 1983 the mandatory age was set at 60, but the yen appreciation at the end of 1985 and the ensuing crisis led once again to the enforced retirement of all employees over 55. Because of this, the firm will probably have first age-60 retirement in 1994. Early retirement as a measure of employment adjustment is often bargained with the union and requires a premium on the amount of severance pay. Usually severance pay of blue collars at 55 is 15 million yen. A premium for early retirement of 13 months of pay makes the total severance payment 20 million. The underlying idea is that this guarantees the previous income up to the age of 60, given that

1. unemployment benefits can support the retired worker for the first year,

2. the severance premium of one year's salary will take care of an additional year if re-employment does not occur afterwards,

3. after reemployment, the salary in the new firm (usually 60 percent of the previous salary) can be supplemented by interest on, and running down of, the severance premium.

Steelmaker C and shipbuilder D, both hard hit by the yen appreciation, are actually retiring employees at 59 years and are delaying the extension to 60 years up to 1990. On the other hand, firms B and F, which were affected only slightly by the appreciation of the yen, are retiring employees at 60 years of age. Actually these firms are also implementing a retirement scheme for managerial staff, which consists of transferring employees in their fifties to subsidiaries. Both in firm B and in firm C retirement age for managerial staff is 55. Employees over 50 who are university graduates have to go through a very strict selection in order to become top management. Those who do not make it become top management in affiliated companies.

In firm D extension of the retirement age beyond 58 years does not apply to managerial staff from section chief up. About 90 percent of managerial employees are transferred permanently to an affiliated company by the age of 55.5. This is equivalent to the termination of their employment relationship with their original firm. In the new firm employment is guaranteed up to age 60. In the same fashion, managerial staff in firm A over 50 have to submit to an interview. Those who fail are transferred permanently to an affiliated company. Both in firms A and D, only 10 percent of university graduates remain with the firm up to mandatory retirement. On the other hand, in firm B, which has faced fewer problems than firms A and D, the percentage of university graduates remaining with the parent firm up to retirement is 50 percent. In this firm the mandatory retirement system for graduate employees works as follows:

1. Thirty percent remain as managers until mandatory retirement.

2. Twenty percent remain up to the mandatory age, but as specialists, in nonmanagerial positions.

3. The remaining 50 percent leave before mandatory age, either by moving to an affiliated firm (30 percent) or by early retirement.

Thus, even if retirement at 60 is encouraged by law, employment adjustment has delayed its application. In particular, the lifetime employment system has become an elusive ideal for white-collar university graduates; the best they can hope for is employment up to 60 (or sometimes a little beyond) guaranteed only within the wider sphere of the industrial group.

Part-time and Dispatched Workers

In contrast to the shrinking of the core of workers who enjoy the lifetime employment system, there has been an increase in the relative importance of part-timers, dispatched workers, and the marginal labor force. It is not easy to give a clear-cut estimate of the size of part-time employment in Japan.[6]

Three different definitions are available:

1. Workers who work no more than 35 hours a week (*Labor Force Survey*, Office of the Prime Minister).

2. Workers who are defined as part-timers or as close substitutes of part-timers in the firm (*Survey on the Employment Structure*, Office of the Prime Minister).

3. Regularly employed workers who work fewer standard hours a day or fewer days a week than the standard regular worker (*Survey on the Wage Structure and Survey on Employment Trends*, Ministry of Labor).

The last definition is the closest to the definition chosen by the Central Committee on Labor Standards in October 1984 (Ichino 1989).

Of the three definitions above, the first includes among part-timers regular workers who, because of temporary holidays, are working shorter hours than usual. On the other hand, it excludes those part-timers who work more than 35 hours, something not unusual in Japan. According to this definition, part-timers have increased from 2,780,000 in 1973 (7.9 percent of nonagricultural employment net of those who are temporarily out of work) to 5,030,000 workers in 1986 (11.7 percent of the total). According to the *Survey on the Wage Structure*, which divides female employment between regulars and part-timers, the share of female part-timers out of total female employment increased from 4.8 percent in 1972 to 19.3 percent in 1987.

Ichino (1989) has extended the data from the *Survey on the Wage Structure* to include the fishing industry, government employees, and firms with fewer than 9 workers and has estimated that female part-timers increased from 510,000 in 1972 to about 3 million in 1987. According to the *Survey on the Employment Structure*, however, part-timers in 1987 were 4.68 million (220,000 men and the rest women).

Among part-time workers, dispatched employees have played an important role since the first oil shock. The Law on Employment Stability (1947)

---

6. Okunishi (1988) presents a detailed analysis of the statistical definition of part-timers.

excluded in principle fee-taking private employment agencies, with the exception of special occupations such as "music and artistic performance and other occupations which require special skills" (Art. 32). Those special-skill occupations were deemed to include scientists, physicians, dentists, pharmacists, midwives, nurses, hospital technicians, designers, lawyers, movie directors and technicians, certified accountants, tax consultants, managers, makers of traditional cakes (*namagashi*), domestic servants, beauty parlor operators, models, bartenders, cleaning experts, interpreters, cooks, and so on. After the first oil shock, however, the explosion of the service sector led to a widening of the range of occupations covered by agencies that dispatch employees (mainly part-time females). The law of July 1985 on employment dispatchment agencies authorized this business for 16 new occupations. By November 1988 there were 21,001 authorized agencies employing 59,821 regular employees and 37,663 temporary workers. These new occupations include general accounting, office automation operators, secretarial jobs, computer software, design, building maintenance, and related activities.

Furthermore the expansion of the service and catering sectors brought into the labor force an increasing number of students doing part-time jobs. Koyama (1988) estimates that about 3 million high school and college students work part-time out of a total of 10 million. A Survey by the Tokyo Labor Research Center (1988) reports a large number of students working in fast food establishments, pubs, department stores, and supermarkets.

In general, this increase in the number of part-time and dispatched workers increases the flexibility of the labor market. It does not necessarily mean, however, a reduction in the proportionate size of the "stable labor force" or in the importance of long tenures. Among part-timers the share of workers with long tenures may be increasing, and more important, the tenures of those who remain as core regular employees are likely to lengthen.

Ichino (1989), for instance, uses the *Basic Survey on the Wage Structure* to work out a "stability rate" for female employees—the percentage of workers with one year's service in a given year who remain as workers with five years' service five years later. For full-time workers there was an increase from 47 to 55 percent from the 1977–82 cohort to the 1982–87 cohort. For part-time workers there was a slight decline from 48 percent for the 1980–85 cohort to 45 percent for the 1982–87 cohort.

The recent trend in human resource management of large Japanese firms is well explained by the theory of employment determination in labor-minded firms formalized by Komiya (1988). The principle is that employment of core "member" workers is held back to the point at which the marginal product of labor equals the average net product of labor. This principle contrasts with the principle that determines the employment of peripheral workers, namely to equalize the market wage with the marginal product of labor. Temporary workers, subcontractors, part-timers, and dispatched workers come in this peripheral "non member" category, whereas employees transferred to subsidiaries are in between "member" and "non-member" workers.

## 12.4 Relationship among Wages, Bonuses, and Employment

An outstanding feature of Japanese human resource management is the remuneration system. As pointed out by Komiya (1988), large Japanese firms behave as if they were maximizing the per capita income of (core) employees. Komiya states that

... in large Japanese firms an important part of profits is allocated to employees and executives.... Empirical evidence on this point, however is not conclusive. Thus there is a need for a detailed analysis of the renumeration system within the firm. In particular, one should investigate the relationship between net profits, bonuses and wages at the firm level. (p. 57)

Actually, the sort of empirical research advocated by Komiya was carried out in the 1960s by Sano (1967, 1970) and later by the Ministry of Labor (1973) and Koshiro (1980, 1986). The results of recent research on bonus and wage determination in large Japanese corporations are outlined below. If one says that employees in large Japanese firms receive the going market wage plus a premium that amounts to a share in profits, how is this share distributed? In general the distribution can occur by means of

1. the standard wage (net of overtime),

2. bonuses,

3. severance pay and fringes,

4. entertainment expenses.

In what follows I will focus on points 1 and 2.

Responsiveness of Standard Wages to Profits

Since 1955 wage settlements in Japan have occurred during the Spring Wage Offensive. The Labor Administration section of the Labor Ministry

**Table 12.7**
Average wage increases in main private corporations (Δws)

| Sector and sample period | Explanatory variables | | | | | $\bar{R}^2$ | DW | Profit elasticity of wages[a] |
|---|---|---|---|---|---|---|---|---|
| | Constant | PCS[b] | UYS[c] | $\pi/L$ | DMY[d] | | | |
| Average for all industries | | | | | | | | |
| 1973–85 | 687.0 (0.36) | 673.5 (7.16) | 5,301.5 (3.50) | 2,286.6 (2.71) | — | 0.9128 | 2.46 | 0.252 |
| 1973–86 | 800.2 (0.44) | 675.1 (7.53) | 5,268.9 (3.65) | 2,194.2 (2.90) | — | 0.9162 | 2.43 | 0.263 |
| 1973–87 | 800.2 (0.47) | 675.1 (8.09) | 5,266.4 (3.84) | 2,192.5 (3.05) | — | 0.9226 | 2.44 | 0.263 |
| 1973–88 | 1,091.2 (0.68) | 681.0 (8.41) | 5,057.1 (3.91) | 2,054.8 (3.09) | — | 0.9222 | 2.42 | 0.263 |
| Average for all industries | | | | | | | | |
| 1973–85 | 2,740.4 (2.47) | 561.3 (10.15) | 4,528.6 (5.49) | 1,470.1 (3.06) | 3,704.0 (4.86) | 0.9752 | 3.10 | 0.177 |
| 1973–86 | 2,732.1 (2.68) | 561.3 (10.18) | 4,531.2 (6.19) | 1,476.1 (3.49) | 3,700.4 (5.19) | 0.9767 | 3.10 | 0.177 |
| 1973–87 | 2,732.1 (2.82) | 561.6 (11.57) | 4,529.4 (6.19) | 1,474.8 (3.70) | 3,700.5 (5.47) | 0.9787 | 3.10 | 0.177 |
| 1973–88 | 2,853.0 (3.21) | 562.3 (12.06) | 4,449.4 (6.56) | 1,419.8 (3.92) | 3,739.6 (5.81) | 0.9791 | 3.11 | 0.185 |

Note: DW is based on data of the Labor Administration section of the Ministry of Labor. After 1980 the date is weighted by numbers of union members. Before 1980 the data are simple averages. 290 firms in 1988.
a. $p/L$ (profits per employee) is based on data on 895 firms from the NEEDS databank. The variable is expressed in million yen.
b. PCS is the rate of growth of the consumer price index over the previous year (January–March period).
c. UYS is the effective job offers/job seekers ratio (January–March of each year).
d. DMY is a dummy that takes the value 1 in the years 1974 and 1982, and zero otherwise. It is meant to capture shifts in industrial relations.

has collected from 1956 data on wage settlements of large private enterprises. These corporations, belonging both to the Tokyo and to the Osaka Stock Exchanges, have at least 200 million of paid-in capital, more than 1,000 employees, and are unionized. The current size of the sample is 290 firms. Sano (1967) has used these data disaggregated at the industry level from 1965 to study the correlation between average wage hikes and current profits per employee. The data on profits are from the *Economic Indicators of Main Private Firms* by the Bank of Japan. Sano found that this correlation was significant during the high-growth era.

After the first oil shock Koshiro (1980) slightly modified Sano's model and extended the sample period up to 1980. Table 12.7 shows both the results based on the 1973–88 sample period and the results from regressions that extend the sample year by year beyond 1985.

Rows 1 through 8 of the table show that spring wage settlements (inclusive of automatic increases) are significantly related to current profits per employee measured at the end of the fiscal year (March). For instance, row 8 shows that if profits per employee increase by 1 million yen, wages increase by 1,420 yen. In the case of the 1989 wage settlement, profits per head increased by about 3.11 million yen. According to the estimates, this should have implied a wage hike of 4,416 yen (1,419.8 × 3.11). The increase at 12,747 yen, was about three times larger; profits explain about a third of its increase. The average profit elasticity of wages, however, though increasing in the past few years, reached only 0.1846 in row 8, a rather small number. The implication is that wage hikes are sensitive to labor market conditions as a whole (as shown by the significant coefficients of the job offers/job seekers ratio) and to price hikes. The fact that wages also respond to profits, however, should not be overlooked.

Relationship between Bonuses and Profits

The responsiveness of Japanese bonuses to the business cycle is considered to be the main ingredient of real wage flexibility in this country. This opinion is widely held in Europe and the United States. Hashimoto (1979), Gordon (1979), OECD (1983, 1984, 1986), and Weitzman (1984) represent this view. For instance, the OECD (1984) reports:

... the Japanese economy combines employment stability with the bonus system, which ensures that remuneration is flexible.... The question is whether the allocation of labor resources is more efficient in Japan than elsewhere. If the answer is positive, the next question is why.... in Japan and especially in large firms, employment security is not challenged by demand shocks. The adjustment role lies on the bonus system, which allows labor and management to split the costs. (p. 67)

Moreover Hashimoto (1979) argues that the bonus system represents a share in profit derived from investment in human capital. In the empirical evidence presented by Hashimoto, he calculates an index of production responsiveness to business cycle fluctuations by industry sector—the co-efficient in the regression of the logarithm of industrial production on the logarithm of GNP. He also calculates for each sector a similar index for the bonus/wage ratio (RB) by regressing the logarithm of RB on the logarithm of GNP. He then shows that the correlation between these two is quite high. The variable RB should increase with an expansion and decrease with a contraction if the bonus component of total renumeration is more flexible than the rest. This method, however, does not allow a direct analysis of the relationship between bonuses and profits. Moreover no explanation is given of whether bonuses are more flexible than the remaining components of total remuneration.[7]

The European and American view of the flexibility of Japanese bonuses is exaggerated. There are two reasons for this. First, the history of the development of the bonus systems after the Second World War is largely ignored. Second, limits to data availability abroad do not allow a direct measurement of the relationship between bonus and profit variations.

The Japanese bonus system before the Second World War was almost exclusively limited to white-collar workers. Blue-collar workers were paid in allowances to buy food and presents when they went back to their families at midsummer and year end.[8] The payment of bonuses to blue-collar workers started with the labor movement after the end of the Second World War, which led to the abolition of differences based on occupation. During the severe inflation of the late 1940s, however, bonus payments took the form of supplementary payments to keep up with living costs. Because of this, current payments were strongly tied to previous payments and were very sticky downward. So they are today. For instance, the Confederation of Private Railway Workers adopted in 1972 the formula of negotiating bonus level in terms of "months' worth" of regular wages (5.4 months in 1987). The Electrical Engineering Workers Federation set a stan-

---

7. Mizuno (1985) criticizes the view held by Hashimoto, Gordon, and Kahn (1984) that bonuses are more flexible than wages. He argues that (1) the ratio of special wage payments (which include the bonus and other wage adjustments) to contractual wages (gross over-time) does not exceed 26.1 percent and (2) the contribution of bonuses to total wage flexibility was 9 percent during 1960–83 and 16.4 percent during 1974–83. Thus the main source of wage flexibility in Japan is the behavior of contractual wages, which cover 75 percent of total payments.

8. End-of-period bonuses, which correspond to actual bonuses, were not paid to most factory workers. Those who were lucky received something between ¥5 and ¥50. (Hazama 1978, 366; see also Showa dojinkai 1960; Kagiyama 1977).

dard of "at least five months paid out as bonuses." Moreover Toyota Motors paid the same 6.1 months of regular pay as bonuses from 1967 to 1986. Even the unions in big shipbuilders, a depressed industry, established a minimum of three months' pay as a bonus "as a necessary supplement to cover living expenses." In the wake of the 1987 expansion they asked for 120,000 yen plus 3.5 months of regular pay as bonuses.

On the other hand, a profit-sharing component in bonuses cannot be denied. The determination of bonuses is often based on some profit-sharing formula. According to The *Survey on the Determination of Wages and Working Hours* by the Ministry of Labor (1983), 32 percent of the surveyed firms have such a mechanism of bonus determination that takes profit performance into account (52.5 percent of these firms make this mechanism explicit); 68.3 percent of firms use the assessment of individual performance as a criterion for the determination of the bonus. The proportion of the bonus linked to such personal assessments ranged from 13 to 20 percent.

Link between Profits and Bonuses

A representative case of the regulation of bonus payments within the framework of a labor agreement is that of Asahi Kasei and its union, which is affiliated to the All Textiles Workers Industrial Union (see Koshiro 1988b). The negotiation of bonuses at Asahi Kasei occurs once a year and determines both the winter and the following summer bonus payment. The criteria are two. One is the return on capital $(\pi/K)$; the other is a fixed ratio between total pay and current profits. For instance, the summer bonus for 1987 in number of months of regular pay $(Y)$ was given by

$$Y = 0.0471\left(\frac{\pi}{wN}\right) + 2.187, \tag{12.1}$$

where

$$\frac{\pi}{K} = \frac{\text{Current profits in second part of fiscal year 1986 (million ¥)}}{\text{Average capital employed in fiscal year 1986}} \times 100,$$

$$\frac{\pi}{wN} = \frac{\text{Current profits in second part of fiscal year 1986 (million ¥)}}{\begin{array}{l}\text{Average monthly base of}\\ \text{union members at 15 March 1987}\\ \times \text{ Average number of}\\ \text{employees in fiscal year 1986–87}\end{array}} \times 100.$$

The parameters in equation (12.1) were obtained from the regression of actual past bonuses (in number of months) on the profit indicators $\pi/K$ and $\pi/wN$ on the sample period summer 1979–summer 1986.

$$Y_1 = \frac{0.0893\pi}{K} + 2.1443, \tag{12.2}$$

$$Y_2 = \frac{0.0679\pi}{wN} + 2.1862. \tag{12.3}$$

The simple (rounded) average of (12.2) and (12.3) is given by

$$Y = \frac{Y_1 + Y_2}{2} = \frac{0.00447\pi}{K} = \frac{0.034\pi}{wN} = 2.1653. \tag{12.4}$$

If we insert into (12.4) the performance of the first part of fiscal year 1986 ($\pi/K = 4.45\Pi/wN = 4.59$), we get

$$Y^* = 2.52. \tag{12.5}$$

Taking equation (12.5) as the basis, collective bargaining makes the final adjustment to get equation (12.1) as the formula for the summer bonus of 1987. The number of months paid under that formula was 2.563. Of that sum, 85 percent (2.187 months) was contributed by the constant term, so the profit-related portion was only 15 percent.

Clearly even in a firm such as Asahi Kasei, which uses an explicit link between bonuses and profits, the bonus component that varies with profit fluctuations is limited, and bonuses as a whole exhibit a higher than expected degree of downward rigidity, though this is not to deny the notion that bonuses can be seen as a share in profits.[9]

Responsiveness of Bonuses to Profits

The White Paper on Labor by the Ministry of Labor (1973) shows that bonuses ($B$) in Japanese main corporations can be explained simply as

---

9. This conclusion is perhaps in line with the work done by Otake (1988), who challenges the conventional view that Japanese real wages are flexible. Otake studies the rate of adjustment of real wages to their equilibrium level in five countries (Japan, the United States, Britain, West Germany, and France) and shows that the rate is lowest in Japan, where it is equal to 0.13 (0.88 in Britain, 0.36 in West Germany, 0.24 in the United States, and 0.31 in France). The rate of adjustment of worker hours is rather 0.52, as in West Germany, which is lower than in the United States (0.80) but consistent. For other studies on the flexibility of the labor market, see Chinloy and Stromsdorfer (1987), Koshiro (1989a, 1989b), and Starfati and Kobrin (1988).

$$B_{it} = a + b\left(\frac{\pi}{L}\right)_{it} + B_{i,t-1}, \tag{12.7}$$

where $\pi/L$ is profits per head. Koshiro (1986) applies this formula to the data on bonuses by industry sector of the Labor Administration Section of the Labor Ministry (1973–84) and obtains good results with the exception of private railways and public utilities. Here I present the results for the industrial sector as a whole (equation 12.8).

$$B_t = 178.847 + 0.05833\left(\frac{\pi}{L}\right)t + 0.742B_{t-1},$$

$$(4.77) \quad (2.14) \quad\quad\quad (9.59)$$

$R = 0.9721$,    Durbin $h = -1.51$ ($Z_{0.05} = 1.65$).

The estimates are based on the OLS method. Since the Durbin $h$ is well under the critical value at the 5 percent level of confidence, there is no serial correlation. For the private industrial sector as a whole, the bonus paid is significantly correlated with profits per head. If we calculate the profit elasticities of bonuses, we find that the short-term elasticity is 0.100 whereas the long-term elasticity (calculated by setting $B_t = B_{t-1}$) is 0.3879. The last number is much larger than the profit elasticity of regular wages computed above. At a more disaggregated level, the long-run elasticity ranges from 0.7593 in the shipbuilding and general equipment industry to 0.2864 in the steel industry and 0.3448 in textiles.

If we disaggregate further to the firm level, equation (12.7) does not perform so well. There are cases where replacing current with operating profits and profits per employee with profits as a percentage of sales improves results. For instance, in the case of the five major steelmakers, $AR_1$ estimates produce better results with sales margins ($\pi/S$) than with profits per head ($\pi/L$) (see table 12.8). For Nippon Kokan the degree of fit is lower than for other firms, and the estimated coefficient of first-order serial correlation is higher, with the danger of serially correlated errors. This result could be explained with the fact that Nippon Kokan has a large shipbuilding division, which performed much worse than steel after the first oil shock. This performance notwithstanding, bonuses at Nippon Kokan have remained very much in line with bonuses paid by major competitors. Not included in table 12.8 are the results based on data from small and medium steelmakers. These results are generally good with the exception of two makers of special steel (Aichi Steel and Mitsubishi Steel). In these two firms the sign of profits per head is negative. If we focus on the profit elasticity

**Table 12.8**
Relationship between bonuses and profits in the steel industry

|  | Constant | $(\pi/S)_{t-1}$ | $B_{t-1}$ | $\bar{R}^2$ | DW | $\rho$ |
|---|---|---|---|---|---|---|
| Industry as a whole | 85,402 (2.0917) | 21,276 (5.0161) | 0.87999 (20.091) | 0.978559 | 2.0384 | −0.11814 (−0.35340) |
| Five major firms | 95,638 (1.1439) | 23,860 (4.6639) | 0.85579 (9.3440) | 0.946830 | 1.9014 | 0.32889 (1.1391) |
| Nippon Steel | 57,833 (0.88514) | 25,624 (6.3716) | 0.89527 (12.284) | 0.962850 | 1.8582 | 0.33179 (1.1643) |
| Nippon Kokan | −85,689 (−0.25593) | 40,302 (2.6754) | 1.0398 (3.0243) | 0.526825 | 2.5827 | 0.65006 (4.1283) |
| Sumitomo Kinzoku | 107,080 (1.4872) | 16,250 (2.7350) | 0.85376 (10.688) | 0.935828 | 2.0097 | 0.17276 (0.52182) |
| Kobe Seiko | 87,037 (1.3787) | 22,136 (3.8151) | 0.89161 (12.399) | 0.958169 | 2.0030 | 0.14358 (0.46243) |
| Kawasaki Seiko | 126,860 (3.0464) | 15,828 (4.8967) | 0.83854 (18.003) | 0.975574 | 1.7486 | −0.11776 (−0.43123) |
| Small and medium firms | 119,010 (3.7409) | 16,237 (5.0868) | 0.86697 (22.523 | 0.981348 | 2.2968 | −0.24241 (−0.70909) |

Note: Estimate by $AR_1$.

of bonuses, the short-term elasticity for the five major steelmakers is 0.0945, whereas the long-run elasticity is 0.655. In the case of the 16 medium and small steelmakers, these elasticities are, respectively, 0.0536 and 0.403. Other experiments with car makers, textile firms, shipbuilders, and electrical engineering firms do not lead to satisfactory results.

The Case of Public Utilities

Public utilities are usually constrained in their pricing policies. So, even if they are private corporations, the determination of bonuses cannot simply be explained by firm profits. Here I consider the case of the 12 major private railways (Tobu, Tokyu, Kintetsu, Nankai, Hankyu, Hanshin, Keihan, Keikyu, Keisai, Keio, Meitetsu, and Seitetsu). The regression analysis uses profits per head $(\pi/L)$ as well of kilometers of service done per head $(RK/L)$. Results are presented in equation (12.9). Equation (12.10) instead presents the estimates of a similar equation for the 9 electric power companies. In this case I use electric power sold per employee as a measure of profitability. In both types of public utilities the measures of physical productivity have an important role to play. In the case of electric power, the elasticity of bonuses to productivity is 0.64—a rather large number.

*Private Railways (1976–85)*

$$B_t = -880.475 + 82,085 \left(\frac{\pi}{L}\right)_t + 111,875 \left(\frac{RK}{L}\right)_t, \qquad (12.9)$$

$$(-17.84) \quad (2.92) \qquad\qquad (32.04)$$

$\bar{R}^2 = 0.9973, \quad DW = 2.04.$

*Electric Power (1976–86)*

$$B_t = -222,149 + 0.5994 B_{t-1} + 1.4617 \left(\frac{KW}{L}\right)_t, \qquad (12.10)$$

$$(-2.06) \quad (2.86) \qquad\qquad (2.27)$$

$\bar{R}^2 = 0.9718, \quad DW = 2.07, \quad \text{Durbin } h = -0.1645.$

In this section I have considered profit-sharing characteristics of bonuses and disregarded the view expressed by Hamada (1985), who argues that bonuses are lump-sum payments for overtime. This view is based on the critique of implicit contract models by Topel and Welch (1982) and the shirking models of Lazear (1979, 1981). Hamada claims that bonuses as payment for overtime can be understood as a means to prevent a decline in efficiency where imperfect information could make an accurate monitoring of workers' "abilities" and performances difficult. The empirical analysis of Hamada's model is, however, unsatisfactory, since he finds that bonuses are strongly correlated with profits rather than with overtime hours (as predicted by his theory). In fact in Japanese large firms—with their developed internal labor markets, lifetime employment, annual wage hikes, and twice a year bonuses—the monitoring of abilities and effort is achieved through a detailed evaluation of individual performance. Thus the shirking model discussed by Lazear does not seem to be relevant (on this see chapter 14).

## 12.5 Conclusions

I have discussed the Japanese employment system by keeping in mind the debate on labor market flexibility. The Japanese lifetime employment system, a special form of human resource management, was analyzed for the period after the first oil shock both from the employment and the wage perspective.

The Japanese employment system can basically be explained by the neoclassical theory of human capital and the theory of internal labor markets, with the important qualification that this system is close to that of a labor-managed firm. The lifetime-employment system is not a social custom but the result of legal regulation, of employment security (particularly judicial precedents), and hard labor bargaining after the Second World War.

These restrictions notwithstanding, the structural adjustment that followed the oil shocks and the yen appreciation led to substantial employment adjustment. Several devices sought to reduce the number of lifetime employees and to expand the size of a more flexible labor force. The practice of adjusting to production fluctuations by changing hours of work was also reinforced. As a consequence the very sluggish adjustment of employment during the 1973–87 period (20 years to reach the optimal level) was in sharp contrast with the rather flexible adjustment of worker hours (in 2 years to reach the optimum). The speed of adjustment, however, is slowing down with respect to the period immediately after the first oil shock.

After the second oil shock and the yen appreciation, negative adjustment policies were increasingly coupled with positive measures such as the entry into new lines of business, the creation of subsidiaries, the intensive use of transfers, dispatched workers, and part-timers, and the development of a new human resource management strategy. This point is made clear in the chapter with the results of the eight-firm survey begun in autumn 1985. The major trends are the increased importance of planning, research and development, and sales departments (with the ensuing increased significance of white-collar workers), the reduction in the importance of female labor in large firms, and the transfer and the early retirement of male employees over 50. In particular, the extension of mandatory retirement to 60 years has been delayed by structurally depressed firms, with important consequences for the lifetime employment system.

The policy of limiting the number of core employees and responding to economic fluctuations by adjusting the number of temporary workers and working hours is typical of a labor-managed firm. In this type of firm core employees are paid more than the market wage because they share profits. In Japan large corporations pay both regular wages and bonuses by adjusting their payments to fluctuations in profits. This point has been made quite clear in the chapter both for bonuses and for wage hikes. For instance, 20 percent of the bonuses, which covers one-third of wages, is explained with movements in profits. The profit elasticities of bonuses and wages are, however, 0.4 and 0.17, respectively—not very large. Bonuses in particular exhibit a strong downward rigidity. This indicates that they are not simply a form of profit sharing but derive historically from their postwar role of maintaining living standards. In sum, Japanese firms have managed to adapt the rigidity of the lifetime employment system to economic fluctuations thanks to the existence of transfers within and beyond the firm, the creation of subsidiaries, and flexible overtime, on the one hand, and the flexibility of temporary and part-time employment, on the other, with supplementary help from the responsiveness of wages and profits to economic conditions.

# 13    Intellectual Skills and
        Long-Term Competition

Kazuo Koike

The chapter seeks to explain two factors affecting the behavior of workers in Japanese firms: intellectual skills and long-term competition. By "intellectual skills" I mean the techniques that workers learn on the job—what one might call the "software" of the human brain. Workers are encouraged to upgrade this knowledge through institutionally supported long-term competition. These two dependent factors may explain why workers in different countries will behave differently under the same environmental conditions, in the same industries, and with the same "hard" technologies.

One could go on at length about the special features of labor relations in large Japanese firms, but here I will consider three problem areas and will confine my discussion to a few words about each.

## 13.1  Special Features of Labor Relations in Japanese Firms

*Problem 1: What is the meaning of diligence?*

It means working better than workers in other countries, paying attention to the job and filling any gaps in job descriptions, and accepting responsibility, even at the lowest rank.

"Working better" does not involve working longer hours but rather working more efficiently. The common assertion is not that *all* Japanese workers, using the same machinery and equipment, have a higher productivity per hour than workers in Europe or America; that is, production workers in large firms and white-collar workers below middle-management levels. Whether higher-level Japanese managers are really better than their European or American counterparts is doubtful. Likewise the superior productivity of large-firm production workers does not apply to the whole period of Japan's industrialization; it is a recent phenomenon.

As for the vagueness of job descriptions, the fact that neither the scope nor contents of jobs are clearly written down, and workers need to fill in gaps, has not been researched thoroughly, despite a large literature making such assertions. (See Ishida 1985 for a discussion based on a questionnaire survey of Japanese managers running overseas plants.) Those who have written about the overseas applicability of Japanese managerial techniques affirm almost without exception that this differentiates Japanese from the foreign practice of specifying detailed job descriptions and that it leads to greater efficiency. They usually ascribe to it "group orientation," which is defined as a culturally specific Japanese way of thinking. The extent of this difference and the reasons for it, however, require further analysis.

The acceptance of responsibility overlaps with vagueness of job descriptions. Work is not carried out only on orders from above; there is delegation of decision making to lower ranks. Again, this often explained on the basis of "groupism," but is this really the case?

*Problem 2: What does long-term employment mean?*

Long-term employment involves fairly broad systems of promotion from within and definitive personnel selection after long time periods.

If the preceding question was concerned with outputs, here we are concerned with mechanisms that produce those outputs. It is quite conventional to point to long-term employment as a Japanese specialty (the so-called lifetime employment theory), but long-term employment is found among male Western white-collar workers and some blue-collar workers as well (Hall 1982; OECD 1984; Koike 1977, 1981). If one looks for special Japanese features perhaps they are to be found in the promotion system, and the way it gives blue-collar workers a broad range of experience. I found in a comparison of workshops in Japanese and American heavy and chemical industries (Koike 1977) not that Japanese workers do all kinds of work within the firm but that their promotions take place within two or three workshops that are closely related technologically. (Moving to an unrelated workshop is called by a different term, "transfer" and is not a promotion.) This contrasts with the U.S. system where promotion is usually within a single workshop. Why and what difference does it make?

By definitive selection, I have in mind the selection of candidates for higher management. The most significant difference between Japanese and European or American firms is that workers are selected quite early for promotion to higher management in the latter, but only after their work performance has been observed for 10 to 15 years in Japan.

Early promotion is good for the training of management. One can give people important job experience from the start, which prepares them for future work. At the same time the many who are passed over for promotion are discouraged, and their efficiency falls. In Japan's late-promotion system, some clearly inadequate workers may of course drop out of competition, but most stay to compete, maintaining their morale, through their initial 10 to 15 years. Moreover the definitive selection for promotion can be based on the evaluation of performance over many years, not short-period work performance or school records. Selection by either method will reflect the subjective judgments of evaluators (superiors), but the later it takes place, the larger will be the number of evaluations filed by different supervisors in the personnel office. This helps to reduce subjectivity and arbitrariness. The disadvantage of not allowing time to train leaders remains.

*Problem 3: What are the Methods of Compensation?*

These are primarily explained in terms of the so-called seniority curve and wages unrelated to the worker's specific job.

The seniority curve is often regarded as a special feature of the Japanese firm. Yet it is not uncommon for Western white-collar workers (Koike 1981, ch. 2). Its extension to blue-collar workers in large firms is, however, a special feature of Japan, and this needs explaining.

As for the relation of wages to specific jobs, the system of regular annual wage increases over time (which means that wages continue to rise even if the worker continues to do exactly the same job—what is sometimes also called a "qualification-related" rather than "job-related" wage system) is well known. The system is also referred to as "wages by qualification." There has been insufficient research in this area, but it appears to be very similar to the payment system of white-collar workers in the West. Its extension to blue-collar workers in large Japanese firms is a matter that needs detailed examination.

How well have existing theories been able to explain these phenomena? I have space here only for a brief answer. There is first the "long working hours theory." Once Japanese industry was thought to be competitive because of low wages; now the explanation has turned to long work hours. But this does not account for the higher productivity per hour.

Second, there is the "culture determination theory," the idea that the main variables are the Japanese esteem for workmanship and the propensity to see the firm as a group to which members should contribute. These allegedly explain why Japanese work well, are attentive and productive despite the vagueness of their job descriptions. There may be something to this explanation for the first area listed above, but for the second and third areas the culture theory has little to say about the material basis promoting groupism, namely the seniority wage curve and long-term employment. As I have already indicated, these are also characteristic of white-collar employment in large firms and even of some blue-collar workers in the West. Can one explain Western white-collar workers' behavior by a groupist culture?

## 13.2   Intellectual Skills

Adjustments to Change

The main thrust of my hypothesis is that high worker efficiency occurs on the shop floor because most workers in large Japanese firms' productive shops are sufficiently prepared intellectually to be able to react appropriately to changes and emergencies. Empirical research on this matter has only recently begun. I can only rely on my own studies over the last few years of nine workshops in six firms (I began with a much larger sample and carried out observations at least twice; see Koike, Muramatsu, and Hisamoto 1987; Koike and Inoki 1987). The nine workshops in my study were one workshop each in the mass production of food, chemicals, and cement, and in engineering, two workshops with highly automated assembly lines, two workshops making precision products to order, and two workshops with a considerable degree of mass production; all involved large firms.

Even in mass-production operations which seem at first glance not to require much skill, over the long term a single worker can be observed to have two tasks: normal working and deviations from normal working. Normal working involves highly standardized and repetitive work in which high efficiency depends on rapid and precise movements. These tasks are gradually taken over by machinery. For only repetitive work one might conclude that no skill level is necessary. However, if one observes carefully, it becomes apparent that even repetitive mass-production jobs involve more changes and problems than might be expected.

These deviations lead to what I will call "unusual operations," which may be subdivided into two categories: adjustments to changes and adjustment to problems. Changes occur in five ways: introduction of new products, changes in product mix, changes in scale of production, changes in production methods, and changes within the work groups themselves. To save space, I will consider mainly changes in the product mix and the introduction of new products.

Many different products with minor variations can move along a single assembly line. A firm must react quickly to keep up with the variations because of changes in demand, since a separate line for each product variety requires too much equipment. If the product changes, sometimes a worker must change tools and jigs. After a change, defects may be introduced unless there is fine tuning. It makes a great difference in efficiency whether the tool changes and fine adjustments are done well. A worker's ability to make adjustments to changes in a modern workshop is obviously a very important skill.

Add to this the problem of introducing a new product, and the production procedures and the types of tools and jigs acquire further importance. Initially engineers determine designs and production techniques, but only when production actually begins can one observe how smoothly the plan goes in practice. If there are production workers able and willing to suggest improvements, efficiency can be raised. For this, knowledge of the structures and mechanisms of the product is critical in determining technique. When trouble occurs, such knowledge is essential for resolving it.

Dealing with Problems

There is no such thing as a trouble-free work place. The higher the quality standards are raised, the more inescapable trouble and product defects (including small defects) become. Handling such problems efficiently is at the core of our contemporary concept of skill. It involves three steps:

First, there is inspection and the removal of defective products. If this is done immediately, one can reduce unnecessary work. After assembly is completed, finding defects is not an easy matter. To remove them, one must know what they look like, and since defects take many forms, this requires long experience.

Second one must determine the cause of the trouble. This is particularly important in order to prevent the recurrence of the trouble. If the cause cannot be discovered, defects in output will continue, or production will shut down for a while, so efficiency will fall quickly. Indeed the ability to diagnose difficulties is at the core of present-day technology.

Third is dealing with the problem once the cause has been determined. Even if major alterations are still left to specialized technicians, efficiency is increased when ordinary production workers can make minor adjustments themselves, and this requires an understanding of the structure of the product and of the production machinery—the source of most defects. Since the required understanding of production technology is somewhat similar to that of engineers, I call it "intellectual skill."

Questions will probably be raised about this. Even though "coping with changes and problems" is important, is it really central to the daily tasks of factory workers? Of a sample of six firms, the main task of workers in four of them was actually dealing with changes and problems. These four cover a variety of workshop technologies. Among mechanical industries the examples included highly automated assembly lines, a workshop producing one-off custom precision machinery, and of course equipment manufacture.

An illustration will make this easier to understand. I take a workshop that represents the direction of future trends in a large-scale manufacturing company with highly automated machining lines. In this workplace 10 to 20 machines form a manufacturing assembly line with a single operator in charge. The manufacture itself may be entirely automatic on each shift. At one end of the line, parts are supplied automatically and machined one after the other; at the other end, the finished products emerge. Therefore the only function of the operator is to deal with changes and problems. When things go smoothly, the operator has nothing to do. The principal change is an alteration in the flow of parts, which occurs several times a day. Then the operator must change the jigs, the tools, and so on.

The more complex the equipment, and the worse the maladjustments, the more defects appear, and the more frequently problems arise. Efficiency is higher the faster the operator can pinpoint the cause of a problem and correct it. When there is a major problem, the firm relies on specialized repair personnel, but ordinary workers observe carefully what the repair people do and learn more about the mechanism. It is being able to cope with such problems that makes one an experienced worker. Coping with such problems is a daily task; it has little or no relation to the so-called QC circles. It is sometimes called QC activity, but it is really a matter of individual workers figuring things out.

A Matter of Increasing Importance

Intellectual skill will become an increasingly important factor as mechanization progresses. It is often said that skills become less important the more mechanization advances, but from actual observations the skills involved suggest the opposite case. The area in which mechanization reduces the need for the worker is repetitive work; more people are needed for non-repetitive work. The more complex the machinery and equipment, the more difficult it becomes to acquire the understanding to deal with problems. In the example given of automated machinery with electronic controls, the worker has to understand not only the structure of the machinery but also the mechanisms of the oil and air pressures that control it, and the worker must have knowledge of at least elementary electronics.

The logical question is, Is it not possible to standardize the "approach to changes and problems?" If it could be done, we would not require such high skill from production workers. As far as I can observe in workshops, standardization is not easy; the variety of problems and changes is too great. A manual that describes all the operations necessary to deal with problems would be too bulky to use. By the time it were written, it would be out of date.

Even if one could standardize methods of coping with difficulties, efficiency would fall. Let me give an example. In the fermentation workshop of a biochemical company, the control of the oxygen quantity is a matter of decisive importance. Standardization means to set upper and lower limits for the oxygen quantity, and make adjustments if this quantity gets too high or too low. A veteran worker, however, can make adjustments within even narrower limits than the tolerance standard and thus increase the yield from a given amount of raw materials.

Although the work looks repetitive at first glance, there are actually continual adjustments to make. Efficiency varies greatly depending on the number of people who can deal with such situations. We have talked about production workers, but the same applies to white-collar workers handling complex transactions with many different people, for example.

Skill-Formation Methods

How do people acquire the skills that raise their efficiency? In the final analysis the basic method is long-term on-the-job training (OJT) within the firm. This means starting with simple tasks in one workshop or in several closely related workshops, then progressing to more difficult tasks, receiving promotions, and so making a career. The intellectual skill accumulated is an understanding of the workings of the machinery and of the end products, which are often specific to the industry or the workshop. Even if the machines are of a general type, frequently they are assembled, automated, and connected in a specific way. To understand these specifics and the flow of production, one needs the wide experience of working in that particular workshop.

There are two additional methods of skill formation. One is a special sort of OJT—participation in taking machines apart and repairing them. When a technician is repairing a breakdown, the operator observes the work with care and ends up helping on the job, with the result that he acquires the skill required for smaller repairs, so for these repairs technicians need not be called. Since problem resolution is difficult to standardize, the production worker records his experience with various problems that have actually occurred, notes how they should be handled, discusses them with fellow workers, and tries to discover their causes.

The other additional method is the use of classroom training off the job (off-JT) to provide brief general training. However different may be the arrangement of machinery in different workshops, the principles of mechanics are generally the same. The principles of cutting, oil pressure, air pressure, and electronic engineering are likewise quite general. Every few years, in the course of OJT, the production worker may attend short outside courses of two to three days, or even one week, to consolidate his experience.

Clearly these intellectual skills are the basis of superior efficiency on the shop floor, and to attain such efficiency long-term employment in the same firm is necessary. Still some mechanism is necessary to encourage workers to acquire these skills, and because of the nature of the intellectual skill itself, these mechanisms must be complex. They include long-term evaluations, a system of wage payments, and competition over the longer term. To these I will turn next.

## 13.3  Long-Term Competition

The meaning of long-term competition may be understood by distinguishing it from short-term competition. Short-term competition as represented in textbooks makes various assumptions, as in the uniform quality of a commodity. Apply this to the labor market, and you have unrealistic assumptions such as the quality of labor being fixed at the point of transaction in recruitments, dismissals, and awards of new contracts.

The rationale of competition over the longer term, however, involves the more realistic assumption that workers' skills can improve with experience. Competition over the longer term means that workers who improve their skills advance to higher positions and further their career, while those who do not advance more slowly, or not at all, and may in extreme cases be dismissed.

Long-term competition of this sort works well where a high level of skill is essential and can be expected to develop over time; otherwise, short-term competition prevails. In large Japanese firms, for example, not all workers are long-term employees. Not only are there the "dispatched workers" and part-timers that are so often mentioned, but firms can assign work to on-site subcontractors and associated companies on a regular basis. In large steel plants, more than half of the on-site work force has typically been subcontracted outsiders. Which work gets assigned to outsiders and which to regular employees is largely a matter of the skills needed and the extent to which they are improved by experience. If a firm just wants cheap labor, it can rely entirely on nonregular workers.

This is very different from the standard theory of the internal labor market, as developed in the work of Doeringer and Piore (1971). They explain the growth of internal labor markets by the efficiency value of the knowledge that workers develop about the peculiarities of different machines and the characters and habits of fellow workers. There is surely something in this, but this reasoning is too general. Machines and fellow workers have peculiarities everywhere, so there ought to be internal labor markets everywhere. But both in America and in Japan they are largely limited to large firms. This point cannot be explained by the standard internal labor market theory. The theory I have suggested which stresses the importance of the technical conditions under which long service raises skill levels better fits the facts.

Much the same criticism can be applied to organization theories that see the creation of firms as a way of saving on transaction costs (again assuming uniform quality of labor in hiring transactions), or the attempt to go beyond that assumption with information-cost theories that stress the impossibility of knowing beforehand how well a worker will perform. Both miss an important aspect of reality by not taking account of the way workers increase their skills during employment over the long term.

Evaluation

Up to this point, the focus of my discussion has been on the meaning of "long term." Next I will consider the meaning of "competition." My explanation will weigh the mechanisms of both evaluation and compensation.

To instill competition in job performance, one must first provide a means of evaluating performance in a fair way. A 100-meter race cannot be run without some fair method of deciding who is the fastest. Of course in the case of intellectual skill formation, the questions of evaluation are more difficult. But they are easier to understand after comparison with the short-run case.

In the short term a firm can ignore the development of skill. It is enough to evaluate and pay a worker according to the difficulty of the job the worker does and his credentials. Over the long term, however, the worker's skill increases, even if he stays in the same job. This manifests itself in two ways. First, even in the same position, performance differs among workers because people differ in dealing with changes and difficulties. Some handle them well, while others cannot handle them at all. If workers had the same evaluation and pay, no one would invest in skill development to deal with problems and changes. Second, two people in the same position may differ in their value to the firm, by differences in their previous experience. A worker who, in addition to mastering his present job, has mastered other jobs within the workplace can substitute when someone is absent or teach new recruits. More important, the wider the experience of the worker in other jobs, the more easily he will understand the flow of production and develop intellectual skills. Unless recognition is given to such broad experience, intellectual skill and the ability to deal with potential problems will not develop.

For evaluation purposes one must rely on people who know a good deal about skill levels. In simple repetitive work, skill can be judged by the quantity of output. But for more complex and higher-level jobs, the evaluation and assessment must come from the supervisor who knows the job well. But however well the supervisor may know the work, his assessment cannot avoid subjectivity. If this leads to arbitrariness in that workers cannot expect high evaluations no matter how well they work, it is unlikely that they will work very hard.

To reduce arbitrariness, modern factories can draw up "job-matrix charts." These take two forms. One indicates the breadth of the worker's experience while the other assesses the worker's skill in handling problems and changes. Table 13.1 gives an example of the former. The rows list the workers by name, the columns show the principal workplace positions. For each job that a worker has experienced, the skill level is indicated by a number. A number 1 indicates that the worker has had some training on the job, 2 that he can work without supervision, 3 that he can do setups, and 4 that he is qualified to train other workers. The chart is revised every three months as skills improve. Sometimes it is put up on the wall, so that everyone's evaluation can itself be seen by the workers, thereby reducing subjectivity.

Table 13.2 gives a simplified version of the second chart, which indicates the level at which the worker handles unusual operations (3 means "can handle"; 4 means "can teach others"). These two evaluation charts are an

**Table 13.1**
Job-matrix chart 1, breadth of experience

| Worker's name | Shearing machines | NC lathes | Horizontal milling machines | Cylindrical grinders |
|---|---|---|---|---|
| Abe | 4 | 1 | 2 | 4 |
| Ito | | 2 | 4 | |
| Ugai | 4 | 4 | 1 | 3 |
| Eto | 1 | 4 | | |
| Ogata | | 2 | 2 | |

**Table 13.2**
Job-matrix chart 2, depth of experience

| Worker's name | Correcting Programs | Dealing with product defects | Making mechanical repairs | Making electrical repairs |
|---|---|---|---|---|
| Abe | | 4 | 4 | 3 |
| Ito | | | 4 | 3 |
| Ugai | 4 | 3 | | 3 |
| Eto | 3 | 3 | 3 | |
| Ogata | | 3 | | |

important basis for determining annual pay raises and promotions to higher positions (which come every few years). Consequently workers' skills and compensation tend to coincide in the medium and long term. The reasons why wages are not based simply on current jobs should by now be clear. It is also obvious, since skills are formed over the long term, why there are incentives and rewards for long service—the point of annual increments and the seniority wage curve.

## 13.4 Remaining Problems

Of the problem areas I have selected in this chapter there remain yet (1) vague job descriptions and downward delegation of decision making and (2) delayed definitive selection for top managerial positions.

Vague Job Descriptions

The recorded evidence on whether job descriptions in Japan are less detailed than elsewhere is slim (Dore 1973, 243–44). While elsewhere job

descriptions and standardized work methods are thought to improve efficiency, it is alleged that in Japan where there is a "groupist" culture efficiency levels can still be high without these measures.

The evidence from six of my factory studies shows that apart from the
charts indicating workers' job capabilities just described, recorded in writing were reports of problems that had arisen and how to deal with them.
Familiar problems that workers knew how to handle were not written up;
only recent problems that had given some trouble were recorded—by the
worker who encountered them—with an indication of the solutions found.

In four of the workshops the foreman kept a written record of individual
workers' job assignments. Such records are valuable in showing the pattern
of job rotation practiced intermittently or an a daily basis in Japanese
workshops. The pattern varies, even within the same firm. In two of the
four, job positions were stable, often over a period of years, with the record
showing only substitutions in cases of absence. In the other two rotation
was very frequent.

According to the line supervisors, there were several reasons for keeping
records: first, in customer complaint cases, to identify the worker responsible, and second to provide a clear factual basis for worker evaluation. This
is in sharp contrast with the commonly held view that groupism and team
work prevails in Japan. How is it that the existence of records such as
these is not noted in the literature? The logical answer is that they are kept
by supervisor and not turned over to the office. So researchers who got no
further than the personnel office or the production manager's office did not
learn about them.

Clearly then for the large firms the assumption that Japanese workshops
do not use written records is far from true. What about the assumption that
written job descriptions and standardized methods improve efficiency? To
be sure, in workshops where changes and problems are frequent and cannot
be anticipated, handling them is a highly skilled task that cannot be standardized easily. In fact, efficiency would fall if changes and problems were
subjected to standardized methods. As Knight once pointed out (1971, esp.
ch. 10) problems and changes abound in workshops, so it is an illusion to
think that efficiency can be improved by written directions and standardization. Such are second- or third-best methods to be used when one cannot
get workers with adequate intellectual skills.

This brings the argument back to my primary point—a system where
workers themselves can and do bear responsibility is the preferable system.
Unanticipated problems whose solutions cannot be standardized also cannot be directed from above. In general, as Hayek put it (1945, passim, but
esp. p. 524), in handling problems, one needs to know who is the best

problem solver in the workshop, and only "the man on the spot" knows that. If he is not allowed to handle a problem, that problem may simply be overlooked. Downward delegation of responsibility is the only way to ensure efficiency where handling change and problems is an essential part of the job.

Implications of the Slow-Promotion System

Japanese blue-collar production workers in large firms have considerably broader and less specialized careers than American workers in similar workshops—a point I first noted ten years ago from observations and records in chemical and heavy industrial plants in the two countries. How this helps to develop an understanding of the production process and accumulate intellectual skills, has already been discussed (Koike 1977). In this chapter I have also discussed the late-promotion system and here need only reiterate what was said above, that delaying definitive selection of white-collar workers for the career tracks that lead to top managerial positions for 10 or 15 years stimulates long-term competition, motivates the acquisition of skills, and ensures fairness and objectivity in the selection process which is necessary for that motivation to be effective.

**13.5   Conclusions**

I would like to make two final points. The first is about individualism, the second about national and cross-national variables. The chapter's argument is decidely opposed to the "group consciousness" hypothesis and takes an individualist position. The strongest ground for regarding the Japanese firm's behavior as "groupist" has been the vagueness of job descriptions, as noted in section 3.4 above. But as this chapter has shown, each worker's individual responsibility is very clear for routine work. There no vagueness there. If it is not clear which worker tightens each bit, how can an automobile assembly line work smoothly? This point needs making because it is often thought that in a Japanese workshop each individual's job is not well defined, so that workers function as a team.

   Even for unexpected changes or problems, it is not a group but rather an individual who handles the problem. What looks like vagueness means only that (1) there are differences in ability among workers in handling problems, and (2) problems are too numerous to be either written down or foreseen. In short, it is not that vagueness of job specifications indicates groupism but only that for efficiency's sake one does not overregulate; where there is some vagueness, individuals' work fills the gaps. Likewise in the West, the "team work"I observed in the white-collar work places was always an important category in worker evaluation. Clearly anywhere where work involves judgment full standardization of tasks is impossible.

The clearest evidence of individualism are the mechanisms that promote the improvement of workers' intellectual skills. Those mechanisms are individualistic; individual skills are evaluated, and each individual's compensation is based on that evaluation. At first glance the fact that veteran workers train recruits, and the fact that workers make suggestions for improving tools when new products and methods are introduced, can be easily mistaken for groupism. These are certainly contributions to the group, but what encourages them is the evaluation, which takes account of such individual contributions.

The second point is this: Intellectual skill and long-term competition (both emphasized here repeatedly) are real intervening variables. But there are powerful independent variables as well, such as exogenous conditions. Of course the effects of underlying variables are not small. Holding exogenous conditions constant, consider the example of the production workshops of large steel plants, where the career element is somewhat greater in Japan than in America. But, when we compare production workshops in large steel plants with, say, carpentry workshops, there are large differences within each country. In both Japan and America, in steel plants where skills are acquired through lengthy training on the job, industrial relations are based on the organization of the factory or firm. Yet in both countries carpentry workers form craft unions that center on the occupation, not the workplace, and industrial relations differ greatly from those of the steel industry. These differences, which are similar in Japan and in America, result primarily from factors exogenous to the firm.

Even the intervening variables, which cause intercountry differences, cannot be wholly ascribed to peculiarities within a country unless one brings in the variable of "culture." However, the development of intellectual skills can be thought of as a kind of "software." Regarded as a technology, it can be transmitted to other countries given appropriate circumstances. Long-term competition is a an institutionalized practice, and institutionalized practices, which take time to establish or to change, are the product of repeated behavior. There is really no reason why, given a period of time to develop, such intellectual skills cannot be transmitted from country to country. So it is with long-term competition. What is needed is the determination to introduce it, to create the necessary conditions, and to allow it to persist over time.

# 14

# On the Determinants of Bonuses and Basic Wages in Large Japanese Firms

Isao Ohashi

Hashimoto (1979), Gordon (1982), Kahn (1984), and Freeman and Weitzman (1987) have argued that the bonus system is critical for explaining the Japanese labor market. According to the "Monthly Labor Survey" (Ministry of Labor 1985), 97 percent of firms with 30 employees or more pay bonuses twice a year to regular workers. Even in establishments with between 30 and 99 employees, over 20 percent of a regular worker's total cash earnings are received in the form of bonus payments.[1] Since this type of bonus system can be found only in Japan, many European and American economists view it as a useful concept in analyzing the combination of wage flexibility and employment stability in the Japanese labor market.

However, as this chapter shows, many Japanese labor economists such as Mizuno (1985), Koshiro (1986), and Brunello and Ohtake (1987) are reluctant to accept this view. They have attempted to verify the correlation between bonuses and profits, and test the hypothesis that the bonus system allows wages to fluctuate with business conditions and helps to stabilize employment in Japan. The results are not favorable to the hypothesis. Therefore it is worth considering other hypotheses such as the traditional wage model, which interprets bonuses as being a part of wage payments, and the overtime work compensation model developed by Hamada (1985).

This chapter attempts to develop a further explanation of how bonuses are determined, to test it on two-digit classified manufacturing industries

An earlier version of this chapter was presented at the NBER-TCER-CEPR Conference on "Labor Relations and the Enterprise: A Comparative Perspective" and at the conference on "The Japanese Enterprise" in 1989. Substantially the same paper has appeared in the *Journal of the Japanese and International Economies*, vol. 3, 451–79 (1989). The author thanks M. Hashimoto, K. Muramatsu, K. Koike, H. Miyazaki, H. Yoshikawa, M. Okuno-Fujiwara, R. Komiya, and K. Imai for their valuable comments, and J. Nemoto for helpful advice on econometrics.
1. For a brief survey on the bonus system and its background in Japan, see Suruga (1987) and Freeman and Weitzman (1987).

and for microdata on individual firms, and to compare its goodness of fit with that of the profit-sharing hypothesis. In particular, it looks at whether bonuses are paid by firms to compensate employees for the intensity of work experienced during the last period.[2] This idea also stresses a distinction between the determination of bonuses and basic wages. Even though both forms of remuneration are strongly influenced by labor market conditions, bonuses are basically seen as a reward for past work intensity, while basic wages are characterized as compensation based on organizational elements (e.g., *nenko* wages). This distinction will be ascertained empirically.

## 14.1 Overview

There are currently three hypotheses to explain bonus determination. The first interprets bonus payments within the framework of the traditional model of wage determination. According to this hypothesis, bonuses are essentially the same as basic wages and are determined by the supply and demand for labor. This implies that the individual firm must pay the market-level bonus to maintain the labor force it requires. Empirical studies that estimate the Phillips relation by regressing the rate of change in total cash earnings, including bonuses, to the unemployment rate and consumer price index are based on this interpretation. Recent studies by Yoshikawa and Takeuchi (1988) using microdata on the labor costs of individual firms, by Mizuno (1985) disputing that there is a large difference in the behavior between bonuses and basic wages, by Koshiro (1986) insisting on the weakness of the correlation between bonuses and profits, and by Brunello and Ohtake (1987) pointing out the significance of market effects appear to consider the determination of bonuses within the framework of the traditional model.

The second type of hypothesis emphasizes the positive correlation between profits and bonuses. Models of this type are the share economy model developed by Weitzman (1984), the specific training model of Hashimoto (1979), and the incentive bonus model of Okuno (1984).[3] Although Aoki (1980) does not make direct reference to the bonus system,

---

2. In order to motivate workers to work hard, firms need to measure workers' productivity precisely and to make compensation closely related to it. But it is actually very difficult for large firms because they adopt the team production system. Okuno (1984) argued that they can solve this incentive problem by introducing the bonus system under the custom of firm ostracism.
3. See Yellen (1984) or Stiglitz (1984).

**Table 14.1**
Ratio of firms with formal gain or profit-sharing contracts (in %)

| Firm scale | Firms paying bonuses | Firms with formal contract for gain or profit sharing | | | | Firms without formal contract |
|---|---|---|---|---|---|---|
| | | Subtotal | Related to production or sales | Related to value added | Related to profits | |
| Average | 100.0 | 32.0 | 14.7 | 4.2 | 24.6 | 68.0 |
| Over 1,000 employees | 100.0 | 16.4 | 8.0 | 3.0 | 13.0 | 83.6 |
| 100–999 employees | 100.0 | 33.8 | 16.5 | 5.6 | 25.4 | 66.2 |
| 30–99 employees | 100.0 | 31.7 | 14.2 | 3.7 | 24.6 | 68.3 |

Source: General survey of wages and hours worked, Ministry of Labor (1983).

his cooperative game model of the firm falls in this category. He argues that in firms where employees acquire firm-specific collective skills and where team spirit is said to exist, wages including bonuses are determined by Nash bargaining between the employer and the employees.

Actually there are two ways in which a firm can reflect profits in the determination of bonuses. It can use a schedule, explicitly contracted between management and labor, to link bonuses with certain business indicators such as profits, sales, and production. According to a Ministry of Labor (MOL 1983) survey, 32 percent of bonus-paying firms practiced such a contracted system (table 14.1). It should be stressed here that sales and production different from profits—they are closely related to the intensity of work—but other empirical studies treat them together (see section 14.5).

It is interesting to note that the percentage of firms having a formal profit-sharing contract is 13 percent for large-scale firms (with 1,000 employees or more ) and 25 percent, for smaller-scale firms (with 999 employees or less). This appears to run contrary to the expectation that the lifetime employment and the profit-sharing systems are well established in large-scale firms.

The other method is less concrete. That is, profits are also reflected in bonus determination even when there is only a tacit understanding between both the employer and the employee that business performance is a suitable criterion. In a profit-sharing firm such an acceptance is probably based on a sense of community which the workers and the management share, and in a monopolistic or oligopolistic firm it is probably based on the fact that profits indicate the firm's ability to pay.

The third type of hypothesis interprets bonuses as being compensation for the volatility of overtime work. Hamada (1985) discusses the overtime work compensation model in the following way. It is well known that in Japan, compared to fluctuations in output, employment is stable, but hours worked fluctuate greatly. Japanese employees are often required to work overtime and on holidays, yet overtime premiums are low at 25 to 30 percent compared to the American premium of 50 percent. For this reason in Japan large increases in working hours often result in a falling average hourly compensation. Thus, to compensate for the volatility of overtime work and hence wage income, it is necessary for firms to pay bonuses. Such an argument, however, can easily be refuted. That is, there are many workers who welcome overtime work for the reason that a premium is paid to it. It is said that often workers will select employment on the basis of total income including payment for overtime work. In such cases, as the worker desires extra hours, the firm need not compensate increased hours by paying bonuses. The effort compensation model can avoid this criticism because it assumes that bonuses are paid for work intensity but not for overtime hours.

## 14.2   Effort Compensation Model

The model that I develop in this study is based on the efficiency wage hypothesis. According to this hypothesis, an increase in the wage rate will induce higher labor productivity. This proposition can be explained by several analytical tools. Of these the so-called incentive model introduces the following labor effort function:[4]

$$e = e\left(\frac{W}{P} - rV\right), \qquad e' > 0,$$

where $e$ is the effort level of the employee, $W$ is the total wage payment including basic wage, bonus, and allowances, $r$ is the interest rate, $P$ is the consumer price index, and $V$ is the expected real income when an employee leaves his or her current job. This function states that a worker's incentive is dependent on the differential between the real wage currently received and the expected total income upon leaving one's current employment (more specifically, the interest yielded in each term, $rV$). In other words, it is dependent on the loss the worker will suffer upon losing his or her current employment.

Let us incorporate this function into the firm's wage and employment adjustment process. A firm modifying planned production in response to changing demand is able to adjust three factors—namely the level of employment, working hours, and labor intensity. Of these a short-term adjustment of employment is extremely costly. A firm facing exogenous shocks will therefore regulate, in the short term, working hours and labor intensity (e.g., by altering the speed of the production line). If a firm becomes busier and labor intensity increases, then greater effort is required of the workers. Therefore there is a need to develop a system of compensation for such increases in labor intensity, in the same way that overtime working hours are compensated for by the premium wage system. In Japan the bonus system has come to play such a role. More specifically, when determining the bonus size, the firm will consider the level of activity, that

---

4. See Shapiro and Stiglitz (1984) for the derivation of this effort supply function. The author (1989) has incorporated hours worked into the efficiency wage model to analyze the adjustment process of wages, hours worked, and employment.

is, the labor intensity experienced since the last payment. The bonus has in effect become a compensation for past effort. In other words, a worker's current effort will be reflected in the next bonus payment.

Two criticisms of this view may be anticipated. One is that in the usual formulation of the efficiency wage hypothesis, a higher wage causes more effort (while in this study, more effort causes a higher bonus). My answer is that the causality is not important in a repeated situation with long-term contracts. More specifically, if the firm does not compensate for hard work in the last period, the employees will retaliate for it by reducing effort or will not work hard at the next busy time. The other concerns why the firm compensates hard work in the form of a lump-sum bonus payment twice a year. This is because it is costly to contract and measure the intensity of work at each point of time and the lump-sum payment can save the transaction costs required for measurement and negotiation.

Some different aspects of bonuses and basic wages will be discussed herein. According to Baily (1974), risk-averse employees with insufficient personal capital will form implicit contracts with risk-neutral firms that can offer wage stability because they prefer stable income subject to only slight fluctuations. This analysis explains a situation where the firm functions as a kind of financial institution for the employee by stabilizing income flow. Hall (1980) discusses the implications of such a concept on the long-run employment relationship. When a long-term employment relationship exists, a firm need not compensate a worker directly for his or her productivity at each point in time but can instead divide the payment over the entire period of employment. In this case actual payments will be lower than productivity in the early periods of employment and higher in later periods. This results in a characteristic upward-sloping wage profile and will provide incentives for workers and also prevent skilled workers from quitting.

Hall applies this logic to explain the rigidities of wages with relation to short-run business fluctuations. His argument describes well the characteristics for basic wages made by Japanese large firms, which adjust the basic wage rates each year during the *shunto* negotiation rounds. This adjustment (recently nearly always an increase) can be divided into a regular increase component and a "base-up" component. The former, which is the change in the basic wage payment along an age-wage profile, is influenced by organizational factors such as training systems, promotions, and labor incentives, as already stated. The latter adjusts mainly to changes in economic conditions. In this sense the "base-up" component is critical when discussing bonus payments.

The base-up component reflects not only current price levels and labor market conditions but also the expected changes in business conditions. However, real conditions are not accurately forecast and often require the employees to work with intensity beyond expectations. For this reason basic wage increases often do not fully compensate the workers. It is the bonus system that allows the firm to periodically adjust compensation levels when such insufficiencies arise. It should be stressed here that this interpretation based on the effort compensation model is distinguished from that of the traditional wage model, which interprets bonuses in the same way as basic wages.

Freeman and Weitzman (1987) found that basic wages have a negative effect on employment, while bonuses have a positive one. It is easy to explain this fact with the effort compensation model. When increased product demand is expected to continue in the long run, the firm eventually has to increase employment since it cannot keep up with the long-run trend of the increased demand only through overtime and work on holidays.

One problem encountered when researching the effort compensation model is the measurement of effort. How should it be measured? As actual measurement proves to be near impossible, it is necessary for us to find a substitute variable. There are in fact several: overtime hours and hours worked on holidays, actual hours worked, and productivity indexes. Of these overtime hours will be chosen as the most appropriate, the rationale being that overtime hours are thought to reasonably indicate times when the level of business and labor intensity increase.

One may argue that since workers are satisfied with overtime wage rates, the need for bonus payments is debatable. The answer is simple. Overtime wage rates are payments only for extra hours worked not for the extra effort required. It is important to remember when overtime work is necessary, employees are also busy during regular working hours. How is this high intensity of work during regular hours compensated for?

One may also argue as follows: If overtime is a good proxy for hard work, why not adjust the overtime premium for this? The premium is only 25 to 30 percent in Japan while it is 50 percent in the United States. Why do the firms not raise the premium to 50 percent, or why do workers not strongly demand it in Japan? The answer to this question is the following: If the premium were raised to 50 percent, for example, the firm would come to adjust the level of employment in response to fluctuations in production and reduce overtime hours on average. The high premium would bring unstable employment and reduced income form overtime work, which are not favorable to workers. It would also be unfavorable to the firm not only because it raises hourly labor costs but also because shorter working hours prolong the period for recouping human investments.

It is probable that in busy times company profits will grow. If this is the case, in what way do the implications of the effort compensation model differ from those of the profit-sharing model? First and most important, there are differences in the effects of labor market conditions. Since the profit-sharing model postulates that bonus payments are literally a sharing of the profits, profit is the primary factor in bonus determination. Consequently how labor market conditions affect bonuses is not extensively discussed. While this model acknowledges that the ratio of profits shared with employees may in part depend on labor market conditions, the exact relationship is far from clear. The effort compensation mode, on the other hand, based on the efficiency wage model, explains bonus payments that are influenced considerably by labor market conditions.

The second important difference is how market demand for a firm's output is assumed to affect bonus determination. For example, suppose that despite an increase in labor intensity during the bonus period, profits do not increase, possibly because of a severe exchange rate or an exogenous price disturbance such as the oil shocks. In such a case the profit-sharing model postulates that workers will accept lower bonus payments. The effort compensation model, however, implies that since bonuses are a reward for hard work, employees will be reluctant to accept a reduced payment. They will in fact attribute the failure in profit to the employer, and not to themselves. Of course, despite such feelings, it cannot be denied that the financial standing of the firm will affect the actual bonus bargaining process.

## 14.3 Empirical Method

The purpose of this study is to examine the validity of the three hypotheses outlined in the previous section by analyzing two-digit manufacturing industry data for establishments with more that 1,000 employees, and micro-data on individual firms. The sample period is from fiscal year 1971 to fiscal year 1986.[5] Data for 1970, however, are actually utilized in this analysis because of a one-year time lag.

---

5. The reason for considering this restricted period is that for earlier periods only aggregate data for firms with more than 500 employees are available. Restricting the survey to only large-scale enterprises is thought to be justifiable because generally both the profit-sharing and the wage efficiency models are accepted as being relevant to large-scale enterprises. Fiscal year data are employed because, the profit-sharing model postulates that bonuses cannot be determined without accurate profit figures, which are in fiscal terms such as those calculated for public and especially stockholder reports.

In a study using only industry-specific data, it is impossible to interpret the influence of the market wage and market bonus to which both the employer and employees will look with first priority during the negotiation period. More specifically, according to another MOL survey (*Survey on the State of Wage Increases, etc.* 1986), the most important factors in decisions by firms are the wage rates set by leading or comparably-sized companies in the same industry. In fact in all the manufacturing industries more than 80 percent of firms with more than 1,000 employees rank this factor as the most important. Only 15 percent of the surveyed firms rank higher other factors, such as the rates set by firms in other industries, firms in the same geographic region, and affiliated firms.

While the 1986 data on priorities during the negotiation period are for basic wages and not bonuses, classified industry data for bonuses can be found in the 1970 data from the Ministry of Labor. Even though this study is rather old, the results do not vary greatly from those of the 1986 data, except for the food and the furniture industries. Therefore it is possible to use the average wage rate of an industry as an approximation for the market level. Such an assumption is valid only in the case of individual firm data and not in the case of industry data. However, the difficulty in assessing suitable market rates is not a large problem, since we use the effective job offer rate as an index that reflects labor market conditions. The implications of this issue need to be discussed in more detail.

The models that explicitly incorporate the market rate as an explanatory variable of wage and bonus determination are the traditional and the efficiency wage models. In the former model, because the market wage is considered to be determined by the demand and supply for labor, it is possible to evaluate the effectiveness of the model by studying the elasticity of wage payments to labor market conditions. That is, the market rate is only a signal to inform workers of the wages they could get by moving to other firms, and it functions as an intermediary connecting the demand and supply for labor and wage determination. If the market is operating smoothly, the wages paid by a firm following the market will directly reflect labor market conditions. It is clear then that even though market rates are the most important for individual economic agents, it is more essential for us to find a suitable index that expresses a specific industry's labor supply and demand conditions. Unfortunately, however, at this stage we cannot find a good industry-specific index. The only likely candidate is the effective job offer rate for the whole economy.

The market rate also plays a crucial role in the efficiency wage model. We already know from the labor effort function that a worker's incentive depends not only on the currently received real wage but also on the expected income from other job opportunities, $V$. Therefore, if $V$ changes in line with the market rate, a firm is forced to adjust its own real wages to prevent a fall in workers' incentive. This adjustment in turn will result in a wage spillover effect. Note that this spillover mechanism is substantially different from that of the traditional model, which states that spillover is brought on by labor mobility between firms.

In this sense the market rate is an important variable for the efficiency wage model when explaining wage determination. Unfortunately for this model though, the effective job offer rate cannot be considered as a suitable approximation for the market rate. The reason is that the model analyzes wage determination in an economy where the improper functioning of the labor market is the primary cause of involuntary unemployment.[6] Therefore the relationship between the market rate and the labor supply and demand conditions differs from that assumed in the traditional model. For example, consider the case of an economy where the market rates are relatively high yet job opportunities are scarce. Even though the level of $V$ is low, the firm facing the increased demand for the products and hence requiring overtime work will still have to pay a high wage to maintain workers' incentive. In such a case, even if the job offer rate is controlled, overtime hours representing labor intensity will have a significant effect on the determination of bonuses.

Another aspect of this model that will be examined concerns the time lag structures of the explanatory variables on bonus determination. The impact of time lag greatly depends on the frequency and timing of bonus negotiations. Table 14.2 from the *State of Annual Wages and Bonuses* (Institute of Labor Administration 1982, 1983, 1984) shows the different methods of bonus negotiations used by large firms. More than 20 percent of the firms surveyed in the food, chemical, and electric industries use the "lump-sum-in-winter" method. That is, a negotiation that takes place during the winter period simultaneously determines both the winter and the following summer bonus payments. In general, however, two other methods are much more common. Under the first, the "short-run" method, negotiations are held in both winter and summer to determine the bonus payment for each respective period. The second, the "lump-sum-in-summer" method, is a straight reversal of the lump-sum-in-winter method. Therefore, if the

---

6. Normally the efficiency wage hypothesis is used to justify the rigidity of wages. Therefore it can be questioned why it is used to justify the volatility of wages in this chapter. I would stress that the efficiency wage hypothesis deals with an economy in which wages, although flexible, do not clear the excess supply of labor.

**Table 14.2**
Bonus bargaining system

| Industry | Total | Short run | Lump-sum in summer | Lump-sum in winter |
|---|---|---|---|---|
| Food manufacturing | 27 (100) | 5 (18.5) | 15 (55.6) | 7 (25.9) |
| Textiles | 10 (100) | 9 (90) | 1 (10) | 0 (0) |
| Pulp, paper, and related products | 6 (100) | 6 (100) | 0 (0) | 0 (0) |
| Chemicals | 47 (100) | 29 (61.7) | 7 (14.9) | 11 (23.4) |
| Rubbers products | 3 (100) | 1 (33.3) | 2 (66.7) | 0 (0) |
| Iron and steel | 7 (100) | 1 (14.3) | 6 (85.7) | 0 (0) |
| Nonferrous metals and metal products | 9 (100) | 7 (77.8) | 2 (22.2) | 0 (0) |
| Machinery | 45 (100) | 17 (37.8) | 25 (55.5) | 3 (6.7) |
| Electric appliances | 31 (100) | 14 (45.2) | 2 (6.5) | 15 (48.4) |
| Transportation equipment | 20 (100) | 1 (5) | 19 (95) | 0 (0) |
| Precision instruments | 11 (100) | 2 (18.2) | 7 (63.6) | 0 (0) |
| Average | 216 (100) | 92 (42.6) | 86 (39.8) | 38 (17.6) |

Source: State of annual wage and bonuses, Institute of Labor Administration, 1983, 1984, 1985.
Note: Values are numbers of firms, with percentages in parentheses.

information acquisition process of the workers is taken into consideration, introduction of lag variables for profits and the consumer price level into the empirical framework is necessary.

## 14.4 Empirical Results

For the two categories of workers—production workers (blue-collar workers) and managerial, clerical, and technological workers (white-collar workers)—of each industry, we regressed BONUS (real bonuses) on the explanatory variables: namely PROF (real profits), PROF($-1$), OH (overtime hours), OH ($-1$), VACAN (the ratio of effective job vacancies to job searchers, D (dummy variable), and T (time trend), where ($-1$) is a lagged variable for the immediate past period (see the appendix, section 14.7, for definitions and data sources). Since in the textile, chemical, and electric industries lump-sum bonus bargaining in winter or short-run bargaining are prevalent, as shown in table 14.2, CPI is used as the denominator when converting nominal BONUS to the real. This is because it can be conjectured that during bonus bargaining the current period CPI is the most important data for both parties considering current and next period price behavior. In turn, for the other industries in which the lump-sum bargaining in summer is prevalent, CPI($-1$) is used as the denominator. In fact, when we used current CPI as the denominator in these industries, the results were unfavorable; that is , the estimated effects of the explanatory variables were not statistically significant in most cases. Unfortunately, because of incomplete data, regression equations for all the two-digit manufacturing industries could not be computed. Moreover, owing to differences in the data sources for PROF and OH, the number of industries for which profit-sharing equations are estimated is one less (the rubber industry) than the number for which overtime equations are estimated.[7]

At the outset, in order to see the lag structure effect of the explanatory variables in each industry, we regressed both OH and OH($-1$), and PROF and PROF($-1$), on BONUS and obtained the following results: The industries in which the lagged variable is more favorable than the current are rubber, iron and steel, nonferrous metals, general machinery, and transportation equipment. For these industries the lagged variable, as was expected, is more significant than the current variable (in the respect that the $t$ value is larger). Table 14.2 indicates that most of the firms in the industries referred to above (excluding nonferrous metals) determine bonuses by lump-sum bargaining in summer. In turn the industries for which the current explanatory variables of OH and PROF are more significant are textiles, chemicals, and electrical appliances. In these industries bonuses are determined mainly by lump-sum bargaining in winter or short-run bargaining in both summer and winter. As for the pulp and paper industry, in which the short-run bargaining method is prevalent, the lagged and current variables are both significant. It is possible that the current variables of OH and PROF are more significant in industries that use lump-sum winter or short-run bonus bargaining methods because interim business results are available for the bargaining rounds. However, a word of caution is necessary regarding these results; because the sample is relatively small, the implications of table 14.2 are limited.

Overtime versus Profits

Given the results discussed above, we can specify the lag structure for each equation and estimate the effect of OH, OH($-1$), PROF, PROF($-1$), and VACAN on bonus payments. Table 14.3 gives the overtime equations and tables 14.4 and 14.5 the profit-sharing equations. Since the Durbin-Watson

---

7. Also the data on profits in the precision instruments industry cover only 1967 to 1986.

statistic estimated by the ordinary least squares methods is far larger or smaller than 2 for most of the equations, the values were calculated using a maximum likelihood estimator, assuming a first-order serial correlation of error.

According to table 14.3, the effect of overtime as a proxy variable for work intensity is statistically significant at the 5 percent level of confidence for both blue- and white-collar workers in four industries, namely pulp and paper, nonferrous metal products, general machinery, and electrical appliances. Furthermore overtime is significant at the 5 percent level of confidence for white-collar workers in the rubber, iron and steel, metal products, and precision instrument industries and for blue-collar workers in the textile industry, and at the 10 percent level of confidence for blue-collar workers in the iron and steel industry. On the other hand, the estimated effect of OH or OH($-1$) is not significant even at the 10 percent level of confidence for both blue- and white-collar workers in the food and tobacco, chemical, and transportation industries.[8]

As for the transportation industry, as shown above, the effect of overtime is not significant at the ordinary level of confidence, but it is interesting that in November 1988 the Toyota Motor Corp paid its employees an average of ¥50,000 as a special payment for cooperation (*kyoryoku iro kin*) to employees for increased work loads. Toyota said that its employees had had an increased load for the last year, and had worked an average of about 35 hours overtime per month. We will discuss the chemical industry later.

To sum up, overtime is a statistically significant variable at the 10 percent level in 14 equations but not in 10. Thus one might say the results in table 14.3 support the hypothesis of this chapter that bonus payments depend on how busy the workers were during the last period. One could also use as a proxy for work intensity other variables such as production index, sales, and total hours worked (scheduled hours plus overtime) and regress each of them on BONUS, but the effects are significant at the ordinary level of confidence in fewer industries.

In all the estimated overtime equations the effect of VACAN on BONUS is also statistically significant, as was expected, at the 5 percent level

---

8. Overtime may not be a suitable proxy for work intensity because in a business recession firms often reduce scheduled hours by a cutback operation and temporary days off. Therefore I tried to adjust overtime hours by adding the residual between the actual and the fitted value of scheduled hours, which was obtained by the estimated equation of $S = ab/T$, where $S$ is scheduled hours and $T$ is time. Unfortunately, the results obtained by this method are similar, or less favorable, to those obtained by the simple method used in the chapter.

**Table 14.3**
Estimates of overtime equations

| Industry | Occupation | OH | OH(−1) | VACAN | D | T | Constant | $\bar{R}^2$ | DW |
|---|---|---|---|---|---|---|---|---|---|
| Food manufacturing and cigarettes | Blue | | −28.80 (1.30) | 2,325[b] (8.39) | −85.03[b] (3.96) | −2,773[b] (11.1) | 5,349 (14.2) | 0.968 | 2.10 |
| | White | | −18.96 (0.40) | 3,739[b] (5.06) | −56.29 (1.70) | −3,033[b] (4.86) | 7,732 (6.93) | 0.752 | 1.81 |
| Textiles | Blue | 233.8[b] (2.59) | | 2,544[b] (2.67) | −1,725[a] (1.97) | 64.08 (0.93) | −913.0 (0.99) | 0.752 | 1.97 |
| | White | 0.108 (0.00) | | 4,154[b] (6.73) | −1,504[a] (1.86) | 216.5[b] (3.94) | 1,951 (2.38) | 0.800 | 1.63 |
| Pulp, paper, and related products | Blue | 172.5[b] (5.32) | 53.22[a] (2.19) | 3,977[b] (9.25) | −5,349[b] (12.6) | −75.62 (1.76) | 1,293 (1.64) | 0.936 | 1.46 |
| | White | 318.8[b] (9.71) | 91.95[b] (3.62) | 5,415[b] (24.3) | −6,975[b] (30.1) | −122.4[b] (7.56) | 1,241 (4.86) | 0.995 | 1.85 |
| Chemicals | Blue | −43.44 (0.61) | | 1,091[b] (3.12) | −257.4 (0.59) | 282.7[b] (5.63) | 3,330 (9.73) | 0.984 | 2.35 |
| | White | −168.0 (1.61) | | 1,805[b] (4.33) | −296.5[b] (0.55) | 324.6[b] (5.27) | 6,238 (1.39) | 0.976 | 1.87 |
| Rubber products | Blue | | 0.510 (0.02) | 2,703[b] (6.28) | −3,174[b] (8.49) | −21.85 (0.65) | 4,518 (12.0) | 0.829 | 1.99 |
| | White | | 113.2[b] (2.75) | 3,455[b] (6.26) | −3,846[b] (6.89) | −51.01 (1.44) | 5,101 (8.69) | 0.727 | 1.98 |
| Iron and steel | Blue | | 52.04[a] (2.19) | 2,724[b] (5.31) | −3,754[b] (7.91) | 48.81[a] (1.92) | 3,971 (6.46) | 0.902 | 1.97 |
| | White | | 202.5[b] (2.25) | 4,805[b] (4.90) | −6,118[b] (6.48) | 148.3[b] (2.84) | 6,135 (4.41) | 0.906 | 2.11 |

| | | | | | | | Constant | $\bar{R}^2$ | DW |
|---|---|---|---|---|---|---|---|---|---|
| Nonferrous metals | Blue | 34.52 (3.53) | | 2,682[b] (8.70) | −3,387[b] (11.6) | −71.04[b] (3.34) | 3,850 (12.2) | 0.873 | 1.65 |
| | White | 99.55[b] (4.23) | | 3,138[b] (7.04) | −3,669[b] (8.18) | 3.071 (0.09) | 4,792 (8.52) | 0.874 | 2.12 |
| Metal products | Blue | 26.54 (1.65) | | 1,404[b] (4.89) | −1,744[b] (6.44) | 29.61 (1.78) | 3,436 (11.0) | 0.714 | 1.77 |
| | White | 118.0[b] (2.91) | | 3,152[b] (7.60) | −2,833[b] (6.11) | 75.24[a] (1.95) | 2,074 (2.77) | 0.868 | 1.89 |
| Machinery | Blue | 31.69[b] (2.58) | | 2,550[b] (7.14) | −2,824[b] (8.28) | −16.39 (0.72) | 4,068 (10.3) | 0.772 | 1.64 |
| | White | 55.00[b] (2.44) | | 3,443[b] (7.43) | −3,795[b] (8.28) | −26.23 (0.86) | 5,532 (9.06) | 0.814 | 1.73 |
| Electric appliances | Blue | | 21.60[b] (2.62) | 615.9[b] (4.38) | −1,236[b] (9.26) | 31.70[b] (2.82) | 3,911 (29.4) | 0.990 | 2.27 |
| | White | | 34.46[b] (2.37) | 811.9[b] (4.19) | −1,091[b] (5.75) | 142.4[b] (6.95) | 5,053 (25.4) | 0.983 | 1.73 |
| Transportation equipment | Blue | 9.016 (0.69) | | 1,423[b] (4.37) | 45.78[b] (2.37) | −1,949[b] (6.24) | 4,630 (12.3) | 0.755 | 1.94 |
| | White | 52.03 (1.55) | | 2,213[b] (3.51) | −2,792[b] (4.34) | 34.01 (0.86) | 5,894 (6.66) | 0.556 | 1.53 |
| Precision instruments | Blue | 0.388 (0.012) | | 1,086[b] (3.64) | −1,692[b] (5.96) | −7.127 (0.25) | 5,782 (21.8) | 0.954 | 2.15 |
| | White | 233.4[b] (3.64) | | 4,667[b] (8.21) | −6,269[b] (9.26) | −262.4[b] (3.45) | 5,753 (11.3) | 0.945 | 2.28 |

Note: Estimated by the maximum likelihood (first-order serial correction of the error). $t$ statistics are in parentheses (absolute values). $\bar{R}^2$ and DW stand for the adjusted $R^2$ and the Durbin-Watson statistic, respectively.
a. Significant at the 10 percent level of confidence in a two-sided test.
b. Significant at the 5 percent level of confidence in a two-sided test.

**Table 14.4**
Estimates of the profit-sharing equations

| Industry | Occupation | PROF | PROF(−1) | D | T | Constant | R | DW |
|---|---|---|---|---|---|---|---|---|
| Food manufacturing | Blue | 94.81 (1.49) | | −1,610[b] (3.44) | −148.2[b] (3.95) | 5,728 (7.37) | 0.490 | 1.88 |
| | White | | 18,368[a] (1.86) | −1,075 (1.42) | −121.8[b] (1.89) | 8,147 (6.30) | 0.278 | 1.75 |
| Textiles | Blue | 107,212[a] (1.85) | | −668.3 (0.71) | 106.8 (1.25) | 2,394 (2.53) | 0.271 | 1.53 |
| | White | 214,207[b] (3.95) | | −1,307[b] (1.60) | 6.01 (0.09) | 6,838 (9.25) | 0.555 | 1.76 |
| Pulp, paper, and related products | Blue | 10,854[b] (4.06) | 9,764[b] (4.29) | −1,538[b] (3.55) | −68.17 (1.75) | 5,685 (15.0) | 0.842 | 2.00 |
| | White | 16,324[b] (4.51) | 12,904[b] (4.24) | −2,422[b] (4.27) | −175.7[b] (3.47) | 8,071 (16.7) | 0.849 | 2.07 |
| Chemicals | Blue | 47,146[b] (3.03) | | −130.7 (0.63) | 200.2[b] (9.93) | 3,858 (24.4) | 0.986 | 2.56 |
| | White | 75,054[b] (3.88) | | −496.3[a] (1.91) | 143.6[b] (5.72) | 6,848 (34.7) | 0.982 | 2.37 |
| Iron and steel | Blue | | 5,390[b] (2.26) | −1,135[a] (2.01) | 60.13 (1.05) | 5,845 (7.98) | 0.385 | 1.45 |
| | White | | 9,839[b] (2.29) | −1,484 (1.58) | 112.4 (1.30) | 10,453 (9.34) | 0.276 | 1.64 |
| Nonferrous metals | Blue | | 5,083[a] (1.94) | −1,127[a] (2.10) | −31.01 (0.61) | 5,949 (9.38) | 0.198 | 1.53 |
| | White | | 6,378[a] (2.00) | −842.9 (1.26) | 51.03 (0.78) | 7,602 (9.77) | 0.321 | 1.69 |

| | | | | | | | |
|---|---|---|---|---|---|---|---|
| Metal products | Blue | 5,666 (1.71) | | −619.2 (1.96) | 8,135 (0.26) | 44.96 (12.1) | 0.295 | 1.47 |
| | White | 1,342[b] (2.19) | | −162.8 (0.28) | 38.6 (0.66) | 4,439 (7.25) | 0.264 | 1.44 |
| Machinery | Blue | 10,005 (1.22) | | −972.7[a] (1.83) | −21.9 (0.42) | 5,510 (6.42) | 0.762 | 1.55 |
| | White | 11,974 (1.13) | | −1,252[a] (1.81) | −33.3 (0.47) | 7,666 (6.57) | 0.211 | 1.54 |
| Electric appliances | Blue | | 1,527 (0.94) | −692.6[b] (4.12) | 46.76[b] (2.71) | 4,382 (27.1) | 0.824 | 1.58 |
| | White | | 5,336[b] (3.35) | −564.3[b] (3.19) | 145.7[b] (7.8) | 5,720 (29.5) | 0.918 | 1.59 |
| Transportation equipment | Blue | 1,975 (0.43) | | −942.9[b] (2.45) | 39.08 (0.97) | 5,628 (12.0) | 0.297 | 1.64 |
| | White | 8,851 (1.22) | | −1,312[a] (2.03) | −3,572 (0.48) | 7,673 (8.62) | 0.461 | 1.35 |
| Precision instruments | Blue | −3,461 (2.08) | | | 6,193 (0.42) | 6,730 (43.7) | 0.987 | 2.33 |
| | White | −2,228 (0.21) | | | 62.27 (0.96) | 8,499 (12.4) | 0.807 | 1.20 |

Note: Estimated by the maximum likelihood. With regard to the symbols, see the notes in table 14.3. The regressions on the precision instrument industry cover only 1967–86 and hence have no dummy.
a. Significant at the 10 percent level of confidence in a two-tail test.
b. Significant at the 5 percent level of confidence in a two-tail test.

**Table 14.5**
Estimates of the profit-sharing equations including VACAN

| Industry | Occupation | PROF | PROF(−1) | VACAN | D | T | Constant | $\bar{R}^2$ | DW |
|---|---|---|---|---|---|---|---|---|---|
| Food manufacturing and cigarettes | Blue | 2,707 (0.93) | | 2,255[b] (6.99) | 2,894[b] (11.0) | −117.0[b] (7.40) | 4,786 (14.1) | 0.949 | 2.05 |
| | White | | 11,798[a] (2.03) | 3,377[b] (5.24) | 3,206[b] (5.89) | 92.65[b] (2.82) | 6,470 (9.05) | 0.798 | 1.91 |
| Textiles | Blue | 72,245 (0.72) | | 766.6 (0.44) | 816.2 (0.80) | 136.8 (1.23) | 1,598 (0.78) | 0.228 | 1.63 |
| | White | 7,893 (0.14) | | 4,042[b] (3.94) | 1,519[b] (2.47) | 209.6[b] (3.10) | 2,094 (1.73) | 0.799 | 1.64 |
| Pulp, paper, and related products | Blue | 6,339 (1.33) | 8,476[b] (3.45) | 1,486 (1.17) | 2,164[b] (3.21) | 11.68 (0.18) | 4,528 (4.21) | 0.822 | 1.93 |
| | White | 9,845 (1.54) | 11,183[b] (3.40) | 2,071 (1.23) | 3,257[b] (3.71) | 94.18 (1.13) | 6,431 (4.51) | 0.848 | 1.97 |
| Chemicals | Blue | 19,801 (0.68) | | 667.8 (1.10) | 383.0 (1.25) | 231.1[b] (6.70) | 3,418 (7.94) | 0.986 | 2.58 |
| | White | 38,386 (1.01) | | 942.0 (1.26) | 849.1[a] (2.26) | 187.4[b] (4.41) | 6,226 (11.8) | 0.983 | 2.31 |
| Iron and steel | Blue | | 4,339[b] (2.67) | 2,174[b] (3.99) | 2,767[b] (5.14) | 47.83 (1.33) | 4,649 (8.21) | 0.620 | 1.67 |
| | White | | 7,655[b] (2.36) | 3,572[b] (3.27) | 4,112[b] (4.02) | 106.8 (1.76) | 8,329 (7.98) | 0.586 | 1.84 |
| Nonferrous metals | Blue | | 3,392[b] (3.41) | 2,685[b] (8.64) | 3,042[b] (9.93) | 33.29 (1.55) | 4,260 (13.5) | 0.889 | 1.44 |
| | White | | 4,043[b] (2.32) | 2,947[b] (5.40) | 3,474[b] (5.89) | 11.71 (0.20) | 6,333 (8.63) | 0.861 | 1.73 |

| | | | | | | | | | |
|---|---|---|---|---|---|---|---|---|---|
| Metal products | Blue | 4,026[a] (2.17) | | 1,492[b] (5.67) | 1,585[b] (6.99) | 20.45 (1.29) | 3,523 (15.07) | 0.816 | 1.85 |
| | White | 10,520[b] (4.30) | | 2,850[b] (8.20) | 1,877[b] (5.08) | 52.86 (1.52) | 3,045 (6.42) | 0.915 | 1.42 |
| Machinery | Blue | 10,115[b] (2.92) | | 2,567[b] (7.53) | 2,741[b] (8.41) | 18.55 (0.83) | 3,711 (8.70) | 0.802 | 1.68 |
| | White | 12,497[b] (2.74) | | 3,254[b] (7.47) | 3,513[b] (8.16) | 32.20 (1.01) | 5,472 (9.03) | 0.855 | 1.70 |
| Electric appliances | Blue | | 1,394 (1.25) | 606.0[b] (3.50) | 1,149[b] (7.38) | 46.24[b] (4.04) | 4,005 (25.9) | 0.980 | 2.05 |
| | White | | 3,785[b] (5.21) | 809.9[b] (7.25) | 1,005[b] (9.95) | 160.6[b] (21.5) | 5,183 (52.3) | 0.998 | 2.20 |
| Transportation equipment | Blue | −4,215 (1.65) | | 1,569[b] (5.33) | 1,805[b] (6.73) | 75.5[b] (3.77) | 4,937 (17.4) | 0.940 | 1.99 |
| | White | 3,157 (0.52) | | 2,021[b] (2.86) | 2,520[b] (3.73) | 20.10 (0.35) | 6,784 (8.99) | 0.580 | 1.49 |
| Precision instruments | Blue | −4,294 (2.05) | | 580.6 (0.71) | | 9,223 (0.57) | 6,416 (13.6) | 0.985 | 2.41 |
| | White | −1,536 (0.25) | | 1,061 (0.48) | | 59.38 (0.89) | 7,883 (5.25) | 0.737 | 1.24 |

Note: See the notes to table 14.3.

of confidence. This implies that not only the condition of the industry but also the general condition of the labor market affects bonus payments. Such a dependence on general labor market conditions is explained by the efficiency wage model. That is, labor market conditions influence the expected real income which an employee could obtain upon leaving his or her current job. Using microdata of the firm, Sano (1981), Muramatsu (1986), and Brunello and Ohtake (1987) stress the importance of market wages as points of reference for the individual firm in determining wages. As indicated also by the present study the significance of VACAN shows that the market level of bonus (which is equivalent to BONUS in this chapter because BONUS data are an average in each industry) is responsive to labor market conditions. (Note, however, that this chapter does not assume that the market mechanism will operate to clear any excess demand or supply of labor.) The notion that the market mechanism is not perfect is compatible with the percepts of the efficiency wage hypothesis which, among other things, aims to explain the existence of involuntary unemployment.

According to table 14.4, which shows the estimates of the profit-sharing equations, the effect of PROF or PROF(−1) on BONUS, as expected, is statistically significant at the 5 percent level of confidence for both blue- and white-collar workers in four industries—namely in textiles, pulp and paper, chemicals, and iron and steel—and for only white-collar workers in two industries—namely in metal products and electric appliances. In turn the estimated effect of PROF or PROF(−1) is not significant at the 10 percent level of confidence for either blue- and white-collar workers in the three industries of machinery, transportation, and precision instruments. These results are on the whole similar to the trends exhibited in the statistical significance results of overtime, although there are some exceptions. One is that the effect of profits is significant at the 5 percent level of confidence for both blue- and white-collar workers in the chemical industry but not in the machinery industry, while the effect of overtime is the reverse.

It is possible that in the chemical industry overtime hours is not a good indicator for work intensity, or even that work intensity is not a convincing criterior for determining bonuses because it is typically a capital-intensive industry where the main functions of labor are to maintain equipment and monitor gauges. But it is also difficult to conclude that profits influence bonuses in the chemical industry as the effect of PROF is not significant at an ordinary level of confidence when VACAN is included as an explanatory variable, as shown in table 14.5.

**Table 14.6**
Partial correlations

| Industry | Occupation | PROF | PROF(−1) | VACAN |
|---|---|---|---|---|
| Food manufacturing and cigarettes | Blue | | 0.073 | 0.814 |
| | White | | 0.273 | 0.714 |
| Textiles | Blue | 0.045 | | 0.017 |
| | White | 0.002 | | 0.585 |
| Pulp and paper | Blue | 0.150 | 0.543 | 0.120 |
| | White | 0.192 | 0.536 | 0.131 |
| Chemicals | Blue | 0.040 | | 0.099 |
| | White | 0.085 | | 0.126 |
| Iron and steel | Blue | | 0.393 | 0.591 |
| | White | | 0.336 | 0.557 |
| Nonferrous metals | Blue | | 0.514 | 0.872 |
| | White | | 0.329 | 0.726 |
| Metal products | Blue | | 0.299 | 0.745 |
| | White | | 0.627 | 0.859 |
| Machinery | Blue | | 0.437 | 0.838 |
| | White | | 0.406 | 0.835 |
| Electric appliances | Blue | 0.124 | | 0.527 |
| | White | 0.712 | | 0.830 |
| Transportation equipment | Blue | | — | — |
| | White | | 0.024 | 0.426 |

Note: The estimated coefficient of PROF(−1) is negative in the profit-sharing equation for blue-collar workers in the transportation equipment industry.

In the author's opinion, because the very aim of the profit-sharing model is to explain how a firm uses bonuses to stabilize its internal labor force against fluctuations in output, it pays little attention to how labor market conditions are reflected in bonus determination.[9] In turn the effort compensation model based on the efficiency wage hypothesis explicitly incorporates the mechanism of labor market conditions affecting bonus determination. Therefore it is interesting to see how labor market conditions actually affect bonuses in the profit-sharing model. Table 14.5 shows the estimates of the profit-sharing equations including VACAN. A comparison with table 14.6 shows that at the 10 percent level of confidence the effect of profits on bonuses is not significant in the textile and chemical industries, while it is significant at the 5 percent level of confidence in the machinery

9. It appears that according to Weitzman (1985) labor market conditions affect wages, including bonuses, through changing employment and hence profits (value added). If this interpretation is correct, it would be sufficient to introduce only profits as the explanatory variable in order to explain the behavior of bonuses.

industry. From these one knows that the estimations are suffering from multicolinearity caused by a strong interrelationship between PROF and VACAN. However, we should not leave out the labor market condition as an explanatory variable for two reasons. First, VACAN is significant at the 5 percent level of confidence in most of the estimated industries. The two exceptions are the pulp and paper, and precision instruments. Second, the adjusted $\bar{R}^2$ values drastically improve for both blue- and white-collar workers in many industries, for example, food manufacturing and cigarettes, nonferrous metals, metal products, machinery, and transportation equipment.

To determine which is more "important" as an explanatory variable, profits or labor market conditions, we must focus on the partial correlations. Table 14.6 shows the partial correlation coefficients of PROF or PROF($-1$) and VACAN to BONUS, which were calculated from the estimated equations of the profit-sharing model including VACAN. From this table we can see that the partial correlation coefficient of VACAN is larger than that of PROF or PROF($-1$) in all the estimated equations excluding only those for blue-collar workers in the textile industry and for both blue- and white-collar workers in the pulp and paper industry. That is, labor market conditions explain a larger part of the residual, which is left unexplained after the other variables are included, than profits do. Therefore it is an exaggeration to say that the bonus system functions as a profit-sharing scheme and makes wages more flexible in response to business fluctuations in Japan. Rather bonuses are responsive to labor market conditions in Japan.

Nonnested Test Results

We can now test the goodness of fit for the two models, namely the effort compensation model (E model) and the profit-sharing model (P model) in the cases where the estimated signs of both overtime and profits are positive, as expected, in the preceding estimations. There are 16 such industries and occupations (table 14.7). In this calculation I used the Akaike Information Criterion (AIC) and Davidson and Mackinnon's (1981) test, which is a simplified Cox test called the "J test."

We must first compare the P model excluding VACAN with the E model. According to AIC, in all 16 cases the results are more favorable to the E model. In other words, the AIC statistic is larger in the P model in all cases, as we can easily infer from the adjusted $\bar{R}^2$ values in table 14.3 and 14.4. In the J test there are 6 cases in which the null hypothesis—that the

**Table 14.7**
Non-nested test

| Industry | Occupation | Equation | AIC | J test |
|---|---|---|---|---|
| Textiles | Blue | Profit | 204 | 1.640 |
| | | Overtime | 212 | 0.205 |
| | White | Profit | 199 | 0.189 |
| | | Overtime | 201 | 1.016 |
| Pulp, paper, and related products | Blue | Profit | 197 | 1.945[a] |
| | | Overtime | 192 | 1.407 |
| | White | Profit | 207 | 2.983[b] |
| | | Overtime | 173 | 0.304 |
| Iron and steel | Blue | Profit | 193 | −0.863 |
| | | Overtime | 192 | 0.694 |
| | White | Profit | 213 | −0.486 |
| | | Overtime | 215 | 1.188 |
| Nonferrous metals | Blue | Profit | 176 | 1.611 |
| | | Overtime | 174 | 0.993 |
| | White | Profit | 196 | 2.767[b] |
| | | Overtime | 187 | −0.306 |
| Metal products | Blue | Profit | 167 | −0.403 |
| | | Overtime | 170 | 1.556 |
| | White | Profit | 187 | −0.606 |
| | | Overtime | 191 | 1.952[a] |
| Machinery | Blue | Profit | 178 | 0.296 |
| | | Overtime | 179 | 0.996 |
| | White | Profit | 189 | −0.558 |
| | | Overtime | 189 | 0.608 |
| Electric appliances | Blue | Profit | 159 | 1.762 |
| | | Overtime | 156 | −0.782 |
| | White | Profit | 148 | −1.212 |
| | | Overtime | 159 | 3.574[b] |
| Transportation | White | Profit | 200 | 2.083[a] |
| | | Overtime | 198 | −1.686 |

Note: AIC stands for the Akaike Information Criterion. The statistic in the J test, which was proposed by Davidson and Mackinnon (1981), has a student's t distribution.
a. Denotes that the null hypothesis of one model against the alternative being true is rejected at the 5 percent level of confidence.
b. Denotes that the null hypothesis is rejected at the 10 percent level of confidence.

P model is true against the E model—is rejected at the 10 percent level of confidence and the opposite is not. Unfortunately, there are 3 cases in which both null hypotheses are rejected at the 10 percent level of confidence. It is difficult for us to interpret these cases. But we can conclude that the results show that the E model is more effective in explaining bonus determination than the P model excluding VACAN.

Next we compare the P model including VACAN with the E model. The test results by AIC and the J test are also shown in table 14.7. AIC results show that the two models are equally effective, since the AIC statistic for the P model is smaller in 7 equations than that of the E model. In turn the J test results are slightly more favorable to the E model. More specifically the above null hypothesis is rejected at the 10 percent level, and the opposite is not for blue-collar workers in the pulp and paper and transportation industries and for white-collar workers in the pulp and paper and nonferrous metals industries. On the other hand, the null hypothesis of the E model against the P model is rejected, and the opposite is not for white-collar workers in the metal products and the electric appliance industries. Furthermore, note the cases for blue-collar workers in the textile, nonferrous metals, and electric appliance industries in which the statistic in the J test is more than 1.6 for the null hypothesis of the P model against the E model and less than 1 for the opposite. Thus we can say that even if VACAN is incorporated into the P model, the E model is still more effective in explaining bonus determination.

Blue- and White-Collar Workers

There are several reasons for separating blue-collar (production) and white-collar (management, clerical, and technical) workers in this study. First, overtime hours may not be a pertinent substitute variable for labor intensity in the case of white-collar workers. Their working hours are probably underreported because it is difficult to survey unpaid hours worked by overtime. Second, as Alchian and Demsetz (1972) discuss, for firms to motivate white-collar workers whose jobs involve the supervision, management, and control of manual workers and the assessment of output, they must be paid wages closely tied to business performance. Because of these two factors, the significances of OH and PROF differ between blue- and white-collar workers.

This point is illustrated in table 14.3 and 14.4. First table 14.4 shows that at the 5 percent level PROF or PROF($-1$) is significant for white- but not for blue-collar workers in the metal and electrical appliance industries. At the 10 percent level the same applies to the food industry. There are no industries for which the reverse case holds true. Business profits, then, are a meaningful factor to explain the bonuses of white-collar workers, which is consistent with Alchian and Demsetz (1972).

On the other hand, the effects of OH and OH(−1) are puzzling (table 14.3). At the 5 percent level of confidence OH or OH(−1) is a significant variable for blue- but not for white-collar workers only in the textile industry, but conversely significant for white- and not blue-collar workers in the rubber, metal, and precision machinery industries. Does this mean that paid overtime hours can be considered to accurately express the level of activity and labor intensity of white-collar workers? Probably not; rather it highlights the fact that in Japan both blue- and white-collar workers belong to the same enterprise union, which conducts wage and bonus negotiations for both categories of workers. The difference between blue- and white-collar bonuses arises after the total bonus figure is decided. Bonuses are usually distributed among employees on the basis of the basic wages they receive. The differences between blue- and white-collar workers therefore arises at the distribution stage, and the internal wage structure plays an important role in this.

Differences between Bonuses and Basic Wages

To help clarify the special characteristics of bonus determination, a brief discussion of basic wage fixing follows. Each year during the "spring wage offensive" (shunto) an overall rise in a basic wage is decided upon. This rise can be divided into two components: a "regular-rise" (set annual wage rise) and a "base-up" component. The former is the rise accounting for long-term contractual agreements and is the factor that solidifies the behavior of wages. On the other hand, the base-up component depends on the economic conditions at the time of the negotiation. It is the portion that to some degree is a response to the business environment. Recently the ratio of the "base-up" to the regular-rise component has become relatively smaller. This is a result of the low economic growth rates experienced since the oil shocks. We can infer that basic wages in Japan are now solidifying.

The results for the regressions of OH, OH(−1), and VACAN to increments in real basic wages (BASICW) are shown in table 14.8. Although the significance of these variables fell somewhat, the effect of VACAN remained significant. Similar results were also obtained from regressing PROF, PROF(−1), and VACAN on increments in BASICW. These findings are consistent with those of Mizuno (1985), who argued that based on

**Table 14.8**
The effects of overtime hours and labor market conditions on basic wage increments

| Industry | Occupation | OH | OH(-1) | VACAN | D | T | CONST. | $\bar{R}^2$ | DW |
|---|---|---|---|---|---|---|---|---|---|
| Food manufacturing | Blue | 3.65 | -6.46 | 279.8[b] | -63.89 | 4.38 | -186.35 | 0.633 | 2.20 |
| | | (0.39) | (0.62) | (3.61) | (0.86) | (0.72) | (1.67) | | |
| | White | -16.24 | 21.52[b] | 293.51[b] | -65.17 | 1.72 | -306.0 | 0.73 | 2.19 |
| | | (2.25) | (3.38) | (3.43) | (0.48) | (0.48) | (2.06) | | |
| Textiles | Blue | 1.27 | 12.51 | 199.01 | -133.41 | -7.02 | -146.29 | -0.144 | 1.90 |
| | | (0.74) | (0.70) | (1.23) | (0.77) | (0.51) | (0.94) | | |
| | White | -2.18 | 21.68 | 336.63[b] | -154.96 | 2.42 | -352.0 | 0.56 | 1.86 |
| | | (0.77) | (1.67) | (3.66) | (1.15) | (0.34) | (2.57) | | |
| Pulp, paper, and related products | Blue | 8.35 | 3.39 | 23.02[b] | -123.71 | -4.95 | -278.0 | 0.65 | 2.16 |
| | | (1.06) | (0.64) | (3.30) | (1.56) | (0.92) | (2.95) | | |
| | White | 19.33* | -8.64 | 243.5[b] | -78.88 | -4.99 | -238.7 | 0.81 | 2.12 |
| | | (2.14) | (1.24) | (3.93) | (1.22) | (1.11) | (3.34) | | |
| Chemicals | Blue | 17.33 | 0.52 | 171.66[b] | -113.18[a] | -10.38 | -179.1 | 0.82 | 2.59 |
| | | (1.51) | (0.89) | (3.68) | (1.95) | (1.50) | (4.01) | | |
| | White | 62.64[b] | -16.54 | 184.9[b] | -197.9[b] | -24.90[b] | -292.9 | 0.84 | 2.11 |
| | | (3.42) | (1.75) | (3.31) | (2.81) | (2.96) | (4.90) | | |
| Rubber products | Blue | -0.72 | 3.16 | 144.1[b] | 31.12 | -2.77 | 56.73 | 0.76 | 2.50 |
| | | (0.14) | (0.80) | (2.45) | (0.57) | (0.63) | (1.20) | | |
| | White | 14.19 | 3.97 | 161.1[b] | -147.8[a] | -12.20 | -177.9 | 0.81 | 2.48 |
| | | (1.73) | (0.92) | (3.20) | (2.06) | (1.82) | (4.05) | | |
| Iron and steel | Blue | 12.51[a] | 0.97 | 97.95 | -64.46 | 2.10 | -229.8 | 0.82 | 2.30 |
| | | (2.04) | (0.37) | (1.19) | (1.52) | (0.96) | (4.43) | | |
| | White | 12.17 | -0.80 | 234.2[b] | -74.21 | 3.89 | -264.0 | 0.74 | 2.40 |
| | | (0.81) | (0.96) | (2.31) | (1.11) | (1.11) | (2.79) | | |

| | | | | | | | | | |
|---|---|---|---|---|---|---|---|---|---|
| Nonferrous metals | Blue | -3.30 (1.59) | 7.50$^b$ (4.73) | 148.6$^b$ (3.59) | -68.23 (1.30) | -7.42 (1.59) | -121.3 (3.41) | 0.72 | 2.30 |
| | White | 7.32 (1.18) | 5.18 (1.37) | 235.9$^b$ (4.01) | -111.74 (1.53) | -7.93 (1.27) | -245.8 (4.29) | 0.82 | 2.23 |
| Metal products | Blue | -9.27 (2.16) | 16.24$^b$ (5.87) | -8.70 (0.16) | 8.13 (0.99) | -0.75 (0.30) | -77.83 (1.20) | 0.90 | 2.21 |
| | White | 11.54 (1.12) | 3.29 (0.45) | 197.8$^b$ (2.83) | -180.1 (1.61) | -7.09 (1.28) | -223.7 (2.46) | 0.64 | 2.41 |
| Machinery | Blue | -2.05 (0.76) | 2.66 (1.45) | 193.0$^b$ (3.79) | -26.43 (0.65) | 0.69 (0.16) | -136.4 (3.51) | 0.83 | 2.48 |
| | White | -2.22 (0.59) | 3.40 (1.27) | 186.6$^b$ (4.10) | -15.26 (0.34) | 0.83 (0.23) | 144.5 (2.97) | 0.84 | 2.55 |
| Electric appliances | Blue | -3.01 (1.21) | 2.45 (0.86) | 116.9$^b$ (2.54) | 14.44 (0.37) | 0.30 (0.72) | -59.75 (1.53) | 0.79 | 2.29 |
| | White | -0.47 (0.13) | 3.74 (1.03) | 175.5$^b$ (3.42) | -26.18 (0.51) | -2.76 (0.45) | -143.2 (2.79) | 0.79 | 2.42 |
| Transportation equipment | Blue | -0.97 (0.38) | 2.05 (1.06) | 160.5$^b$ (3.64) | -15.90 (0.35) | 0.56 (0.16) | -127.6 (2.67) | 0.82 | 2.48 |
| | White | 1.58 (0.30) | 4.72 (1.36) | 172.6$^b$ (3.01) | -52.41 (0.71) | 1.20 (0.29) | -211.8 (2.60) | 0.75 | 2.21 |
| Precision instruments | Blue | -1.46 (0.35) | 1.48 (0.40) | 123.2$^b$ (3.51) | -20.91 (0.57) | 0.25 (0.68) | -69.76 (2.22) | 0.72 | 1.95 |
| | White | 3.82 (0.58) | 6.10 (1.00) | 172.0$^b$ (3.20) | -80.03 (1.01) | -10.31 (0.96) | -129.6 (2.55) | 0.71 | 2.17 |

Note: Estimated by the maximum likelihood. See the notes to table 14.3.

**Table 14.9**
Microdata analysis of bonuses, 1971–86

| Explained variable | ln MSALE | ln MSALE(−1) | MPROF | MPROF(−1) | BONUS | VACAN | MAGE | MLENG | D | T | $\bar{R}^2$ | DW |
|---|---|---|---|---|---|---|---|---|---|---|---|---|
| MBONUS | 0.496 | | | | 0.458 | 0.938 | 0.006 | −0.057 | −0.926 | 0.027 | 0.791 | 1.776 |
| | (2.97)[b] | | | | (9.98)[b] | (6.14)[b] | (0.15) | (1.15) | (6.44)[b] | (0.03) | | |
| | | 0.193 | | | 0.439 | 1.107 | −0.183 | 0.078 | −1.700 | 0.018 | 0.695 | 1.710 |
| | | (1.29) | | | (6.81)[b] | (5.04)[b] | (3.29) | (1.32) | (6.92)[b] | (0.56) | | |
| | | | 26.31 | | 0.384 | 0.875 | 0.006 | 0.035 | −1.204 | 0.037 | 0.801 | 1.832 |
| | | | (7.93)[b] | | (8.89)[b] | (6.40)[b] | (0.16) | (0.75) | (9.43)[b] | (2.13)[b] | | |
| | | | | 28.61 | 0.320 | 1.381 | −0.185 | 0.084 | −2.048 | 0.024 | 0.717 | 1.725 |
| | | | | (5.77)[b] | (4.93)[b] | (6.38)[b] | (3.47) | (1.50) | (8.57)[b] | (0.90) | | |

Note: Estimated by the maximum likelihood (first-order serial correlation of the error). With regard to the symbols, see the appendix, section 14.7. The unit value of BONUS has changed to ¥1,000, and likewise that of MBONUS, MSALE, and MPROF.

**Table 14.10**
Microdata analysis on average wages, 1972–86

| Explained variable | Δln MSALE(−1) | ΔMPROF(−1) | ΔBASICW | VACAN(−1) | MAGE | MLENG | R̄² | DW |
|---|---|---|---|---|---|---|---|---|
| ΔMWAGE of RS | 0.054 | | 0.391 | 0.057 | −0.004 | −0.008 | 0.529 | 1.885 |
| | (2.38)** | | (5.02)** | (3.34)** | (0.64) | (1.42) | | |
| | | 0.075 | 0.419 | 0.059 | −0.003 | −0.008 | 0.524 | 1.873 |
| | | (0.16) | (5.41)** | (3.44)** | (0.60) | (1.37) | | |
| ΔMWAGE of CRLA | −0.006 | | 0.912 | −0.129 | −0.036 | 0.029 | 0.876 | 1.924 |
| | (0.31) | | (24.4)** | (11.6) | (7.28) | (6.00)** | | |
| | | −2.536 | 0.953 | 0.128 | −0.031 | 0.026 | 0.885 | 1.936 |
| | | (6.29) | (26.7)** | (12.3) | (6.64) | (5.68)** | | |

Note: Estimated by the maximum likelihood (first-order serial correlation of the error). Δln MSALE(−1) = ln MSALE(−1) − ln MSALE(−2). ΔMPROF(−1) = MPROF(−1) − MPROF(−2). RS is the "Report on Securities," and CRLA is the "Current Report on Labor Administration." The unit value of BASICW has changed to ¥1,000.

whole industry data basic wages as well as bonuses are responsive to labor market conditions, but the former are less responsive to profits than the latter. These results also confirm my hypothesis that the bonus system is a device to adjust wages in line with industry-specific (firm-specific) factors such as past work intensity.

## 14.5 Analysis by Microdata

In this section the results of my analysis using microdata for large manufacturing firms are discussed. I chose the top 3 or 4 companies in each industry where possible, for a total of 50 companies. Microdata for profits and sales were taken from the *Report on Securities* (Yuka Shoken Hokokusho), data for bonuses from the *Current Report on Labor Administration* (Rosei Jiho), and data for average wages per employee from both data sources. Here, instead of overtime hours whose microdata unfortunately was not available, I used sales as a proxy for intensity of labor, since it seemed to accurately approximate work loads. Sales are more closely associated with the intensity of labor than the current profit figure, which includes not only operating profit but also nonoperating receipts such as capital gains and royalties earned on security and patent holdings. Furthermore, despite increased production, it is possible for a firm not to make a profit. Many firms experienced this situation during the oil shocks and more recently during the period of high exchange rates. Sales, however, are not as good a proxy for work intensity as overtime because they depend on the product prices, which do not necessarily move congruously with production and work intensity.

The analysis based on microdata makes it possible to test the effects of market levels on bonuses and basic wages. We can now use industry aggregate data for market levels, that is, BONUS and BASICW, defined in the previous section. We can regard them as being given to individual companies. As discussed in section 14.3, the factors to which most companies attach greater importance in deciding bonuses and wages are the levels set by leading or comparable size companies in the same industry. Thus we can specify the estimation equations of both the models including the market level by each industry, and estimate them for the pooled data, using company dummies.

In the estimation of bonus determination I used current sales and profits as explanatory variables for all the companies in the textile, pulp and paper, chemical, nonferrous metal, and electric industries, one company in the machinery industry, and two in the precision instrument industry because in these companies bonuses are determined through lump-sum-in-winter or short-run bargaining. For the companies in the other industries I used the lagged variable of sales and profits since lump-sum-in-summer bargaining is prevalent there. The estimates results are shown in table 14.9.

According to table 14.9 the logarithm of total sales (MSALES) and profits (MPROF) have a positive effect on bonuses, as expected, and their effects are statistically significant at the 5 percent level of confidence except the effect of sales in the equation estimated for the companies adopting the method of the lump-sum-in-summer bargaining. More important, the effects of both labor market conditions (VACAN) and the market level of bonuses (BONUS) are significant at the 5 percent level of confidence with expected signs. These results can be explained reasonably by the effort compensation model based on the efficiency wage hypothesis, which insists that both labor market conditions and the market level affect wages including bonuses through changing the expected real income an employee could get by leaving his or her current job.

I also regressed increments in average wages per employee (MWAGE) on increases in the logarithm of MSALE or MPROF, VACAN, BASICW, MAGE (average ages), and MLENG (length of service) for the pooled data, using company dummies. In so doing, since basic wages are determined in the spring wage offensive, I used the lagged variable for ln MSALE and MPROF and obtained MWAGE, ln MSALE, AMPROF, and BASICW by using CPI($-1$). The estimated results are shown in table 14.10.

First, the results based on the wage data from the *Reports on Securities* show that the effect of sales on real wages is statistically significant at the ordinary level of confidence while that of profits is not. But the effect of sales should not be overemphasized as an explanatory variable since, if ln MSALE($-1$) is left out of the estimation equation, $\bar{R}^2$ changes only slightly from 0.529 to 0.525. In turn labor market conditions and the market rate are significant in both equations with expected sign. These results are consistent with the discussion in section 14.2 that basic wages are mainly affected by the general condition of the labor market and industry-specific conditions, and not by company-specific conditions.

The average wage data of the *Reports on Securities* are different from those of the *Current Report on Labor Administration*. In particular, the former includes both payments for overtime worked and nonunion members' salaries while the latter does not. Therefore it is useful to conduct the same analysis on the data of the latter. Unfortunately, the results are a little puzzling; as shown in table 14.10, only BASICW is significant at the ordinary level of significance, and both ln MSALE($-1$) and VACAN($-1$) do not have the expected sign. Here one can say only that basic wages strongly depend on the market rate and the average length of service of employees.

## 14.6 Conclusions

The main arguments in this chapter are as follows:

1. According to empirical results based on both the macro- and microdata, overtime hours as well as labor market conditions have a positive and significant effect on bonuses. This supports the effort compensation model that bonuses are paid to compensate employees for the intensity of work experienced during the last period.

2. The profit-sharing model needs to explain the mechanism of how labor market conditions affect bonuses, since the goodness of fit of this model is low without labor market conditions included as an explanatory variable.

3. Judging from the statistical significance of the effect on bonuses and from the partial correlation, labor market conditions are more influential than profits, overtime, and sales in the determination of bonuses and basic wages. This implies that wage flexibility in Japan should be explained by the response of wages to labor market conditions. In this sense the problem of why Japanese wages are flexible remains unsolved.

4. Bonuses are more responsive to economic conditions than basic wages are. This fact was also found by Freeman and Weitzman (1987) and Suruga (1987). The microdata analysis of this chapter shows that bonuses are more responsive to firm-specific conditions than basic wages are.

5. There is no distinct difference in the wage determination between white- and blue-collar workers. This is probably because in Japan both belong to the same enterprise union, and hence the negotiations of bonuses and wages are held together for both categories of workers.

6. Microdata analysis shows that the effect of the market rate is significant on both bonuses and basic wage increments, that the demand-supply condition in the whole economy is significantly effective on bonuses and, from data from the *Reports on Securities*, on average wage increments. In turn the effects of firm-specific conditions such as profits and sales are demonstrated for bonuses but not basic wages.

## 14.7    Appendix: Definitions and Data Sources of Variables

BONUS = Total sum of "bonuses and special payments" per regular worker in a fiscal year (*Monthly Labor Survey*, Ministry of Labor). Unit = yen.

OH = Monthly average of "overtime worked" per regular worker in a fiscal year (*Monthly Labor Survey*, Ministry of Labor). Unit = hours.

PROF = Annual "ordinary profits" per employee for companies capitalized at more than one billion yen (*Financial Statements of Incorporated Businesses*, Ministry of Finance). Unit = million yen.

VACAN = Ratio of effective job vacancies to effective job searchers (*Employment Exchange Statistics*, Ministry of Labor).

CPI = Consumer price index (*Monthly Survey of Consumer Price Index*, Bank of Japan).

BASICW = Basic wages. To remove overtime payments from "contractual cash earnings including payments for overtime worked" (*Monthly Labor Survey* Ministry of Labor), I divided through by [1 + 1.28 (overtime hours/scheduled hours), where 1.28 is the average premium for overtime in manufacturing firms with 1,000 employees or more (*General Survey of Wages and Hours Worked*, Ministry of Labor, 1976). Unit = yen.

D = Dummy variable. D takes a value of 1 for the period from 1971 to 1973 and 0 for all other years.

T = Time trend.

MBONUS = Total bonus per employee in a fiscal year (*Current Report on Labor Administration*, Institute of Labor Administration). Unit = 1,000 yen.

MNWAGE = Monthly average of wages per employee (*Current Report on Labor Administration*, Institute of Labor Administration and *Report on Securities*, Ministry of Finance). Unit = 1,000 yen.

MPROF = Annual ordinary profits per employee (*Report on Securities*). Unit = million yen.

MAGE = Average age of employees (*Report on Securities*).

MLENGTH = Average length of service of employees (*Report on Securities*).

# V

# Public and Cooperative Enterprises

# 15      The Privatization of Public Enterprises: Background and Results

Masu Uekusa

Direct government regulations of enterprise activity may be classified as either economic or social according to their purpose (Weiss and Klass 1981). Economic regulations are often applied to natural monopoly sectors. To ensure efficient resource allocation and equitable distribution, governments control the entry-exit, pricing, investment, and financing of firms. Social regulations are usually aimed at handling problems posed by negative externalities. They concern the maintenance of health and safety, preservation of the environment, and prevention of pollution. Although some regulations are difficult to classify as economic and not social, sectors covered by economic regulations—consisting primarily of public utilities, transportation, communications, and finance (banking, securities, and insurance)—are responsible for about one-third of Japanese GNP (Gyokakushin 1989). Economic regulations apply to (1) sectors where only private enterprises exist (e.g., the securities industry), (2) sectors where only public enterprises exist (e.g., postal delivery), and (3) sectors where private and public enterprises coexist (i.e., most industries subject to economic regulation). Furthermore the government has established numerous public enterprises to administer social regulations. As a result Japan has had a rather large number of public enterprises.

The major developed countries, including Japan, have deregulated controlled industries and privatized public enterprises since the 1970s. In the United States, for example, finance (banking, securities, and insurance), transportation (railroads and trucking), energy (natural gas and oil), telecommunications, and other industries have been deregulated (Weiss and Klass 1981; Wenders 1987), and privatization of public enterprises appears to be forthcoming (President's Commission Report 1988). In Britain, France, West Germany, and other major European countries, privatization has been more prevalent than deregulation, but the telecommunications sector has been deregulated (Kiemeyer and Quaden 1986; Kay, Mayer and

Thompson 1986), and EC members are aiming at large-scale deregulation of other sectors as part of the process of integration by 1992.

Three factors constitute the background to deregulation and privatization. First, the oil shock of the early 1970s pushed many economies into stagnation, and thereby caused government deficits to expand. Eventually "small government" became a slogan to reduce the size of government sectors characterized by deficits and ballooning administrative costs, and the need arose to raise productivity in regulated industries which had grown inefficient under government protection and excessive regulation. Second, the rapidly unfolding technological revolution centered especially on information technology created the technical basis both for interindustry mergers and for the entry of firms into sectors formerly dominated by natural monopolies or oligopolies. Consequently the economic basis for maintaining monopolies and highly concentrated oligopolies by public regulations was eroded. The technological revolution also resulted in a new industrial structure (characterized by greatly expanded information and service sectors) and new industrial organization (network-form industrial organization and "new business" sectors), and necessitated relaxation of regulations acting as impediments to such changes. Third, the strengthening of international relationships among economies since the 1970s in the areas of people, goods, money, and information necessitated the removal of regulations hindering international movement.

These three factors were operative in Japan, as elsewhere. In the 1980s the Provisional Commission for Administrative Reform (1981–83), the Provisional Council for the Promotion of Administrative Reform (1983–87,) and the New Provisional Council for the Promotion of Administrative Reform (1987–90) were organized as direct organs of the prime minister's office, and they issued bold declarations in favor of privatization and deregulation. The three largest public companies were privatized, and regulations were relaxed for finance, telecommunications, transportation, energy, wholesale and retail trade, and agriculture.

This chapter will focus on the public enterprises that have constituted a substantial share of Japan's enterprises and will analyze not only public enterprise management (particularly its inefficiency) but also the history and the results of privatization. Section 15.1 gives an initial overview of Japan's public enterprises by providing a simple survey of the forms and numbers of public enterprises, the context of regulations, and the share of public and regulated enterprises in the economy as a whole. Section 15.2 outlines the background to privatization of Japan's major public corporations since 1985, and section 15.3 analyzes in greater detail the important issue of public enterprise inefficiency. In section 15.4 I attempt to clarify the impact of privatization on former public enterprises, the industries in which they operated, and the economy as a whole and then to evaluate the policy of privatization.

## 15.1  Japan's Public Enterprises

Classification of Public Enterprises

Generally speaking, public enterprises are enterprises with capital wholly or partially owned by the national government or local public bodies (*chiho kokyo dantai*). Public enterprises owned by the national government are called state enterprises, while those owned by local public bodies are called local public enterprises. Such enterprises take a variety of forms, but it is possible to divide them broadly into three types: (1) departmental undertakings (*gengyo*), operations belonging to the departments of the national or local governments and managed with some degree of independence by the head of the department; (2) public corporations (*kokyo hojin*), which are enterprises established according to special laws with corporate status, all equity supplied by the national government or local public bodies, and management entrusted to an enterprise manager; and (3) mixed enterprises (*koshi kongo kigyo*), enterprises having a portion of their equity owned by the government and generally taking the form of a joint-stock or limited-liability company.

Because public enterprises have obtained their capital from public funds (from national or local taxes), they are subject to public regulations to ensure their fair operation ("public finance democracy") regardless of which particular organizational form they take. But the regulatory body and the content of regulations varies according to the organizational form.

First, for departmental undertakings of the national government, the most important regulatory body is the national Diet. The Diet supervises departmental undertakings and has the right to determine their budgets, settlement of accounts, prices, plans, fund raising, disposal of profits and other matters. The budgets, settlements of accounts, and plans of departmental undertakings also require the approval of the Ministry of Finance, and, from the standpoint of price stability, price changes of goods and services supplied by departmental undertakings require the approval of the Economic Planning Agency. Departmental undertakings are subject to the examination of the Board of Audit and the Administrative Inspection Bureau of the Management and Coordination Agency. Thus, in addition to the "vertical" regulations of the national Diet, they are subject to the "horizontal regulations" of the Ministry of Finance, the Economic Planning Agency, the Board of Audit, and the Administrative Investigation Bureau of the Management and Coordination Agency. The departmental undertakings of local public bodies are subject to both vertical regulation of the prefectural assemblies and horizontal regulation of the budget bureaus, and the substance of their operations is subject to the vertical regulations of the Ministry of Home Affairs.

Second, like departmental undertakings, public corporations come under the regulation of both the legislative and the administrative branches of government. In contrast to departmental undertakings, public corporations are enterprises in which management and ownership are separated. Hence the managers of public corporations have more independence, with less room for supervision than departmental undertakings. But among public corporations the large-scale enterprises (the former JNR, NTT, and Japan Monopoly Public Corporation; the Japan Development Bank, and various public finance corporations) came to be subject to about as much government regulation as departmental undertakings. Diet regulation of smaller-scale public corporations (the *kodan* and the *jigyodan*) was less severe. In addition to the regulation of the legislative and administrative branches of government, public corporations are subject to the regulation of the bureaucracies in their particular areas of operation. In finance (banks, securities, and insurance), transportation (railroads, busing, trucking, taxis, air transport, and water transport), communications (postal services, telecommunications, and broadcasting), public utilities (electricity, gas, water, and heating) and other industries, industry laws exist that regulate both private and public enterprises.

Third, mixed enterprises are identical to private enterprises in being joint-stock or limited-liability companies according to civil and commercial law, and therefore their accounting is the same as that of private enterprises and differs from public governmental accounting. Other than regulations regarding state jurisdiction, government regulation of mixed enterprises had become rather mild. Diet regulation has been abolished in principle, and the Diet maintains only the right to conduct surveys.

Regarding the content of public enterprise regulation, the regulations are divided into (1) regulations based on public enterprise law, such as the Public Finance Law and the Special Legislation Law, and (2) regulations based on particular industry laws. Regulations based on the former relate to the composition of activities; organization; appointment, dismissal and terms of office of directors; budgets and settlement of accounts; issue of bonds; limits on the amount of borrowing; disposal of profits; plans for new programs; restrictions on the right to strike; and so on. Regulations based on the latter are the economic regulations mentioned above, and they concern entry and exit, prices, quantities supplied, quality, mergers, investments in new projects, and accounts and finance.

To summarize, public enterprises are owned by the national government or local public bodies and are subject to regulations under various laws established on the basis of public ownership. While public enterprises have a "public character" from public ownership and regulation, as enterprises they do manage certain operations and acquire operating revenues with a degree of independence. In some public enterprises, operating revenues greatly exceed expenditures (e.g., the Japan Monopoly Public Corporation), some are regulated so as to realize balanced revenues and expenditures, and others receive subsidies if expenditure exceeds revenue. Public enterprises also differ according to when and why they were established.

Numbers and Forms of Public Enterprises

How many Japanese public enterprises are there? First, let us consider state enterprises. There are 38 departmental undertakings designated in Special Accounts. But since almost half of these are dependent on subsidies for most of their revenue, it is more sensible to classify them as "general government activity" than as public enterprises. From this perspective the New System of National Accounts (SNA) identifies 18 operations as departmental undertakings, and this chapter will follow the same classification.

Public corporations and mixed public enterprises excluding departmental undertakings are called Special Corporations. As of January 1985 there were 99 Special Corporations: 3 public companies, 13 public foundations (*kodan*), 17 enterprise foundations (*jigyodan*), 9 financial corporations (*koko*), 4 financial depositories (*kinko*) and banks, 1 management foundation (*eidan*), 10 special companies (*tokushu kaisha*), 42 "other special corporations." Setting aside the small-scale public enterprises that comprise "other special corporations," the remaining 57 may be classified by enterprise form into 39 public corporations, 17 mixed public enterprises, and one other company (which is still classified as a Special Corporation although government-supplied funds have been repaid; Uekusa 1983).

State enterprises have been established in a wide range of economic sectors, but the central sectors of activity of present-day enterprises are the directly regulated sectors previously discussed, and socially supplied services (medical services, preventative hygiene, waste disposal, social education, social insurance, social welfare, etc.; Uekusa 1979, 1983).

As for local public enterprises, at the end of the 1986 fiscal year there were 3,300 local public bodies operating departmental undertakings and providing funds for public corporations and mixed enterprises, and 3,650 departmental undertakings involved in such activities as managing water supply, sewer systems, hospitals, and tourism. At the beginning of 1987 there were 1,451 local public corporations (for land development, roads, and housing supply) and 3,172 mixed enterprises. The share in the Japanese economy of national and local public enterprises is indicated by 1985 statistics which show that national and local public enterprises accounted for 11 percent of total fixed capital formation and 9.2 percent of total employees.

## 15.2 The Privatization of Public Enterprises

Forms of Privatization

Since 1985 Japan's major public enterprises have been privatized. Strictly speaking, the privatization of public enterprises involves the sale to the private sector of the government-owned capital of the public enterprise, the transformation of the enterprise into a private one, and the abolition of associated regulations according to public enterprise law. But in Japan (more exactly, among those connected with the administrative reform movement and among journalists) the term "privatization of public enterprise" has been used to include the following three meanings. First, it refers to the reorganization of public corporations into public enterprises of the joint-stock company form (and this includes enterprises for which plans exist to sell successively to the private sector parts of the government-owned share capital). Second, it refers to the reorganization of public corporations into "Chartered Corporations." Third, there is privatization proper, the reorganization of public corporations and mixed enterprises into private corporations, a form of reorganization called "complete privatization." Here the term "privatization" is used to refer to all three meanings.

Table 15.1 lists the state enterprises that have been privatized since 1985 on the basis of reports issued by the Provisional Commission for Administrative Reform (hereafter referred to by its abbreviated Japanese title Rincho). Three companies underwent transformation to Special Company status, nine were reorganized as Chartered Corporations, and four were completely privatized. Privatization had three outstanding features. First,

**Table 15.1**
Privatization of public enterprises since 1985

| Before change | After change | Date of change |
|---|---|---|
| **Turned into special companies** | | |
| Nihon Telegraph and Telephone | Nihon Telegraph and Telephone Corp. | April 1, 1985 |
| Japan Monopoly Public Corp. | Japan Tobacco Industry Corp. | April 1, 1985 |
| Japan National Railways | JR Hokkaido | April 1, 1987 |
| | JR East Japan | April 1, 1987 |
| | JR Tokai | April 1, 1987 |
| | JR West Japan | April 1, 1987 |
| | JR Shikoku | April 1, 1987 |
| | JR Kyushu | April 1, 1987 |
| | Japan Freight Railway Company | April 1, 1987 |
| | Japan National Railway Settlement Corp. | April 1, 1987 |
| | Shinkansen Holding Organization | April 1, 1985 |
| **Turned into chartered corporations** | | |
| Central Bank for Agriculture and Forestry | Central Bank for Agriculture and Forestry | April 1, 1986 |
| Tokyo Small Business Investment Company | SME BIC | April 1, 1986 |
| Nagoya SBIC | SME BIC | April 1, 1986 |
| Osaka SBIC | SME BIC | April 1, 1986 |
| High Pressure Gas Maintenance Association | High Pressure Gas Maintenance Association | April 1, 1986 |
| Japan Electrical Measuring Equipment Inspection Center | Japan Electrical Measuring Equipment Inspection Center | April 1, 1986 |
| Japan Fire Prevention Inspection Association | Japan Fire Prevention Inspection Association | April 1, 1986 |
| Forestry Credit Bank | Attached to Agriculture, Forestry, and Fishery Trust Fund | April 1, 1986 |
| Agriculture Mechanization Research Centre | Attached to Institute for Promotion of Biological Equipment | April 1, 1986 |
| **Full privatization** | | |
| Japan Automobile Terminal Coy | Japan Automobile Terminal Coy | April 23, 1985 |
| Tohoku Development Coy | Tohoku Development Coy | October 6, 1985 |
| Japan Airlines | Japan Airlines | November 18, 1987 |
| Okinawa Electric Power Coy | Okinawa Electric Power Coy | Within 1988 |

Source: Management and Coordination Agency ed. *Tokushu hojin soran* (Special Corporation Conspectus), various years.
Note: JNR Settlement Corp. and Shinkansen Holding Organization are not special companies but public corporations.

Japan's three largest public enterprises were reorganized as Special Companies. Neither NTT nor the Japan Monopoly Public Corporation (JM) were broken up, but JNR was split into seven joint-stock companies and two public corporations. All seven joint-stock companies are scheduled to sell a portion of their shares to the public in the near future, and sale of NTT shares to the public has already begun. Second, of the ten Special Companies existing as of early 1985, only two—Kokusai Denshin Denwa Kaisha (KDD) and Kansai International Airport Company—exist today, and thus due to Rincho almost all mixed enterprises and Special Companies have been privatized. Third, Rincho erected a policy of privatizing public enterprises that were not monopoly enterprises or that were special public enterprises without public ownership, and it investigated which enterprises corresponded to those characteristics. But Rincho stopped at turning the Norin Chukin Bank and a fraction of the "Other Special Corporations" into Chartered Corporations.

Background to Privatization

The background to the establishment of Rincho in the first half of the 1980s and the subsequent privatization of public enterprises promoted by the administrative reform movement is similar to the background to deregulation and privatization in the rest of the world. To avoid repetition, I will focus on the major public enterprises (NTT, JM, JNR and JAL), and consider in detail the evolution behind their privatizations.

Privatization of NTT

In its first report Rincho advocated reorganizing NTT into a mixed enterprise (Special Company) and hiving off certain business and regional divisions. In fact the NTT Public Corporation became the NTT joint-stock company without any hiving off. Moreover it is significant that the privatization of NTT was accompanied by deregulation of the telecommunications industry. The Telecommunications Industry Law, which was passed in the same year, advanced the policy of allowing new entrants into the telecommunications industry, and the law greatly changed the market structure that had prevailed until that time in which the NTT and KDD monopolized , respectively, the domestic and the international communications markets.

Three points need to be emphasized regarding the privatization of NTT which accompanied telecommunications deregulation. First, the inefficiency of NTT was a major reason for its privatization. Except for the two times the main fares were revised, the NTT Public Corporation recorded a constant rate of profit since its formation as a balanced revenue–expenditure enterprise in 1952, and it pioneered many leading technological innovations. But immediately prior to privatization NTT employed about 330,000 persons, and according to the Rincho approximately one-third of them were superfluous or redundant. Likewise Rincho pointed out that NTT had concentrated its procurement of intermediate goods on a group of enterprises known as the "NTT family" and had developed the inefficient habit of paying high prices for them. As will be explained later in this chapter, the reasons for such inefficiency were (1) restrictions on management imposed by various public regulations on the enterprise as a public enterprise and (2) a monopolistic market structure that provided no exposure to the harsh winds of competition.

Second, the privatization of NTT was related to the revolution in information technology. As a consequence of the unfolding revolution in various information technologies relating to telecommunications (integrated circuits, computers, fiber optics, satellite transmissions, and the emergence of value-added networks and other "new media"), industries have merged in many areas of the information transmission industry (Uekusa 1989). Technological innovation and the expansion of market sizes have further made possible the provision of services through small-scale networks capable of competing against the large-scale networks, and it has become technologically feasible to secure communications interfaces between enterprises. The convergence of these and other conditions has been the basis for major changes in the competitive structure of the telecommunications industry.

Third, the desire for privatization that existed within NTT must be recognized, particularly the desire to avoid regulation by the national Diet, to maintain the independence of management, and to realize greater enterprise efficiency. Since the NTT Public Corporation required Diet approval of its budgeting and settlement of accounts, it did not have the right to determine independently the wages of its personnel (nor even the annual pay-increase rate). It had to go through the process of applying to the Minister of Finance, making an arbitration request to the Public Corporation and State Enterprise Labor Committee (*Koroi*), and obtaining Diet approval before finally determining the structure of wages. NTT management wanted to avoid such procedures, to freely determine wages and stimulate the incentive to work, and to increase management efficiency by acquiring the right to determine freely personnel transfers and entry into related fields. Since these objectives could all be achieved by privatization, NTT management cooperated with the privatization policy of the Provisional Commission for Administrative Reform. Thus the privatization of NTT was carried out with fewer hitches than other privatizations.

Privatization of the Japan Monopoly Public Corporation (JM)

The privatization of JM, like that of NTT, had greater efficiency as its main purpose. JM had been given monopoly rights for the manufacture and sale of tobacco and salt, mainly to secure tax revenues. In the JM accounts for the 1985 fiscal year, 60 percent of the ¥2.5 trillion sales revenue consisted of sales taxes going to national revenues and tobacco consumption taxes going to the revenue of local public bodies. Of the remaining 40 percent of sales revenues, 34 percent consisted of costs and administrative expenses, and 6 percent counted as profits. The salt business, however, registered losses and had to be supported by cross-subsidization from the tobacco business. Furthermore, under the influence of the government's agricultural protection policies, JM was obliged to purchase domestically produced tobacco leaves at three times the price of foreign-produced tobacco leaves, and hence faced a severe limitation to reducing expenses. Rincho originally advanced a plan that in conjunction with privatization the enterprise would be given the right to make tobacco leaf purchases freely. The Rincho plan, however, drew opposition from many Diet members, and ultimately the obligation to purchase domestic tobacco leaves was retained. It was also decided that after privatization the enterprise would retain monopoly rights regarding production and sales in order to secure tax revenues and to protect Japanese tobacco growing and manufacture. Accordingly, after passing through the political process, the privatization of JM diverged from the original proposals. But due to the market liberalization campaign of the American tobacco companies, the entry of new enterprises into cigarette sales was finally allowed. American tobacco companies entered the market and soon secured a market share of nearly 10 percent.

Privatization of JNR

JNR's massive accumulated debt was particularly notable. In the 1964 fiscal year JNR registered its first postwar deficit on overall accounts, and thereafter the deficit mushroomed, reaching a net loss in the 1980 fiscal year of about ¥1 trillion or 30 percent of operating revenues. By the 1982 fiscal year the accumulated debt had reached ¥25 trillion, or ¥37 trillion if the debts of the Japanese Railway Construction Public Corporation are included.

JNR registered deficits since 1964 because of (1) stagnation of the freight business due to lack of initiative in responding to highway alternatives; (2) except for the Shinkansen (Bullet Train line) and the commuter lines in the largest metropolitan areas; cumulative deficits on almost all lines, especially on regional transportation lines, (3) an exceedingly large number of personnel amounting to about 330,000 persons; (4) mushrooming retirement allowances and pensions; and (5) massive interest payments that accompanied the rapid expansion of accumulated debt.

But the root of the problem was that (1) the Diet, the agency responsible for regulating the JNR, was less interested in supervising the management activities of JNR than with establishing regional transportation lines and extending the Shinkansen (an example of the "politicization of regulation"); (2) with the deterioration of labor-management relations left unresolved, the internal motivation of the enterprise to increase efficiency declined dramatically; and (3) the continuation of losses did not pose the threat of bankruptcy for the enterprise.

The Rincho reports called for the division and rationalization of JNR together with rationalization and unification of regional transportation lines, large-scale trimming of personnel, and integration of JNR pensions into the National Pension System (Kokumin Nenkin). The passenger and freight operations of the enterprise were separated, with passenger operations divided among six passenger rail companies (known as JR) and freight operations handed over to the Japan Freight Railway Company (Nihon Kamotsu Tetsudo Kaisha). Further the Japanese National Railway Settlement Corporation was established to deal with JNR's accumulated debt, and the Shinkansen Holding Organization was established to control the assets of the Shinkansen. JNR then was split into nine different companies. The division of passenger operations into six companies and the separation of the Japan Freight Railway Company were ostensibly directed toward efficient management through small-scale organization and specialization, but the intention of dismantling the main JNR labor unions is undeniable. Also undeniable is that one motive for establishing seven Special Companies was to escape the politicization of regulations.

Japan Air Lines (JAL)

JAL was a classical a mixed-enterprise type of joint stock company established in 1953 with funds from both the government and the private sector.

Although a system of competition with private enterprises was established for domestic air routes, JAL was the only Japanese enterprise permitted access to international routes. While maintaining a high market share in domestic air travel, JAL also registered large profits on international routes (especially on Pacific Ocean and European routes). Yet not only were labor-management relations unstable, but politics was continually a factor in upper management appointments, and there was perpetual conflict within the management group. As pointed out by Rincho, JAL had such problems as the highest accident rate among domestic airlines. To solve these problems, Rincho put forth a proposal for complete privatization, which was implemented in 1987. The privatization of JAL also aimed at eliminating the politicization of regulation and reforming labor-management relations, thereby raising internal organization efficiency.

### 15.3   Factors behind the Inefficiency of Public Enterprises

The "inefficiency of public enterprise" is part of the common background to the privatization of the big three public companies and JAL. But what explains the emergence of such inefficiency? In the previous section fragmentary references were made to the relevant factors, which will now be explained systematically.

An enterprise is fully efficient if (1) when it purchases inputs, it purchases them at prices set by competition in input markets; (2) given the technological level attainable during the period, the enterprise realizes the optimal combination of inputs; (3) production occurs at the optimal scale of production; (4) sales are carried out through optimal sales channels at minimum expense; and (5) there is no "managerial slack" in personnel administration or in finance. In reality even private enterprises in competitive markets are not always optimally efficient. Yet public enterprises typically realize performance levels far below those of private ones. The three public companies were much more lax than typical private enterprises in terms of optimal purchasing activities and optimal combination of inputs, particularly concerning the purchase of supplies and plant and equipment, and they exhibited a great deal of managerial slack, as did JAL.

The three public companies and JAL were not departmental undertakings but corporate enterprises, and being "Japanese enterprises" all of them exhibited the characteristic features of Japanese-style management. They had (1) enterprise unions, (2) lifetime employment and seniority wages, (3) a system of rotation among different jobs and the formation of intellectual skills within the enterprise, (4) unified personnel administration, and (5) a system of advancement to upper-level managerial positions. If such features determine the efficiency of Japanese enterprises, it might be expected that the three public companies and JAL would have attained the average level of efficiency of Japan's large private enterprises. What then explains their inefficiency? In the author's opinion, the explanation lies in the public ownership and their resultant public regulation (including whether or not they acquired monopoly rights of supply). From this perspective the enterprise form of the three public companies differed from that of JAL and consequently so did the degree of public regulation they experienced. The inefficiency of the three public companies must therefore be analyzed separately from that of JAL.

The three public companies were departmental undertakings in the pre–World War II period, but during the Occupation they were reorganized into public companies known as public enterprise bodies. Reorganization was intended to promote enterprise efficiency by contributing to the independence of management through its separation from ownership. But in fact, as symbolized by two points, the Diet did not limit the application of direct regulations to departmental undertakings. First, the accounting system of public companies was based on the public enterprise accounting system, and it became necessary to obtain the approval of the Diet for enterprise budgeting and settlement of accounts. Second, the Diet had to give approval to enterprise plans, profit allocation, prices, and personnel administration; the composition of business was perpetually under the supervision of the Diet; and other matters (e.g., the issue of bonds and borrowing from banks) required the approval of the relevant minister.

The budgeting and settlement of accounts system within public enterprise accounting is the most important cause of the inefficiency of public enterprises (and of the government bureaucracy as well). Budgets are usually drawn up by adding to the previous year's results the factors expected to change during the current year (e.g., price movements), and further, for newly established operations, the budget is based on all of the expenses expected to arise during the current fiscal year. Because the budget is constructed on the basis of the results of the previous fiscal year—for example, in most cases the purchase costs of materials and equipment (including research and development expenses) will be registered in the budget without adjustment—incentives to economize on the purchasing costs of materials and equipment are missing. Incentives to economize are further weakened because (1) the purchase of materials and equipment at list prices makes for fewer complications if the accounts are investigated and (2) it is common practice to exhaust budgets during the current fiscal year. Extreme restrictions on shifting expenses incurred for one particular category to some other category impede efficient budget utilization. This budgeting and settlement of accounts system, which is especially rigid for the accounts of the government bureaucracy, has undoubtedly been an important factor blocking optimal input purchase, combination of inputs, scale of production, and the selection of sales outlets.

Let us next consider the issue of managerial slack. First, the three public companies required Diet approval of members of their boards of directors and appointments were the responsibility of the prime minister. If promotion to top executive positions is not carried out within the firm, there is a strong tendency for managers above a certain level to cease internal competition for promotion, and rather to hustle about establishing connections with outside politicians or to seek transfers (*amakudari*) to affiliated companies (and to increase attention paid to political contributions and affiliated companies). Second, if managers require Diet approval regarding pricing, investment, financing, and so on, they cannot independently determine their goals. Goal determination was even further restricted because public regulations are also the concern of ministries such as the Ministry of Finance. Since the decisions of the Diet and the various Ministries were not always consistent, comprehensive policy decisions were impossible, and often the location of final responsibility for such decisions was unclear. Unified action within the administration of the enterprise became difficult, notably in response to labor unions. The complicated contributions of the Ministry of Finance, the Diet, and the Public Corporation and State Enterprise Labor Relations Committee to decisions regarding the base rate of pay increases in wage negotiations served to severely restrict managements' powers of decision making and ultimately resulted in irresponsible personnel administration. The efficiency of public enterprises then was impeded by overlapping and inconsistent supervision of the regulating bodies and by the blurring of the location of responsibility for regulation.

One cannot overemphasize the importance of "politicization of regulation" in fostering inefficiency in the three public companies, as illustrated by the JNR problem of establishing regional transportation lines and the JM problem of purchasing domestic tobacco leaves. In addition the Diet as the most important regulatory agency never set out long-term goals for any of the three public companies. In the absence of a clear, long-term "concept," public companies were used to carry out the economic policies of the time. The public enterprises sometimes became entwined in pork barrel politics. The Diet failed to utilize specialist knowledge regarding pricing policy (two-part pricing, peak-load pricing, Ramsey pricing, etc.), and there was seldom any debate about pricing policy for the purpose of raising the efficiency of resource allocation.

Among other causes of management inefficiency of the three public companies (particularly NTT and JM) monopoly supply rights were prominent. These have already been mentioned in the previous section, and elaboration is probably unnecessary. The related issue of the subsidy-dependent character of public enterprises,however, merits further discussion. Not all public enterprises can balance revenues and expenditures, and some can only continue to operate thanks to subsidies (e.g., enterprises supplying semipublic goods or devoted to research and development). Even for other public enterprises subsidies are introduced to cover for losses. And because public enterprises are enterprises with government-owned equity (according to the philosophy of the Public Finance Law), they are not allowed to go bankrupt. Public enterprises are also protected from the danger of being absorbed by, or merged with, other enterprises, since the approval of the Diet and the relevant minister is required.

Finally, the behavioral motivation of public enterprises merits discussion. The main motives driving private Japanese enterprises are the growth motive and the long-term profit motive (long-term, stable achievement of a certain rate of profit). Japan's public enterprises have also held a growth motive for maintaining and developing the organization, and balanced revenue-expenditure enterprises have held a long-term profit motive within the scope of securing fair returns. But, limiting discussion to the three public companies, they concentrated on providing the most stable and safe supply possible, to avoid having the Diet or various ministries intervene because conflict with the purchasers of their goods and services. In other words the motives of stable supply and conflict avoidance (or "trouble minimization") were dominant. These motives resulted in excessive investment in equipment and employment in order to avoid incidents, as well as in the payment of large sums as "political costs" to avoid investigation by the Diet and ministries. These contributed to inefficiency. The expansion of such costs, it should be noted, caused a diminution in the cost consciousness of employees and managers, a diminution that was particularly strong for the three public companies.

In sum, the factors that contributed to the inefficiency of the three public companies were (1) a rigid accounting system equivalent to that of the government bureaucracy, (2) restriction by regulation of management independence, (3) a system of overlapping regulations and the blurring of the location of responsibility for regulations, (4) the politicization of regulation, (5) monopoly supply, (6) the protected character of public enterprises, and

(7) stable supply and trouble minimization motives. Because JAL was a public enterprise of joint-stock company form, it was free from the government bureaucracy accounting system; it had greater independence of management than the three public companies; and its chief regulatory agency was not the Diet, but the Ministry of Transportation. Hence the impact of regulatory restrictions on JAL was less than for the three companies, although it had less management independence than representative private enterprises. Also (1) the politicization of regulations affected JAL, (2) it was the only Japanese enterprise authorized to operate on international air routes, and (3) it exhibited the protected character of a public enterprise. With stable supply and trouble minimization motives, JAL also experienced an expansion of political costs, which led to inefficiency.

### 15.4   The Results and Difficulties of Privatization

As noted above, the main purpose of the privatization of Japan's key public enterprises was to rectify their inefficiency. Since inefficiency stemmed above all from the weakness of managers' incentives to raise efficiency, and since the weakness of public enterprise incentives stemmed from Diet regulation and the politicization of regulations, privatization became necessary. Because monopoly supply privileges of some public enterprises were an additional factor giving rise to their inefficiency, it also became unavoidable that competition be introduced when technological innovation had weakened the basis for natural monopoly. If the efficiency of the main public enterprises were improved and goods and services of higher quality and/or lower prices provided, and if the habit of depending on state finance (particularly in the case of JNR) were rectified, the whole national economy would be made more efficient. From this perspective, as well, it was absolutely necessary that the major public enterprises be privatized. What have been the results of privatization and deregulation, and what problems have remained? (JAL has only recently been privatized, so it will not be discussed here for lack of evidence).

Nihon Telegraph and Telephone (NTT)

Based on reorganization as a joint-stock company organization and the substantial acquisition of management's right of independent goal determination, NTT (1) introduced a system of business divisions, (2) expanded its marketing and sales system, (3) advanced into new areas of business and established new subsidiaries, (4) separated its data headquarters, (5) expanded new services and improved service quality, (6) reduced costs, (7) introduced an ability-based system of personnel administration, and (8) reconstructed its research and development organization. Cost reduction is particularly notable. It mainly stems from a reduction in the number of employees; improved efficiency of plant investment, purchase of materials and machinery, and fund raising; and the rationalization of unprofitable business sections. Specifically, NTT has reduced employment by 6,000 persons per year by not replacing retirees and by transfer of employees to (at present 177) affiliated companies. Improved efficiency of equipment investment is largely due to economization of investment funds through the purchase of the latest small-scale, high-capacity equipment and the switch to a concentrated system of control by six major centers over the equipment investment of the various telephone exchanges. Improved efficiency of materials and machinery purchases stems mainly from increased severity of control over purchase prices, a product of liberation from the government bureaucracy system of budgeting and settlement of accounts. Improved fund-raising efficiency stems from the move to seek funds at the lowest rate of interest whether on domestic or international markets. Through rationalization efforts the deficit of the business section most in the red—the telegram service—has been reduced year by year and should turn to profits within a few years. With the contribution of these cost reduction efforts, the 1987 budget showed recurring profits of about ¥500 billion, the second highest profits among Japanese companies. These recurring profits may be somewhat excessive if judged by the fair return principle for privately owned public utilities. But that aside, what needs to be emphasized is that these reforms are a consequence of heightened internal incentives brought about by privatization. NTT's attempts to raise internal efficiency have not been without controversy (reduction of employees, rationalization of deficit business sections) but while comprehensive evaluation is not yet possible, the achievements of privatization have certainly been substantial.

The changes at NTT reflect not only privatization but also deregulation. Since the passage of the Telecommunications Industry Law entry into the industry has rapidly intensified. As of June 1988 there were 36 new common carrier companies (NCC) and 20 nationwide VAN businesses. The number of SME VAN businesses was 533. The entry of new enterprises stimulated NTT on a number of fronts, but let us first consider rates. With new entries foreseen, even before deregulation began NTT introduced weekend discount rates and reduced rates for dedicated lines (*senyo sen*) and long-distance calls. When large NCCs began to supply dedicated lines and regular phone services at an average 20 percent discount per call, NTT responded with several cuts in rates for long-distance calls. A substantial gap still exists between NCC and NTT fares, however, largely because the Ministry of Posts and Telecommunications (MPT) has restrained the extent of NTT price decreases as part of a policy to foster NCC growth.

Turning to other results of competition, NTT carried over from its public company days a history of major achievements in R&D, and with that background of R&D ability, it began to supply not only basic telecommunications services but also various information handling services like VAN. In the monopoly period the system of NTT fares was distorted by internal cross-subsidization, but competition has rectified such distortions and has promoted the supply of a variety of services. (In the first three years after privatization NTT introduced around 100 new services.) From this perspective, deregulation can be evaluated as having produced major positive results.

Next let us consider the sale of government-owned shares that accompanied the privatization of NTT. Of the ¥780 billion share capital belonging to NTT, originally one-third was to be government owned, while the other two-thirds would become privately owned. At present, however, plans exist to sell half of the share capital to the private sector. Already three sales have been staged, and 37.5 percent of the total share capital has been sold. The government has received some ¥10.2 trillion from such sales, which has been used to retire government bonds, undertake public works, an foster private sector activity. In addition the government obtains dividend revenue from its shares. Thus the privatization of NTT has contributed to the expansion of the government's financial resources.

The privatization of NTT and the deregulation of the telecommunications industry have not been problem free. First, since the privatization of NTT and the passage of the Telecommunications Industry Law, responsibility for regulatory restrictions on the telecommunications industry has shifted form the Diet to the MPT. Various conflicts have arisen between NTT (and KDD), which had expected to obtain freedom of management as a result of privatization and deregulation, and the MPT, concerned with the maintenance of regulatory restrictions. In particular, because the ministry has been attempting to foster a competitive telecommunications industry through "asymmetric regulation"—strong regulation of NTT and KDD and mild regulation of NCC—NTT and KDD have been dissatisfied with the state of affairs, and have reacted against the MPT fare regulations and other regulatory policies. According to NTT and others, the present administrative costs are greater than those during the era of Diet regulation.

Even now NTT and KDD are market-dominating enterprises in the telecommunications industry. They form a structure of partial monopoly, and in many regional markets NTT is the monopoly supplier. Some regulation is therefore necessary, but there must be a steady rectification of the present fare determination characterized by cartel-like adjustments directed at NCC (Wenders 1987), asymmetric regulation, and excessive intervention toward both new and established enterprises. Also the basis for ministerial restrictions on new entry (e.g., in satellite communications and cellular telephones) may not be expressed in writing, and such opaque administration must be reformed. In any event, public regulation should be more open, both to the regulated enterprises and to society at large.

The JR Companies

Since being privatized the JR companies have (1) promoted demand and strengthened management, (2) upgraded services and renovated facilities, and (3) made management diversification a major goal. To promote demand, JR companies have supplied services to meet the needs of different regions and users, introduced various types of discount fare systems, operated special events trains, developed new complementary travel products such as accommodation facilities, and have put great efforts into sales of "orange (automated) cards" by all employees. They have endeavored to improve service by upgrading manuals on customer relations, strengthening training in the field of customer relations, and raising the quality of station facilities. With goals such as expanding revenues, creating employment, and stabilizing management, the JR companies have effectively utilized railroad facilities and other internal management resources to actively enter the travel, restaurant and bar, and real estate industries.

Such endeavours have significantly upgraded the quality of service, and the composition of business has been improved. A symbol of the turnaround is that one year after the privatization of JNR, all of the JR companies were registering current profits. Actually JR Hokkaido, JR Shikoku, and JR Kyushu all registered deficits on their income and expenditure accounts but received subsidies form a special fund of the Japan National Railway Settlement Corporation and thereby registered current profits. If one considers the finances of the former JNR, however, the deficits of the companies were surprisingly low, and the surpluses of the other JR companies were surprisingly large. If the present situation continues the character of government finance dependence of the JNR era will be rectified. Also, of the employees of the three public companies that were privatized, the change of consciousness of the JR employees has been most noticeable. The self-motivated sales efforts (of "orange cards," etc.) outside of working hours could probably not even have been imagined in the JNR era, and service extended to customers has been improved to a marked degree. All of these developments may be evaluated as the accomplishments of efforts to improve managerial efficiency in the period since privatization.

Efforts by JR companies to improve the quality of their service have been a stimulus to numerous private and local public railroad enterprises. Also JR (specifically JR Tokai) has announced plans to lay tracks for a "linear motorcar" operating between Tokyo and Osaka. The plans have not yet influenced the national economy, since track completion will not be realized until the next century; nevertheless, the intensification of competition among the railroads and other transportation companies to develop new means of high-speed transportation is significant.

Japan Tobacco Industry Joint-Stock Company (NTI)

NTI has also witnessed an improvement in its income statements since privatization. But (1) its advance into related businesses (particularly biotechnology) is not progressing well, (2) neither the reform of its internal organization nor the reform of employee "consciousness" is proceeding as well as in NTT and JR , and (3) entry of foreign enterprises into the tobacco sales business as a potential source of stimulus to the management of NTI is not yet reflected in NTI management practices. These problems are appear to be related to the continued politicization of regulation centered on the obligation to purchase domestically produced tobacco leaves and the associated fact that competition has not been introduced. The influence of ministry regulation on top management personnel remains strong. To resolve the domestic tobacco problem, it will be necessary to strengthen the system of competition, including the liberalization of the manufacture and the sales price of tobacco. It will also be necessary to have NTI actively pursue entry into related businesses and transform the composition of its business.

In summary, the Provisional Council (Gyokakushin) report of 1989 suggests that deregulation and privatization have resulted in desirable performance as evidenced by (1) lowering of fare levels, (2) rectification of fare systems (the reform of internal cross-subsidization), (3) diversification of services, (4) rationalization of enterprises,and (5) vitalization of investment. As with my own analysis, the evidence of the report suggests that in Japan, as elsewhere, deregulation and privatization have had major positive results.

## 15.5 Conclusion

In 1985 Japan had about 120 national and about 7,000 local public enterprises with a combined share of 11 percent of total fixed capital formation and 9 percent of total employees. The expansion of government deficits after the 1973 oil price shock, technological revolution, and internationalization of the economy were factors behind the privatization of public enterprises that had constituted a significant share of Japanese economy.

While these factors were behind privatization of the three major public enterprises and JAL, rectification of the enterprises' inefficiency was particularly important. The major factors giving rise to this inefficiency were identified as (1) a government bureaucracy accounting system, (2) restriction of management independence by regulation, (3) a system of overlapping regulations and the blurring of the locus of responsibility for regulations, (4) politicization of regulations, (5) monopolistic organization of supply, (6) the protected character of public enterprises, and (7) their stable supply and "trouble minimization" motives.

Public enterprises have been established in response to the socioeconomic needs of various eras, but they face the inherent organizational and systemic problem of the development and expansion of inefficiency. When continuation as a public enterprise loses its meaning, reorganization becomes inevitable. In economies that rely on the market mechanism, the result is movement toward complete privatization.

This chapter has made clear that the introduction of competition and deregulation in industries that had been monopolized by public enterprises served to greatly improve performance. Deregulation of all economically regulated industries is presently being advocated in Japan, most importantly by the New Provisional Council for the Promotion of Administrative Reform, and in the next year or so deregulation of many regulated industries should be implemented. Only when unfolding changes in the Japanese economic system (enterprise organization, industry organization, industrial structure, and macroeconomic structure in both domestic and international spheres) have been analyzed will it be possible to evaluate satisfactorily the major reforms of privatization and deregulation. Since the reforms have only just begun, subsequent reevaluation will be necessary.

# 16

# Public Utilities: The Gas and Electric Power Utilities

Tetsuya Kishimoto

Firms can be classified into three groups according to the degree of their scope for management discretion (see Uekusa 1979). The first group analyzed in parts I to IV of this book contains private firms where management is entrusted to the free discretion of the firm. The second group treated in Uekusa's chapter 15 contains public enterprises that are established and managed by the government for some policy reason. This chapter deals with the third group containing private firms whose management discretion is restricted by government regulation.

Private firms in the first group are also subject to various government regulations. In the banking and securities industries, certain conditions must be satisfied when a new business is established or when new branches are opened, and bank interest rates are regulated. Safety standards are also set for manufactured goods, including foodstuffs, pharmaceuticals, and electrical appliances. However, these regulations try to impose a fixed framework and do not try to actively interfere with company management. In principle the regulations leave decisions to market competition and the firm's management discretion.

In contrast, regulations on firms in the third group impinge on management details and restrict the firm's scope for discretion. This type of regulation is seen in the field of public utilities. Public utilities are firms providing essential services using large-scale fixed facilities (including networks for the supply of services). Examples of public utilities are electric power, gas, waterworks, postal services, communications, railways, airlines, and buses. For industries with the characteristics of a natural monopoly, in that the existence of several suppliers leads to inefficiency, regulations on corporate behavior are imposed in order to sanction a geographic monopoly and to suppress the ill effects of monopoly. The electric power and gas industries are examples.

In this chapter the characteristics of the power and gas industries are investigated from several angles. In section 16.1, I explain the legal basis for the geographic monopoly of these firms and examine the regulations imposed on the firms in exchange for the guarantee of a geographic monopoly. In section 16.2, I show that these firms are exposed to competition notwithstanding the guarantee of a geographic monopoly but that difficulties may arise when rate-of-return regulations are imposed on them. Japanese public utilities are assumed to be worker-managed firms, that is, they seek to maximize the income per employee. It can be shown that the worker-managed firms facing a rate-of-return regulation may respond undesirably from the point of view of consumer welfare. Finally, the performance of Japan's electric power and gas utilities is evaluated.

## 16.1  Japanese Electric Power and Gas Utilities: The Legal Environment

The production and supply of electric power and gas require massive facilities. Thus both industries exhibit characteristics of natural monopolies and there are legal restrictions on entry. The approval of the Minister of International Trade and Industry must be obtained in order to operate a general electric power utility or a general gas utility (Electric Power Business Law, Art. 5; Gas Business Law, Art. 5) General electric power utilities and general gas utilities supply electric power or gas to an unspecified number of customers and, in the case of gas utilities, use pipes to supply gas (rather than cylinders). One license criterion is that the supply facilities "be not remarkably excessive" in all or part of that supply area (Electric Power Business Law, Art. 5; Gas Business Law, Art. 5). In the electric Power Business Law and the Gas Business Law it is not clearly specified that only one supplier will be approved in a given area, but in the application of these laws, for all practical purposes, geographic monopolies have been approved because entry into a supply area by suppliers in adjoining areas is not permitted. The Antimonopoly Law which applies to conventional private firms does not apply to general electric power and gas utilities (Antimonopoly Law, Art. 21).

The Guarantee of a Geographic Monopoly

There are ten companies supplying electric power. Each has a geographical monopoly, and each is a private stock company[1] with generation and

---

1. Okinawa Electric, a special enterprise established with 100 percent government capital, was privatized in 1987. However, the government's shareholding still exceeds 70 percent because sales of shares to the public are still under way.

distribution being performed jointly.[2] The sales revenue of the top three companies in 1987 was ¥3.94 trillion for Tokyo Electric, ¥2.01 trillion for Kansai Electric, and ¥1.63 trillion for Chubu Electric. These three companies sold 67 percent of the total quantity of electric power sold nationally. Sales revenue of the smallest company, Okinawa Electric, was ¥95.6 billion.

On the other hand, 174 privately managed firms and 73 publicly managed firms are approved as monopolistic suppliers of town gas in their areas. The sales revenue of the top three companies in 1987 were ¥677.6 billion for Tokyo Gas, ¥552.4 billion for Osaka Gas, and ¥145.7 billion for Toho Gas. These three companies sold 73 percent of the total quantity of gas sold nationally in 1986.

In return for the guarantee of a geographic monopoly, various restrictions are imposed. The two main regulations are price regulation with an accompanying supply obligation and regulations on carrying out side businesses. In addition there are accounting and safety regulations, but these are not considered here because they do not impose significant constraints on managerial discretion.

Price Regulation and the Supply Obligation

Given that electric power and gas utilities are granted a geographic monopoly, there is a fear that a monopoly price would be established and supply would be restricted if the utilities were allowed to set prices freely. Regulations on price setting are implemented to avoid these negative effects. The Electric Power Business Law and the Gas Business Law both provide that "the supply regulation will determine the prices and other supply conditions, and the approval of the Minister of International Trade and Industry must be obtained." A condition for the approval of prices is that "the price yields a reasonable profit added to reasonable cost under efficient management" (Electric Power Business Law, Art. 19; Gas Business Law, Art. 17). The specific formula for determining the price is specified in the Supply Regulation which defines reasonable cost, reasonable profit, and rate base as

$$\text{Reasonable cost} = \text{Operating expenses} + \text{Depreciation costs} + \text{Taxes},$$

2. In France and Italy the joint production and distribution of electricity is performed, respectively, by a public corporation and a state-operated utility, each with national monopolies. In the United States and West Germany there are many different companies at each stage of the generation, transmission, and distribution of electricity.

$$\frac{\text{Reasonable profit}}{\text{(fair compensation)}} = \frac{\text{Rate}}{\text{base}} \times \frac{\text{Fair rate}}{\text{of return,}}$$

$$\frac{\text{Rate}}{\text{base}} = \frac{\text{Fixed business}}{\text{assets}} + \frac{\text{Assets under construction}}{\text{(half of construction expense account)}}$$

$$+ \frac{1.5 \text{ months operating}}{\text{expenses as working capital}} + \frac{\text{Fuel costs}}{\text{(for nuclear power plants).}}$$

Price is established so that a reasonable profit can be earned. The price-setting regulation calls for a fair rate of return (known simply as *rate-of-return regulation*) whereby a reasonable profit is determined by multiplying the fair rate of return by net worth. The fair rate of return is currently set at 7 to 8 percent.

In addition there is regulation of supply in that the utilities cannot refuse to respond to demand arising within their supply area at the given price (Electric Power Business Law, Art. 18; Gas Business Law, Art. 16). Price calculations are performed on the premise that all the demand arising at that price will be covered. If such a supply obligation were not imposed, the utility could achieve a profit that exceeds the reasonable profit by not responding to any demand that would lead to higher costs. Supply regulation is necessary in order to preclude such strategic behavior based on price regulation. Another reason for regulating supply is that electric power and gas are largely necessary commodities.

The regulation of price and the obligation to supply at that price would appear to negatively affect the firm's discretion regarding production and sales, removing incentives to reduce costs. But even with apparently diminished incentives to reduce costs, firms regulated in this way can still exercise their discretion because the reasonable cost and reasonable profit recovered depends on the production method employed.

The supply regulation requires efficient management but does not impose a production method. A firm can increase profits by adopting a production method with a large rate base, especially a production method that has large fixed business assets (e.g., see Averch and Johnson 1962). The price approved by the regulatory authorities changes in response to this, so the firm can move the point on the demand curve determined by the regulatory authorities. Some discretion is therefore retained in selecting the production method that determines the most advantageous price in achieving the objective (e.g., profit maximization) the firm pursues. In this respect the firm has an incentive to achieve efficient production, that is, a situation where it is not possible to produce the same level of output using fewer inputs (see Bailey 1973, ch. 3). Of course, if the firm that is freed from competitive pressures by the geographic monopoly is satisfied with the reasonable return guaranteed by the fair rate of return and gives up on maximization of its activities , the incentive for efficient production will not work.

## Regulations on Carrying out Side Businesses

General electric power utilities and general gas utilities cannot conduct businesses outside their man business areas unless they receive the approval of the Minister for International Trade and Industry. A necessary condition for the approval of side businesses is that "there be no fear that it will cause a hindrance to the proper prosecution" of the main business (Electric Power Business Law, Art. 12; Gas Business Law, Art. 12). The purpose of this statute is to prevent the undermining of a main business by internal subsidies for personnel and capital to the side businesses since this would result in a loss (through higher prices, etc.) for the users of electric power and gas. Another reason is that entry into another market may damage fair competition in that market, for the firm's business power would be protected in a geographic monopoly.

Both reasons are not particularly persuasive. Large-scale internal subsidization between the main business and the side business are not likely to occur because the expenses and revenue of the main business and the side business must be sharply delineated when the rate base and costs are computed to determine prices. Any damage to competition in the market entered could be dealt with by the Antimonopoly Law. There are two grounds for arguing that regulations on side businesses hinder efficient corporate management. Diversification activities can have positive effects on management, stimulating even the main line of business. Where this is precluded, and a single business is continued over a long period, there is a danger of managerial inertia, a decline in management vitality, and eventually inefficiencies in the supply of electric power and gas. This can apply to enterprises in any country, but it may be particularly deleterious in the case of Japan. As noted in part I of this book, large Japanese firms try to avoid as much as possible laying off employees. When layoffs cannot be avoided, firms with businesses outside their main business can solve this problem by dispatching excess workers to the side businesses. Firms that do not have side businesses will carry excess workers, and their production costs will increase.

How strictly are regulations on side businesses enforced? In the electric power industry there are very few side businesses, and regulations are strictly enforced. Revenue other than that from the sale of electric power does not even reach 1 percent of the total sales of Tokyo Electric and Kansai Electric. In the gas industry Article 12 of the Gas Business Law requires that side businesses be approved by the Minister of International Trade and Industry, but exceptions of side businesses that can be conducted without approval have been established (Gas Business Law, Enforcement Regulation, Art. 13). Included are the sale of by-products (coke, tar, LNG, and ammonium sulphate), liquefied nitrogen or liquefied oxygen produced using LNG, the repair of gas meters, the repair and sale of gas utensils, and pipe laying, all of which are related to the main business. From a legal perspective, regulations on side businesses in the gas industry are far more lenient than those in the electric power industry, and as a result gas utilities engage in quite a wide range of side businesses. The approved side businesses of Osaka Gas include the production and sale of pitch coke, the sale of LPG and LNG, the sale of gas meters, the sale of all types of gas-related machinery (excluding utensils and machinery for area heating and cooling), the processing of entrusted LNG, and the management of dining rooms in gas buildings.[3] Revenue other than from gas sales was 24.7 percent of total revenue for Osaka Gas and 22.8 percent for Tokyo Gas in 1987. Since, unlike in the electric power industry, regulations on side business in the gas industry have not been strictly applied, sales from these activities have reached significant levels.

On the other hand, there are no regulations on establishing related companies (where the parent company holds 20 percent or more of the shares) and engaging in activities outside the main businesses through that company. As a result electric power utilities and gas utilities have established many related companies. Tokyo Electric has 41 related companies and Kansai Electric has 30, and the total number of employees in these companies is 61.4 and 71.8 percent of the number of employees in their respective parent companies (Toyo Keizai Shiposha 1988). The business of the related companies also extends from the production of items closely associated with the main business—such as sale of materials for electric machinery, electric and engineering construction, and production of insulators and electricity meters—to the repairing and leasing of vehicles, office

---

3. Processing of entrusted LNG is the business of gas utilities using their own facilities to store or gasify the imported LNG of electric power utilities that do not have their own LNG tanks or LNG gasification facilities and delivering the LNG to the power utilities.

leasing, the management of real estate, electronic communications, and regional development. In the gas industry Osaka Gas has 41 related companies, and Tokyo Gas has 31. The total number of the employees in their related companies is 46.7 and 28.1 percent of the number of employees in their respective parent companies. The businesses of the related companies also extend over a wide area, from the production of items closely related to their main business—including the sale of coke, gas-related engineering work, the sale and repair of gas equipment, and the production and sale of gas utensils—to the management of restaurants, the development of computer software, leasing and the management of real estate, buildings, and car parks.[4]

As noted earlier, regulations on side businesses are strictly applied, especially in the electric power industry. Yet, because the investment of funds in separate companies is not regulated, many related companies have been established, and the effects of the regulation on side businesses have been mitigated.

## 16.2   Some Economic Issues: Alternative Competition and the Rate-of-Return Regulation

In both the gas and electric power industries, geographic monopolies are guaranteed, but this practice only prevents the entry of other general gas utilities and general electric power utilities. There is competition between electric power and gas, competition from other energies including oil and LPG, and, possible competition from private power generators producing for their own consumption. If the degree of competition is strong, the ill effects of monopoly will be mitigated even if the price regulation does not function adequately.

Competition in the Electric Power and Gas Industries

First, let us start with competition in the gas industry. The competitive situation in the Osaka Gas supply area is presented in table 16.1 which

---

4. Here we provide details on the ratio of the number of employees in related companies to the number of employees in the parent company for several large firms of a comparable size to the electric power and gas utilities already cited. Companies with a high ratio compared to the electric power and gas utilities are Nippon Oil (3.56 times), Sumitomo Chemicals (2.16 times), and Hitachi Ltd. (1.79 times). In particular, the ratio is 7.16 times for the Tokyu Corporation which is a public railroad utility not subject to regulations on side businesses. There are also companies that have a very small ratio including the Kajima Corporation (0.22) and Nippon Express (0.19).

**Table 16.1**
Breakdown of city gas sold by use compared with other energy sources (fiscal year 1987; in %)

| | Household use | | | General use | | | |
| | Hot water | Cooking | Heating | Cooking | Boiler | Air-conditioning | Industrial use |
|---|---|---|---|---|---|---|---|
| Share of city gas sold | 30.2 | 14.1 | 6.0 | 9.4 | 5.9 | 6.0 | 28.4 |
| Gas | 88 | 85 | 24 | 80 | 23 | 15 | 18 |
| Electricity | 8 | 15 | 17 | 10 | 0 | 83 | 0 |
| Kerosene, etc. | 4 | 0 | 59 | 10 | 77 | 2 | 82 |

Source: Osaka Gas estimates.
Note: The three household uses are for fiscal year 1986.

gives a breakdown of gas sales by use and the shares of various energies for different uses. Households use 50.3 percent of the gas sold, general businesses (commercial, medical, and public) 15.3 percent, air-conditioning 6.0 percent, and industrial plants 28.4 percent. Gas holds a monopolistic share close to 90 percent for household hot water and cooking uses. Gas also has a monopolistic share of 80 percent for cooking in general business establishments. These monopolistic uses account for 53.7 percent of total gas sales. However, the share of gas held by other uses (the remaining 46.3 percent of total gas sales) is at the low level of around 20 percent. In these other uses gas faces strong competition from other energy sources.[5]

Similar data on energy use could not be obtained for electric power. It is safe to say that electric power generates about 100 percent of the lighting, household air-conditioning, and industrial power used in Japan, with an additional almost 90 percent for business air-conditioning (see table 16.1). Household use accounted for one-third, and business and industrial uses accounted for two-thirds of the revenue of Tokyo Electric and Kansai Electric in 1987 (Ministry of Finance 1988). As seen in table 16.1, the shares of electric power for household hot water supply, household cooking, and household heating are small. Some large-scale industrial users have their own electric power generators. Their share of total electric power consumption is 26.4 percent in the Tokyo Electric supply area and 17.3 percent in the Kansai Electric supply area. Their average share in the power areas of the ten electric power companies is 24.9 percent, with the highest share

---

5. Electric stoves cannot currently emulate gas cookers given that the voltage for household use is 100 volts. There is a possibility that electric stoves would intensify competition for the household gas cooking if the voltage were changed to 200 volts.

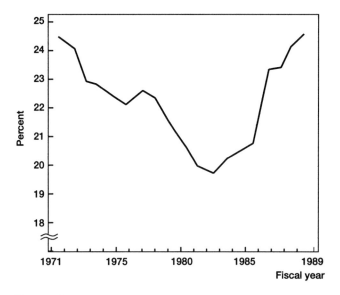

**Figure 16.1**
Private electric power generation (estimates used for 1987–89). Source: Ministry of International Trade and Industry (1988b).

being 58.5 percent in the Hokkaido Electric supply area and lowest 11.2 percent in the Hokuriku Electric supply area (see Ministry of International Trade and Industry 1988a).

Compared to the supply cost of electric power utilities, privately generated electric power responds sensitively to fuel prices, including the price of heavy crude oil, because the cost of electricity transmission is eliminated. As a result the relative cost of private electric power generation fell from 1982 due to a fall in the dollar price of crude oil, together with the yen appreciation. As can be seen in figure 16.1, the share of private generation in large-scale energy demand is increasing rapidly. Even for electric power where the degree of competition with other energies is relatively small, a degree of competition from private-generation arises. Cogeneration that supplies electric power and heat using gas turbines or fuel cells has a high fuel efficiency. If cost reductions through technical innovation occur, cogeneration will become an extremely desirable source of private generation and will strengthen the degree of competition with electric power utilities.

Rate-of-Return Regulation and the Worker-Managed Public Utility

To prevent a firm that is guaranteed a monopoly by entry restrictions from restricting supply and harming the efficiency of resource allocation, price regulations are implemented, as discussed earlier. The price is determined to bring in an amount that adds a reasonable profit to costs. Through this, the firm can choose to supply a larger quantity, and the ill effects due to the monopoly will be mitigated somewhat compared to when there is no regulation.

Large Japanese firms tend to maximize income per employee like worker-managed firms (see Komiya 1988; Ireland and Law 1982). Given this characterization, Japan's public utilities, being large enterprises, would also have this tendency. For firms that pursue a different objective than the conventional profit-maximizing firm, the issue of whether the quantity supplied increases when a rate-of-return regulation is implemented must be considered. There are cases where the implementation of a rate-of-return regulation on a worker-managed firm has not caused the quantity supplied to change or even to fall. Of course the quantity supplied may rise as well, as in the case of the conventional profit-maximizing firm.

## 16.3  Conclusion

Incentives for management to reduce costs are not particularly strong in the public utility that is guaranteed a geographic monopoly. In exchange for being sheltered from competition in its supply area through entry restrictions, the firm's management is subject to the control of regulatory authorities. Since the quantity supplied by a Japanese public utility may be lower under a rate-of-return regulation than when the price is regulated, it would seem unreasonable to expect efficiency in resource allocation for public utilities in Japan. However, private power generation, competition between electricity and gas utilities, and competition among energies mitigate this difficulty. Take the case of large-scale electric power for industrial use. If we set a price level $p^*$ as the boundary price, as shown in figure 16.2, for rates greater than $p^*$ those who supply their own electric power through private generators increase rapidly in number, and large-scale electricity demand to power utilities falls rapidly. If power utilities neglect to minimize costs and the regulatory authorities do not recognize this and approve a high price $p$ that reflects these high costs, demand may become exceedingly small and the sales of electric power utilities greatly reduced. Accordingly, when monopoly behavior is permitted, the probability is high that a price $p^*$ will be chosen whether a conventional profit-maximizing firm or a worker-managed firm is considered. As noted earlier, a worker-managed firm may respond to a rate-of-return regulation by increasing the price and reducing supply. But the firm will ultimately behave by setting a

**Price**

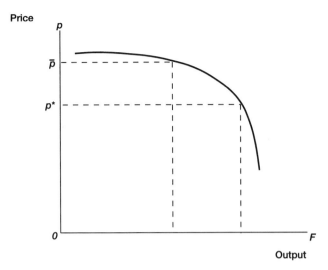

**Figure 16.2**
The effect of competition on electric power prices

price that is not far from $p^*$ because sales will fall if the price is raised. By reducing supply when faced with a rate-of-return regulation, the worker-managed firm is able to mitigate the negative effects.

If we consider the fact that private generator technology will cause $p^*$ to gradually fall, the electric power utilities must arrive at a level of costs that can counteract this. There is an incentive for management to reduce costs. Even if this competition arises only for large-scale industrial power generation, it will reduce the prices for all uses because the resulting cost reduction by power companies will also reduce the reasonable costs of power for household and business uses.

In this way competition reduces the negative effects of monopoly in the Japanese electric power and gas industries. In the case of side businesses, Japanese public utilities are subject to restrictions with the negative effect of closing off the possibilities of moving excess workers to side businesses or stimulating management performance through diversification. Compared with an unregulated monopoly, rate-of-return regulation is expected to cause supply to increase. The special characteristics of the Japanese public utility prevent this from happening. But for all practical purposes, competition in the main business of public utilities mitigates the difficulties that may be expected in the efficient allocation of resources.

# 17    The Cooperative as a
         Business Enterprise

Naomi Saeki

Three main issues are involved in considering the enterprise characteristics of cooperatives: management in comparison with capitalist enterprises (or stock companies), management of different types of cooperatives, and management of Japanese cooperatives from an international perspective. The first involves a "morphological" approach, the second a typological approach, and the third a comparative approach. Most research in Japan has focused on the first of these, and only very recently have the second and third received substantial attention. Below I will give some brief comments on each.

There has been much debate about the characteristics of cooperative management from an early date, both in Japan and abroad. Broadly speaking, some authors have viewed cooperatives as essentially joint undertakings by individuals. Such authors include Liefman (1923), Phillips (1957), Tohata (1932), and Kinoshita (1959). Others such as Triffon (1961), Kondo (1934), and Wakabayashi (1964) view cooperatives as continual decision-making bodies in their own right, thus as special types of enterprises. Such differences arise from diverging judgments over the degree of decision-making autonomy of the cooperative management; weak versus strong. This, however, varies with the scale and type of cooperative. The first view focuses on relatively new, small-scale cooperatives, and the second on large-scale, fully developed cooperatives. The differences therefore are relative, and there is a tendency for cooperatives to evolve from joint undertaking or use toward independent enterprise.

As for the second issue, there are various types of cooperative depending on their organizational base. In Japan there are farmers' agricultural cooperatives, fishermens' cooperatives, foresters' cooperatives, consumer cooperatives, small and medium-sized enterprise (SME) trust associations and cooperatives, business cooperatives, workers' trust associations, workers' mutual aid societies, and so on. Each type differs in its legal base, scale, and institutional framework as well as type and scope of activity, hence management characteristics differ accordingly. At one extreme trust associations have grown so big that they retain few cooperative features, becoming more and more like regular enterprises. At the other extreme are small business cooperatives that merely involve joint facility use. Both are called cooperatives but differ vastly in nature. Typological analysis according to historical circumstance is thus an important but unfortunately neglected part of cooperative research.

One reason in Japan has been the importance of agricultural—particularly multipurpose—cooperatives in the cooperative movement. In terms of membership, business volume, and social influence they have long been dominant, and other types of cooperative much less influential. This is reflected in cooperative studies. As a result there have been few studies comparing different types of cooperative alongside each other, a belated start being made only when the diversity became apparent during the high economic growth period. In 1981 the Japan Cooperative Association Conference was started, and comparative studies of different types has slowly gained momentum.

The third issue relates to international comparisons. Broadly speaking, stock companies organize "things," aiming for business efficiency, while cooperatives organize "people," aiming to expand economic benefits to members. Because people—their customs, cultures, and societies—differ across nations, differences are very likely to appear in cooperatives. Comparative literature is scarce, however. Of course exchanges have developed since the war through the International Cooperative Alliance (ICA), and there is a wealth of information about cooperatives in other countries compared to the prewar period. But this mainly concerns formal institutions, numbers of members, and volumes of business, and little is known about the actual mechanics of management, business, and organization and social and cultural influences on these. By way of example, Britain is known in Japan principally as the home of consumer cooperatives. A. F. Laidlaw upset conventional images of these cooperatives when he argued that they were not so much a special movement of consumers but a type of big business striving like private companies to expand market share and win the interest of their customers (*Zenkoku nokyo chuokai* 1980, 158). The same has been said of agricultural cooperatives in the United States. The notion of members weighing up the pros and cons of selling produce to the cooperative or to merchants, with the cooperatives run by managers scouted from regular companies and a businesslike relationship between the two, is quite alien from that of agricultural cooperatives in Japan.

International comparisons must penetrate these deeper levels of business and management.

It is beyond the scope of this chapter to examine all three issues in detail. I would like to concentrate on the first two, with references to the third. First I will outline the main characteristics of cooperatives compared with capitalist enterprises, and how these are expressed in terms of member organization, staff, business policies, management, and finances. Then I will discuss the types of cooperatives in Japan and their place in the Japanese economy. Finally, I will compare two representative cooperative types in Japan, multipurpose agricultural cooperatives and consumer or "living" cooperatives.

## 17.1 Enterprise Characteristics of Cooperatives

Cooperatives in capitalist societies tend to be associations of the economically less powerful, and that gives their objectives, organization structures, business, and management policies different features from general capitalist enterprises. ICA principles express these in general terms—freedom of entry and exit, one vote per member, dividends by extent of use, limitations on investor dividends, and so on—and there are further regulations by country and cooperative relating to such matters as use by outsiders, region, and financing. These aim to strengthen internal cohesion and realize joint economic profits.

Compared to stock companies, however, it means that cooperatives operate under many restrictions. Investment is linked to membership, which limits freedom to buy and sell, and given the restrictions on investor dividends, there are serious constraints on capital formation. Basic decision making does not depend upon investment but reflects overall opinion through the one member–one vote system. Much time and effort are required for this compared with the average annual general meeting of stock companies. Restrictions on outsider use, region and type of activity limit cooperatives' scope to pursue advantageous business opportunities. Weak members from the management view must be carried with everyone else. Finally, given restrictions on investor dividends and rules on dividends by use, it is much more difficult than for stock companies to accumulate retained earnings.

Such handicaps are balanced by human factors and subjective collective power. By working together through the cooperative, individual members can achieve scale profits of mass sales and purchasing. Such subjective consciousness is vital for the cooperative, hence the saying "cooperative activities begin and end with education." The cooperative often develops as a "movement." This is why cooperatives are called participatory organizations. Members are in principle investors, managers and users (customers) all in one. In theory, they invest their own capital and carry out business by themselves for themselves. This was particularly so in early, spontaneously formed cooperatives. Like-minded farmers (or consumers) joined together to sell (or buy) jointly, decision making took place democratically, and profits were naturally shared. There were no structurally inherent managerial problems. These appear when it becomes necessary to develop a management structure to facilitate the cooperative's business. The cooperative expands in competition with outside capitalist enterprises, its activities becoming increasingly complex and specialized. A management structure grows, and demands to promote the cooperative as a going concern have to be set against member participation and equality. The following management problems of cooperatives in advanced capitalist countries today largely derive from this situation. First is the problem of maintaining close relations between members, and between members and the cooperative. Cooperatives are built upon the premise of face-to-face, human relations. As the cooperative expands, such relations weaken. Members no longer know each others' names, and links between members and the cooperative become more distant and formal. To cope with this, members are divided into smaller groups according to locality, occupation, age, sex, and/or interests. Such subunits become the substantive base for cooperative activities and determine the extent of member participation and cooperative efficiency. They are thus an important measure of the cooperative. Second, at the other pole, is the issue of top management. As cooperatives expand the role of management becomes increasingly important, and various problems arise. A gap inevitably develops between the representative and specialist attributes of directors. Important for the former are leadership and ability to organize, while overall evaluative ability based on specialist knowledge is desirable for the latter. Seldom does the same person have both. To resolve this dilemma in the United States, the board of directors restricts itself to basic policies, and the daily running of the cooperative may be entrusted to professional managers brought in from outside, but this approach has not taken root in Japan. A system of general manager councilors is one alternative. Quite a few cooperatives actually have internally promoted councilors, but in practice the system does not always function well. A further problem is the election of directors. In principle directors are elected directly by all members at a general meeting, but these become difficult to organize as cooperatives grow. Indirect elections by delegates or representatives take place. If the subunits that support them are not active, member democracy may be lost. The one person–one vote principle can actually end up supporting management domination. Life insurance companies with a similar mutual system provide a clear example of this.

Third, there is the problem of staff, who link members and top managers. As cooperatives grow, a stratum of administrative staff with specialist knowledge also grows. Yet, although the staff members actually run the cooperatives, their position both in theory and in practice is ambiguous. Theoretically, are they activists or laborers, and in practice how is the trade-off between maximizing returns to members and improving their wages and conditions to be treated? This dilemma is heightened by the SME management scale of most cooperatives; both members and staff are in a weak economic position. The normal answer is that responsibilities should be clearly delineated and staff participation in management recognized, but this is not always accomplished. The changing social base of staff members, and a shift in their consciousness to that of "salaried worker" makes this a difficult problem. In Japanese corporate thinking the company must meet the triple interests of shareholders, managers, and employees. The cooperative, however, must match the fourfold interests of investors, managers, users, and employees. A fourth problem is how to maintain and utilize the "cooperative" features in business activities. Cooperatives organize sales and purchases. Orders or supplies from members must be determined beforehand and plans for purchasing, delivery, and shipment made accordingly. Member involvement in these is one form of participation, and a means of reducing distribution costs. This is a key in cooperatives' ability to compete with other enterprises despite the restrictions they operate under. They can do this because their clientele is not an undetermined mass but a defined membership. Not all business is carried out in this manner, however. Depending on the product and cooperative, spot purchase and sales may be made, and shop outlets little different from other enterprises are increasing. This is perhaps inevitable as cooperatives grow and diversify and compete with outside enterprises.

Fifth, there are various problems concerning finance. Provision of capital is strongly linked to identified individuals, unlike stock companies in which shares may be acquired for investment. This has the merit that capital providers are "safe shareholders," but it also means that agreement must be reached at a general meeting to increase capital. Further there is a strong tendency toward short-term user dividend maximization, which means that little is held over, and because bonds cannot be issued, there are limitations on raising low-interest capital. This places severe restraints on management when large amounts of fixed capital are needed, as in recent years. Insufficient self-capital is a problem common to most cooperatives that extends beyond finance to fundamental cooperative principles such as self-accumulation and user dividends.

There are clear institutional and morphological differences between stock companies and cooperatives. In practice, however, the differences may be slight. A tendency toward corporatization of consumer cooperatives in Britain has been mentioned. In Japan too there have been cases like Snow Brand Dairy Products that started out as cooperatives but became stock companies as they expanded. Even without switching, many cooperatives resemble stock companies, and stock-company subsidiaries of cooperatives are common. Abstract discussion over which type is superior is unproductive. What is important is to examine to what extent and in what way each type incorporates the basic cooperative features of member participation and democratic operation. If the social responsibility of modern stock companies is to be debated, so is the efficiency of cooperatives, and how they can maintain their "human face" while raising their efficiency.

## 17.2   Types of Cooperatives

Various types of cooperatives exist in Japan. Before the war they were all placed under the Industrial Cooperative Law, but after the war they were divided by sector. The regulatory framework then became very complicated, with various administrating agencies. There are different types of cooperatives even within agriculture, notably multipurpose and single purpose, with different organization principles and management characteristics. There are big differences between student and regional consumer cooperatives too. It is impossible to lump them all together. Table 17.1 gives an overview of cooperatives in Japan.

The table suggest that there are around 60,000 cooperatives with 38 million members in Japan today, although each cooperative has its own organization principles and requirements, so a simple addition is hazardous. Even allowing for multiple membership, however, the importance of cooperatives in Japan's economy is beyond doubt. What activities do these cooperatives engage in, how do they go about them, and what do they actually mean for the Japanese economy? Cooperative activities can be broadly divided into trust (finance), mutual aid (insurance), purchasing, sales, medical, production, use, guidance, liaison, and others. The largest cooperatives with the broadest organization are those of credit and mutual

**Table 17.1**
Overview of cooperatives in Japan, 1983

| Members | Area | Types | Number of cooperatives | Number of members (in 10,000) |
|---|---|---|---|---|
| Farmers | Agriculture[a] | Multipurpose, single-purpose, noncapitalized | 9,316 | 799 |
| Fishermen | Marine products | Coastal area, inland water coops by industry, fish production processing | 4,325 | 59 |
| Foresters | Forestry | | 1,821 | 178 |
| Consumers | Consumption | Regional, residential area, workplace, school, university, medical | 656 | 844 |
| SME owners | Shinkin banks[b] | | 456 | 621 |
| SME owners | Credit coops | Regional, industrial, occupational | 468 | 359 |
| SME owners | Business | | 40,276 | 40 |
| Workers[c] | Credit associations | | 47 | 96 |
| Workers | Mutual aid coops | | 54 | 1,000 |

Source: Ie no hikari hyōkai, *Shinpan kyōdō kumiai jiten* (New Edition Cooperative Dictionary), 1986.
Note: Federations are not included.
a. Agriculture coop. member numbers are for multipurpose cooperatives only.
b. Members of shinkin banks are restricted to borrowers; those who make deposits only are excluded.
c. Worker (labor) coops include associate members.

aid, the latter in particular being integrated into nationwide organizations (Zenrosai, Nokyo kyosai, Kasai kyosai), while financing cooperatives are attempting to expand beyond their regular membership. Cooperatives that purchase for members, especially those with stores, show a similar tendency if not quite as pronounced. In contrast to such centrifugal tendencies, sales, use, and processing cooperatives are centripetal, clearly delineating the extent of their membership. The extreme case is production, typically worker (or farmer) producer cooperatives, where all-round cooperation is rare, and partial cooperation or joint distribution is the norm. As can be seen from table 17.1, the highest member/cooperative ratios are in workers' mutual aid societies and trust associations, while the lowest ratios are in business and fisheries cooperatives.

Naturally the enterprise characteristics of these cooperatives are different, as can be seen in the extreme examples of mutual aid and SME business cooperatives. There are differences between Zenrosai and Nokyo kyosai (agricultural cooperative mutual aid), but again both are national in scope with clear enterprise characteristics, carrying out their business in a similar fashion to life insurance and nonlife insurance companies. SME business cooperatives, on the other hand, are limited to specific industries and regions and often have only around ten members. Their activities may be limited to information gathering, underleasing loans, joint education and training, liasing, and so on, with few enterprise characteristics. Wholesale rice cooperatives are an exception here.

Major differences in scale exist even between cooperatives of the same type. Consumer cooperatives, for example, include Nada Kobe, which in 1985 had 770,000 members and a turnover of ¥255.6 billion, and the Welfare Promotion Living Cooperative with around 400 members and a turnover of only ¥10 million. Similarly some multipurpose agriculture cooperatives have more than 10,000 members, while many have less than 200. Needless to say, the nature of these cooperatives is quite different.

Business volume is probably a more reliable measure of cooperative size than member numbers. People may be registered as members but not participate, and in cases like workers' credit associations, and mutual aid societies where membership is indirect, some may not even be aware they are members. In each area the business volume of the multipurpose agriculture cooperatives (sogo nokyo, or AC) is much higher than other cooperatives. In 1983 combined savings in AC amounted to ¥34 trillion, with ¥12t in loans, ¥6t in sales, ¥5t in purchases, and ¥177t in total long-term mutual aid contracts. This would rank AC among the top banks, trading and insurance companies. Combined consumer cooperative purchases by comparison amounted to ¥1.5t, or less than one-third of AC, while funds in workers' credit associations were ¥4t, long-term mutual aid contracts in workers' mutual aid societies were ¥16t, and savings in trust cooperatives ¥11t—each between one-third and one-tenth of AC. Only shinkin banks, with ¥43t in deposits, surpassed them in any area. Single AC comfortably surpass the combined total of other cooperatives, attesting to the centrality of agriculture cooperatives in the cooperative movement in Japan, to which I will return in the next section.

Before that I would like to make a rough estimate of the weight of cooperatives in different sectors of the economy. Regarding credit activities, in 1984 outstanding deposits in all financial institutions came to ¥664t, of which ¥101t, or about 15 percent, came from cooperatives (¥36t from agriculture cooperatives, ¥47t from shinkin banks, ¥12t from credit cooperatives, ¥4t from workers' credit associations, and ¥2t from fisheries cooperatives). The role of cooperatives in SME and peoples' financing is very large indeed. Mutual aid estimates are difficult because unified insurance and mutual aid statistics are not complied, but at the end of 1984, 15 percent of total life insurance contracts (¥149t out of ¥1,029t) came from mutual aid life policies. For fire insurance the figure was ¥160t out of ¥425t, or 38 percent (agriculture cooperative mutual aid ¥71t, workers' mutual aid ¥42t, agriculturalist mutual aid ¥39t, and SME mutual aid ¥8t). The higher percentage for fire insurance than life insurance suggests a readier adoption of noncumulative as opposed to cumulative principles in the short history of mutual aid activities. As far as purchasing goes, of ¥97t in small retail outlet sales in 1985, around ¥7.1t came from cooperatives, or over 7 percent (agriculture cooperatives ¥5.1t, fisheries cooperatives ¥0.3t, consumer cooperatives ¥1.5t). This is a smaller proportion than for finance-related activities but still very significant. In certain sectors such as agriculture the weight is much higher. AC sold 61 percent of the produce of farming households in 1985, and together with single-purpose agriculture cooperatives the share exceeded 70 percent. Thus, while varying by sector and business, cooperatives constitute a significant entity in the national economy.

Finally, I would like to say a few words about cooperative development. Unlike general enterprises, most cooperatives develop through the participation of all members as a movement. As a rough typology, we might say that agriculture and fisheries cooperatives are local or regional types, trust associations and cooperatives are nonmovement types, business cooperatives are occupational bonding types, workers' credit associations and mutual aid societies are whole industry types, and consumer cooperatives are conscious participation types. The degree and nature of member participation differ according to the type. Of course this typology is rough and subcategorizations can be made. Single-purpose agriculture cooperatives, for example, are occupational bonding types, and consumer cooperatives include student and other whole workplace cooperatives. Nonetheless, behavioral differences of Japanese cooperatives can be explained to quite an extent by this typology. Membership of credit associations and cooperatives is largely a formality, there is no member organization and no participation in a movement. They tend to be "financial enterprises with the form of cooperatives for convenience' sake" (Takeda 1982, 61), and many even tend to avoid using the word "cooperative." Workers' credit associations and mutual aid societies claim membership in whole industries, which results in high membership figures but a low sense of participation. As the expression "30 percent workers' credit, 30 percent workers' mutual aid" suggests that there is a low level of usage, and this is a major weakness of these cooperatives. I now turn to a discussion of agriculture and consumer cooperatives.

## 17.3   Agriculture and Consumer Cooperatives

Multipurpose agriculture cooperatives (*sogo nokyo*, or AC) and local consumer cooperatives (*chiiki seikyo*, or CC) are representative of cooperatives in Japan today. Not only are they significant in terms of business and membership, but they provide a good contrast in the early and new aspects of the cooperative movement. AC have existed for more than 100 years, while with exceptions such as Nada Kobe, consumer cooperatives (CC) have a history of only 20 or 30 years. AC are involved in credit, sales, purchasing, mutual aid, production, use, and consulting, while most CC are involved only in local purchasing for members. Whereas rural households constitute the membership of AC—namely a male-oriented society—the constituent members of CC are women. An even more fundamental difference is in motivation for participation. In practice all farming households in a given locality belong to AC as a matter of course. The purpose is seldom questioned, whereas membership in a CC, while local too, is a deliberate choice designed to attain something beyond that which is available in local supermarkets.

Finally, their policy positions and political stances are vastly different. AC have consistently been involved in policies to protect small farmers and have benefited from numerous policy measures. Thus they are normally pro-government and establishment. The top-down style of decision making reflects this policy involvement. The opposite is the case for CC. The prewar *seikyo* movement was heavily suppressed, and policy measures in the postwar period have done nothing to help it. The political stance of CC is thus pro-opposition party and anti-establishment. There is a strong tendency for bottom-up decision making, and individual cooperatives are relatively independent. So although both are cooperatives, AC and CC are very different. The differences go beyond their rural and urban settings to the core of their organization. One might even say that they represent two aspects of the relation between the individual and the group in modern Japan—the submersion of the individual in existing groups, and the formation by individuals of new groups.

Table 17.2 shows trends in membership and business volume of AC and CC. As can be seen from the table, the rapid growth of the CC contrasts strongly with the AC, whose membership and sales have con-

**Table 17.2**
Changes in membership, business volume of SN and CS (in 1,000 people; ¥100 million)

|  | FY1980 | 1981 | 1982 | 1983 | 1984 | 1985 | 1986 |
|---|---|---|---|---|---|---|---|
| **SN** | | | | | | | |
| Cooperatives | 4,528 | 4,473 | 4,373 | 4,317 | 4,303 | 4,267 | 4,205 |
| Members | 7,885 | 7,930 | 7,958 | 7,987 | 8,013 | 8,068 | 8,154 |
| Savings | 268,455 | 294,916 | 317,094 | 337,268 | 361,861 | 387,361 | 407,261 |
| Loans | 106,393 | 111,581 | 113,893 | 115,928 | 116,484 | 117,371 | 115,721 |
| Sales | 55,009 | 56,009 | 58,139 | 60,686 | 65,420 | 66,961 | 65,734 |
| Purchases | 47,004 | 49,222 | 49,809 | 50,867 | 52,165 | 52,279 | 50,314 |
| Long-term mutual aid holdings | 1,212,052 | 1,410,732 | 1,598,604 | 1,773,916 | 1,945,921 | 2,120,354 | 2,300,405 |
| **CS** | | | | | | | |
| Cooperatives | 647 | 662 | 652 | 647 | 635 | 652 | 648 |
| Members | 12,009 | 15,767 | 16,230 | 17,355 | 18,845 | 20,357 | 21,670 |
| Supplies | 3,970 | 78,322 | 90,599 | 9,826 | 11,007 | 12,476 | 14,228 |

Source: MAFF, *Sōgō Nōkyō Tōkei Hyō* (AC Statistical Tables); MHW, *Shōhi Seikatsu Kyōdō Kumiai Chōsa Kekka Hyō* (*Consumer "Living" Cooperative Survey Results*).

tinued to increase slightly, but with decreasing vitality in the 1980s. The membership of CC increased by 80 percent in the first six years of the 1980s, and goods supplied trebled in volume.

Regarding organization, two points are worth noting. First, while the membership of AC is very stable, that of the CC is very fluid. AC increased their membership by roughly 270,000 (3 percent in the six years), but almost all new members were affiliates. There was little change in the number of regular members. CC, on the other hand, almost doubled their membership from 12 million to 22 million. Behind these figures is a large-scale joining and leaving of members. According to a Nisseikyo (1988) survey, CC experienced yearly membership increases of 29.5 percent, and separation rates of 14.5 percent. Some of this was due to job transfers, and so on, but the figures also reflect the selective element of membership, which stands in sharp contrast to the AC.

Second, there are divergences between AC and CC in terms of member organization. AC are slowly moving toward greater diversity. There has been a shift from collective (village) organization to crop or product-based branch organization to individual and back to collective organization. Starting from the natural unit of the village, in other words, organization became differentiated with increased differentiation of farming, then the axis moved from family unit membership to individual categories such as wives and successors, and recently has been shifting back toward the reformation of local communities. Underlying these shifts have been economic and perceptual changes since the 1960s—the rapid rise of part-time farming, specialization, depletion of young members, mixed residence, and so on, which cooperatives have had to respond to organizationally.

The driving force behind CC growth, on the other hand, has been the distinctively Japanese small group *han* organization. The *han* was identified as the basic organizational unit of consumer cooperatives in 1962. Since then it has spread rapidly, and in 1985, 37 percent of members were organized in one (Tanigawa 1987, 7). There are 6.6 members in a *han* on average, and in this unit anything from joint purchasing, information sharing, receipt collection, and other daily administrative work to new product development, product testing, and formulation of requests to the cooperative is carried out. Problems identified in the *han* are taken up at the *han* leader and block delegate meetings. Thus the *han* is both the basic unit of member participation as well as business activities, and it is the secret behind the success of the CC in Japan. While AC took the natural group of the village as their organizational unit, CC consciously opted for purpose-made small groups.

Regarding business activities, the following characteristics and differences may be observed. First, AC business is all inclusive, while that of CC
is limited and focused. The four main AC activities are credit, sales, purchasing, and mutual aid, but they also include medicine, broadcasting,
consulting, gasoline stands—anything related to local community needs,
literally from cradle to grave, from nurseries to funeral parlors. Most CC,
on the other hand, focus on purchasing, 80 percent of which is food. Both
approaches have merits and demerits. It is difficult for AC to find a focus
and accumulate specialist knowledge, but there is a natural synergy between many of the activities, which makes them easy to develop (e.g.,
loans and insurance for car sales), and there is considerable stability. For CC
there is the advantage of concentration but disadvantages of limited scope
and lack of stability. To overcome this, some CC are branching out into
consumer durables, mutual aid, and so on.

Second, member usage is generally high for AC and low for CC. This is
more closely related to the activities and products involved than to differences in loyalty. Member usage rates (proportion of cooperative to total
use) average about 50 percent for AC credit and mutual aid, 70 to 80
percent for sales, and 60 to 70 percent for purchasing, while for CC (there
are wide variations by cooperative) the figure tends to be around 20 percent. Behind the high usage rates for the AC however, are price support
policies for crops such as rice and barley, and bulk purchase and standardized inputs like fertilizer and feed. Usage rates of freely distributed goods
is not so high, and for goods like food, where there are numerous types,
qualities, and makers, usage rates are estimated at around only 20 percent,
similar to CC.

Third, one characteristic of cooperatives is organized purchase and sales,
but there are differences here as well. AC cooperative sales have been
based on a rigid application of the three principles of unconditional con-
signment, averaged sales, and joint accounting. Recently, however, there
has been a revision of this policy and a trend toward greater flexibility. It
is probably feared that mechanistic application will weaken cooperative
authority and result in an exodus of large-scale farmers and floating members. As for CC, there are some club-type cooperatives with 100 percent
organized purchasing and no stores, but most now do have stores and have
had to accept casual purchasing. That does not mean, however, that they
are becoming regular supermarkets. Activities that expresses their "cooperativeness" include the development of coop goods and direct purchasing
from producers. The former are made to order according to the specifications of the cooperatives themselves, and bear cooperative brand names,

and the latter represent direct tie-ups with producers such as agriculture and fisheries cooperatives without market intermediation. Both respond to member orientations and constitute a practical criticism of mass production and mass distribution. These are factors in the rapid growth of consumer cooperatives since the 1960s in the face of competition from supermarkets and other mass retailers.

Fourth, AC have developed in a three-tier functional structure, while CC tend toward self-sufficiency. AC federations (prefectural and national) play a large role, and most business requires all three tiers. For example, 90 percent of the sales of individual cooperatives is through prefectural federations (Keizairen), and 70 percent of this is in turn sold through the national federation (Zenno). Purchasing and credit activities are similar, and all mutual aid is carried out through the national Zenkyoren. Individual self-sufficiency in this functional division is very low. This used to be viewed positively as showing the collective power of agricultural cooperatives. But more recently the rigid and bureaucratic aspects have been stressed, and there are growing calls for reform. This is not surprising, since the three-tier system was basically a response to the logic of public administration and policy. The reverse applies to CC; less than 20 percent of their purchases are done through federations. Prefectural federations serve mainly as communications organs, and the purchasing function of the national confederation Nisseikyo is also small. Recently, however, with the growing need for large-scale distribution systems, involvement in wholesale rice purchase, and so on, some have been calling for an enlargement of federation functions. Thus the functions of AC federations are being reduced and simplified, while growth and strengthening of those of CC are being sought.

Finally, I will look briefly at AC and CC management. Contrasting performance trends during the 1980s can be observed, attributable to the socioeconomic environment. AC registered overall declines in growth in all business areas, as shown in table 17.3 by the decline in operating profits from 19.5 percent in 1983 to 5.2 percent in 1986. CC, on the other hand, registered significant increases in operating profits, supported by rapid growth in membership and business volume. As shown in table 17.4, operating profits increased from 1.3 percent in 1980 to 2.3 percent in 1987. These figures, it should be noted, are averages which contain significant variations. According to the MAFF's *sogo nokyo* statistical tables, in 1986 only 71 AC (1.7 percent) experienced losses, while in 1987 22 CC (11.3 percent) were in deficit (table 17.5). Most of these were small cooperatives, including 31 percent of CC with a turnover of less than ¥100 million and

**Table 17.3**
Growth and profits of AC (in ¥1,000; %)

| | FY1979 | 1980 | 1981 | 1982 | 1983 | 1984 | 1985 | 1986 | FY1986 profits/ member |
|---|---|---|---|---|---|---|---|---|---|
| Gross business profits | 9.0 | 2.4 | 6.4 | 7.6 | 6.9 | 5.6 | 4.6 | 3.9 | 516,300 |
| Administrative costs | 8.1 | 6.7 | 6.5 | 5.2 | 4.2 | 4.4 | 4.1 | 3.3 | 431,014 |
| (labor costs) | 7.6 | 4.8 | 6.4 | 6.1 | 3.7 | 4.0 | 3.6 | 3.1 | 316,380 |
| Business profits | 14.8 | −21.3 | 5.0 | 27.3 | 26.2 | 12.7 | 7.5 | 7.1 | 85,286 |
| Operating profits | — | — | — | — | 19.5 | 11.5 | 6.9 | 5.2 | 88,622 |

Source: Zenkoku nōkyō chūōkai, *Sōgō Nōkyō Keiei Sokuhō Chōsa Hōkoku* (Advance Survey Report on AC Management).

**Table 17.4**
Trends in operating profits of CS (in ¥ millions)

|                      | FY1980  | 1985   | 1986   | 1987   |
| -------------------- | ------- | ------ | ------ | ------ |
| Members              | 15,309  | 29,689 | 31,632 | 44,158 |
| Capital              | 150     | 403    | 481    | 786    |
| Gross business       | 3,591   | 6,988  | 7,238  | 10,319 |
| Operating profit rate | 1.3    | 2.0    | 2.1    | 2.3    |

Source: Nisseikyō, *Seikyō no Keiei Tōkei* (Management Statistics of "Living" Cooperatives). Note: Data are only for cooperatives affiliated with Nisseikyō. The operating profit rate is for gross business.

**Table 17.5**
Profits of CS by size (in ¥100 million)

|                         | < 1  | 1–5  | 5–10 | 10–30 | 30–50 | > 50 | Total |
| ----------------------- | ---- | ---- | ---- | ----- | ----- | ---- | ----- |
| Coops showing profits   | 9    | 31   | 18   | 41    | 17    | 57   | 173   |
| Coops showing losses    | 4    | 6    | 1    | 6     | 3     | 2    | 22    |
| Percentage with losses  | 30.8 | 16.2 | 5.3  | 12.8  | 15.0  | 3.4  | 11.3  |

Source: Nisseikyō, *Seikyō no Keiei Tōkei* (Management Statistics of "Living" Cooperatives).

16 percent with between ¥100 and ¥500 million. There has been a growing disparity in performance by size. In sum, AC have been characterized by low, stable growth and CC by high, unstable growth.

Financial liberalization has increased pressure on management but has had a different impact on the two. AC's credit activities have been one of their greatest management strengths, and profits from these and mutual aid lines have covered for deficits in other areas. Financial liberalization, however, has stunted the growth of credit activities, profit margins have been reduced and the contribution to overall management has declined. As can be seen from Figure 17.1, the 2.86 percent profit margin of credit activities in 1976 declined to 1.93 percent in 1986. Planned liberalization of interest rates for small accounts in 1989 will further spur this trend. CC, on the other hand, do not have credit activities, and have been forced to finance their rapid growth chiefly through loans. At one time a large part of these came from members in the form of cooperative bonds. Financial liberalization has helped businesses like large supermarkets to raise capital through new share offerings at market rates and convertable bonds, but CC which cannot utilize such direct financing from capital markets are at a disadvantage. If AC have problems with surplus capital, CC have been placed at a disadvantage through capital diversification.

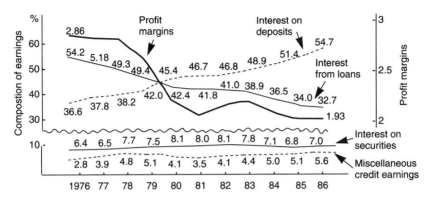

**Figure 17.1**
Interest on credit and earnings and profit margins for agriculture cooperatives. Source:
Zenkoku nokyo chuokai (1987).

Third, director backgrounds contrast strongly. The age of AC directors
is advanced and rising. According to a survey by the central cooperatives'
association Zenchu in 1987, 47.5 percent of cooperative presidents were
aged between 60 and 69, a further 18.4 percent were 70 or over, with only
2.3 percent less than 50. The proportion of directors aged 60 or over had
risen from 63.7 percent in 1971 to 74.8 percent. In the past many were
leading farmers of their village, but with the increased scale of operations,
political skills have become more important. Roughly 30 percent of presidents are now concurrently involved in local government, and some are
even town or village mayors. Apart from the matter of neutrality, clearly
the management of modern AC is too complicated to be handled part time
by local politicians. Comparable statistics are lacking for CC, but most
leaders are aged between 40 and 50, and many are housewives. Most have
become leaders through *han* activities, and are organizers. Also prominent
in top positions are males from university cooperatives. University cooperatives differ from CC in many respects, but they are nonetheless an important source of young managers. Thus, while AC tend to be led from top
down, CC are fed from the bottom up.

Management of AC, it has been argued, is characterized by its "indigenous stability," rooted in Japan's culture and customs (Ariga 1978, 1983).
Contrary to the common view that there are no real managers of AC, this
view posits that it is this very nonmanager-type management that has
enabled members to be organized and agriculture cooperative business
activities to grow so fast. I partly agree and partly disagree with this view.

I disagree with the notion of agriculture cooperative business growing because there were no managers. It grew in the high-growth period because of certain favorable conditions. If there had been managers it would probably have grown even faster. The real management test will come in the difficult period from now. I agree, however, that agriculture cooperative management is a product of Japanese culture and customs. Compared with joint stock companies, agriculture cooperatives and indeed most cooperatives are very human enterprises. Naturally different national cultures and customs are reflected more strongly in them. If the village (*mura*) organization principle with unconditional allegiance to the group underpins Japanese enterprises, this is particularly clearly expressed in cooperative enterprises, and especially AC, whose basis is literally the all-encompassing village.

What can we say, then, about CC? The rapid growth of CC since the high-growth period has occurred in the major urban areas outside such villages and traditional customs. Perhaps it is the result of people seeking to reconstruct local communities, albeit along different lines from those in rural areas. CC are functional groups formed for specific purposes, and not simply economically rational entities. They may have been organized originally for joint purchasing at lower costs, but over time their criticism of the existing distribution system has strengthened, and personal links and exchanges between producers and consumers have become more important. Similarities and differences with the *mura* principle are the subject of debate which I will not go into, except to note that the all encompassing principles of AC are gradually giving way to functional principles, while CC have been moving in the other direction, reducing the distance between the two.

## 17.4  Conclusion

Compared with capitalist enterprises, cooperatives are a very particular type of enterprise. Their fundamental purpose is not the pursuit of profit but the expansion of economic gain for members. Because of this, and their organization structures, decision-making procedures, ways of doing business, distribution of profits, and so on, cooperatives operate under a number of institutional and practical limitations. Their expansion and specialization within capitalist economies, however, has resulted in greater independence for management and blurred some differences with capitalist enterprises. A common problem facing cooperatives today is how to maintain their cooperative characteristics while improving managerial efficiency.

There are differences between types of cooperatives. Cooperatives are generally organizations of the financially disadvantaged such as farmers, small company owners, workers, and consumers. Not only are the organization principles, activities, and scale of business different for these groups, but they also differ in their management. At one extreme in Japan are credit associations and cooperatives, where member participation—a fundamental cooperative principle—is minimal and the distinction with capitalist enterprises blurred. At the other extreme are agriculture and consumer cooperatives, which have tried various measures to maintain their cooperativeness while expanding. Particularly noteworthy for the future of the cooperative movement in Japan are the AC (multipurpose agriculture cooperatives) and CC (local living or consumer cooperatives).

On one level AC and CC seem to differ in all respects. AC represent the old style cooperative, based on the *mura* (village) organization principle encompassing a broad range of business, and they are triple-tiered, are strongly dependent on politics, and have low but stable growth. CC represent the new style cooperative, based on associations of modern individuals, and they are involved in a limited scope of business (particularly purchasing), are strongly independent and critical of politics, and have high but unstable growth. Both types are organized on a regional or local basis but have developed in very different ways. What underlies these differences? What aspects of modern Japanese society do they represent, and how are these changing? Incorporating such issues into comparative studies with cooperatives in other countries is an important task for the future.

# 18

## The Life Insurance Company as a Business Enterprise

Ryutaro Komiya

Life insurance companies are of interest to students of the Japanese firm. To begin with they occupy an important segment of the economy. The market value of their shares amounts to 12.8 percent of all listed companies. The banks have 22.2 percent, but there are more than 80 banks (as defined before the 1988 law permitted conversion of mutual credit banks to ordinary banks), and a mere 25 life insurance companies.[1]

Moreover, of the corporate shareholders of listed companies, all the banks and most business corporations (ownership share 30.1 percent) are joint-stock companies, which are in turn largely owned by other joint-stock companies. By contrast, 16 of the life insurance companies that account for the greater part of the industry are not joint-stock companies but mutual companies. If the intercompany shareholdings of joint-stock companies are netted out so that ownership is attributed only to the "ultimate," non-joint-stock company owners, the mutual life insurance companies would rank with individuals as the owners of the vast bulk of listed companies' capital.

Capitalism in Japan is translated as *shihonshugi*, where *shugi* means an ideology (an "ism"), a doctrine, or a tenet. That is clearly a mistake. "Capitalism" is like "mechanism," "metabolism," or "organism," a system with particular functions. *Shihonsei* would be more accurate. But translation apart, the appropriateness of the word for describing the Japanese economy is questionable. "Capital," meaning control of general purchasing power over a given period of time, and the "capitalists" who own it, play only a limited role in the modern Japanese economy (Komiya 1989, 352). Capitalists in the original meaning of the word—that is, individuals who themselves bear all the risk of the enterprise and manage it—are indeed active in the medium- and small-enterprise sector. But in the roughly 40 years

---

1. Of these twenty-five companies, five are Japanese companies that were established since 1975 partially or wholly with foreign capital. The business scale of these five companies is still small. There are also five foreign companies that have established branches in Japan.

since the Second World War capitalists in the big business sector of Japan have largely disappeared. In the place of the former mighty capitalists, the position of life insurance companies as owners of firms has strengthened. If we think of the ownership of capital as being accompanied by control, then a meager 16 mutual life insurance companies are the most influential "owners" of Japanese big business.

Japan's life insurance companies are also of great interest for economists concerned with the theory of the firm. Excluding the five post-1975 foreign firms, of the 20 long-established Japanese life insurance companies, 16 are mutual companies and 4 are joint-stock companies. What effect does this difference in legal form have on their structure and behavior? Since the comparative method is the social scientist's only substitute for the natural scientists' experiments, mutual life insurance companies should provide important evidence for the verification of theory.

What follows is not a general account of the industry but an examination of structural characteristics, management goals, the performance of life insurance companies, and their behavior as business firms. Section 18.1 explains how mutual life insurance companies differ in structure from joint-stock companies. Sections 18.2 and 18.3 describe how the "surplus," the fruit of their activities, is distributed as dividends to policyholders, as salaries or bonuses to employees, and as retained earnings, and what it is that mutual life insurance companies seem to be maximizing. I also show the error of the widely accepted notion that the so-called convoy system serves to make the top companies ever fatter. Section 18.4 discusses the joint-stock life insurance companies, and section 18.5 the relationship between large Japanese enterprises and life insurance companies that may be their important shareholders or have some other kind of close relationship with them. The last section tries to draw conclusions from the chapter's argument about the theory of the firm in general.

## 18.1 Distinctive Structural Features of Mutual Companies

In their organizational structures there seems to be little difference between a mutual life insurance company and an ordinary joint-stock company (see, e.g., Komiya 1988, 1989, ch. 3). A limited number of senior directors, centering on the president and chairman, make decisions on important matters. Meetings of the board of directors stop at formalities, and it is rare for votes or substantial discussions to take place.

For the election of directors, the board makes nominations which are voted on (i.e., confirmed) by the meeting of representative policyholders.

As in other companies most of the directors have worked as employees of the company for a long time, and there are very few outside directors. Election to the posts of president, chairman, deputy president, executive director, and managing director is formally by an election of the board of directors, but actually it appears to be decided by a few senior directors centering on the company president. This is largely the same as for the regular large Japanese firm.

Meeting of Representative Policyholders

The mutual company's chief decision-making entity is the meeting of representative policyholders. It differs here from an ordinary company. In principle a mutual life insurance company is a corporation created by any hundred or more people who pool their "funds" for the purpose of mutual cooperative support relating to insurance. Legally the policyholders' general meeting is empowered to make major decisions, but in practice this has been entrusted to the representative policyholders. Representatives number from 50 to 150. Candidates are proposed by a nomination committee, and their names are publicly announced in the newspapers. Unless more than a specified number of policyholders object, these candidates are elected. The election of the nomination committee itself is on recommendations made by the board to the meeting of representative policyholders, which the latter approves.

In effect, the policyholders' representatives choose the board, the board chooses the nomination committee, and the nomination committee chooses the policyholders' representatives—or at least proposes the candidates. Of the three a substantial and active role is played by the board, or rather the core directors including the president.[2] The other two bodies are a marginal force for two reasons. First, the stake that a policyholder has in the firm and its welfare is inevitably very small compared to that of the employee directors or of the other employees who see the directors as their representatives. Second, the life insurance business and especially its financial statements and the means of calculating policyholders' dividends, are extremely complex, so only policyholders' representatives who are lawyers or accountants are likely to be able to understand them.

The meeting of representative policyholders in addition to (1) electing directors and (2) electing members of the nomination committee of

---

2. In addition some mutual companies have established a "Board of Councilors." The Board states opinions regarding company management but has no decisive power.

candidates for representative policyholders, (3) approves proposals for the disposition of surplus funds, and (4) deliberates on the distribution of dividend funds to policyholders and other matters. It is usual for nearly all the representative policyholders to attend these meetings, and for them to finish within an hour without objection to any of the formal items of business. This is a remarkable contrast to the shareholders' meetings of some famous large joint-stock companies since the recent revision of the Commercial Law. They have been frequently disorderly and lengthy, in at least one case extending more than ten hours.

Labor Unions

Labor unions are organized on an enterprise basis in mutual as well as joint-stock life insurance companies, though commonly not in a single unitary union. There are frequently two unions—one for office workers and one for sales workers—or even three, with the sales workers being divided into two types. Recently, however, mergers have been taking place at the enterprise level, and in 1969 what had been two national federations—one for office workers founded in 1946 and one for sales representatives founded in 1949—were merged into a single national Life Insurance Labor Federation.

### 18.2 Distribution and Enterprise Behavior: Policyholder Dividends and the "Convoy System"

What goals, what maximands does a mutual life insurance company have? There is no doubt that the mutual life insurance company is a "firm," but how would my microeconomist colleagues teaching the "theory of the firm" treat it?

From very simple and abstract economic theory, and the principles of the law, one might say that the mutual life insurance company's goal is to minimize the cost for a policyholder of receiving a fixed insurance service. This is, indeed, included in the documents such companies produce to describe their fundamental management principles. But such statements also talk of "increasing broad social welfare," "improving the livelihood of employees," and "developing the industry." Similar statements from the joint-stock life companies also talk about the "policyholder-first principle" (the shareholders come second?) and sometimes about management for (by?) the "trinity of policyholders, shareholders, and employees"—all more designed to obscure than to clarify matters for the economic theorist.

Distribution of the Surplus: Dividends to Policyholders

In mutual companies, what an economist would define as the surplus, the product of the firm's activities, appears to be distributed in the following forms:

1. As dividends to policyholders.

2. As salaries and bonuses of employees and executives (the part that exceeds the standard benefits of people engaged in the same sort of work).

3. As extra expenses within the company or as donations to projects that are thought to be socially significant.

4. As retained earnings.

The dividends to policyholders are paid on their policies; the funds invested as "capital" in these companies have long since been repaid. These dividends are determined in a very complicated way according to the type of insurance, the number of years since the policy was taken out, and other items. Premiums paid are standard as between companies, being determined by the Ministry of Finance's so-called convoy system and the industry cartel. But dividend ratios do differ depending on the company's business performance, so that for the policyholder there is a differential in the real cost of insurance. Information is not easily available. It appears that in some companies, for a 20- to 30-year endowment insurance for ¥1 million, the dividend on final payout can be as high as ¥600,000, but in poorly performing companies it is far less.

Exactly what the range of difference is, is hard to find out—partly because the types of insurance offered by each company are extremely numerous and dividend formulas complicated, and partly because comparisons seem never to be published. Few policyholders (e.g., not the writer) know how much better or worse the dividend rates of their company are than those of others.

Lack of information is compounded by the fact that because mutual companies are not listed on the stock exchange, documents equivalent to financial statements are not published. Comparisons of various financial ratios that indicate management performance—including the ratio of earnings to net worth, the ratio of operating profits to the amount of sales as in the case of stock companies, and financial analyses of each company based on these ratios—have never been published.

## Peculiarities Deriving from the Fact that Customers Are Also Owners

One would expect some information flow between potential consumers, especially as time passes, and one would expect that to affect consumer choice. One would not expect that large differences in dividend ratios would continue for long, even if companies do offer their policyholders additional (but charged-for) services. In competitive markets for footloose customers, economic theory would expect that poorly performing companies would lose policyholders, and they would find it harder and harder to survive. In the end only the fittest would survive.

In joint-stock companies a difference in the business management performance is fundamentally reflected in a difference in the ratio of operating profit to capital, and that is reflected in the dividend rate for shares or in the share price. This fact produces a difference in the relative difficulty of raising funds and will, to some extent, influence the company's growth rate. But it does not immediately affect the customers. Even if the net profit to net worth ratio is substantially higher for Toyota than for Nissan, this is hardly a matter of interest for firms and consumers about to buy passenger vehicles. They want to know about the quality and design of the product, after-sales service, and the price. Poor management performance may affect sales of durable goods if there is anxiety about future after-sales service. But for nondurables, even that effect is lacking.

The case is different for life insurance. First, the term of the contract generally extends over a very long period of time, and second, the returns to the customer policyholder (who is also an owner) depend on his dividends, which depend on the performance of the company. A rational customer would investigate the financial performance of each life insurance company, especially the company's retained earnings and, if possible, its "hidden assets" before taking out a life insurance contract. The difference from an ordinary manufacturing company or a bank is sharp, and essential to understanding the nature of a mutual company.

Agricultural and fisheries cooperatives are also enterprises where the members are "owners" and simultaneously customers, but they operate in limited areas and are usually not competing for custom in national markets like life insurance companies. Consumer cooperatives are more similar, however, in that they compete for footloose customers (members) over a relatively large area. One imagines that once a consumer cooperative association has got into difficulties and begun to lose members, revitalization becomes extremely difficult in the face of competition from other retailers or (in metropolitan areas like Tokyo and Osaka-Kobe) rival consumer cooperatives.

## Popular Conceptions about the Convoy System

The convoy system in banking and life insurance refers to the regulations and administrative guidance that kept bank interest rates, both for deposits and loans and for life insurance premiums, uniform. However, in the case of the mutual companies, because policyholders also got dividends out of profits, there *was* a form of price competition. The situation was different from that of the banks or the accident insurance companies that are joint-stock companies. In those companies, under the convoy system, differences in management performance show up primarily as differences in their ratio of operating profit to capital, their operating profit per share or their share price, or as changes in those indicators. For mutual life insurance companies, part of the fruits of superior performance go into better policyholder dividends.

It is popularly, but I think mistakenly, believed about the life insurance industry that (1) the Ministry of Finance's convoy system was a cartel that restricted competition, (2) under the system companies with the worst management performance did not go bankrupt because they were protected, and (3) large economies of scale in the life insurance industry enabled larger life insurance companies to get fatter because premiums were held at a level necessary for the survival of the weak ones. Let us examine these propositions.

## A Comparison of Selected Management Indexes

Table 18.1 uses easily available sources to compare, for the major companies, (1) increases in their total assets over the past two, five, and ten years; (2) dividends paid to policyholders as a ratio of insurance premium revenue; and (3) the ratio of the current (annual) surplus to total assets at the end of the financial year.

On the first count, total assets, the difference between the largest and the smallest company is extremely large, about 140 to 1. As for growth of assets over the past two years, the 20-company average is close to a rapid growth rate of 50 percent. The five companies with the highest rates of growth are the 16th, 13th, 10th, 11th, and 9th in order of total assets at the end of 1987. If we take the last five years, the average growth rate of assets was as much as 129 percent, and over the last ten years, 365 percent. Companies with the highest growth rates were those that ranked between 16th and 10th according to the size of total assets in 1987. The scale of

**Table 18.1**
Total assets of life insurance companies (in ¥ trillion; %)

| Company name | End-of-year total assets at | | | | | Ratio of dividend payments to premium income and rank | | | | Ratio of surplus to assets and rank | | | |
|---|---|---|---|---|---|---|---|---|---|---|---|---|---|
| | 1987 | Rate of increase 1985–87 | Rank of rate of increase 1985–87 | Rank of rate of increase 1982–87 | Rank of rate of increase 1977–87 | 1987 | 1987 rank | 1986 rank | 1985 maks | 1987 | 1987 rank | 1986 rank | 1985 rank |
| Nippon | 18.16 | 44.1 | 10 | 11 | 10 | 12.0 | 6 | 6 | 5 | 3.74 | 9 | 11 | 5 |
| Dai-Ichi | 12.50 | 49.7 | 7 | 6 | 7 | 12.9 | 2 | 7 | 7 | 3.70 | 10 | 8 | 12 |
| Sumitomo | 10.49 | 50.1 | 6 | 5 | 6 | 10.4 | 9 | 11 | 9 | 3.61 | 12 | 13 | 15 |
| Meiji | 6.80 | 48.8 | 8 | 8 | 8 | 11.0 | 7 | 8 | 9 | 3.49 | 13 | 12 | 13 |
| Asahi | 5.74 | 40.3 | 12 | 14 | 14 | 12.8 | 3 | 5 | 6 | 3.87 | 6 | 8 | 14 |
| Mitsui | 4.39 | 43.0 | 11 | 12 | 9 | 12.3 | 5 | 4 | 1 | 3.84 | 7 | 8 | 11 |
| Yasuda | 3.67 | 39.0 | 16 | 13 | 11 | 12.6 | 4 | 2 | 2 | 4.56 | 1 | 1 | 1 |
| Taiyo | 3.18 | 35.3 | 17 | 18 | 16 | 4.6 | 20 | 20 | 20 | 1.84 | 19 | 19 | 19 |
| Chiyoda | 2.60 | 52.1 | 5 | 10 | 12 | 10.3 | 11 | 3 | 2 | 4.40 | 2 | 5 | 10 |
| Tōhō | 2.55 | 72.3 | 3 | 1 | 5 | 9.2 | 12 | 16 | 16 | 2.80 | 15 | 15 | 8 |
| Kyōei* | 1.90 | 57.0 | 4 | 4 | 1 | 9.1 | 14 | 13 | 12 | 3.62 | 11 | 7 | 7 |
| Daihyaku | 1.48 | 39.6 | 15 | 16 | 15 | 5.7 | 17 | 18 | 18 | 2.33 | 18 | 18 | 18 |
| Daidō | 1.47 | 72.9 | 2 | 3 | 2 | 8.1 | 15 | 15 | 13 | 394 | 5 | 2 | 2 |
| Fukoku | 1.33 | 47.8 | 9 | 9 | 13 | 10.6 | 8 | 10 | 8 | 3.84 | 7 | 6 | 4 |
| Nippon Dantai* | 1.12 | 40.0 | 13 | 7 | 3 | 10.4 | 9 | 9 | 14 | 4.09 | 4 | 6 | 5 |
| Nissan | 0.70 | 89.2 | 1 | 2 | 4 | 4.8 | 18 | 12 | 11 | 2.51 | 17 | 14 | 8 |
| Tokio | 0.53 | 32.5 | 19 | 19 | 17 | 13.5 | 1 | 1 | 4 | 4.24 | 3 | 3 | 3 |
| Heiwa* | 0.27 | 35.0 | 18 | 15 | 20 | 7.2 | 16 | 16 | 17 | 2.76 | 16 | 17 | 17 |
| Yamato | 0.14 | 40.0 | 13 | 17 | 18 | 9.2 | 12 | 14 | 15 | 2.99 | 14 | 16 | 16 |
| Taishō* | 0.13 | 30.0 | 20 | 19 | 19 | 4.7 | 19 | 19 | 19 | 1.59 | 20 | 20 | 20 |
| Company average | 3.96 | 47.2 | | | | 10.9 | | | | 3.62 | | | |

Source: Hoken kenkyūjo (Insurance Research Institute), Insuransu: seimei hoken tōkeigō (Insurance: Life Insurance Statistics), various years.
Note: The comparison of twenty life insurance companies excludes recent entrants. The * indicates a stock company; all other companies are mutual companies. For stock companies the surplus is the total of (after-tax) undistributed profits and amounts transferred to the life insurance policyholder's dividend reserve fund.

these companies is relatively small, being between 1/26 and 1/7 of the scale of the top company in the industry. From these facts it is clear that the idea that "the top companies simply get fatter" is mistaken.

For the second ratio, policyholder's dividends as a proportion of premium income, interpretation is difficult because the ratio depends on various factors like the composition of the various types of insurance that each company issues and the maturity composition of these contracts. For example, if there are many contracts that have only just been signed, then the ratio will be low. It will tend to be high when a large portion of the contracts are close to maturity, where liberal retained reserves for each type of insurance contract are held and where there are many long-term contracts maturing in companies that pay out a large part of the dividends on a contract's maturity. Nevertheless, when a company's dividend to insurance premium revenue ratio is high over a number of years, this means that the cost of insurance to policyholders has been low. Such companies can be said to have produced a superior performance for the benefit of policyholders.

In the third ratio, the numerator (the surplus) is the equivalent of a joint-stock company's current net profits (after corporation tax), and a substantial part of it (in most companies more than 99 percent) is transferred to the policyholders' dividend reserve fund. An extremely small portion goes as bonuses to executives (in Nippon Life Insurance, the document of incorporation says "not more than 5 percent"; in practice it has been about 0.03 percent), and the rest is transferred to voluntary reserves. Accordingly this ratio is an index of how effectively the company has managed its total assets, which in a mutual company are the policyholders' joint property. It is similar to a joint-stock company's ratio of net profit to net worth.

As the table shows, there is quite a difference in the management performance of the life insurance companies when both ratios are considered. Prospective policyholders may face the same premiums, but the real cost of insurance varies from company to company. There is also a tendency for companies having a high surplus-to-total-assets ratio to have a high ratio of dividends to premiums and in companies where the former is low for the latter to be low. But there is not such a close relationship between the surplus-to-total-assets ratio and company size as measured by total assets. Over three years, the six companies with the highest ratio were, in terms of size, the 7th, 17th, 13h, 15th, 9th, and 14th ranked companies. Clearly the popular conceptions concerning the convoy system are mistaken.

## 18.3   Distribution Structure and Enterprise Behavior: Salaries and Retained Earnings

I will now discuss the distribution of the mutual life insurance company's surplus as salaries and bonuses to employees and executives and as retained earnings. This discussion will include some simple hypotheses concerning the behavioral principles of mutual life insurance companies.

### Differences in the Level of Salaries across Companies

Several years ago a newspaper article noted that the total remuneration received by an employee who entered Nippon Life after graduating from university and retired at age of 60 exceeded ¥400 million. This greatly exceeded the corresponding lifetime remuneration for a similar employee of most large listed companies, although the article did not indicate how pension and social insurance payments were treated nor how net present values were calculated. It appears to be common knowledge that the level of salaries in Nippon Life is extremely high.

There are what one might call 20 established companies, excluding recent new entrants. Between the largest established company, Nippon Life, and the smallest established company, there is a difference of 140 to one in the size of total assets and a difference in annual surplus of 300 to 1 (see table 18.1). Unlike in the banking industry where there are several types of banks, and where some banks operate only in restricted geographical areas, all life insurance companies operate nationwide, and there are no large differences in the duties of similar employees in different companies. Notwithstanding this, there are extremely large differences in salary levels across companies. There appears to be a graduated salary structure where salaries are highest in Nippon Life and become successively lower as the size of the life insurance company gets smaller.

There is no published information on the level of salaries paid by individual life insurance companies, but anecdotal evidence obtained from executives, midranking employees, and trade union leaders in the life insurance industry suggests there are sizable differences in the salary levels of core employees according to the position of the company in the industry. There are four groups: the top two companies (Nippon Life and Dai-ichi), the next five top companies, the midranking companies, and the bottom companies. For example, there appears to be a difference of around ¥2 million to ¥4 million in the average annual earnings of department chiefs aged 45 to 55 working in the top- and midranking companies.

There is some detailed firm data available on the annual incomes (including bonus payments) paid for standard working hours in the accident insurance industry (see *Sangyo rodo chosasho* 1988). A comparison of data for Tokio Marine and Fire Insurance, the top company in the accident insurance industry, and Taiyo Fire Insurance, a bottom-ranking company, is insightful. According to these data, in 1988 the average annual income of a 45-year-old section chief who had worked continuously with Tokio Marine for 23 years after graduating from university was ¥13.4 million compared with less than two-thirds of that, ¥8.8 million, for a similar individual in Taiyo Fire. A 35-year-old employee who had worked continually for 17 years after graduating from high school had an average annual income of ¥5.65 million in Tokio Marine but less than 70 percent of that, ¥3.92 million, in Taiyo. Biographical evidence obtained from individuals in the life insurance industry who were shown this data indicates a similar pattern for life insurance companies.

Although it is sometimes asserted that there are not large salary differentials for workers performing the same sort of work, the firm data just cited show that this assertion is clearly wrong. My assertion in Komiya (1989, ch. 3) that large Japanese firms behave like worker-managed firms where core employees share in the distribution (or a part) of the profits seems highly appropriate.

Distinctive Features of Sales Representatives

There is a significant difference in the extent to which office workers and sales representatives share in the distribution of profits. For sales representatives the commission portion of their salary is large. A comparison of commissions paid across companies is again difficult, but biographical evidence suggests that the salary level of sales representatives in Nippon Life is not necessarily the highest in the industry.

Sales representatives of life insurance companies, much like female employees of large enterprises, exist in a kind of gray zone, somewhere between the status of male white-collar employee under the umbrella of lifetime employment and promotion by the seniority system, and temporary part-time employee. In many ways they are closer to part-time employees. Nearly 90 percent of the sales representatives of life insurance companies are female, and a large portion of their income depends on their sales performance. Promotion by seniority is rare, and the average length of service is six to seven years. Each year new sales representatives enter in large numbers, and about two-thirds of them resign in their second year of service.

As a result the only employees of life insurance companies that share in the distribution of surplus are the permanent office workers, which for the most part are male white-collar workers with long periods of continual service (and a very small number of sales representatives who also have long periods of continual service).

Retained Earnings

If under the convoy system poorly performing life insurance companies are protected from failing, then it is not desirable that large differences in the dividends paid to policyholders occur. In a high-performing life insurance company a large part of its profits is transferred to employees, another part is kept as retained earnings, and the remainder is used for donations or other purposes. The large life insurance companies have each established a foundation for social welfare, as well as scientific or cultural purposes, although there appear to be large differences in the value of donations to these foundations according to company size. The head office buildings of the top life insurance companies and the offices of their executives are grand, but they are generally rather modest in the middle- and lower-ranking companies.

According to the Modigliani-Miller dividend theorem, if a high-performing stock company keeps a large portion of its profits as retained earnings, its share price will rise in accordance with the exact amount retained, and the shareholders immediately receive those profits. In mutual companies there is no such mechanism for policyholders to immediately receive retained profits. In industries like the life insurance industry where payment obligations randomly shift, regulations that strictly control retained earnings or that increase the dividends to policyholders are not appropriate because the maintenance of sufficient retained earnings is an essential necessary condition for the stable management of a life insurance company.[3] However, if retained earnings are increased, management per-

---

3. New entry into the life insurance industry would be quite difficult without some new innovation. A person who concludes a new insurance contract with an established life insurance company will receive a part of the benefits of the retained earnings and hidden assets retained from the insurance premiums paid to the company by past insurance policyholders and current policyholders who have no relationship with the new policyholder. This is because at the time an insurance contract lapses, the insurance company has not paid out all the retained earnings relating to that contract. New entrants will have neither these retained earnings nor any hidden assets.

formance will improve because income from the next period will generally increase due to the investment of these retained earnings.

Individuals in the industry have tended to emphasize differences in the size of retained earnings and the hidden assets held by each company as major reasons for the differences in the performances of life insurance companies. My conjecture is that the influence of these differences has been very limited because of recent rapid growth in the industry. The net increase in assets over the past five years was equal to 56.3 percent of the life insurance companies' total assets of ¥80 trillion. The gross inflow of new funds exceeds that. The ratio of hidden assets to total assets (at book value) has been rapidly watered down by the addition of these funds from new policyholders. This watering down, or dilution, refers to a reduction in the ratio of retained earnings and hidden assets to total assets (or net worth). The idea that the hidden assets of life insurance companies are still extremely large after this rapid inflow of new funds must be largely discounted.[4]

In stock companies a dilution of net worth indicates that either the rate of increase in capital through issues at market prices is too fast or the share price of these issues is too low and that the existing shareholders are sustaining losses. If in mutual companies the inflow of new funds is too fast, a similar dilution occurs as new policyholders participate to some extent in the distribution of profits from existing retained earnings (including hidden assets). When a mutual life insurance company grows rapidly, its management performance deteriorates and accordingly acts as an automatic brake on rapid growth. Hence theoretically it is not possible for the top companies in the life insurance industry to feed on the trend for very long.

---

However, if all the life insurance companies paid inadequate compensation to policyholders, made excessive profits without returning them to policyholders, and kept dividends unreasonably low, entry into the group insurance industry would occur. For example, in the case of group life insurance for the employees of universities and high schools, seven or more sponsors who recruit 100 or more policyholders can establish a mutual company and begin group insurance business. The fact that no entry occurs suggests that the existing life insurance companies behave competitively and are generally managed with high efficiency. In addition the competition from Kanpo Life Insurance, the Life Benefit Associations of the Agricultural, Fisheries, and Liverlihood Cooperatives, and Workers Benefit Associations cannot be ignored.

4. Over the past three to four years this dilution phenomenon has perhaps hardly occurred because of the rapid rise in real estate and share prices. However, there is no question that the ratios of retained earnings to total assets and hidden assets to total assets have fallen in companies experiencing a rapid inflow of new funds compared to those experiencing a slow inflow of new funds.

What Do Mutual Life Insurance Companies Maximize?
A Behavioral Hypothesis

Let us return to the question of what does the mutual life insurance company maximize? It is now clear that a systematic mechanism to ensure that management seeks to exclusively maximize the benefits of the footloose policyholders does not actually exist and cannot be created. For example, let us assume that a top-ranking life insurance company wishes to donate a massive sum of money to establish a foundation that has social or academic significance but that produces hardly any benefits for the policyholders. Even if it were possible to hold a direct vote of policyholders to determine whether to use the funds in this way or to increase the dividends paid to policyholders, the majority opinion would probably be for increasing dividends. However, there is no method for the policyholders to enforce positions contrary to those of management.[5]

This does not mean that the managers of life insurance companies ignore the interests of the policyholders. For both the managers and employees, it is advantageous that the company grow smoothly. To achieve this, the policyholders who are the customers must be adequately rewarded, the dividends distributed to policyholders must be equivalent to or exceed the dividends of other companies, good quality services must be supplied, the number of customers must be increased smoothly, and good quality sales representatives must be secured. If the customers are not rewarded in this way and their numbers do not increase, the mutual life insurance company cannot expand.

In view of these restrictions we may posit, as a simple starting hypothesis, that the mutual life insurance company determines the number of new core employees and the company's growth rate each year in order to maximize the lifetime earnings of its current core employees. Namely it uses a formula for distributing an appropriate portion of the profits to policyholders (customers), with employees (mainly office workers) and executives receiving the rest.

Translating this into a theoretical model means that in thinking statically, the managers of a life insurance company behave to maximize the per

---

5. Even if the company were managed according to the majority wishes of the policyholders—and it was possible for the majority faction of the policyholders to control with certainty the managers—a reduction in the salary levels of employees and managers to a level clearly below the level of salaries in other companies in the industry in order to increase the policyholders' dividends would not be wise. There would be a danger that the employees and managers would lose their enthusiasm for company management and that the company would be unable to recruit and educate talented people.

capita income of the core employees and so determine the number of employees by setting the marginal product of labor equal to its average product. Dynamically they behave to maximize the present value of the expected lifetime income flow of these workers. In a theoretical model where an enterprise acts to maximize the per-capita income of employees, the amount of capital used is determined by setting the marginal product of capital equal to the cost of capital in the external capital market. For an insurance company this means determining the amount of funds accepted (total insurance premium income) and hence the amount of contracted insurance to achieve a rate of return from the management of funds coming from the insurance contracts and a policyholders' dividend ratio that are equal to or, if possible, slightly exceed the rate of return on fund management and the policyholders' dividend ratio expected in other life insurance companies.

### 18.4 Stock Life Insurance Companies

All the recent new entrants into the life insurance industry are stock companies. Of the 20 established life insurance companies, 16 are mutual companies and 4 are stock companies. The four stock companies are Nippon Dantai, Heiwa Life, Taisho Life and Kyoei Life. Group insurance initially was the core activity for Nippon Dantai, but it now also sells individual insurance, although its business situation is slightly different to those of the other life insurance companies. Heiwa Life and Taisho Life are small in size, ranking 18th and 20th in terms of total assets. Kyoei Life was originally a reinsurance company, but it was reorganized and established as an ordinary life insurance company in 1947. At that time many *zaibatsu*-related stock life insurance companies were reorganized as mutual companies under the orders of the General Headquarters of the Occupation Forces. The exact circumstances under which Kyoei was inaugurated as a stock company rather than as a mutual company are not known.[6]

Although a stock company, Kyoei Life is now a middle-ranking life insurance company that seems very similar to a mutual company. First, its capital is a mere ¥90 million, less than 1/20,000 of its total assets. Until 1987 dividends were a mere ¥9 million per year because dividends to

6. According to the Kyoei company history (Kyoei Life Insurance Company 1963, 80–101), the company's management did not appear to understand the circumstances of this period. Kyoei went through the procedures to be established as a mutual company, but it appears that because of the views of the General Headquarters of the Occupation Forces, it was unexpectedly changed into and approved as a stock company.

shareholders were held to less than 10 percent (at an annual rate) of actual capital by administrative guidance from the Ministry of Finance. This was an extremely small amount compared to the amount of distributed profits (about ¥1.5 billion in 1987) and total costs. In addition over 99 percent of the combined value of ordinary and extraordinary profits was transferred to the policyholders' dividend reserve fund each year. Likewise current profits in the shareholders' accounts were extremely small. Kyoei Life's largest shareholder (25 percent) is a foundation established with a donation from Kyoei Life. This foundation trains employees in the life insurance industry in Southeast Asia. The membership and duties of its board of trustees resemble those of a mutual company's board of councilors.

Obviously a stock life insurance company does not have a meeting of representative policyholders. Rather dividends are paid to policyholders on most insurance, so on this point there is hardly any difference with the mutual companies. However, the policy for dividing the operating surplus between dividends to policyholders and the profits of the stock company is not clear. In Kyoei Life's profit-and-loss statement, current profits were less than 1/400 of the transfers to policyholder' dividend reserve fund in 1988.

If a stock life insurance company neglects the interests of its policyholders because they are not the "owners" of that company as in a mutual company, it cannot acquire policyholders. Conversely, it is not that more beneficial economically to join a mutual life insurance company rather than a stock life insurance company just because one can legally become an owner of the company.

In Japan there has been not much difference between mutual and stock life insurance companies, partly due to administrative guidance from the Ministry of Finance. Yet it cannot be said that there is no difference. Stock life insurance companies have little capital and pay small dividends, but shareholders certainly exist. Considering the possibility of liberalization, including the abolition of restrictions on dividends to shareholders, the share prices of the stock companies could rise quite a lot. Heiwa and Taisho each with capital of ¥100 million are among the smallest of the 20 established companies, but it would not be surprising if their share prices increased to 50 to 100 times their par values. The benefits obtained by large shareholders of stock life insurance companies through the provision of capital to related companies also cannot be ignored.

## 18.5 The Life Insurance Company as a Shareholder

As noted previously, Japan's life insurance companies are very important as shareholders of large firms. Nippon Life heads the list of shareholders for over a hundred companies listed on the first section of the stock exchange. Middle-sized life insurance companies also head the list of shareholders or are among the top ten largest shareholders of quite a few listed companies.

### The Life Insurance Company as Major Shareholder

There are several facets to the relationship between a life insurance company and a firm whose shares it holds. In many cases the life insurance company is not just a shareholder but also a lender of funds, in particular long-term funds. The relative importance of loans in the total assets managed by life insurance companies has recently fallen rapidly. Even so, at the end of 1986 it was still 39.2 percent of total assets. This figure is larger than the weight of securities at 17 percent, although securities are largely valued at book value. The share of privately subscribed bonds, which are similar in character to long-term or extra long-term loans in the securities purchased by the life insurance companies, is also extremely high. If ownership of shares and lending of funds (especially long-term funds) could bring about control of an enterprise, then life insurance companies could control many firms. But, since the life insurance companies themselves are mutual companies, do not issues shares or bonds, and hardly have any capital, they are not controlled by other firms. Among a mutual life insurance company's representative policyholders are several managers from enterprises that borrow from the life insurance company or that have it as a shareholder. These representative policyholders probably cannot make very critical comments regarding the management of the life insurance company at the meeting of representative policyholders.

On the other hand, the life insurance company's control of firms in which it is a shareholder, a lender of funds, or just its voice in the firm's management generally appears to be limited. A major shareholder's voice is far weaker when compared to that of a bank, or at least a leading bank. The number of managers dispatched to firms from life insurance companies is small compared to those dispatched from banks. The reason for this is that while banks, which are the frequent sources of short-term funds, become general advisers or supervisors for a firm's finances and fund management, life insurance companies have little to do with a firm's short-term lending or fund management.

In the past ten or so years there appear to have been some changes. Bank control of firms has weakened remarkably due to the slowing of the rate of economic growth of the Japanese economy, the trend for companies to have an excess of funds, and the diversification of fund raising due to the liberalization and internationalization of finance. On the other hand, pressure from overseas, especially from the United States, that the Japanese government take a more open policy concerning takeovers has increased, as have cases of attempted share cornering and takeovers by domestic or foreign invaders. As a result takeover fears have risen among managers of small-and medium-scale listed Japanese firms. Under these circumstances the practice of firms having life insurance companies as stable shareholders is becoming more important.

The firm is also an important client for the insurance company in the group insurance and enterprise pension markets where the life insurance companies compete vigorously with each other (and with trust banks in the enterprise pension market) to acquire customers. If a life insurance company behaves in a high-handed fashion as a shareholder or as a lender, it will suffer retaliation by the firm as a customer.[7] It is rare to find a firm that has only one life insurance company as a large shareholder and that does not have another life insurance company or trust bank as another large share-holder.

### Life Insurance Companies and Enterprise Groups—The *Keiretsu* Phenomenon

I wish to touch on the relationship between the Japanese enterprise group, or *keiretsu*, and the life insurance company. A firm's attachment to an enterprise group, or *keiretsu*, could be defined by the criteria of whether its shares are held by other companies in the same group and whether its borrowings of funds come from the group's core financial institutions. Then, since the top-ranking Japanese life insurance companies are all mutual companies and do not borrow funds from other financial institutions nor issue debentures, none of the mutual life insurance companies are affiliated with a particular enterprise group. However, it is common knowledge in the Japanese financial world that five life insurance companies belong to former *zaibatsu*-related groups: Sumitomo Life and Mitsui Life both belong to groups bearing the same name, Meiji belongs to the Mitsubishi group; Yasuda Life belongs to the Fuji Bank or Fuyo group (the former Yasuda group), and Asahi Life belongs to Dai-Ichi Kangyo Bank group (the former

---

7. On August 9, 1988, the *Asahi Shimbun* reported that in March 1988 Asahi Life sold a portion of its Japan Industrial Bank shares and that subsequently its share of the group insurance for Japan Industrial Bank employees was reduced. Asahi Life probably judged that the profits from the management of the funds made available by the sale of the bank shares with an extremely low dividend exceeded the losses associated with the group insurance contracts.

Furukawa group). In contrast, two companies—Dai-Ichi Life, one of the three companies that has been a mutual company since before the war, and Nippon Life, the largest company—cannot be said to belong to a specific enterprise group.[8]

Even if a life insurance company is affiliated with a former *zaibatsu*-related group, it does not mean that it is subordinate to the group. The relationship between any of the previously mentioned five life insurance companies and its respective group is a historical product. A life insurance company cannot be compelled into any unprofitable transactions by other companies in the group.

The life insurance companies of the former *zaibatsu* groups were originally stock companies, and the great majority of their shares were held by the main *zaibatsu* company and the firms within the group. They were certainly under the control of the *zaibatsu*. At the time of the dissolution of the *zaibatsu* by the Occupation Forces after the Second World War, these life insurance companies were organized as mutual companies. In addition the companies that were formerly conscription insurance companies— (Toho, Daihyaku, and Daiwa)—and other large life insurance companies made a fresh start as mutual companies. The General Headquarters of the Occupation Forces promoted the organizational switch of stock life insurance companies to mutual companies as part of a policy of privatizing the Japanese economy to reduce as much as possible the remaining influence of the *zaibatsu* and because many of the leading life insurance companies in the United States and Britain are mutual companies.

There are many examples of the group life insurance company and group trust bank appearing in the list of the major shareholders of group companies. However, as already stated, in most cases other life insurance companies and trust banks (including Nippon Life and Dai-Ichi Life) also appear.

The group life insurance company appears to have a dominant position in relation to the group insurance, corporate pensions, and individual insurance contracts of firms in the former *zaibatsu*-related groups. In this case the group life insurance company provides terms as good as or better than its competitors with respect to insurance premiums, service, and other conditions. It is not possible that just because the firms are in the same group

---

8. Since Nippon Life is a member of the presidents' club of the Sanwa group, it is generally considered to belong to this group. But I am sceptical about the existence of a Sanwa group (see *Komiya* 1988b, 62, n. 2, 1989, 137–38). In any case Nippon Life does not appear to have a close relationship with many of the enterprises that are said to be related to the Sanwa group.

that they will conclude insurance or pension contracts where the price conditions or service are inferior. Intragroup transactions in Japan today are extremely close to being at arm's length.

Finally, although life insurance companies are large shareholders and important lenders of funds (especially long-term funds) for many large enterprises, this does not give them strong control over the enterprises. The relationship appears, on the whole, to be an equal one. It is only in exceptional cases like bankruptcy that a life insurance company will use its position as a lender of funds or as a shareholder to speak out and intervene in the management of a firm.

## 18.6 Conclusion

The main purpose of this chapter was not to discuss life insurance but, through an examination of mutual life insurance companies, to throw light on the features of the Japanese firm and the theory of the firm. The main conclusions of the chapter may be summarized as follows.

First, the legal position regarding who actually controls the firm—who makes the important decisions for the firm and who fully participates in those decisions—cannot be ignored but is not decisive. For all firms the people who control the firm are those who have specialist knowledge regarding business management in the field where the firm operates and have actually accumulated a large stake in the firm. Because the typical individual shareholder who is not an owner-manager of a stock company, the policyholders and representative policyholders of a mutual life insurance company, and most of the corporate shareholders do not satisfy the two attributes noted above they can hardly realize any of the functions of control even if they are the owners of the company.

Second, the people who satisfy these two attributes and influence firms' policies in Japan are present managers and those core employees with long continual service from among whose ranks the next generation of managers will be chosen. This is true for both stock and mutual companies.

Third, there is a mechanism to distribute part of the profits to this group of people, and this provides an incentive for efficient management. My view of the large Japanese firm as being to a considerable degree like a worker-managed firm where core employees share in the distribution of profits is also appropriate for the mutual life insurance companies and their core employees (office workers).

In the golden age of Western capitalism, the captains of its industry were simultaneously the managers and financiers of the major firms, and they risked all. Any success was their own, and they also bore any losses. In the modern big business world where large funds are required and a high degree of specialist knowledge is necessary for corporate management that sort of capitalist system cannot function effectively. The large Japanese enterprise with its pivotal systems of lifetime employment and promotion by *nenko* is a system that quite cleverly solves the problems of stakes, control, and incentives.

Fourth, there is a widely accepted view that the top companies in the life insurance industry are getting fatter. The reasons suggested are that they in fact operate as a cartel sanctioned by the Ministry of Finance's convoy system policy in which the small-scale weak companies are protected as well. This view is fundamentally wrong. For mutual life insurance companies where the insurance contractor is simultaneously a customer and an owner, a full-scale cartel would not survive over a long period of time because differences in the management performances across companies would eventually be reflected in the real burdens/interests of the policy-holders. Theoretically it is difficult for the top companies to get ever fatter. Empirically it has not occurred because the rapid growth of each mutual life insurance company has brought about a dilution of retained earnings and hidden profits due to the distinctive structural features of the mutual company. An examination of data for the past five to ten years indicates that life insurance companies with the highest growth rates are all middle- or lower-ranking companies.

Fifth, Japanese life insurance companies are large shareholders of many firms and are also lenders of funds, especially long-term funds, to firms. These firms are clients of the life insurance company in the markets for group insurance and enterprise pensions where competition between insurance companies is fierce. A life insurance company's voice as a shareholder in relation to firm management is rather limited. The major exceptions to this are when the firm becomes bankrupt or is directly faced with a takeover.

Sixth, the owners of a company be it a stock or a mutual company cannot exercise control, but their interests are not ignored. The important mechanisms that guarantee the interests of the shareholders and policy-holders are disclosure of the firm's financial position and market situation— the capital market, and the market where insurance services are demanded and supplied—rather than the legal system of shareholders meetings and the meetings of representative policyholders. When determining the distribution of the profits, the decisive factor is whether the firm can smoothly and profitably raise the funds in the capital markets necessary for the company's growth if the company is a stock company and whether it can smoothly recruit new policyholders if it is a mutual company. The biggest threats to the core employees and managers of large stock companies are the market whips of the capital, product, and service markets rather than shareholders' meetings or the meeting of representatives policyholders. For a mutual life insurance company, the market whip of the insurance services market acts as the combined whip of the product market and the capital market.

# Bibliography

Abegglen, J. C. 1958. *The Japanese Factory: Aspects of Its Social Organization.* Glencoe, Il: Free Press.

Abegglen, J. C., and G. Stalk, Jr. 1985. *Kaisha: The Japanese Corporation.* New York: Basic Books.

Abernathy, W. J. et al. 1981. The new industrial competition. *Harvard Business Review* (September–October).

Aghion, P., and P. Bolton. 1988. An "incomplete contract" approach to bankruptcy and the financial structure of the firm. MIT Department of Economics Working Paper no. 484.

Akerlof, G. 1970. The market for lemons: Qualitative uncertainty and the market mechanism. *Quarterly Journal of Economics* 84:488–500.

Albert, M. 1991. *Capitalisme contre capitalisme.* Paris: Editions Seuil.

Alchian, G. A., and H. Demsetz. 1972. Production, information costs, and organization. *American Economic Review* 62:777–95.

Allen, T. J. 1966. Study of the problem-solving process in engineering design. *IEEE Transactions on Engineering Management* (June).

Ando, A., and A. Auerbach. 1988. The corporate cost of capital in Japan and the United States: A comparison. In J. B. Shoven (ed.), *Government Policy towards Industry in the United States and Japan.* Cambridge: Cambridge University Press, pp. 21–49.

Ando, A., and A. J. Auerbach. 1988. The cost of capital in the United States and Japan: A comparison. *Journal of the Japanese and International Economies* 2:134–58.

Aoki, M., and H. Itami. 1985. *Kigyo no Keizaigaku* (The Economics of Corporations). Tokyo: Iwanami Shoten.

Aoki, M., and N. Rosenberg. 1989. The Japanese firm as an innovating institution, In T. Shiraishi and S. Tsuru, eds., *Economic Institutions in a Dynamic Society.* London: Macmillan, pp. 137–54

Aoki, M., K. Koike, and I. Nakatani. 1989. *Nihon Kigyo Gurobaruka no Kenkyu: Joho-Sisutemu, R&D, Jinzai Ikusei* (The Globalization of the Japanese Firm: Information Systems, R&D, Personnel Training). Tokyo: PHP.

Aoki, M. 1977. *Keizai Taiseiron Dai-ikkan: Keizaigakuteki Kiso.* (Economic Structure, Vol 1: Economic Fundamentals) Tokyo: Toyo Keizai Shinposha.

Aoki, M. 1980. Equilibrium growth of the hierarchical firm: Shareholder-employee cooperative game approach. *American Economic Review* 70:1097–1110.

Aoki, M. 1984. Shareholders' non-unanimity on investment financing: Banks vs. individual investors. In M. Aoki, ed., *The Economic Analysis of the Japanese Firm*. Amsterdam: North Holland.

Aoki, M. 1984. *Gendai no Kigyo* (The Contemporary Corporation). Tokyo: Iwanami Shoten.

Aoki, M. 1984. *Gendai no Kigyo—Gemu Riron kara Mita Ho to Keizai, Dai Ichi-bu* (Contemporary Corporations: A Game Theory Perspective of Law and Economics, Part 1). Tokyo: Iwanami Shoten.

Aoki, M. 1985. Horizontal vs. vertical information structure of the firm. *American Economic Review* (May).

Aoki, M. 1986. *Decentralization-Centralization in Japanese Organizations*. Kyoto: Kyoto University, Institute of Economic Research.

Aoki, M. 1988. *Information, Incentives, and Bargaining in the Japanese Economy*. Cambridge: Cambridge University Press.

Aoki, M. 1984a. *The Co-operative Game Theory of the Firm*. Oxford: Oxford University Press.

Aoki, M. 1986. Horizontal vs. vertical information structure of the firm. *American Economic Review* 76:971–83.

Aoki, M. 1988a. *Information, Incentives, and Bargaining in the Japanese Economy*. Cambridge: Cambridge University Press.

Aoki, M. 1988b. Decentralization-centralization in Japanese organization: A duality principle. Mimeo. University of Kyoto. (To appear in S. Kumon and H. Rosovsky, eds., *The Political Economy of Japan*, vol. 3. Stanford: Stanford University Press.)

Aoki, M. 1989. The participatory generation of information rents and the theory of the firm. In M. Aoki, B. Gustafasson, and O. E. Williamson, eds., *The Firm as a Nexus of Treaties*. London: Sage Publications, pp. 26–51.

Archibald, G. C. 1987. The theory of the firm. *The New Palgrave: A Dictionary of Economics*, vol 2. London: Macmillan, pp.357–63.

Argyris, C., and D. Schon. 1978. *Organizational Learning*. Reading, MA: Addison Wesley.

Ariga, F. 1983. *Nokyo no Keiei Seisaku* (The Management Policies of Agriculture Cooperatives). Tokyo: Nihon Keizai Hyoronsha.

Ariga, F. 1978. *Nokyo Keiei no Ronri—Sono Dochakuteki Anteisei* (The Logic of Agriculture Cooperative Management: Indigenous Stability). Tokyo: Nihon Keizai Hyoronsha.

Ariizumi, T. 1963. *Rodo Kijun-Ho* (The Labor Standards Law). Tokyo.

Arisawa. H. 1963. *Showa Keizai Shi* (Showa Economic History). Tokyo: Nihon Keizai Shimposha.

Arrow, K. J. 1974. *The Limits of Organization*. New York: Norton.

Asanuma, B. 1985. The organization of parts Japanese automotive industry. *Japanese Economic Studies* 13:32–53.

Asanuma, B. 1989. Manufacturer-supplier relationships in Japan and the concept of relation specific skill. *Journal of the Japanese and International Economies* 3:1–30.

Asanuma, B. 1984. Jidosha-sangyo ni okeru buhin-torihiki no kozo (The structure of parts trading in the automotive industry). *Kikan Gendai Keizai* (summer): 58.

Asanuma, B. 1984. Nihon ni okeru buhin-torihiki no kozo (The structure of parts trading in Japan). *Keizai Ronso*.

Ashby, W. 1955. *An Introduction to Cybernetics*. London: Chapman and Hall.

Atkinson, A. 1973. Worker management and the modern industrial enterprise. *Quarterly Journal of Economics* 87. 375–92.

Averch, H., and L. L. Johnson. 1962. Behavior of the firm under regulatory constraint. *American Economic Review* 52:1053–69.

Axelrod, R. 1981. The emergence of cooperation among egoists. *American Political Science Review*.

Azariadis, C. 1975. Implicit contracts and underemployment equilibria. *Journal of Political Economy* 83:1183–1202.

Bailey, E. E. 1973. *Economic Theory of Regulatory Constraint*. Lexington, MA: D.C. Heath.

Baily, M. 1977. On the theory of layoffs and underemployment. *Econometrica* 45:1043–64.

Baily, M. N. 1974. Wages and employment under uncertain demand. *Review of Economic Studies* 41:37–50.

Baldwin, C. Y. 1986. The capital factor: Competing for capital in a global environment. In M. E. Porter, ed., *Competition in Global Industries*. Boston: Harvard Business School Press, pp. 185–223.

Barrett, M. E., L. N. Price, and J. A. Gehrke. 1974. Japan: Some background for security analysts. *Financial Analysts Journal* (March–April): 60–67.

Bateson, G. 1979. *Mind and Nature*. New York: John Brockman Associates.

Becker, G. S. 1981. *A Treatise on the Family*. Cambridge: Harvard University Press.

Becker, G. S. 1964. *Human capital: Theoretical and empirical analysis with special reference to education*. New York: Columbia University Press.

Bell, W. D., and C. G. Hansen. 1987. *Profit Sharing and Profitability*. London: Kogan Page.

Berglof, E. 1989. Capital structure as a mechanism of control—A comparison of financial systems. In M. Aoki, B. Gustafsson, and O. E. Williamson, eds. *The Firm as a Nexus of Treaties*. London: Sage Publications, pp. 237–62.

Berle, A. A., and G. C. Means. 1932. *The Modern Corporations and Private Property*. Chicago: Commerce Clearing House.

Bernheim, B. D., and J. B. Shoven. 1989. Comparison of the Cost of Capital in the U.S. and Japan: The Role of Risk and Taxes. Mimeo. Stanford University Press.

Binder, A. 1992. Should the former socialist economies look east or west for a model? Keynote address to International Economic Association Congress, Moscow. August.

Binmore, K., A. Rubinstein, and A. Wolinsky. 1986. The Nash bargaining solution in economic modelling. *Rand Journal of Economics*. 17:176–88.

Blanpain, R. 1980. Job security and industrial relations. *Bulletin of Comparative Labour Relations*. Bulletin 11. Deventer, The Netherlands: Kluwer.

Blau, P. M. 1964. *Exchange and Power in Social Life*. New York: Wiley.

Bozeman, B., and A. N. Link. 1983. *Investments in Technology: Corporate Strategies and Public Policy Alternatives*. New York: Praeger.

Branton, N. 1966. *Economic Organization of Modern Britain*. London: English Universities Press.

Brown, K. M. 1984. The elusive carrot: Tax incentives for R&D. *Regulation* 8:33–38.

Brunello, G., and F. Otake. 1987. Boonasu, chingin no kettei mekanizumu to koyo: Kigyo-betsu deeta ni yoru saiko (Employment and the mechanisms for determining bonuses and wages: A reconsideration in the light of firm-level data). *Osaka-daigaku Keizaigaku* (Osaka University Economics) (June): 28–41.

Bulow, J. I., J. D. Geanakoplos, and P. D. Klemperer. 1985. Multimarket oligopoly: Strategic substitutes and complements. *Journal of Political Economy* 93:488–511.

Caves, R. E., and M. Uekusa. 1976. *Industrial Organization in Japan*. Washington, DC: Brookings Institution.

Chandler, Jr., A. D. 1988. Administrative coordination, allocation and monitoring: concepts and comparisons. In T. K. McGraw, ed., *The Essential Alfred Chandler*. Boston: Harvard Business School Press.

Chandler, Jr., A. D. 1988b. Markets and hierarchies. In T. K. McGraw, ed., *The Essential Alfred Chandler*. Boston: Harvard Business School.

Chinloy, P. T., and E. Stromsdorfer, eds. 1987. *Labor Market Adjustments in the Pacific Basin*. Deventers, The Netherlands: Kluwer-Nijhorf.

Choi, F. D., H. Hino, S. K. Min, S. O. Nam, J. Ujiie, and A. I. Stonehill 1983. Analyzing foreign financial statements: The use and misuse of international ratio analysis. *Journal of International Business Studies* 14:113–32.

Clark, K. B., W. B. Chew, and T. Fujimoto 1987. Product development in the world auto industry. *Brookings Paper on Economics Activity* no. 3.

Coase, R. H. 1972. Industrial orgainization: A proposal for research. In V. R. Fuchs, ed., *Policy Issues and Research Opportunities in Industrial Organization*. New York: National Bureau of Economic Research, pp. 59–73.

Cole, R., and T. Yakushiji. 1984. *The American and Japanese Auto Industries in Transition*. Ann Arbor: Center for Japanese Studies, University of Michigan.

Coombes, D. 1971. *States Enterprise: Business or Politics?* London: George Allen & Unwin.

Cremer, J. 1989. Common Knowledge and the Coordination of Economic Activities. In M. Aoki, B. Gustaffson, and O. E. Williamson, eds., *The Firm as a Nexus of Treaties*. London: Sage Publications, pp. 53–76.

Cusamano, M. A. 1985. *The Japanese Automobile Industry: Technology and Management at Nissan and Toyota*. Cambridge: Harvard University Press.

Daniel, W. W., and E. Stilgoe. 1978. *The Impact of Employment Protection Laws*, vol. 44. London: Policy Studies Institute.

Davidson, R., and J. H. MacKinnon. 1981. Several Tests for Model Specification in the Presence of Alternative Hypothesis. *Econometrica* 49:781–93.

Demsetz, H. 1973. Industry structure, market rivalry, and public policy. *Journal of Law and Economics* 16:113–32.

Dertouzos, M. L., R. K. Lester, and R. M. Solow. 1989. *Made in America*. Cambridge: MIT Press.

Doeringer, P. B., and M. Piore. 1971. *Internal Labor Markets and Manpower Analysis*. Lexington, MA: D.C. Heath.

Domowitz, I., R. G. Hubbard, and B. C. Petersen. 1986. Business cycles and the relationship between concentration and price-cost margins. *Rand Journal of Economics* 17:1–17.

Dore, R. 1973. *British Factory, Japanese Factory: The Origin of National Diversity in Industrial Relations*. Berkeley: University of California Press (Japanese trans. by S. Yamanouchi and K. Nagai. 1987. Tokyo: Chikuma Shobo).

Dore, R. 1986. *Flexible Rigidities*. London: Athlone Press.

Drucker, P. F. 1981. Behind Japan's success. *Harvard Business Review* (January–February).

Eades, G. C., and R. R, Nelson. 1986. Japanese high technology policy: What lessons for the United States? In H. Patrick, ed., *Japan's High Technology Industries*. Seattle/Tokyo: University of Washington Press/University of Tokyo Press.

Eigen, M. 1971. Self-organization of matter and the evolution of biological macromolecules. *Naturwissenschaften* 58.

Emerson, R. M. 1962. Power Dependence Relations. *American Sociological Review* 27:31–41.

Foulkes, F. 1980. *Personnel Policies in Large Non-union Companies*. Englewood Cliffs, NJ: Prentice-Hall.

Freeman, C. 1981. *The Economics of Industrial Innvoation*. Cambridge: MIT Press.

Freeman, R. B., and M. L. Weitzman. 1987. Bonuses and employment in Japan. *Journal of the Japanese and International Economies* 1:168–94.

Friedman, W., ed. 1954. *The Public Corporation: A Comparative Symposium*. Toronto: Carswell.

Fuss, M. A., and L. Waverman. 1985. Productivity growth in the automobile industry

1970–1980: A comparison of Canada, Japan and the United States. National Bureau of Economic Research Paper, no. 1735. (Forthcoming in C. H. and J. R. Norsworthy, eds., *Productivity Growth in the United States and Japan.*, NBER Studies in Income and Wealth. Chicago: University of Chicago Press.)

Gordon, R. J. 1982. Why U.S. wage and employment behavior differs from that in Britain and Japan. *Economic Journal* 92:13–44.

Goto, A., and W. Takahira. 1984. Gijutsu Seisaku (Technology policy). In R. Komiya, M. Okuno, and K. Suzumura, eds., *Nihon no Sangyo Seisaku* (Japan's Industrial Policy). Tokyo: Tokyo University Press.

Goto, A. 1982. Business Groups in a Market Economy. *European Economic Review* 19.

Grossman, S., and O. Hart. 1986. The costs and benefits of ownership: A theory of vertical integration. *Journal of Political Economy* 94:691–719.

Gutchess, J. F. 1985. *Employment Security in Action: Strategies That Work.* Work in America Institute Series. New York: Pergamon.

Hagen, H. 1985. *The Shaping of Nature and Social Order (Shizen no Zokei to Shakai no Chitsujo),* trans. by T. Takagi. Tokyo: Tokai-daigaku Shuppansha.

Hall, R. E. 1980. Employment fluctuation and wage rigidity. *Brookings Papers on Economic Activity,* no. 1, pp. 91–123.

Hall. R. E. 1982. The importance of lifetime jobs in the US economy. *American Economic Review* (September).

Hamada, K. 1985. Bonus payments in Japan: Profit sharing vs. overtime work compensation. Mimeo. Keio University.

Hamada, Y. 1985. Shoyo seido no keizai bunseki—Chukan Hokoku (An economic analysis of the bonus system: Interim report). In *Tokei Kenkyukai Rodoryoku Jukyu Kozo no Henka to Koyo Seisaku ni kansuru Kenkyu* (Research of the Change in the Structure of Labor Supply and Demand and Recruitment Policy.)

Hanami, T. 1979. *Labor Law and Industrial Relations in Japan.* Deventer, The Netherlands: Kluwer.

Hart, O., and B. Holmstrom. 1987. The theory of contracts. In T. Bewley (ed.), *Advances in Economic Theory.* Cambridge: Cambridge University Press.

Hashimoto, M., and J. Raisian. 1985. Employment tenure and earnings profiles in Japan and the United States. *American Economic Review* 75:721–35.

Hashimoto, M. 1979. Bonus payments, on-the-job training, and lifetime employment in Japan. *Journal of Political Economy,* vol. 87, no. 5

Hatsopoulos, G. N., P. R. Krugman, and L. H. Summers. 1988. U.S. competitiveness: Beyond the trade deficit. *Science* (July 15): 299–307.

Hayek, F. A. 1945. The use of knowledge in society. *American Economic Review* 35.

Hayes, R. H. 1981. Why Japanese factories work. *Harvard Business Review* (July–August).

Hazama, H. 1978. *Nihon Romu-Kanrishi no Kenkyu* (The History of Personnel Management in Japan). Tokyo: Ochanomizu Shobo (reprint 1984).

Hedlund, G. 1986. The hypermodern MNC—A hierarchy? *Human Resource Management*, vol. 25, no. 1.

Hill, T. P. 1979. *Profits and Rates of Return*. Paris: OECD.

Hirschman, A. O. 1970. *Exit, Voice and Loyalty*. Cambridge: Harvard University Press.

Holland, D. M., ed. 1984. *Measuring Profitability and Capital Costs*. Lexington, MA.: Lexington Books.

Horiuchi, A., F. Packer, and S. Fukuda. 1988. What role has the main bank played in Japan? *Journal of the Japanese and International Economies* 2:159–80.

Hyodo, T. 1971. *Nihon ni okeru Roshi Kankei no Tenkai* (The Development of Labor and Capital Relations in Japan). Tokyo: Tokyo Daigaku Shuppankai.

Ichino, S. 1989. Pahtotaimu rodo shijo no henbo katei (The transformation process of the part-time labor market). *Nihon Rodo Kyokai Zasshi* (Japan's Labor Union Journal), no. 356, p. 5.

Ihara, T., and Y. Okada. 1988. Sabisu to niyu bijinesu no soshiki (Service and new business organization). In K. Imai et al., eds., *Nihon no Soshiki* (Japan's Organizations), vol 9. Tokyo: Daiichi Hoki Shuppan.

Imai, K., and H. Itami. 1984. Interpenetration of market and organization. *International Journal of Industrial Organization* (December).

Imai, K. and Y. Kaneko. 1988. *Nettowaaku Soshiki Ron* (Network Organization Theory). Tokyo: Iwanami Shoten.

Imai, K. 1976. *Gendai Sangyo Soshiki* (Contemporary Industrial Organization). Tokyo: Iwanami Shoten.

Imai, K. 1986a. Nihon no kigyo nettowaku (Japan's corporate network). *Economics Today* (fall).

Imai, K. 1986b. Nettowaku soshiki: Tenbo (Network organization: A survey). *Soshiki Kagaku* (Organizational Science 20).

Imai, K. 1987. The corporate network in Japan. *Japanese Economic Studies* (winter).

Imai, K., H. Itami, and K. Koike. 1982. *Naibu Soshiki no Keizaigaku* (Economics of Internal Organization). Tokyo: Toyo Keizai Shinposha.

Imai, K., H. Uzawa, R. Komiya, Takashi Negishi, and Yasusuke Murakami. 1971. *Kakaku Riron* (Price Theory). Tokyo: Iwanami Shoten.

Imai, K., I. Nonaka, and H. Takeuchi. 1985. Managing the product development process: How Japanese companies learn and unlearn. In K. Clark, R. Hayes, and C. Lorenz, (eds.), *The Uneasy Alliance: Managing the Productivity-Technology Dilemma*. Boston: Harvard Business School Press, ch. 8.

Industry Research System. 1985. Hitachi gurupu Keiretsuka no jittai. (The Formation of the Hitachi Group Keiretsu.)

Ireland, N. J., and P. J. Law. 1982. *The Economics of Labour-Managed Enterprises*. London: Croom Helm.

Ishida, H. 1985. *Nihon Kigyo no Kokusai Jinji Kanri* (International Personnel Management by Japanese Corporations). Tokyo: Nihon Rodo Kyokai.

Ishida, H., and T. Umezawa. 1989. *Ristorakucharingu no Jinzai; Soshiki Senryaku; Yakushin 12 Sha no Kesu Stahdy* (Human Capital and the Process of Restructuring; Organizational Strategy; Progress. A Case Study of 12 Companies). Tokyo: Nikkan kogyo shimbun sha.

Ishida, M. 1988. Igirisu no chingin seido no genjo. (The wage system in Britain). *Nihon Rodo Kyokai Zasshi* no. 344 (April).

Itami, H., and T. Kagono. 1989. *Zeminaru Keieigaku Nyumon* (Management Science: An Introductory Seminar). Tokyo: Nihon Keizai Shinbunsha.

Itami, H., T. Kagono, T. Kobayashi, K. Sakakibara, and M. Ito. 1988. *Kyoso to Kakushin— Jidosha Sangyo Seicho* (Competition and Innovation: The Growth of Firms in the Automobile Industry). Tokyo: Toyo Keizai Shinposha.

Itami. H. 1987. *Jinponshugi Kigyo* (Human Capital-ist Corporations). Tokyo: Chikuma shobo.

Itami, H. and Y. Matsunaga. 1985. Chukan rodo shijoron (Intermediate labor market theory). *Nihon Rodo Kyokai Zasshi*, vol. 27.

Ito, M., M. Kiyono, M. Okuno, and K. Suzumura. 1988. *Sangyo Seisaku no Keizai Bunseki* (Economic Analysis of Industrial Policy). Tokyo: Tokyo Daigaku Shuppankai.

Itoh, H. 1987. Information processing capacities of the firm. *Journal of the Japanese and International Economies* 1:299–326.

Itoh, M., and A. Matsui. 1986. An economic analysis of organizational transactions: An aspect of Japanese-style transactions. Mimeo.

Itoh, M., and A. Matsui. 1989. Kigyo: Nihonteki torihiki keitai. (Enterprises: The Japanese mode of trading). In M. Ito and K. Nishimura, eds., *Oyo Mikuro Keizaigaku (Applied Microeconomics)*. Tokyo: Tokyo University Press, ch. 1.

Iwai, K. 1988. Jyugyoin kanri kigyo toshite no Nihon kigyo (Japanese corporations as employee management enterprises). In K. Iwata and N. Ishikawa, *Nihon Keizai Kenkyu*. eds., Tokyo: Tokyo Daigaku Shuppankai.

Iwata, R. 1977. *Nihonteki Keiei no Hensei Genri* (The Organization Principles of Japanese Management). Tokyo: Bunshindo Press.

Jaikumar, R., and R. E. Bohn. 1986. The development of intelligent systems for industrial use: A conceptual framework. In *Research on Technological Innovation, Management and Policy*, vol. 3. Tokyo: JAI Press.

Jansen, M. B., ed. 1965. *Nihon ni okeru Kindaika no Mondai*. Tokyo: Iwanami shoten. Japanese trans. of M. B. Jansen, ed., *Aspects of Japanese Modernization*. Princeton: Princeton University Press.

Japan Productivity Center. 1985. *Kenkyu Kaihatsu Gijutsusha no Shogu nikansuru Chosa Hokoku* (Survey Report on Remuneration of R&D Engineers). Tokyo.

Japan Productivity Center. 1987. *Jishu Gijutsu Kaihatsu to Soshiki Jinji Senryaku*. (Independent Technological Development and Corporate Strategy). Tokyo.

Japan Productivity Center. 1988. *Jishu Gijustu Kaihatsu Jidai no Gijutsusha*. (Engineers of the Era of Independent Technological Deveopment). Tokyo.

Jensen, M., and W. Meckling. Theory of the firm: Managerial behavior, agency costs and capital structure. *Journal of Financial Economics* 4:305−60.

Johansson. J., and L. G. Mattsson. 1987. Interorganizational relations in industrial systems: A network approach compared with the transaction cost approach. *International Studies Management and Organization* 17.

Kagano, T., I. Nonaka, K. Sakakibara, and A. Okumura. 1983. *Nichi-bei Kigyo no Keiei Hikaku* (Comparisons of American and Japanese Corporate Management). Tokyo: Nihon Keizai Shinbunsha.

Kagiyama, Y. 1977. *Shoyo to Seika Haibun* (Bonuses and Profit Distribution). Tokyo: Hakucho shobo.

Kahn, A. E. 1988. *The Economics of Regulation: Principles and Institutions*. Cambridge: MIT Press.

Kahn, G. A. 1984. International differences in wage behavior: Real, nominal or exaggerated? *American Economic Review* 74:155−59.

Katz, M. L. 1986. An analysis of cooperative research and development. *Rand Journal of Economics* 17:527−43.

Kawasaki. S., and J. McMillan. 1987. The design of contracts: Evidence from Japanese subcontracting. *Journal of the Japanese and International Economies* (September): 327−49.

Kay, J., C. Mayer, and D. Thompson, eds. 1986. *Privatization and Regulation: The UK Experience*. Oxford: Clarendon.

Kinoshita, K. 1959. Kyodo kumiai no keizai kozo (The economic structure of cooperatives). In S. Tohata's 60th Birthday Memorial Publication *Keizai Hatten to Nogyo Mondai* (Economic Development and Problems of Agriculture). Tokyo: Iwanami Shoten.

Klein, B., R. G. Crawford, and A. A. Alchian. 1979. Vertical Intergration, Appropriable Rents and the Competitive Contracting Process. *Journal of Law and Economics*: 297−326.

Klein, S., and N. Rosenberg. 1986. An Overview of Innovation. In R. Laudau and N. Rosenberg, eds., *The Positive Sum Strategy*. Washington, DC: National Academy Press, pp. 275−305.

Knight, F. H. [1921] 1971. *Risk, Uncertainty and Profit*. Boston: Houghton Mifflin.

Koike, K., and T. Inoki, eds. 1987. *Jinzai-Keisei no Kokusai-Hikaku: Tonan-Ajia to Nihon* (An International Comparison of Human Resource Creation: South-East Asia and Japan). Tokyo: Toyo Keizai Shimposha.

Koike, K., K. Muramatsu, and N. Hisamoto. 1987. Chiteki Jukuren no Keisei—Aichiken no Kigyo (Formation of intellectual skills: Firms in Aichi Prefecture). Nagoya: Aichiken.

Koike, K. 1977. Shokuba no Rodo Kumiai to Sanka—Roshi Kankei no Nichibei Hikaku (Labor Unions in the Workplace and Participation: Comparison of Industrial Relations in Japan and the U.S.). Tokyo: Toyo Keizai Shimposha.

Koike, K. 1981. Nihon no Jukuren (Skills in Japan). Tokyo: Yuhikaku.

Koike, K. 1984. Skill formation systems in the U.S. and Japan: A comparative study. In M. Aoki, ed., The Economic Analysis of the Japanese Firm. Amsterdam: North Holland, pp. 47–75.

Koike, K. 1988. Understanding Industrial Relations in Modern Japan. London: Macmillan.

Koike, K. 1989. Intellectual skill and the role of empoloyees as constituent members of large firms in contemporary Japan. In M. Aoki, B. Gustafsson, and O. E. Williamson, eds., The Firm as a Nexus of Treaties. London: Sage Publications, pp. 185–208.

Koike, K. 1988. Choki kyoso to chiteki jukuren (Long-term competition and intellectual skills). Business Review 35. no. 1.

Komiya R., M. Okuno, and K. Suzumura. 1984. Nihon no Sangyo Seisaku (Japanese Industrial Policy). Tokyo: Tokyo Daigaku Shuppankai.

Komiya, R., and K. Iwata. 1970. Kigyokinyu no Riron (Theory of Corporate Finance). 3d ed. Tokyo: Nihon Keizai Shimbunsha.

Komiya, R. 1987. Japanese firms, Chinese firms: Problems for economic reforms in China, Part I. Journal of the Japanese and International Economies 1.

Komiya, R. 1987. Japanese firms, Chinese firms: Problems for economic reform in China, Part II. Journal of the Japanese and International Economies 3:97–145.

Komiya, R. 1988. Nihon Kigyo no Kozoteki, Kodoteki Tokucho (Structural and behavioral characteristics of Japanese enterprises). In Keizaigakuronshu, vol. 54. Tokyo: Daigaku Shuppankai. (Also in Komiya, R. 1989. Gendai Chugoku Keizai. Tokyo: Tokyo Daigaku Shuppankai.)

Komiya, R. 1988b. Gendai Chugoku Keizai: Nitchu no Hikaku—Kosatsu (The contemporary Chinese Economy: A Comparative Study of Japan and China). Tokyo: Tokyo University Press.

Kondo, Y. 1934. Kyodo Kumiai Genron (Principles of Cooperatives). Tokyo: Koyo shoin.

Koshiro, K. 1986. Gainsharing, wage flexibility and macro-economic peformance in Japan. Discussion Paper Series. Faculty of Economics. Yokohama National University.

Koshiro, K. 1980. Dai-ni-ji sekiyu kikika no chingin kettei (Wage determination during the second oil crisis). Nihon Rodo Kyokai Zasshi 5.

Koshiro, K. 1983a. Naibu rodo shijo no koyo hendo (Changes in the internal labor market employment). Rodo Mondai Research Center, Kinkei Shinzu 65.

Koshiro, K. 1983b. Nihon no Roshi Kankei (Japanese Industrial Relations). Tokyo: Yuhikaku.

Koshiro, K. 1986. Chingin shinshukusei no kokusai hikaku (An international survey of wage flexibility). In *Kokusaiteki shiten kara mita waga kuni rodo shijo no junansei ni kan suru chosa kenkyu* (Studies in Japanese labor market flexibility in an international perspective), no. 8. Kinkei Shirizu. Rodo Mondai Research Center.

Koshiro, K. 1988a. *Kozo Chosei ni Taio Suru Kigyo no Hosaku ni Kan Suru Jittai Chosa* (Survey Related to Planning in Corporations Undergoing Structural Adjustment). Tokyo: Koyo shokugyo sogo kenkyujo/Nihon seisansei honbu.

Koshiro, K. 1988b. Kigyo reberu ni okeru shoyo no shinshukusei—senigyo no jirei o chushin toshite (The flexibility of bonuses at the corporate level: Using textiles as the central example. *Tei seicho ka no kozo chosei to rodo shijo no henka* (Structural adjustment in the slow-growth phase and changes in labor market). Tokyo: Tokei kenkyukai.

Koshiro, K. 1986. Labor market flexibility in Japan. Discussion Paper Series, 86-2. Center for International Trade Studies. Yokohama National University (included in Koshiro 1989b).

Koshiro, K. 1989a. Labor market flexibility and new empolyment patterns in Japan. Presented to the International Industrial Relations Association, 8th World Congress. Brussels (September).

Koshiro, K., ed. 1989b. *Empolyment Security and Labor Market Flexibility: Proceedings of the Yokohama Symposium*. Detroit: Wayne State University Press.

Koyama, S. 1988. Gakusei arubaito no genjo bunseki (Analysis of the situation for part-time jobs for students). Tokyo: Tokei kenkyukai rodo shijobukai miniconfarensu. *Rodo shijo bukai minikonfarensu* (Labour Market Group Mini conference) vol. 10.

Kreps. D. 1986. Corporate Culture and Economic Theory. Mimeo.

Kuehn, D. 1975. *Takeovers and the Theory of the Firm*. London: Macmillan.

Kuroda, I., and Y. Oritani. 1979. Wagakuni no kinyu kozo no tokucho no saikento (A reappraisal of the special characteristics of Japan's financial structure). *Nihon ginkoo tokubetsu kenkyuushitsu*. In *Kinyu Kenkyu Shiryo* (Finance Research Documents). no. 2, pp. 1–24.

Kuroda, M., K. Yoshioka, and M. Shimizu. 1987. Keizai seicho: Yoin bunseki to tabumonkan hakyu (Economic growth: Factor analysis and multisectoral affects). In K. Hamada, ed., *Nihon Keizai no Makuro Bunseki* (Macroeconomic Analysis of Japan). Tokyo: Tokyo University Press.

Kuwahara, Y. 1987. Nihonteki keiei wa senshin moderu ka—Aratana paradaimu o motomete (Is Japanese management an advanced model? The need for a new paradigm). Rodo Mondai Senmonka Kokusaikaigi. (International Conference of Labor Experts) *Seijuku Gijutsushakai ni okeru Rodomondai* (The Question of Labor in a Mature Technological Society). Tokyo: Nihon Rodo Kyokai.

Kuwahara, Y. 1988. Nihonteki keieiron saiko—'Kyochoteki' roshi kankei no kitei ni aru mono (Reconsideration of the theory of Japanese management: What lies behind "harmonious" industrial realations). *Nihon Rodo Kyokai Zasshi*, no. 342:1.

Kyoei Life Insurance Company. 1963. *Kyoei Seimei Hoken Kabushiki Kaisha: Shiko* (Kyoei Life Insurance Company: A History). Tokyo: Kyoei Life Insurance Company.

Lall. B. D., ed. 1985. *Economic Dislocation and Job Loss.* New York State School of Industrial and Labor Relations. Ithaca: Cornell University Press.

Lazear, E. 1979. Why is there mandatory retirement? *Journal of Political Economy* 87.

Leibenstein, H. 1976. *Beyond Economic Man—A New Foundation for Microeconomics.* Cambridge: Harvard University Press.

Leibenstein, H. 1987. *Inside the Firm.* Cambridge: Harvard University Press.

Liefmann, R. 1923. *Die Unternehmungsformen,* vol. 3.

Lincoln, J., M. Hanada, and K. McBird. 1986. Organizational structures in Japanese and U.S. manufacturing. *Administrative Science Quarterly* 31:334–64.

MacCulloch, W. S. 1965. A hierarchy of values determined by the topology of nervous nets. In *Embodiment of Mind.* Cambridge: MIT Press.

MacLeod, B. W., and J. M. Malcomson. 1986. Reputation and hierarchy in dynamic models of employment. Mimeo. University of Southampton.

Mailath, G. J., and A. Postlewaite. 1988. Asymmetric information and bargaining problems with many agents. Mimeo. University of Pennsylvania.

Mansfield, E. 1988. Industrial R&D in Japan and the United States: A comparative study. *American Economic Review* 78:223–28.

Marquis, D. B. 1969. *Successful Industrial Innovation.* Washington, DC: National Science Foundation.

Marris, R. L. 1964. *The Economic Theory of "Managerial" Capitalism.* London: Macmillan.

Matsuda, Y. 1984. The dismissal of workers under Japanese law. *Stanford Journal of International Law* 10.

Matsumoto, J. 1983. *Kigyoshugi no Koryu* (The Rise of Corporationism). Tokyo: Japan Productivity Center.

Minami, R. 1981. *Nihon no Keizai Hatten* (The Development of the Japanese Economy). Tokyo: Toyo Keizai Shimposha.

Mincer, J., and Y. Higuchi. 1988. Wage structures and labor turnover in the United States and Japan. *Journal of the Japanese and International Economies* 2:97–133.

Ministry of Finance (Publishing Bureau). 1988. *Yuka shoken hokoku—soran* (Bibliography of Financial Statements). Fiscal year 1988 edition. Tokyo.

Ministry of International Trade and Industry. 1988. *Nichibei Kigyo Kodo Hikaku Chosa Hokokusho* (Report on the Comparative Survey of Japanese and American Enterprise Activities). *Kigyo Kodo ni Kansuru Chosa Kenkyu Iinkai* (Committee on Research into Company Activities). Tokyo: (September).

Ministry of International Trade and Industry. 1988a. *Denki—jigyo no genjo* (The Present Situation of Electricity Utilities). Fiscal year 1988 edition. Public Utility 3 Division, Natural Resources and Energy Agency. Tokyo.

Ministry of International Trade and Industry. 1988b. *Denryoku jukyu no gairyo* (A Summary of Electric Power Supply and Demand). Fiscal year 1988 edition. Tokyo.

Ministry of Labor. 1973 *Rodohakusho* (White Paper on Labor). Tokyo.

Ministry of Labor. 1983. *Rodohakusho* (White Paper on Labor). Tokyo.

Ministry of Labor. 1984. *Chingin rodo jikan seido sogo chosa* (Comprehensive survey of the hourly wage system). Tokyo.

Miwa, Y. 1988. Nihon no kigyo shudan (ron) ni tsuite (Concerning Japanese group theory). Tokyo University Economics Department, 88-J-10.

Miwa, Y. 1976. *Shinsangyo no Mebae* (The Budding of New Industry). In H. Arisawa (ed.), *Showa Keizai Shi* (Showa Economic History). Tokyo: Nihon Keizan Shinbunsha.

Miwa, Y. 1988. Shitauke to chu-sho kigyo deiskasshon peipah (Subcontracting and small and medium enterprises discussion paper). Tokyo: Tokyo Daigaku keizaigakukai, 88-J-7.

Miwa, Y. 1989a. Nihon no chu-sho kigyo no "imeji", "ittai" to "seisaku" (Japanese small and medium firms: Image, reality and policy). *Keizaigakuronshu* 4. (Also in T. Moriaki and Y. Miwa, eds., *Nihon no chu-sho kigyo* [Small and medium Japanese firms] Tokyo: Daigaku Shuppankai, 1989.

Miwa, Y. 1989b. Shitauke kankei: Jidosha sangyo no kesu (Subcontractor relations: Case of the automobile industry). *Keizaigakuronshu* 55.

Miyazaki, H. 1984. Internal bargaining, labor contracts, and a Marshallian theory of the firm. *American Economic Review* 74:381–93.

Mizuno, A. 1985. Chingin shinjukusei to koyo hendo (Wage flexibility and empolyment fluctuation in Japan). In Nakamura, Nishikawa, and Kosai, eds., *Gendai Nihon no Keizai Shisutemu* (The Economic System in Contemporary Japan). Tokyo: Daigaku Shuppankai.

Modigliani, F., and M. Miller. 1958. The cost of capital, corporation finance and the theory of investment. *American Economic Review* 48.

Monden, Y. 1983. *Toyota Production System*. Atlanta: Industrial Engineering and Management Press.

Morgan, G. 1986. *Images of Organization*. Beverly Hills: Sage Publications.

Moritani, M. 1978. *Gendai Nihon Sangyo Gijutsuron* (Technology in Contemporary Japanese Industry). Tokyo: Toyo Keizai Shimposha.

Moroi, K. 1989. *Keiei Zaimu Kogi* (Lectures on Financial Management). 2d ed. Tokyo: Daigaku Shuppankai.

Mowery, D. C., and N. Rosenberg. 1985. Commercial aircraft: Cooperation and competition between the U.S. and Japan. *California Management Review* 27:70–92.

Mueller, D. C. 1986. *Profits in the Long Run*. Cambridge: Cambridge University Press.

Muramatsu, K. 1986. Kaiko rijun chingin (Dismissals, profits and wages). *Academia* 89:399–432.

Muramatsu, K. 1978. Koyo chosei to naibu rodo shijo (Employment adjustment and the internal labor market). *Kikan rodoho bessatsu,* no. 2. (Also in Muramatsu K. 1983. *Nihon no Rodo Shijo Bunseki* [Analysis of Japan's Labor Market].

Nagano, S. 1989. *Kigyo Gurupu-nai Jinzai Ido no Kenkyu* (Research on Personnel Movement within Corporate Groups) Tokyo: Taka Shuppan.

Nakamura, H. 1985. *Chosen Suru Chu-sho Kigyo* (Small and Medium Firms Push Forward). Tokyo: Iwanami Shoten.

Nakamura, T. 1981. *The Postwar Japanese Economy,* trans. by Jacqueline Kaminski. Tokyo: University of Tokyo Press. (Originally published as *Nihonkeizai: Sono seicho to kozo,* 2d ed. Tokyo: University of Tokyo Press, 1980.)

Nakamura, T. 1983. *Chu-sho Kigyo to Dai Kigyo* (Small to Medium Firms and Large Firms). Tokyo: Toyo keizai shimposha.

Nakane, G. 1970. *Japanese Society.* Berkeley: University of California Press.

Nakatani, I. 1983. Rodosha sanka no keizai riron (The economic logic of worker participation). In M. Aoki, ed., *The Economic Analysis of the Japanese Firm.* Amsterdam: Elsevier.

Nakatani, I. 1983. The Economic Role of Financial Corporate Grouping. In M. Aoki, ed., *The Economic Analysis of the Japanese Firm.* Amsterdam: Elsevier.

Nash. J. 1950. The Bargaining Problem. *Econometrica* 18:155–62.

Nasu, H., and S. Tohata. 1932. *Kyodo Kumiai to Nogyo Mondai.* (Cooperative Associations and Problems of Agriculture). Tokyo: Kaizosha.

Nihon seiktasu kyodo kumiai rengokai. 1988. *Kyodo konyu saizensen tankyo jissen hokokusho* (The Front Line of Joint Purchasing: Report on Practice of Single Cooperatives). Tokyo.

Nishida, M. 1987. *Nihon no Gijutsu Shimpo to Sangyo Soshiki.* (Japanese Technological Beliefs and Industrial Organization) Nagoya: Daigaku Shuppankai.

Nishiyama, T. 1981. *Nihon wa Shihonshugi de wa nai* (Japan Is Not Capitalist). Tokyo: Mikasa Shobo.

Nishiyama, T. 1983. *Datsu Shihonshugi Bunseki—Atarashii Shakai no Kaimaku* (The Analysis of Postcapitalism: The Coming of a New Social Order). Tokyo: Bunshindo Press.

Nobes, C., and R. Parker, eds. 1985. *Comparative International Accounting.* 2d ed. Oxford: Philip Allan.

Noll, R.G. ed. 1985. *Regulatory Policy and the Social Sciences.* Berkeley: University of California Press.

Nonaka, Y. 1986. Soshikiteki joho sozo purosesu no manejimento (The management of the information creation process in organisations). In K. Imai, ed., *Innovation to Soshiki (Innovation and Organisation).* Tokyo: Toyo Keizai Shinposha.

Nonaka, Y. 1989. Joho to chishiki sozo no shoshikiron: innovation no soshikikakatei (Organization theory of information and knowledge creation: The orgainisational process of innovation). *Soshiki Kagaku* 22.

Odagiri, H. 1992. *Growth through Competition: Competition through Growth*. Oxford: Clarendon Press.

Odagiri, H., and H. Yamawaki. 1986. A study of company profit-rate time series: Japan and the United States. *International Journal of Industrial Organization* 4:1–23.

Odagiri, H., and H. Yamawaki. 1990. The persistence of profits in Japan. In D. C. Mueller, ed., *The Dynamics of Company Profits: An International Comparison*. Cambridge: Cambridge University Press.

Odagiri, H., and H. Yamawaki. 1990b. The pesistence of profits: An international comparison. In D. C. Mueller, ed., *The Dynamics of Company Profits: An International Comparison*. Cambridge: Cambridge University Press.

Odagiri, H., and T. Yamashita. 1987. Price mark-ups, market structure, and business fluctuation in Japanese manufacturing industries. *Journal of Industrial Economics* 35:317–31.

Odagiri, H., and T. Hase. 1989. Are mergers and acquisitions going to be popular in Japan too? An Empirical Study. *International Journal of Industrial Organization* 7:49–72.

Odaka, K. 1958. *Sangyo shakkaigaku* (Industry Sociology). Tokyo: Daiamondo sha.

Ohashi, I. 1989. *Rodo Shijo no Riron* (Theories of labor markets). Tokyo: Tokyo Keizai Shinposha.

Ohkawa, K., and H. Rosovsky. 1973. *Nihon no Keizai Seicho* (Japan's Economic Growth). Tokyo: Toyo Keizai Shimposha.

Okochi, K., M. Uchihara, and W. Fujita, eds. 1959. *Rodo Kumiai no Kozo to Kino.* (The Structure and Function of Japanese Labor Unions). Tokyo: Daigaku Shuppankai.

Okochi, K. 1952. *Reimeiki no Nihon Rodo Undo..* (Dawn of the Japanese Labor Movement). Tokyo: Iwanami Shoten.

Okuno, M. 1984. Corporate loyalty and bonus payments: An analysis of work incentive in Japan. In M. Aoki, ed. *The Economic Analysis of the Japanese Firm*. Amsterdam: North Holland, pp. 387–411.

Okuno, M., and K. Suzumura. 1985. *Microkeizaigaku* (Microeconomics). 2d ed. Tokyo: Iwanami Shoten.

Okuno, Y., and M. Kodaira. 1988. Pahtotaimah no rodo shijo (The part-time labor market). *Rodo Tokei Chosa Geppo*. Tokyo: Ministry of Labor.

Okuno-Fujiwara, M., and K. Suzumura. 1987. Strategic cost reduction investment and economic welfare. Discussion Paper 87-F-5. Research Institute for the Japanese Economy. University of Tokyo.

Ono, A. 1981. *Nihon no rodoshijo* (The Japanese labor market). Tokyo: Toyo Keizai Shimposha.

Ordover, J. A., and R. D. Willig. 1985. Anti-trust for high-technology industries: Assessing research joint ventures and mergers. *Journal of Law and Economics* 28:311–33.

Organization for Economics Cooperation and Development (OECD). 1973. *Manpower Policy in Japan*. Paris: OECD.

Organization for Economic Cooperation and Development (OECD). 1983. *Economic Outlook*. Paris: OECD.

Organization for Economic Cooperation and Development (OECD). 1984. *Employment Outlook*. Paris: OECD. (July)

Organization for Economic Cooperation and Development (OECD). 1984. *The Importance of Long Term Attachment in OECD Countries*. Paris: OECD.

Organization for Economic Cooperation and Development (OECD). 1986. *Labor Market Flexibility*. Paris: OECD. (September)

Otake, F. 1988. Jishitsu chingin no shinjukusei o megutte (About the real issue of wage flexibility). *Nihon Rodo Kyokai Zasshi* 347.

Otsuka, K., M. Kikuchi, and Y. Hayami. 1986. Community and market in contract choice: Jeepney in Philippines. *Economic Development and Cultural Change*. 34:279–98.

Ouchi, W. G. 1981. *Theory Z: How American Business Can Meet the Japanese Challenge*. Reading, MA: Addison-Wesley.

Pascale, R., and T. Rohlen. 1983. The Mazda turnaround. *Journal of Japanese Studies* 9:219–63.

Phillips, R. 1957. Economic nature of the cooperative association. In M. A. Abrahamsen and C. L. Scroggs, eds., *Agricultural Cooperation: Selected Readings*. Minneapolis: University of Minnesota Press.

Piore, M., and C. E. Sabel. 1984. *The Second Industirial Divide*. New York: Basic Books.

President's Commission on Privatization. 1988. *Privatization: Toward More Effective Government*. Washington, DC: Government Printing Office.

Puchick, V. 1984. Management practices and business strategy in manufacturing firms. In R. L. Tung, ed., *Strategic Mangement in the United States and Japan*. Cambridge, MA: Ballinger.

Puchick, V. 1986. White-collar human resource management in large Japanese manufacturing firms. *Human Resource Managment* 23.

Qualls, P. D. 1979. Market structure and the cyclical flexibility of price-cost margins. *Journal of Business*. 52:305–25

Rees, R. 1976. *Public Enterprise Economics*. London: Weidenfeld and Nicolson.

Rinji Gyosei Kaikaku Suishin Shingikai Jimukyoku. (Bureau of the Provisional Council for the Promotion of Administrative Reform). 1989. *Kisei Kanwa*. (Deregulation). Tokyo.

Rosenberg, N., and W. E. Steinmueller. 1988. Why are Americans such poor imitators? *American Economic Review* 78.

Rosenberg, N. 1976. *Perspectives on Technology*. Cambridge: Cambridge University Press.

Rosow, J. M., and R. Zager. 1984. *Employment Security in a Free Economy*. A Work in America Institute Policy Study. New York: Pergamon.

Rubinstein, A. 1979. Equilibrium in supergames with the overtaking criterion. *Journal of Economic Theory* 21:1–9.

Sachs, J. 1979. Wages, profits, and macroeconomic adjustment: A comparative study. *Brookings Papers in Economic Activity* 2:269–319.

Sakai, K. 1986. *Bunsha-aru Keiei Kankaku* (Branch Companies—One sense of Management). Tokyo: Asahi Shinbunsha.

Sakakura, S. 1988. Minkan kenkyujo o chushin to suru kenkyu kanri no jittai chosa hokoku (An empirical study of research administration priority in the private sector). *Kenkyu Gijutsu Keikaku Gakkai Kenkyu Kanri Bunkakai Hokoku 3*.

Sakamoto, K., and M. Shimotani. 1987. *Gendai Nihon no Kigyo Grupu* (Corporate Groups in Contemporary Japan). Tokyo: Toyo Keizai Shinpo Sha.

Salop, S. C. 1973. Wage differentials in a dynamic theory of the firm. *Journal of Economic Theory* 6:321–44.

Sangyo rodo chosasho (Institute Investigating Industrial Labor). 1988. *Moderuchingin jittai shiryo: 89* (Data on the actual condition of model wages: 89). Tokyo: Sengyo Rodo Shuppan Kyokai.

Sano, Y. 1967. Waga kuni no shunto soba no bunseki to yosoku (The spring offensive going rate: Analysis and outlook). *Roseijiho*, no. 1876.

Sano, Y. 1970. *Chingin kettei no Keiryo Bunseki* (Wage Determination: An Economic Analysis). Tokyo: Toyo Keizai Shimposha.

Sano, Y. 1981. *Chingin to Koyou no Keizaigaku* (The Economics of Wages and Employment). Tokyo: Chuo Keizaisha.

Sarfati, H., and C. Kobrin, eds. 1988. *Labor Market Flexiblity: A Comparative Anthology*. New York: Gower.

Schelling, T. C. 1971. *The Strategy of Conflict*. Cambridge: Harvard University Press.

Scott, J. 1985. Theoretical Framework and Research Design. In F. N. Stokman, R. Ziegler, and J. Scott, eds., *Networks of Corporate Power: A Comparative Anaysis of Ten Countries*. Cambridge, England: Polity Press.

Seike, A. 1983. Koyo chosei seisaku to rodo shijo tokusei (Labor adjustment policy and special characteristics of the labor market). In Koyo shokugyo sogo kenkyujo, *Senshin kogyo koku ni okeru kozo henka to koyo ni kan suru kenkyu* (Research on structural changes in employment in industrially advanced countries).

Seike, A. 1989. The employment patterns of Japan and the United States. In K. Koshiro, ed. *Employment Security and Labor Market Flexibility: Proceedings of the Yokohama Symposium*. Detroit: Wayne State University Press.

Sekitani, K. 1974. Nenkogata Chingin—Shoshinsei (The seniority wage and promotion system). In K. Takada, and T. Hosoi, eds., *Nihonteki Keiei no Tokushitsu* (Aspects of Japanese Managment). Tokyo: Daiyamondosha Press.

Sengenberger, W. 1986. Revisiting the legal and institutional framework for employment security—An international comparative perspective. K. Koshiro, ed., *Employment Security and Labor Market Flexibility: Proceedings of the Yokohama Symposium*. Detroit: Wagne State University Press.

Shapiro, S., and J. E. Stiglitz. 1984. Equilibrium unemployment as a worker discipline device. *Amerian Economic Review* 74:433—44.

Sheard, P. 1989. The main bank system and corporate monitoring and control in Japan *Journal of Economic Behavior Organization* 11:399—422.

Shimada, H., and J. P. Macduffie. 1986. Industrial Relations and "Humanware". Alfred P. Sloan School of Management Working Paper, 1855—1888.

Shimada, H. 1974. The structure of earnings and invertments in human resources: A comparison between the United States and Japan. Ph.D. dissertation. University of Wisconsin-Madison.

Shimada, H. 1981. Rodo shijo kiko no bunseki (Analysis of the labor market mechanism). *Keizai kikakucho kenkyu shirizu*, no. 37.

Shinkai, Y., H. Niida, and T. Negishi. 1988. *Kindai Keizaigaku Shinpan* (Contemporary Economics: New Edition). Tokyo: Dai go-roku sho.

Shinozuka, H., and E. Ishihara. 1977. Oilushokku iko no koyo chosei—4 ka koku hikaku to nihon no kibokan hikaku (Employment adjustment after the Oil Shocks: A comparision of four countries and firm-size differentials in Japan). *Nihon keizai kenkyu 6*.

Shirai, T. 1984. A theory of enterprise union. In T. Shirai, ed., *Contemporary Industrial Relations in Japan*. Madison: University of Wisconsin Press, pp. 117—43.

Showa dojinkai. 1960. *Waga Kuni Chingin Kozo no Shiteki Kosatsu (A Historical Consideration of Japan's Wage System)*. Tokyo: Shiseido.

Simon, H. A. 1979. Rational Decision Making in Business Organization. *American Economic Review 69*.

Smith, P. B., and J. Misumi. 1987. Japanese management: A sun rising in the West. In C. L. Cooper and I. Robertson, eds., *Interational Review of Industrial and Organizational Psychology*. New York: Wiley. (Also in H. Itami, ed., *Jinponshugi Kigyo* [The Humanist Firm]. Tokyo: Chikuma Shobo.)

Solnik, B. 1988. *International Investment*. Reading, MA: Addison-Wesley.

Solow, R. M. 1979. Another Possible Source of Wage Stickiness. *Journal of Macroeconomics* 1:79—82.

Stiglitz, J. E. 1984. Theories of Wage Rigidity. NBER Working Paper Series, no. 1442.

Sugeno, K. 1985. *Rodoho* (Labor Law). Tokyo: Kobundo.

Suruga, J. 1987. Bonusu seido to shinshukuteki chingin (The bouns system and flexible wages). *Nihon Rodo Kyokai Zasshi* (March): 13—21.

Suzuki, M. 1981. *Gemu Riron Nyumon* (Introduction to Game Theory). 6th ed. Tokyo: Kyoritsu Zensho.

Suzuki, Y. 1987. *The Japanese Financial System.* Oxford: Clarendon.

Sweezy, P. M. 1953. Interest groups in the American economy. *The Present as History.* New York: Monthly Review Press.

Tachibanaki, T. 1987 The determination of the promotion process in organizations and of earnings differentials. *Journal Economic Behavior and Organization.* 8:603–16.

Takayama, A. 1969. Behavior of the firm under regulatory constraint. *American Economic Review* 59:255–60.

Takeda, I. Tasai na jitsuzo to kiro ni tatsu rinen—Shinyo kumiai no keiei mondai (Management problems of credit cooperatives: Multifaceted reality and principles at the crossroads. In Nihon kyodo kumiai gakkai ed., *Kyodo kumiai kenkyu* (Research on Cooperative Associations), vol. 2.

Takeshita, S. 1967. Mizushimachiku jidosha buhin kogyo no doko to mondai ten (Motivation and problems in Mizushima's car-parts factory). *Nihon no jidosha buhin kogyo* (Japan's Auto Parts Industry). Annual volume.

Takeuchi, Y., and Y. Nonaka. 1986. Shin seihin kaihatsu no senryaku to soshiki (Strategy and organization of new product development). In K. Imai, ed., *Innovation to Soshiki* (Innovation and Organization). Tokyo: Toyo keizai Shinposha.

Takeuchi, Y., and Y. Nonaka. 1986. The new new product development game. *Harvard Business Review* 64.

Takizawa, K. 1966. Kozo hendo katei ni okeru chu-sho kikai kogyo no sonritsu kiban (The existing base of small and medium machine manufactures in the process of structural change). *Chu-sho kigyo kinyukoko chosa jiho* 7.

Tanigawa, H. 1987. Han o kiso ni shita minshuteki unei o tsyomeru ni wa do subekika (What should be done to strengthen the democratic management based on local groups?). In *Seikyo Unei Shiryo* (Materials on the Management of Seikyo), vol. 113. Tokyo: Nihon seikatsu kyodo kumiai rngokai ed.

Taylor, J. B. 1989. Differences in economic fluctuations in Japan and the United States: The role of nominal rigidities. *Journal of the Japanese and International Economies* 3:127–44.

Thiemeyer, T., and G. Quaden, eds. 1986. *The Privatization of Public Enterprises.* Belgium: CIRIEC.

Topel, R., and F. Welch. 1982. On self-insurance and employment contracts with uncertain demand. Mimeo. University of Chicago.

Toritsu Rodo Kenkyujo (Toritsu Labor Research Center). 1988. *Shutoken rodo shijo ni okeru koyo keitai tayoka no jittai: Gakusei rodoryoku riyo jittai chosa (Labor diversification in the metropolitan area labor market: Survey of the use of student labor).* Tokyo.

Toyoda, E. 1985. *Ketsudan* (Resolution). Tokyo: Nihon keizai shimbunsha.

Triffon, R. 1961. The economics of cooperative ventures. *Journal of Farm Economics* (May).

Tsuda, M. 1977. *Nihonteki Keiei no Ronri.* (The Logic of Japanese-Style Management. Tokyo: Chuokeizaisha.

Ueda, Y. 1983. Kigyo shudan ni okeru yakuin kennin no keiryo bunseki (Statistical analysis of municipal officials in corporate groups). *Shoken Keizai* (December).

Uekusa, M. 1979. Kigyo bunseki josetsu (An introduction to the analysis of public enterprises). *Keizaigaku Ronshu* 44.

Uekusa, M. 1979. Kokigyo bunseki josetsu (An introduction to the analysis of public utilities). *Keizaigaku Ronshu* (Tokyo University) 44:12–30.

Uekusa, M. 1983. Kigyo no Kazu-Keitai-Yakuwari (The number, forms and purposes of public enterprises). In M. Uekusa and Y. Okano, eds., *Nihon no Kokigyo (Japan's Public Enterprises).* Tokyo: University of Tokyo Press.

Uekusa, M. 1985. Dai-san Sekuta no Keiei. (Management of the "third sector"). *Keizai Hyoron* (special July issue on the Reorganization of Japan National Railroads).

Uekusa, M. 1989. The effect of innovations in information technology on corporate and industrial organization in Japan. In T. Shiraishi and S. Tsuru, eds., *Economic Institutions in a Dynamic Society.* London: Macmillan.

Uekusa, M., and A. Torii. 1985. Stochastic production frontier o mochiita Nihon no seizogyo ni okeru gijitsu hikoritsudo no keisoku (Estimation of the degree of technical inefficiency in Japan's manufacturing industry using a stochastic production frontier). *Keizaigaku Ronshu* 51 (October).

Vickers, J., and G. Yarrow. 1988. *Privatization: An Economic Analysis.* Cambridge: MIT Press.

Vogel, E. F. 1979. *Japan as Number One.* Cambridge: Harvard University Press.

von Hippel, E. 1976. The dominant role of users in the scientific instrument innovation process. *Research Policy* (July).

von Hippel, E. 1988. *The Sources of Innovation.* Oxford: Oxford University Press.

Wachtel, H. M., and P. D. Adelsheim. 1977. How recesssion feeds inflation: Price markups in a concentrated economy. *Challenge* 20: 6–13.

Wada, K. 1984. "Jun suichokuteki togo soshiki" no keisei—Toyota no jirei (Quasi integrated organization: The Toyota example). Nagoya: Academia (Nanzan Daigaku).

Wakabayashi, H. 1964. *Asu no Nokyo—Nokyo no Miraizo* (Tomorrow's Agriculture Cooperatives: The Future Image of Nokyo). Tokyo: Meibun shobo.

Wakasugi, R. et. al. 1988. *Nihon no kabuka suijun kenkyu gurupu hokokusho* (Report of Japan's stock price level research group). Tokyo: Nihon shoken keizai kenkyujo.

Wakasugi, R., K. Nishino, F. Konya, and M. Tsuchiya. 1984. Measuring the profitability of the nonfinancial sector in Japan. In D. M. Holland, ed., *Measuring Profitability and Capital Costs:* An International Study Lexington, Mass: Lexington Books, pp. 345–86.

Wakasugi, R. 1986. *Gijutsu Kakushin to Kenkyu Kaihatsu no Keizai Bunseki* (Economic Analysis of Technological Innovation and Research and Development). Tokyo: Toyo Keizai Shimposha.

Wakasugi, R. 1988a. Kyodo kenkyu kaihatsu no keizaiteki kosatsu (An economic study of cooperative research development). *Shinshu Daigaku Keizaigaku Ronshu.* 26.

Wakasugi, R. 1988b. Kenkyu kaihatsu toshi no senryakuteki daitai: Hokan (The strategic alternative of research development investment capital: Supplement). Shinshu University Staff Paper.

Wakasugi, R. 1988c. A consideration of innovative organization: Joint R&D of Japanese firms. Paper presented at the International Schumpeter Conference.

Weiss, L. W., and M. W. Klass, eds. 1981. *Case Studies in Regulation: Revolution and Reform,* Boston: Little, Brown.

Weitzman, M. L. 1984. *The Share Economy.* Cambridge: Harvard University Press.

Weitzman, M. L. 1985. The simple macroeconomics of profit sharing. *American Economic Review* 75:937−53.

Wenders, J. T. 1987. *The Economics of Telecommunications: Theory and Policy.* Cambridge, MA: Ballinger.

Westney, D. E., and K. Sakakibara. 1985. Comparative study of the training, careers, and organization of engineers in the computer industry in Japan and the U.S. Mimeo. Massachusetts Institute of Technology.

Weston, J. F., and T. E. Copeland. 1986. *Managerial Finance,* 8th ed. New York: Dryden.

Williamson, O. E. 1975. *Markets and Hierarchies: Antitrust Implications.* New York: Free Press.

Williamson, O. E. 1983. Credit commitments: Using hostages to support exchange. *American Economic Review* 73:519−40.

Williamson, O. E. 1985. *The Economic Institutions of Capitalism.* New York: Free Press.

Yamada, K. 1984. Koyo seisaku no kadai (The topic of employment policy) In Nihon rodo kyokai (ed.), *80 nendai no roshi kankei* (Industrial relations in the 80's) Tokyo: Nihon rodo kyokai.

Yamamoto, T. 1982. Jinin rodo jikan tahmu de mita koyo chosei no jissho bunseki (Analysis of evidence of empolyment adjustment in items of numbers employed and hours worked). *Mita gakkai zasshi* 75.

Yashiro, A. 1986. *Nihon no Sangyo Soshiki: Kigyo Soshiki to Rodo Shijo.* (Japan's Industrial organization: Corporations and the labor market). In Rodo mondai risachisenta, *Kokusaiteki Shiten Kara Mita Waga Kuni Rodo Shijo no Junansei ni Kansuru Chosa Kenkyu* (Research on the Flexibility of Japanese Labor Market from an International Perspective). Tokyo.

Yasueda, H., and K. Nishimura. 1984. Seirikaiko ni kan suru hanreihori (Judicial precedents of arrangements for redundancy dismissal of employees). In Nihon Rodo Kyokai, *80 Nendai no Roshi Kankei.* (Industrial Relations in the 80's) Tokyo.

Yellen, J. 1984. Efficiency wage models of unemployment. *American Economic Review* 74: 200–205.

Yoneyama, T. 1990. Seiho sangyo soshiki to hoken gyosei (The structure of life insurance industry and life insurance administration). *Hitotsubashi Ronshu* (Hitotsubashi University) 103:555–71.

Yoshihara, H. 1981. *Nihon Kigyoo no Takakuka Senryaku* (Diversification Strategy of Japanese Firms). Tokyo: Nihon keizai shinbunsha.

Yoshihara, K. 1986. *Senryakuteki Kigyo Kakushin* (Strategic Corporate Reform). Tokyo: Toyo Keizai Shimposha.

Yoshikawa, H., and F. Ohtake. 1987. Postwar business cycles in Japan: A quest for the right explanation. *Journal of the Japanese and International Economies* (December).

Yoshikawa, H., and Y. Takeuchi. 1988. Jisshitsu Chingin to Nihon Keizai (Real wages and the Japanese economy). *Kinyu Kenkyu (Monetary Studies)* 7:97–132.

Yoshikawa, H., and Y. Takeuchi. 1989. Real Wages and the Japanese Economy. *Bank of Japan, Monetary and Economic Studies* 7 (April 11).

Zenkoku nokyo chuokai. 1980. *Seireki 2000 Nen no Kyodo Kumiai* (Cooperatives in the Year 2000). Tokyo.

Zenkoku nokyo chuokai. 1983. *Nokyo no Katsudo ni Kansuru Zenkoku Issei Chosa Hokoku* (Nationwide Survey Report of Agriculture Cooperative Activities) 18. Tokyo.

Zenkoku nokyo chuokai. 1987. *Nokyo Keiei Bunseki Chosa Hokokusho* (Survey Report on Nokyo Management Analysis). Tokyo.

# Index

Accountability, in absence of shareholders, 11–14
Accounting practices, and profitability of Japanese corporations, 182–86
Adverse selection, and rank hierarchy, 53–54
Affiliated companies. See also Subcontractors; Subsidiary or subordinate firms
employment adjustment through, 240–42, 246
and information redundancy, 214–15
Agency theory, 68–69
and American view of market, 33
and Japanese system, 3
Agricultural cooperatives, 14, 346, 352, 354–62, 363
and life insurance companies, 371
Aichi Steel, 255
Airlines. See Japan Air Lines
Allocation of funding, for R&D, 166–68, 176
Allocation of resources
and interfirm mobility, 37
for public utilities, 341–42
Altruism, 4–5
American companies
change in governance of, 99–101
cooperatives, 346, 348
and diversification, 238
managerial selection by, 32–33
profitability of, 181–82, 184, 187, 196
and short-term concerns, 202, 203
survival rate of, 180
and work force numbers, 26
Asahi Life, 382
Automobile industry, 141–46

Hayek and decentralization of, 154
production scheduling in, 42–44, 51–52
subcontractors in, 142, 146–55

Bank-oriented business financing, 40
Bank-oriented financial control, 56–61
Bankruptcy, 61
Banks
business information provided by, 36
firms controlled by, 381
main banks, 56–57, 58n, 61, 63, 115
Barriers to exit. See Exit barriers
Blue-collar workers
and bonuses, 252, 287, 294, 298–99, 306
broad experience of, 262
compensation of, incentive system for, 207, 263, 306
and cooperation, 8–9
Bonuses, 6–7, 249, 275–76
and basic wages, 299, 302
determination of, 276–306
and economic conditions, 306
as effort compensation, 279–82, 306
flexibility of, 227
and labor market, 294, 295, 296, 305, 306
and market conditions, 282
and nenko system, 21
and overtime, 278, 281, 286–87, 306
and profits, 251–257, 258–59, 276, 278, 282, 294, 295–96, 305
and wages, 276, 299, 302
British companies
cooperatives, 346, 350
employment system of, 228
profitability of, 181–82, 184
survival rate of, 180
Business schools, in Japan, 205